CHINA URBAN

P9-CAM-050

CHINA URBAN Ethnographies of Contemporary Culture

Edited by Nancy N. Chen, Constance D. Clark, Suzanne Z. Gottschang,

and Lyn Jeffery · *Duke University Press   Durham & London 2001*

© 2001 Duke University Press   All rights reserved
Printed in the United States of America on acid-free paper ∞
Designed by Rebecca M. Giménez   Typeset in Minion
with Futura display by Keystone Typesetting, Inc.
Library of Congress Cataloging-in-Publication Data
appear on the last printed page of this book.

For Sami—NC

For Chaya—CC

To my sisters, Kelley Gottschang
and Michele Meisner—SG

In the spirit of sisterhood that
carried this project, to my sweet
sister Elizabeth Jeffery—LJ

Contents

Editors' Acknowledgments

It has been an exciting and stimulating process to bring to fruition a project that began with a series of discussions among the editors and other anthropologists conducting field research in Beijing during the fall of 1995. Since those meetings, we have received intellectual, financial, and logistical support from numerous people and institutions. We want to especially thank Virginia Cornue for her participation in the formative stages of this project.

The chapters in this volume were first presented at a workshop held on September 27–28, 1997, at the University of California, Santa Cruz. Financial support for the workshop was provided by a Pacific Rim Research Program workshop grant from the University of California Office of the President. Additional support came from the Department of Anthropology and the Center for Cultural Studies at UC Santa Cruz and the Center for Chinese Studies at UC Berkeley. The workshop would not have been possible without Cheryl Barkey's assistance and support. In addition to the contributors in the volume, we would also like to thank Xin Liu, Hai Ren, Dawn Einwalter, and Virginia Cornue for their presentations at the workshop. The presenters benefited from the intellectual insights and suggestions of panel discussants: Ann Anagnost, Aihwa Ong, Lisa Rofel, and Mayfair Yang. Raoul Birnbaum, Gail Hershatter, Emily Honig, and Bruce Larkin generously assisted in chairing the panels. Tani Barlow, Madeleine Dong Yue, Tom Gold, Greg Guldin, and Tim Oakes provided additional inspiration throughout the workshop.

The final version of the volume has benefited from a careful reading and incisive suggestions by Stevan Harrell and an anonymous reviewer on behalf of Duke University Press. In addition, we would like to extend special thanks to Karen L. Turner and Daniel T. Linger for their willingness to read the introduction at various stages. Greg Guldin kindly commented on the introduction at a later phase. We are very grateful to Ken Wissoker for his support in seeing this project to publication. Thanks also to Cheryl Van De Veer at UCSC Document Publishing Center for her able assistance in assembling the final manuscript and to Cathryn Clayton for her swift, outstanding work on the index.

Over the course of the project, as we lived and worked in various locations in the United States and China, we have used nearly every combination of communications technology, from e-mail to conference calls, in the collaboration on and the production of this work. The volume has been sustained by the unflagging support of family and friends, and we wish to thank Karen Turner, Joseph (Bo) Zawadsky, Liu Fendou, Xiaodong Zhang, Darby Li Po Price, and Cheryl Barkey for providing child care and encouragement at every turn, with special thanks to Bo Zawadsky for the frequent flier miles. Finally, we acknowledge the camaraderie and collaboration of the editorial group that brought us through this process.

The transformations in mainland China over the past two decades have given rise to more than their share of hyperbole from all sides. The statements of conservative Western free-market advocates and socialist bureaucrats, for example, coincide with jubilant claims that the People's Republic of China (PRC) has at last discovered the true path to modernity. The American media ceaselessly trot out images of fast food and technology as evidence of a victorious penetration of the "bamboo curtain." For Chinese citizens who are actually living with these changes, however, the transformation of the physical landscape, the virtual reorganization of built space to reflect a new social reality, is a constant, sometimes jarring fact of daily life. Film critic Dai Jinhua describes an urban world in which "the old cities—for example, Shanghai, which is a few hundred years old, or Beijing or Suzhou, which are thousands of years old—quietly recede into oblivion in the explosive transformation. If the spaces of old remain the milestones of individual remembrance and of regional history . . . then the prosperous, cosmopolitan, anonymous big city already truncates its enduring visible history" (Dai 1997: 146). These revised city landscapes have been produced through an uneven mélange of local, regional, national, and transnational influences and reveal an aesthetics and politics that overlap with the past.

This volume had its beginnings in the fall of 1995 in Beijing, when a group of anthropologists met informally to discuss the difficulties of doing fieldwork in urban settings, chaotic and transitory as they are. There, in a city that has witnessed two decades of upheaval as a result of epic reconfigurations in the economy, we sensed an urgent need to reassess the tenor of everyday life. As the walled compounds of state-owned work units and single-story residences became engulfed by skyscrapers, department stores, and high-rise housing, we found our research methodologies inadequate. Entire field sites disappeared, old friends left for faraway places with better economic prospects, and inner city residents were moved by the state to suburban high-rises. How should we conduct field research with actors on the move in a constantly shifting terrain?

While the urban work unit was still important in many of our informants' lives, others were employed outside their work units in small-scale enterprises and the service industry. Migrants from all over China, often seen by urban residents as uniform emblems of rurality, had an increasingly visible presence in urban areas. As some people redecorated their apartments with crown molding, wallpaper, and hardwood flooring, others eked out a living as street peddlers and itinerant laborers at construction sites. We saw continued and growing economic inequality, which was reflected in the lived environment. Like many other researchers, we grappled with fundamental questions about the relationships between field methodology, anthropological theories of culture, and everyday experience. The ethnographies in this volume maintain this sense of the instability of spatial and social realms at the same time that they provide grounds for understanding it. This volume thus represents the collective efforts of thirteen anthropologists to examine "the urban" and urbanization processes in 1990s China.

An understanding of these changes also requires attention to larger questions raised by the economic reforms that began in 1978. With the spatial inequalities of reform measures in these last twenty years, the Chinese economy has become an ever more influential factor in the world economy. This has given rise to an increasingly visible overlap between constructions of global capitalism and the Chinese economy. The chapters in this volume illustrate that the current influx of transnational culture, capital, and people must be understood from within a cultural and economic framework more complex than the simple adoption of Euro-American neo-liberal capitalism.

Four decades ago, Lefebvre, in writing about processes of urbanization then claiming the countryside of France, conceptualized "the urban" as a "new form of sociability where town and country had been abolished" (Kofman and Lebas 1996: 14). This volume broadens the category of the urban to a potential that includes both imagination and practice rather than simply the notion of an urban society or social life that infiltrates nonurban landscapes and ways of life through urbanization and other means (media, stories/myths, migration). It also insists on the cultural specificity of notions of the urban: in China, the urban is particularly framed through two deeply though differently embedded discourses, these being rurality and socialism.

Mao Zedong extolled the virtues of rural life in contrast to the corruption of the city, a sentiment also expressed to varying degrees in elite Confucian ideologies, for instance in the eighteenth and nineteenth centuries among landowning gentry (see Wakeman 1966; Skinner 1977; Mote 1977; Murphey 1984; and Whyte and Paris 1984). Based on the experiences of the peasant-fueled Chinese revolution, Maoist theory deviated from Marxism by identifying the peasants as leaders of the revolutionary struggler rather than ignorant masses beholden to the urban proletariat.[1] Moreover, as Meisner suggests, implicit in Maoism was the association of the city "with what is foreign and reactionary and the countryside with what is truly national and revolutionary" (1982: 64). This theme—the recuperative power of the rural in nation building, prominent in nationalist ideologies elsewhere (Ferguson 1997)—shaped a critique of Western imperialism and foreign occupation of Chinese territory (cf. Meisner 1982). The importance of rural China in establishing socialism played out in development policy as the CCP set up communes and industrialized the countryside in the late 1950s.

In terms of contextualizing urbanity in relation to socialism, 1990s China presents a situation in which the dynamics between West and East, capitalism and socialism, are not easily categorized. Scholars of urbanization such as David Harvey have focused their analyses on global capitalism—a force characterized by an international division of labor, flexible production controlled by the transnational corporation, revolutions in communications and other technologies, and a shifting of national capital—said to be in the process of completely reshaping local cultural practices from labor and consumption to experiences of time and space (Harvey 1989; Lipietz 1986; Pred and Watts 1992; Jameson 1984). More recently, Asia's emergence as an increasingly important sphere of global capitalism has necessitated a rethinking of the historical and geographic specificity of this dynamic (Frank 1997). Ong, for instance, has described the discourse on Asian capitalism as "a paradigm change in capitalism as the West knows it. . . . Chinese modernities are new imaginaries and regimes of domination decentering Western hegemony in the global arena" (1997a: 359). While these processes are visible in contemporary China, the material and social dimensions of capitalism and foreign consumer cultures are built within the cultural structures already established by Chinese socialism. This is true for both the state and ordinary individuals.

The material in this book provides us with a means of going beyond privileging capital as the sole organizing principle of analysis. Chinese landscapes present us with a different intellectual and political history of notions of city and country, and of the role of the state in allocating, designing, and distributing space. In a place where land, bodies, and buildings have only recently been reframed as commodities, the Chinese urban is just as importantly constituted by discourses of socialism, rurality, civilization, gender, ethnicity, class, space and others. And, as ideological and material reconceptions of culture and cities in China are put into place by planners, developers, marketers, and state governing bodies, we believe anthropological critiques should be increasingly important in contextualizing such urban revisions (cf. Ellin 1996; Low 1996).

One outcome of the volume is that contributors present multiple readings about culture in contemporary China. For example, the chapters on the development of new markets and industries such as multilevel marketing, rock music, and the university graduate labor market illuminate the cultural construction of the socialist market within the context of global capitalism. Such disparate realms as a fashion-modeling competition, maternity practices in the hospital, sex tourism, and marriage introduction agencies are examined by other contributors, highlighting the intersections of consumer culture, gender, and the body in a network of socialist institutions and market forces. Themes of morality, place, and the symbolic meaning of space are explored through research on new social geographies of health care and medicinal consumption, the shifting social position of railway workers, and the destruction of Beijing's largest migrant neighborhood. Other contributors consider the nature of the urban as cosmopolitan, a subject approached via studies of cultural production among minority youth, the distinction of the rural and the urban through television programming, and the cultural construction of urban "face" and anonymity.

Urbanization and the Chinese Socialist City   Chinese cities and their inhabitants were radically reconstructed after the revolution of 1949 through a blend of Soviet and Chinese Marxist ideology and praxis. As was the case in the development strategies of other socialist countries, Chinese urbanization was initially assessed in terms of cost-benefit analysis (Naughton 1995: 62). The Chinese Communist Party still sought to promote urban industrialization, but as inexpensively as possible since its large cities had been devastated by the Japanese occupation and the civil war with the Nationalists (Kirkby 1985). State goals to transform cities from consumer (*xiaofei*) to producer (*shengchan*) status, and to reduce economic disparities between city and countryside, affected industrialization efforts and mobility policies. The policy became one of "industrialization without much urbanization" (K. W. Chan 1992: 57; Naughton 1995). As Kwok notes, industrialization in many developing countries has been concentrated in large cities and has been associated with high levels of urban economic and population growth (1992: 66). With Chinese socialist goals of wealth distribution and social equity, however, the links between industrialization and urbanization took a quite different form. Postrevolutionary urban policy addressed several concerns: cost, rural-urban leveling, national security, and a wariness of large cities.

The CCP was not opposed to large cities themselves, but rather to their associations with foreign imperialism and capitalism (Meisner 1982; Pannell 1992). Party authorities considered cities to be wasteful centers of consumption that demanded huge capital expenditures on infrastructure, public transport, electricity, and social services. For these reasons, urban development strategies focused less on the industrialized Northeast and coastal regions (the treaty port cities) and more on creating smaller, less costly urban centers in inland regions closer to the supply of resources (Lewis 1971; Pannell 1992: 21–25; Johnson 1995: 191).

Overall, a primary focus on rapid heavy industrial production, at the expense of developing consumer services and city infrastructure, guided the Party's policies of urbanization after 1949 (Chan 1992; Johnson 1992). The discontinuation of traditional handicrafts and rural factories, which used scarce raw materials and labor, and the channeling of most rural labor into agriculture (97 percent of the rural labor force in 1965) created an agricultural surplus that was transferred to the urban industrial sector (Kwok 1992: 68). At the same time, the state worked to control urban growth and population movement into urban areas by implementing the household registration system (*hukou*) in the late 1950s. For the most part, the system effectively restricted individual mobility, excepting the mass rural movement into the cities during the Great Leap Forward (1958–60) and the urban outflow of youth to the countryside during the decade of the Cultural Revolution (1966–76). The hukou instituted a binary legal and inherited distinction between peasants and nonpeasants (Cohen 1994: 158). Historically, those born into agricultural families (the majority of the population) have had great difficulty converting to non-agricultural status and have been denied perquisites given to those in the urban, state-supported sector (Potter 1983; Kipnis 1997).

Despite the CCP's goal to reduce rural-urban social and economic inequality, the nonpeasant hukou marked the difference between who would or would not receive guaranteed employment, education, medical insurance, household grain allocations, and other subsidies, creating a broad two-tiered system of privilege. Although the urban economy was composed of state-owned, collective, and independent sectors that provided a variable range of benefits, in general urbanites as a group received the greatest share of any resource distribution in Maoist China (cf. Whyte and Parish 1984; Lü and Perry 1997). The state-owned work units (*danwei*) further maintained the hukou system as the main way to control and distribute privileges and necessities, especially housing. The multifunctional danwei, often resembling a walled miniature city, became an integral part of the dramatically reorganized socialist urban landscape (Gaubatz 1995: 30). Residents lived, worked, and socialized within the work unit space. Through the urban danwei, the state controlled urban society and also mobilized residents into political participation (Lu and Perry 1997: 8; Li 1993). Both the hukou and the danwei systems were particular socialist institutions that minimized the movement of Chinese citizens.

Especially after the Cultural Revolution, boundaries marking cities and their surrounding countryside were transformed into inflexible lines of control that were difficult for individuals to cross without extensive documentation (Whyte and Parish 1984: 26). State mobility restrictions also held in check the development of the kinds of large migrant settlements that surrounded metropolises and infused city centers in many Southeast Asian countries (Kirkby 1985; Guldin 1992a). The result of the hukou system was that the city was the preferred place to live and became a steadfast destination of desire for rural dwellers and exiled urbanites. With fairly strict regulation of movement and little state investment in urbanization, large cities experienced almost no growth from the mid-1960s through the late 1970s, retaining their compact physical forms and definitive edges between city limits and countryside. Indeed, Naughton comments that before economic reforms the city centers of Guangzhou, Tianjin, and Shanghai possessed an almost museumlike quality, where building facades remained unchanged since the 1930s (1995: 70).

Urbanization Compared   The process of urban development in China also can be compared productively with that in other countries and regions. Unlike many Latin American countries, which have experienced high levels of urban growth and rural-urban migration since the 1930s (de Oliveira and Roberts 1996: 254), China's urbanization trajectory has been discontinuous. For instance, during the 1960s and 1970s China experienced what may be called underurbanization, as planning policies advocated a containment of urban growth and rural-urban migration (Chen and Parish 1996: 64). A super concentration of population in large metropolitan centers has characterized urbanization in Latin America and the Caribbean, such that three-quarters of the populations live in urban areas. In contrast, in places such as sub-Saharan Africa, India, Indonesia, and China, two-thirds or more of the population still live in rural areas (Gugler 1996: 2). The high rates of urbanization in Latin American cities have been intimately linked with the restructuring of state and society, as was the case for many Asian countries. In post-Mao China, rapid in-migration of ruralites and other people without access to what are considered urban rights has sharpened existing inequalities and engendered a hierarchy of citizenship. Thus, cities have become arenas for the making of new kinds of citizens. Solinger describes this condition at the end of the century as a "contest over citizenship" between a socialist state in transition and a complex, mobile population that is deeply altering the structure of urban society (1999: 3).

Urbanization patterns in reform-era China remain distinct from those in Western industrialized countries. Far from withering under the sweep of city-based urbanization, small towns, primarily through the development of nonstate township enterprises, have contributed to rural-based urbanization (Lefebvre 1996; Guldin 1997: 62). China's prominent anthropologist Fei Xiaotong has noted that the release of surplus labor after rural decollectivization in 1978, which cities couldn't absorb, led a portion of this labor force to migrate and participate in the growth of small rural towns (1992). These towns have become critical nodes in national development processes whose goal has been to keep people in the countryside but not necessarily working the land (Lin 1997). As Dirlik and Zhang note, "one sees that the industrial penetration of the rural also gives rise to a post-urban, decentralized and place-based mode of development that promises to narrow rural-urban disparity and to rebuild rural communities in the market environment" (1997: 6).

The industrialization of small rural centers is not unique to China. Scholars stress the similarity of the urbanization of China's countryside to processes occurring in Asian countries such as Taiwan, Thailand, the Philippines, and Japan (Costa et al. 1989; Jinnai 1995; Kim and Choe 1997; Seabrook 1996). In these countries, the majority of industry is concentrated not in urban centers but in hinterlands serviced by cities (Naughton 1995: 83). A new process of settlement termed *desakota* may be distinctive to Asian regions; it is "a form neither urban nor rural, but a blending of the two wherein a dense web of transactions ties large urban cores to their surrounding regions" (Guldin 1997: 62).

And yet, desakota formations in China do not always reduce rural-urban differences. As the ethnographies in this volume suggest, communities in this market environment are not rebuilding on a level playing field, but along historically and culturally specific axes of urbanity and rurality. For example, the coastal cities have regained their preliberation status as dynamic centers in the forefront of economic growth. Deng era policies have continued to promote the development and investment in these areas, resulting in irregular patterns of wealth accumulation. Southern and seaboard provinces attract far more foreign investment than the Northwest. Moreover, each province is internally marked by highly variable patterns of wealth and poverty.

Chinese Cities in the 1980s and 1990s   In the quest for a fresh national economic identity, Chinese leaders in the early 1980s endorsed the creation of special economic zones (SEZs) in southern China, hitching their development image to that of the economically successful "Asian Tigers" (Singapore, Taiwan, South Korea, and Hong Kong). Several of these zones have developed into booming industrial and commercial cities that represent modernity and progress to Chinese citizens and to the world. With economic reform, these special economic zones have reshaped older models of cities as largely manufacturing bases to centers of commerce, services, consumption, and recreation. The decentralization of taxation authority and control of foreign funds has favored large coastal cities and their surrounding regions (Chen and Parish 1996: 67). For instance, after more than a decade of concentrated foreign-funded development and heightened focus by state officials, Shanghai has regained its pre-1949 cosmopolitan reputation. Chinese authorities have relaxed strictures on population mobility, which has created movements of between 70 and 100 million people throughout the country and has accelerated urban economic and population growth (Solinger 1995, 1999). Although cities and special economic zones have attracted substantial in-migration, China's small towns also have drawn large numbers of migrants. This has been spurred by state policies of rural urbanization and industrialization. Such large-scale mobility has profoundly changed rural and urban social space and is reshaping the future of China's cities and rural regions.

In sum, urbanization, large-scale migration, extensive township and village development, and the increasing presence of transnational cultural forms in China have ruptured boundaries and altered former physical and social distinctions between city and country. This volume emphasizes the fluidity of rural, urban, and global forces and offers a mosaic of anthropological perspectives on contemporary Chinese urbanity.

The book is arranged in four parts: "Xia Hai: Ethnographies of Work and Leisure"; "Gender, Bodies, and Consumer Culture"; "Negotiating Urban Spaces"; and "Expressions of Urbanity and the Urban."

Part One: Xia Hai: Ethnographies of Work and Leisure   *Xia hai*, literally "entering the sea," is the popular term given to participation in China's market economy. In the mid-1980s, most urbanites still viewed the petty merchants of street stalls with more contempt than envy. Yet by the early 1990s many people were feeling pressured to—and sometimes exhilarated by—taking the plunge. Opportunities seemed to lie just at the surface. As the century closed, another wave of changes occurred with the massive layoffs of state-industry workers, and the ocean looked choppier, more dangerous. Unemployment and underemployment are potentially the most serious threats to Chinese market socialism. The chapters in part one speak to changes in Chinese cultural-economic relations and to new regimes of difference produced by the emerging Chinese market.

The chapters deal with the creation of new markets and industries—an understudied area that foregrounds the constructed nature of economic reforms and thus of personal experiences of the market. In analyzing different representations of the market in China (here the network, the labor market, and the social market for Chinese rock and roll music), we take the market to be a cultural product as well as a form of cultural production. All three authors posit an intimate relationship between a Chinese socialist market and the urban, but one that remains unequal and local nonetheless. Jeffery and Efird's chapters outline how the parameters of various markets are drawn through extant cultural categories and an urbanity that is spatially associated with the foreign. Hoffman traces the channeling of the nation's most desirable labor pool—college graduates—into urban labor markets.

While much has been written about the disempowerment of the nation-state in the face of increasingly flexible and mobile capital, in China we see a process of negotiation between the state and new kinds of economic actors (Anagnost 1997). The state and the market are sometimes mutually constitutive, as in Hoffman's chapter, where labor markets turn out to be neither naturalized nor autonomous but a process through which different agents (university employment counselors, employers in state and other institutions, and college graduates) act as interlocutors and constituents of both the state and the market. In other instances, these categories are more ambiguous, more explicitly oppositional, and less state initiated, as in Jeffery and Efird's chapters. In both of these cases, new markets (direct sales and rock music, respectively) sprang up at some distance from the gaze of the state through the efforts of individuals who identified themselves as bearers of indigenized transnational culture. However, neither were wholly independent of the state but were established through the efforts of local and national-level officials.

The equivocal and contradictory position of the state, where officials increasingly find themselves representing the interests of capital, is ironic at the very least given that the nature of relations between labor and capital has been one of the founding moral narratives of the entire socialist era. Hoffman and Jeffery's chapters posit employer-worker relations as a critical moment of struggle over basic values of appropriate personal sacrifice and just rewards, talent, and professionalism.

Hoffman details the transition from the state bureaucratic distribution of labor to a labor distribution process shaped by market forces, in this instance a particular labor market that valorizes certain kinds of urban labor while stigmatizing others. Her study of students, employment officers, and employers at institutions of higher education, themselves strictly urban phenomena, focuses attention on the construction of desirable labor—that is, highly educated urban male intellectuals rather than less educated, female, out of work factory hands or agricultural workers. Jeffery's study, on the other hand, shows an entire industry pathologized by the state. It is the tension around the relationship between direct sales distributors and their companies, which the state is ultimately unable to mediate due to the spatial and social structure of network marketing, that eventually destroyed the industry in 1998. Efird notes that practices viewed by some as outside or even counter to the interests of the state (in this case the creation of a consumer base for Chinese rock music) are not necessarily outside the interests of the market.

Efird's chapter on the development of the Chinese rock music (*yaogun*) market and Jeffery's on the Chinese direct sales industry also contribute analyses of the indigenization of foreign market practices, narratives, and capital. Efird recounts the processes by which yaogun—a phenomenon that takes place largely within urban spaces—mediated between locally defined notions of art and commodification, foreign cachet and local authenticity, and state intervention and private initiatives. Jeffery describes how the promise offered by foreign and cosmopolitan marketing practices, techniques, and skills extends to all-around personal transformation.

The chapters each address the issue of market identities, or new forms of subjectivity that come into being through market discourses, and their relationship to the urban. It is through the practicing and hopeful bodies of university graduates, would-be multilevel marketers, and rock musicians that particular ways of dressing, talking, walking, and other forms of self-expression become authorized at the same time as they devalue older or alternative modes. Ultimately, the contradictions between socialist and market era values are experienced most saliently in terms of identity.

Part Two: Gender, Bodies, and Consumer Culture Part two brings together several overlapping themes to consider experiences of the urban: consumer culture, bodies, and representations of gender. Economic reforms in China have brought the Chinese citizen into increasingly close contact with transnational capitalist goods, ideas, and practices, inundating the Chinese landscape with a consumerism that refigures relationships and self-identities from the ground up. The four chapters in this section provide localized ethnographic analyses about the ways in which commodified ideals, narratives, and practices move around the world via human bodies, technologies, and capital (see Appadurai 1990; Featherstone 1990; King 1997; and Ong and Nonini 1997).

Yet, in considering the growth of a consumer culture, scholars of mainland China must remain attentive to the continuities and breaks with the pre-economic reform era. Indeed, thirty years of anticonsumption, antibourgeois, socialist education have been eroded but continue to shape the present. The 1990s brought about a flood of state-sanctioned and transnationally produced valorizations of consumption. "What comes into being," writes Mayfair Yang, "is a culture of desiring, consuming individuals yearning to be fulfilled" (1997: 303). Changing conceptions and experiences of the body and gender emphasize the individual as a project of self-identity and self-presentation; nevertheless, this project is mediated by state and national agendas (Bourdieu 1977; Turner 1994). These chapters highlight important institutional and social contexts as China seeks to enlarge its presence on the international political and cultural scene, maintain political and social stability, and promote economic development.

Gottschang's chapter explores the position of urban hospitals as representations of modernity and bioscience as well as changing regimes of sexuality and feminine body management. Women are subject to contradictory messages about their bodies and those of their children. In a Beijing hospital, Gottschang analyzes the effect of state birth control policies that place the burden of producing healthy citizens upon women and their bodies. At the same time, however, images of sexually attractive mothers used to promote infant formula products and breast-feeding play on new mothers' concerns with regaining their prepregnancy shapes. In the convergence of motherhood and consumerism in the hospital, self-identity is being reorganized in a way that moves beyond the earlier, socialist model of womanhood, a model that emphasized the strong, asexual woman, to one that also embraces a slim body image and sexual attractiveness.

The chapters in this section also highlight an increased commodification of culture and tradition, concentrated in women's bodies and framed within regional, national, and international interests. Clark describes the production of marriage introduction agency videos that show off young women in Shenzhen to foreign men in which traditional femininity was the most desired quality. Brownell discusses the evaluation of traditional oriental beauty in the context of a mainland "supermodel" contest held by a transnational modeling agency to choose the next Chinese model for international competition. And Hyde illustrates the construction of an ethnic minority "culture" marked as rural, feminine, and sexual.

Clark, Brownell, and Hyde also offer analyses of flows of narrative, imagery, and practice circulated via the media, migrant workers, tourists, athletes, models, and others between countryside and city. Brownell posits the urban as a site for the production of an elite cosmopolitan culture that draws country people to the city with visions of an urbane lifestyle and even an "imagined cosmopolitanism" (Schein, this volume). These imagined lifestyles are part of the promotion of a "misrecognition" of growing social and economic inequality by urban cultural producers such as modeling agencies, media, and other urban institutions (Bourdieu and Passeron 1990: 4–5, 12–15, 177–78). These are also the bodies that represent the nation in international competitions. As such, they shape and are shaped by both a national Chinese identity and the idea of Beijing as the civilizing center in a country fraught with increasingly powerful urban centers. In the bodies of young, female fashion models— who are "made, not born"—we see clearly the production of a concept of feminine beauty that must answer at once to nationalist, culturalist, and transnational market interests. Clark presents a view of Shenzhen, the bustling special economic zone in the South that draws in large numbers of migrant and other workers every year. Her research centers explicitly on young women who move to the city in search of work, adventure, and love—and whose expectations are often dampened by the state's refusal to provide them with legal permanent residency. The borders of the city still represent real barriers to nonresidents—and yet the state is willing to lift national bureaucratic barriers to assist the same women in entering into transnational marriages with Japanese or Singaporean men. Clark's work among marriage introduction agencies shows how these women, still in the process of becoming urbanites, construct themselves as traditional Chinese women in order to appeal to men in other Asian countries. The very female bodies that are unwanted in Shenzhen become transformed into marketable commodities for relatively wealthy foreign men.

Hyde gives an example of an urban site that is developing a marketing niche for itself. In this case, the southwestern city of Jinghong is perceived by the rest of China as an ethnically other, tropical rural paradise brimming with sexually exotic young maidens. At the same time, it operates as an emblem of the urban within the region because of its highly developed prostitution and gambling industries. This city has become a space where migrant women of all ethnicities make a living off rich male tourists by masquerading as eroticized Tai girls and a place where male Han tourists come to fulfill their fantasies of the high life, gambling, and alluring women. Minority Tai, majority Han, and other ethnic groups in Jinghong, argues Hyde, are engaged in a highly disputed process of creating a commodified culture of Tai ethnicity by exploiting and refashioning Tai traditional culture. Together the chapters present diverse ways in which the Chinese female body is being packaged in relation to the growing consumer market, as well as how women are engaged in presentation of a certain bodily self for their own social and economic success.

Part Three: Negotiating Urban Spaces Post-Mao economic reforms have fostered dramatic changes in the relationships between space, time, state, and society. Following Massey's suggestion (1994) that places are never static or empty concepts but reflective of gendered and unequal power relations, the chapters in part three address space, place, and the urban as contested social processes. The transformation of state-society relations and the partial withdrawal of the state from domestic and social life have given rise to increasingly diverse kinds of leisure and personal space. The authors in these chapters suggest that this reshaping of space has been accompanied by changing relationships between the urban, modern, rural, national, and transnational. As new policies displace the planned structures of the socialist order, individuals such as railway workers, migrant laborers, and even ordinary consumers must locate themselves in new markets with vastly different social geographies. The readying of the Chinese population for participation in global capitalism has taken place through a state-initiated civilizing process aimed at re-making subjectivities into those appropriate for a disciplined, efficient work force (Anagnost 1997).

The socialist era was marked by a politicization of domestic, social, and public space through periodic mass campaigns, social movements, and rituals (cf. Anagnost 1997; Brownell 1995; and Rofel 1999). A temporality based on a continuum between a bitter past, a present of deprivation, and a sunny socialist future privileged the future over the present and in the process minimized consumption to increase production (Croll 1994; Rofel 1999). While the opportunities for economic reform have spread unequally across the Chinese landscape, creating hierarchies of investment along axes of hinterland and coast, and Northwest and South, the idea of the nation has become one of multiple times and spaces (cf. Anagnost 1997).

As Verdery has noted for Romania during a similar transformative period, the time-space of a socialist economy was a poor match for the accelerated time-space of post-Fordist global accumulation and production, which is characterized by "just in time" inventories, increasing turnover time, and capital circulation (1996: 34–36). Key features of socialist economies, such as cumbersome bureaucratic planning and distribution and centralized control over the production process, may have had more resonance with the economics of Fordism than with the "nimbleness" of capital attributed to practices of flexible accumulation (ibid.). In the process of moving from plan to market in China, space itself has become commodified. Capitalist practices produce particular kinds of space, yet already inscribed in such space are memories and practices of a socialist era that continue to inform the new.

For example, as the socialist medical system moves toward a profit system, place has gained new significance in the social geographies of health care. Chen describes how access to health care and meanings of health have shifted from more communal and affordable practices, even in forms such as meditation and breathing (*qigong*) or folk dancing (*yangge*), to new practices that speak to an individual consumer who interacts directly with the pharmaceutical market. In her analysis of contemporary modes of healing and medicine consumption, Chen notes how processes of decentralization, greater access to technology in rural areas, and new drug markets have called into question the urban as the privileged site of medical care. She points out that as people bypass hospitals and clinics in their quest for health and the good life, their roles are no longer defined as patients but as consumers or clients who have a certain autonomy from some aspects of the hospital-based medical system. However, as individuals become the focus of marketing ploys by drugstores and pharmaceutical firms, wealth and access to new medicines critically alter the social relations of medicine in rural and urban contexts.

According to Junghans, the spatialization of time during the socialist period immobilized Chinese citizens through the household registration system and fixed specific places in a national developmental hierarchy. Through the narratives of railway workers, she addresses changing geographies of distinction engendered by mobility and market opportunities. In the movement from plan to market, formerly prized railway jobs and places have lost status as a different set of cultural values comes to shape individual positions and self-worth. Railway lines and workers now defined through qualities such as old/young, educated/uneducated, inside/outside, and backward/progressive, are ranked in a hierarchy of modernity and exchange value. Workers tied to unprofitable places within a particular railway station and to lines now seen as less desirable are linked symbolically with the planning era of stasis and centralization, while those on the faster, lucrative, more easterly, and more heavily traveled lines represent the dynamism of the market era. Junghans emphasizes that the current spatialization of the social landscape should be linked to its legacy if we are to understand people's experiences of place and space.

Zhang's portrayal of a migrant community on the outskirts of Beijing offers a clear example of the relationship between space, power, and representation in a challenge over place. Zhang addresses the symbolic and disputed meanings of space as it becomes marked as criminal, unsafe, and private. The migrant entrepreneurs of Zhejiangcun, in the process of building businesses and residences, created a self-governing community perceived by local authorities and Beijing residents as a threat to social order. Part of the socially marginalized "floating population," the entrepreneurs' success pushed the limits of state tolerance for economic and social autonomy as tensions between migrants, local citizens, police, and municipal authorities escalated. The need to enact state legitimacy led to the destruction by authorities of the migrant homes and businesses and their expulsion from the city. As Zhang's analysis highlights, changing state-society relations demand new forms of political resolution that rely upon spatial codes of order.

Collectively, the chapters in part three demonstrate how, even as individual, social, and physical locations shift under market reform, new practices have emerged to counter dislocation and create a sense of belonging.

Part Four: Expressions of the Urban   In the final section, the authors explore some of the ways in which urbanity has been characterized—in scholarly or popular opinion as well as in transnational settings or specific mainland sites. They suggest that historically embedded meanings of the urban continue to have powerful effects on everyday lives and on the ways those lives are represented. The authors urge us to pay attention to the agency of individuals and crowds whether it is the contemporary renegotiation of Chinese urban/rural distinction, as in Schein and Ballew's chapters, or Western social science theories of Chinese rurality and urban anonymity, as in Hertz's chapter.

In the early twentieth century, Chinese urban intellectuals came to see the countryside and its vast peasant population as a primary reason for China's failure to achieve modernity. After the 1949 revolution, however, the oppositions of rural/traditional/backward and urban/modern/cosmopolitan were explicitly contested by the Maoist vision of the restorative potential of peasant labor. In the 1990s, perceptions that rural China was preventing the entire nation from modernizing re-emerged in state and popular rhetoric. Indeed, changes in migration and urbanization brought about by market reforms and China's continuing integration with the global economy have led to increasingly complex interpretations of the relationships between rurality, urbanity, and modernity. One way of understanding how these interpretations are produced is through specific ethnographic cases such as those in this section: Ballew discusses how Shanghai rural factory workers and urban television producers negotiate cosmopolitanism and the representation of rurality; Hertz challenges theories of anonymity and individualization as they apply on crowded Shanghai streets; and Schein details the production of Miao ethnicity through young people's experimentation with rural/minority/urban distinctions in village courting and other rituals and practices.

In Ballew's chapter, we see how Shanghai television producers drew upon cultural assumptions about rural tastes in their work to create a new rural television channel in the early 1990s. Ironically, these very assumptions subverted their project. On a production shoot meant to use the voices of authentic, enthusiastic rural viewers, suburban Shanghai residents contested TV producers' beliefs about rural viewing preferences. Rural Channel producers found their audience surprisingly uninterested in the programming, such as traditional Chinese opera, that was supposed to be appealing to them. This exemplifies how urbanites, planners, and state authorities misrepresented the rural "other" as culturally unsophisticated and frozen in time. Nevertheless, Ballew shows that as urban media producers continue to produce programming that fits their vision of the rural television audience, the audience itself also insists its interests be represented.

Shanghai ruralites' rejection of popular stereotypes is echoed in different ways among members of the Miao ethnic minority group in Schein's chapter. Here the rural/traditional/backward framework is further complicated by the Miao's minority status. As with other minority groups in China, the Miao are valorized by the state as exemplars of tradition. Miao young people, though, experiment with their ethnicity to reposition themselves within the Chinese social structure. In rural Guizhou, Miao youth gain relative proximity to the urban through the selective creation and consumption of courting and marriage practices— some coded as traditional, others as cosmopolitan. This cultural reworking enables Miao young people to take charge of an identity neither burdened by a weighty traditional past nor engulfed by a dominant Han culture. Schein's chapter also underscores the point, as does Ballew's, that accessing the urban is conceived not as moving physically to cities but as appropriating and often reworking goods, ideas, and trends associated with urbanity and urban life. Together these chapters demonstrate the need to go beyond representations of the urban as one pole of rural-urban dualism (cf. Certeau 1984; Shields 1996).

Ellen Hertz, on the other hand, examines urban society on its own terms through an analysis of the cultural construction of anonymity or "facelessness." In discussing moments of urban anonymity, such as crowd behavior, Hertz offers an alternative to what has been described as the relational construction of Chinese personhood, represented by the concept of "face." *Face* refers to one's social status in the eyes of others, which can be accumulated, lost, or given to another and is said to be a key principal guiding relations between Chinese people, rural or urban. Its corollary, facelessness, here expressed through phenomena of "fevers" such as stock market participation, occurs in those moments when individuals willingly abandon the particularistic identities that define their relations with others to a collective, anonymous experience. Interestingly, it is the way people conduct themselves in the context of a fever (*re*), such as making big money on the stock market, that provides a means of gaining individual distinction within the group. Hertz questions the characterization of anonymity in Western societies as a naturalized, un-marked feature of modern urban life. She concludes that in the Chinese urban context, anonymity is embedded within a diverse range of cultural meanings and practices that illuminate the relationship between the collectivity and the individual.

Together these chapters compel us to examine anew popular cultural and scholarly categories such as urbanity and anonymity, all the while remaining attentive to their specific histories and to the diverse ways these categories are lived through individual practice.

It is our hope that the volume expands what historically has been an emphasis on rurality within the anthropology of China. The thirteen essays here offer localized insights about the imagined and practiced urban in China. In the ethnographic particularities of each case, the instability of categories and distinctions about the urban and urbanization are brought to light. At the same time, these essays insist upon the salience of the past in China's present moment.

Note

1   Yet see Cohen on elite invention of the "peasantry" (*nongmin*) as a new cultural category depicted in negative images and considered lacking in leadership ability. Cohen suggests that the term *nongmin* (versus *nongfu,* "farmer") first came about through a deepening of the rural-urban cultural divide and the rise of an urban-based intelligentsia in the early part of the twentieth century. This image was adopted by the Chinese Communist Party (CCP) to implement its own political agenda (1994: 157–58).

Part One Xia Hai: Ethnographies of Work and Leisure

Lyn Jeffery Placing Practices: Transnational
Network Marketing in Mainland China

What we're selling is not product but our characters!—Woman, Chinese
MLM recruit

For many people in China, the last decade of the century was a time of increase: an increase in mobility, in access to a variety of material goods and cultural products, and in varied employment "opportunities." Yet it was also marked by an increase in anxiety about massive state sector layoffs and the loss of state benefits that accompanied those jobs, in anger about corruption among state bureaucrats and local officials, and in uncertainty about the ideological stability of the country's leadership. Established social topographies—cultural and institutional assumptions about who belongs where and what various categories of persons represent—have been substantively reworked since the beginning of economic reforms in the late 1970s. Much of the remapping has relied on new modes of participation in and conceptualizations of global processes, the most important being transnational capitalist markets and their cultural forms. From 1990 to its official ban in 1998, the Chinese multilevel marketing movement (MLM) offered millions of Chinese the opportunity to participate in this type of cultural repositioning, allowing them to partially replace or subvert conventional social geographies.[1] Old and young, male and female, urbanites and peasants alike attended three-day training sessions where they learned to talk, think, and move, ostensibly just like those above them in these transnational marketing networks. By 1997, the multilevel marketing (*chuanxiao*) industry, introduced to China by American, Taiwanese, and Japanese companies, had sold an estimated

U.S.$7 billion of health-related products through networks with some 10 million participants.[2] In times of financial uncertainty, MLM provided quick cash through the recruitment of friends and family organized into networks (also known in English by the pejorative term *pyramids*). Relying on oral presentations and training seminars, chuanxiao mobilized and capitalized upon the legendary Chinese social connections between kin, classmates, colleagues, hometown residents, ethnic groups, and, increasingly, among those of common religious faith and similar age, most notably retirees.[3]

Since the vast majority of participants (also called distributors) had little or no background in sales and marketing, MLM training focused on the transformation of the individual into a multilevel marketer. As with MLM around the world, consumption, sales, and recruitment within one's personal networks were presented as opportunities for life enhancement rather than as the commodification of social relations. And, as with MLM elsewhere, the industry and its practitioners were often viewed with suspicion by others. State concerns centered around the significant financial, moral, and political problems posed by MLM. Not only was it nearly impossible to tax the networks of individuals spread throughout the country, but it was also difficult to control large-scale meetings of several thousand participants, meetings in which chuanxiao's implicit message about the bankruptcy of socialism was heard loud and clear by recently laid-off factory workers. In the larger national environment, where construction of a proper consumer identity had become a significant project of the state, some forms of consumerism were apparently more acceptable than others.[4] Official worries were echoed by anti-chuanxiao narratives I regularly heard from many people outside the MLM community. These comments, often based on direct experience with chuanxiao practitioners, focused on the way marketers capitalized upon their personal relationships, "cheating family, cheating friends."[5] By early 1998, the government had banned the industry outright, making visible the point at which the social costs of the market economy to the state became too great.

As the planned economy system is dismantled under the program of reforms, the ability of the Chinese Communist Party (CCP) to impose the state-sponsored production of culture and knowledge is increasingly being challenged. In a country where thirty years of political movements sought to create a dominant concept of the normal Chinese socialist citizen, who was encouraged to be frugal and self-sacrificing and discouraged from engaging in bourgeois or capitalist activities, widespread opinion now holds that participation in the market is not only inevitable but desirable. Whereas Maoism equated capitalism with immorality, today we find a discourse (both official and popular) of the market as a civilizing practice that implies and confers proximity to the modern. Despite widespread anti-MLM sentiment, chuanxiao made sense to millions of people within the context of this larger progressive narrative.

Not only is the notion of the market mobilized by the state as a tool to transform China into an international superpower, but forms of work such as sales and marketing are said to bring about different personal identities. These relatively newly possible identities are explicitly linked to the dizzying variety of contemporary Chinese notions of Western culture and of life outside the borders of the People's Republic. Mayfair Yang has emphasized the enormous impact of Chinese commercialism in Hong Kong, Taiwan, and elsewhere overseas on contemporary popular imaginaries of the transnational in China (1997). And yet, chuanxiao, represented by and to PRC marketers as an "originally American" practice, offers a striking example of the difficulty of identifying discursive practices as either Western or Asian or of trying to define which is more or less influential in contemporary mainland China. The MLM industry was introduced almost entirely through ethnic overseas Chinese interlocutors, but *their* narratives and representations articulated MLM, as a transnational capitalist practice, to an entire range of qualities, associations, and possibilities such as "the West," freedom, the fulfilled self, independence, filial piety, spontaneity, and many others.[6] This is not to say that chuanxiao did not also resonate with nationalist and culturalist definitions of Chineseness—it did. But it was the power of MLM to redraw the boundaries of established Chinese social geographies of marginality with the space of the network that convinced so many people that the chuanxiao marketer identity was desirable despite the negative opinions of newspapers, television, friends, and family. Itself a culturally marginalized industry, the MLM network by its very nature symbolically and discursively privileges its marginal members, who are the main engine of profit for members higher up in the structure.

As Anna Tsing demonstrated so convincingly in *The Realm of the*

Diamond Queen (1993), local, national, and transnational discourses can create overlapping zones of domination and difference, where people are excluded in multiple ways, some more than others. Within these circumstances, people find endless ways of mobilizing powerful narratives and practices for their own social, emotional, financial, or cultural ends; and sometimes, they are successful. As China becomes ever more engaged with the exclusionary capitalist networks that connect specific nodes of wealth and power, certain other capitalist practices, such as the multilevel marketing network, nevertheless also enable individuals to become part of *inclusionary* networks that subvert conventional notions of rurality, urbanity, and cosmopolitanism. Chinese MLM is thus best understood as a proactive *placing practice,* that is, a practice that situates individuals within an imagined geography (in this case, a commodified geography, a market) and revises their marginality or centrality at multiple levels of meaning.

Below I briefly introduce the establishment of the industry in the PRC and then explore the central chuanxiao idea of "duplication" (*fuzhi*), one of the mechanisms through which the sociospatial hierarchy of transnational networks of Chinese marketers was created. It didn't matter where distributors actually resided as long as they "duplicated" the emotional, physical, intellectual, and social status of those in the network "above them." This duplication replaced new recruits from the edges of the network into its inner webs. It also assigned a market value to certain narrowly defined techniques (dress, comportment, speech, and consumption) that were felt to bring cosmopolitan transnationalism in contact with the body of the individual. At the same time, the vast range of behaviors and beliefs that lay outside of the confines of MLM were devalued and made illegitimate or even immoral, in a neat reversal of generally negative public opinions of chuanxiao.

Leveling the Competition   "Chinese people are born to *chuan,*" said one successful distributor in an interview. The translation "chuanxiao," originally Taiwanese, from the Japanese, from the English, was an apt one: the practice of marketing or selling, *xiao,* was being *chuan,* a versatile word with meanings including "to pass on, hand down, impart, teach, spread, transmit, convey, infect" (Shanghai Jiaotong University 1993: 358). With more than a passing resemblance to another chuan activity—*chuanjiao*, or "doing missionary work"—chuanxiao was spread by word of mouth, literature, videos, and especially group meetings often led by charismatic, articulate marketers. Typically, MLM producers or companies sell directly to consumers, who then become a marketing and advertising force that moves product for the company by building "levels" of consuming sales-people below them into hierarchical networks. As in MLM around the world, new recruits take up their positions "down" the "line" from their "upline" (*shangxian*), the person who introduced them. The vertical line of distributors leads back up to the company of course, and in the case of many MLM firms, beyond Chinese national borders.

This spatial hierarchy is manifested in both practice and profit. The principle of multilevel marketing is elegant in its simplicity: on top of the wholesale price for a product add a hefty markup (up to 60 percent of the final price) and return that markup directly to the sales force. Require salespeople to buy a certain amount of product at the retail price in order to "enter the network" (*ruwang, ruhui*) and obtain the selling rights. Those who have the right to sell are then able to take advantage of the 60 percent commission that is redistributed by the company, ideally the producer. In MLM, an individual makes a commission on not only his or her own sales but on those of several levels of distributors in the network below. From the company's perspective, consumers are also employees: they are marketers, advertisers, personnel managers, and customer rela-tions officers rolled into one. Further, by structuring the sales force in vertically integrated webs one obtains an exponential effect. As MLM ·advocates love to demonstrate on blackboards across the world, if a distributor were to find "only one person a month" to be in his or her network, and each of them was in turn able to find only one person a month, he or she would have a network of 2,048 people after just one year.[7] Under one popular Taiwanese-owned company, such a network would have pulled in 200,000 renminbi (RMB) a month (U.S.$24,000), at least for a certain period of time.[8] The initial investment required to become a distributor ranged from two weeks' to half a year's salary or even more, but this did not seem to stop some people from borrowing money or selling possessions to scrape the sum together. In fact, it was often the poorest who were most attracted to companies with extremely high entrance fees, since these would also yield higher profits in a shorter period of time.

The first chuanxiao companies to arrive in China were based in Taiwan, Hong Kong, Japan, and the United States. Major international firms with global networks began initiating recruits alongside small, fly-by-night outfits that provided shoddy products and left many distributors out of luck and money. Chuanxiao's person to person distribution system allowed companies to conduct sales outside any known Chinese commercial distribution system. According to Chinese economists who have studied the industry, the government seems to have been caught unawares, as these early companies paid little tax and imported goods without being subject to normal commercial regulations.[9] In fact, the state had never encountered this type of marketing on such a large scale.[10] Nevertheless, MLM expanded to every corner of China and huge quantities of products were sold (and huge profits made) by individuals, companies, and local state agencies, including commercial, tax, and public security organs. As in many other national MLM markets, the most popular products in the PRC were health related (exercise machines based on Chinese or Japanese medical principles, Chinese medicinal beverages, calcium, lecithin, fish oil, aloe products, and so on) or home related (shampoo and soap for the body and home, computer and TV screens, and so on).

By definition, MLM avoids formal paid advertising and draws its recruits from personal relationships. In China, company representatives (primarily distributors with their own profit incentives rather than company managers) created a market for the concept by convincing people one on one and then in larger meetings. The key was that they had to recruit *the right* people—people who were ready to hear their mixed message of personal growth and fortune, those who were not wealthy but could imagine wealth within their grasp, who were articulate or at least had a certain amount of social status. The first MLM companies did manage to attract highly placed elites, especially those in the culture industries. After it became apparent to these first participants that they would not be making money as quickly or easily as company propaganda promised, MLM spread to less well positioned people who had farther to climb in terms of upward social and economic status. Foreign marketers started from places where they had access to convenient transportation and communications. Overseas Chinese often had family, friends, and professional contacts in urban centers. A deeply rooted domestic and transnational characterization of the Chinese countryside as backward also engendered the assumption (still common among foreign marketers today) that a "new" idea such as MLM would never be accepted in the village. For these reasons, early recruits were not drawn from villages but from major urban commercial centers across the country—Guangzhou, Shanghai, Beijing, Wuhan, Shenzhen, Dalian, Qingdao, Xiamen, Xuzhou, Chengdu, and others. The first "new soldiers," as they are occasionally referred to in industry parlance, were urban professionals (academics, journalists, and business people), younger people who literally "looked the part" and were picked off the street, and mainland relatives of ethnic Chinese distributors residing in other countries.

Once chuanxiao was introduced to urban Chinese, it spread through their local personal and professional networks and, if they were successful, moved farther afield to their distant relatives, old classmates, fellow war veterans, and so on. Urban migrants (*waidi ren*), who generally have more difficulty establishing local connections, were in a position of strength, for they could take their chuanxiao business away from the major urban centers, back to their villages and hometowns, and introduce it as a new, decidedly urban form. As with the development of MLM in many countries, chuanxiao's message was ultimately most attractive to those who had some difficulty accessing channels to money and power within the extant system—poor, aspiring, or undereducated residents; laid-off urban workers with few marketable skills; educated professionals in state-run "hospitals" and schools; and workers in transportation and manufacturing sectors, whose salaries lagged behind those in the private sector.

In 1997, I attended an informational seminar where one successful northeastern China distributor, Ms. Liu, told an audience of three hundred distributors and potential recruits how she had been recruited to chuanxiao several years earlier.[11] She had been sitting alone, waiting for her husband in a foreign-owned hotel in Dalian (a large northeastern port city) when a well-dressed Taiwanese woman at the next table struck up a conversation with her. Commenting on the fashionable cut of Ms. Liu's clothes, the woman tried to pique her interest. "How would you like to know about a great business opportunity? I've made a fortune for myself in a very short time." The audience roared with appreciation at how Ms. Liu told the Taiwanese woman that she wasn't interested since she already had a successful business—one that "probably makes even more money than yours!" The story ended with a laugh when Ms. Liu described how she agreed to meet the woman anyway. Ms. Liu even offered to send her private car to pick the woman up. Of course, there was no way to verify Liu's story of who she was when she discovered chuanxiao; she and her husband both had high-school educations, and he worked as an engineer for a state-owned mining corporation. She didn't specify what kind of "business" she was engaged in at the time, but the implication was clear—she had been wealthy and successful. In her retrospective, she didn't need the money or the affiliation with wealthy overseas Chinese, yet they formed the foundation of her narrative's allure. Her scenario mobilized a stage set and cast of characters that had long been familiar to the audience from television, literature, and film: expensively clothed women at leisure in a gleaming hotel lobby bar, probably drinking coffee or perhaps even cocktails, and a private automobile.[12] Her story also illustrates how chuanxiao recruiting connections were often made, not through personal relations but by approaching strangers (a fairly unusual behavior in China) who seemed to be in the right kind of place or have the right look (i.e., not a peasant or a worker).

The recruiting of strangers also appeared in the sales pitch performances of Mr. Yang, an articulate and ambitious Beijing man in his late twenties. Mr. Yang had become involved with MLM fairly early. By the time I met him in 1996, he had been in the business five years and was working as a lecturer in a Beijing-owned chuanxiao company. His first encounter with MLM took place on the subway in 1991 as he was on his way to his administrative post in a state-run institution. A business-suited, older Hong Kong man smiled at him on the train, got off at his stop, and pursued him down the street. He then approached Mr. Yang, telling him how urbane he looked and talking about a mysterious "opportunity." Mr. Yang finally accepted his business card and gave him his phone number. For the next week, the man called him twice a day. Eventually, Mr. Yang agreed to hear about the opportunity, went to hear a lecture in a basement with seven other young urbanites, and so entered the world of multilevel marketing.

The public repetition of these kinds of personal narratives highlighted the imported nature of chuanxiao and linked it to the stereotypical accoutrements of an imagined cosmopolitanism. The speakers embodied the promise of MLM as a process through which one could become that well-dressed woman, that Hong Kong businessman. Having made the transition, successful salespeople like Liu and Yang (no matter how they positioned themselves prior to their participation in MLM) showed how the mainland Chinese self-perception of marginalization vis-à-vis overseas Chinese could be reversed in the dynamic of being courted by outsiders. Indeed, the pursuit of those who feel themselves marginalized *in any way* remains one of MLM's most powerful tools, whether it be within a transnational, national, or subnational context.[13] The concept of chuanxiao was thus sold to urban residents in part by appealing to their understanding of "business opportunities," a trope that was downplayed in favor of others (such as health or the acquisition of marketable skills) as the market expanded to include those less confident with their participation in the modernity business.

Once having paid their fee to join, each distributor was doubly positioned at a node in his or her "upline's" network *and* at the "top" of his or her own network; this engendered a potent set of entrepreneurial narratives that valorized the "free" individual such as "being your own boss" (*zuo ziji de zhuren*) and "relying on oneself to support oneself" (*kao ziji yang ziji*). For a significant number of chuanxiao practitioners, this discourse was polarized with the "tradition" of anti-individualist socialism in China. The market was seen by them as a positive, possibly transformative force that opened up spaces in which different kinds of individuals could develop themselves. Consider, for example, the complaint of one forty-six-year-old Shandong village leader, whose status as a government official made him ineligible to (legally) participate in chuanxiao: "I've been oppressed for so many years. I have an energy inside me, it's just that I have no opportunity to realize it." His comments, framed as regret for time wasted in state bureaucracies, echoed MLM training rhetoric without his ever having practiced chuanxiao and illustrate the view of many participants on the liberatory potential for self-realization offered by chuanxiao. One Hainan man in his thirties quit his job in a major municipal government because he, too, felt he was unable to "give rein to himself" (*fahui ziji*).[14] The man, a college graduate who spoke fluent Japanese and English, spent months researching various MLM companies and eventually chose one of the larger, American-based, Taiwanese-led firms. By following in the footsteps of network marketers "at the top"—who were often foreign, overseas Chinese, or at least not poor and rural mainland Chinese—Chinese practitioners felt they might overcome their own marginality, whether vis-à-vis overseas Chinese, "Westerners," or domestic elites and urbanites. I now turn to one of the mechanisms that effected such a process.

Transforming the Margins: Duplication So-called potential training was seen by marketers and critics alike as one of the most controversial recruiting practices in Chinese MLM. Chuanxiao's promise was predicated on the concept of human "potential," said to exist in everyone, waiting only to be accessed or "dug out" through special training.[15] "Success" was based on the performance of the individual and its opposite (namely, poverty) on the failure of the individual to manifest himself or herself properly. Once potential was seen to lie latent within each person, one had only to "develop," "exercise," or "give rein to" one's self to redeem the failed past as well as transform the future.

We were on the second day of a three-day potential training session. Four hundred participants, the majority of whom had not yet joined the company, sat cross-legged on the threadbare red carpet of a second-floor ballroom in a small hotel on the outskirts of Beijing. Black plastic taped over the windows shut out most of the light and a good deal of the air as well. We had played a series of games the day before, which were designed to train both body and mind in the techniques of marketing. Most were aimed at breaking down our inhibitions about spreading the news of the "wonderful opportunity" (of chuanxiao) to our family and friends, even to strangers. We tore off our "false masks," threw them to the floor, and stomped on them; we learned the proper techniques for shaking hands and hugging and practiced on each other; we broke in and out of circles of people; we fell backwards into each other's arms. Each activity was followed by a period of "sharing," including testimonials on the meaning of the games delivered by individual members of the twenty-three small groups. The chuanxiao speaking style was encouraged by a competitive points system, which also increased identification with one's team. By the second day, most people had mastered the style of public self-representation: they introduced themselves with their name and place of residence or origin, and the audience responded by clapping and yelling "So-and-so, I love you!" So-and-so answered "I love you all, too!" This particular expression of emotion was very exciting for participants, most of whom had never voiced this kind of "love" aloud, even in the context of their own families. A palpable thrill coursed throughout the room as person after person performed the act on stage. The speaker then talked about how the game had taught him or her about the principles of chuanxiao and ended with a formulaic, fist-pumping exhortation to success, something along the lines of "You'll definitely succeed!" or "I want to make it to [highest level of distributorship in company]!"

It was then time for one of the "duplication" games, variants of the "telephone" games with which many Americans are familiar, in which a piece of information is passed down a line of people, often reaching its final destination wholly changed. We crowded around as one of the teams was lined up single file down the middle of the room. Mr. Sun, the head lecturer, handed the last person in the line a card with a Chinese saying on it: literally, wolf's heart, dog's lungs (meaning brutal, cold-blooded, or savage). The young man mimed a few different versions of the phrase until Mr. Sun found the one he liked best, a toothy but silent snarl for *wolf*, two hands around the heart for *heart*, running on all fours for *dog*, and chest thumping for *lungs*. The audience was allowed to laugh during this game, whereas some of the other exercises demanded the utmost seriousness on pain of public humiliation. The young man tapped the woman in front of him on the shoulder. She turned around to watch his performance and then tapped the shoulder of the man in front of her, did her version of wolf-heart-dog-lungs, and so on. By the time the person at the head of the line, some sixteen people later, performed the charade, it had morphed into what looked like a cruel imitation of a disabled person. The crowd was in hysterics. But we calmed down when it came to Sharing. "This game taught me that in order to succeed I have to study my upline." "If you don't duplicate well, your whole line will be off kilter." "We must trust our upline." Left unsaid was what else the game had illustrated—how very difficult it was to "duplicate" even a simple mimed phrase, much less an entire identity, and how easily it could end up as something completely different from its original.

One excerpt from a popular chuanxiao series justified duplication as follows:

An upline's biggest contribution toward your success, which is also his or her duty, is to offer a "mold" of the successful person. This mold of the successful person is used to "duplicate" every person within the same MLM system, so that whenever they talk about products, the system, MLM ideas, and so on, almost everyone is on the same track, everyone talks about things in the same way, and people's movements are the same. This is the only way to produce a common recognition, the only way to fuse into a system, and from this to produce feelings of intimacy (Fang 1996: 178)

Feelings of "intimacy" were necessary for several reasons. For MLM in general, the idea of the company as fictive kin serves to dampen the shock of commodifying relations with family and friends. For China, in particular, it may have served as a moral counterpart to the stigmatization of marketing found in both socialist and Confucian theory.

The hierarchy of vertical "lines" that emanated from the company all the way down to the individual distributor was constructed by and enabled this concept of duplication. What needed to be duplicated was the "packaging of the self" (Fang 1996: 72), which included speech, dress, consumption habits, physical habits such as hugging and handshaking, and, most importantly, "mind-set" (*xintai*).[16] In line with widespread social constructions of success and marketing exemplified within the popular Chinese field of "success studies," MLM books encouraged marketers to adopt the "look of a boss" by following "the etiquette of dressing." The marketing of cosmetics in particular required fairly strict adherence to conventional American business dress codes, that is, dark-colored business suits and ties for men and suits, nylons, and high-heeled shoes for women. For other product lines, on the other hand, some distributors deliberately chose not to change their appearance. "You see the clothes I wear," said a wealthy woman who marketed electric massage machines, gesturing toward her winter layers of long underwear, home-knit sweater, dark blue suit jacket, and trousers. "They're no different than anyone else's. I want to be an ordinary person; that way my down-lines feel there's no *distance* between us." Her analysis was quite correct: some viewed it as "closer to" a new self and others as "farther away" from their former practices, but the adoption—or not—of prescribed clothing was a placing practice in relation to a cosmopolitan market identity.

Bodies were further transformed (or sometimes were just said to have been by individuals for marketing purposes) through the consumption of products. Chuanxiao marketers were required to consume to enter the company, and the more they consumed the better. You had to use the product to be able to sell it, companies stressed again and again—though many did not. Few people would admit that they were not consistent consumers, but the fact is that many were too busy to follow consumption regimes and didn't have enough money to maintain that consumption anyway (Farquhar 1994b). However, for a good number of marketers, the discourse on consumption and the creation of healthy bodies was crucial to the way they defined themselves. Through regular use of the product, bodies were modified; through the marketing of the concept of health, some distributors aimed to transform their compatriots' bodies and minds from weak, unhealthy, and ignorant Chinese to strong, healthy, skilled citizens of an international community of capitalist marketers.[17]

Commonplace training in handshaking, hugging, and speechmaking focused on self-presentation and properly loving, enthusiastic interaction with others. By reproducing the international etiquette (a phrase used repeatedly in training) of expressive physical contact, marketers created a new environment within and around themselves.[18] They embodied what they defined as foreign, or at least non–mainland Chinese, culture. Perhaps this is why these physical training activities were a lightning rod for state and popular criticism of chuanxiao. Throughout 1996–98, newspaper reports from around the country wrote about participants being "hypnotized" and embracing each other in dark rooms. The most devastating report appeared on a Zhejiang provincial television station in the summer of 1997. In this instance, a reporter snuck a camera into one of the training sessions, and the resulting pictures of what looked like indiscriminate touching and people "learning to bark like dogs" caused problems for many chuanxiao practitioners. Nevertheless, practitioners still enthusiastically copied choreographed hugging, developed firm handshakes, consumed unknown products, spent time memorizing complicated product descriptions, talked endlessly of the correct mind-set, and contributed to charities. They believed these were the techniques whereby they had transformed themselves from edgy neophytes into marketers with their own locations on the network map.

According to MLM rhetoric (and despite marketers' own experiences in duplication games at training sessions), it was possible to simply replicate not only the body practices of those less marginal than oneself but their emotions, psychological outlooks, and attitudes as well. By accomplishing replication of one's upline, one redrew one's own cultural standing at the same time as one presumably became more deeply embedded in the network. "We begin with human conduct" (*cong zuoren kaishi*), said distributors and trainers over and over again. And the industry was filled with stories about former drug addicts, prostitutes, and gangsters reforming themselves through training, like the one described above, and becoming productive members of the network and society. The emphasis on correct conduct allowed multilevel marketers to distinguish themselves from what they constructed as the immoral practices of "traditional business."[19] A mix of socialist era anticapitalist sentiment and reform era antisocialist rhetoric, traditional business encompassed the supposedly tricky, fraudulent practices of the slick capitalist and the supposed sloth of the state worker, "reading the paper and drinking tea," as well as the corruption associated with both.

The most highly valued attributes of the multilevel marketing identity were honesty, mentorship, concern for others, self-sacrifice, hard work, and moral righteousness. The list suggests that these were trouble spots for many. One of the more famous proponents of Chinese chuanxiao education and theory (Mr. Ai was the top lecturer for China's largest domestically owned MLM company, which in mid-1997 had 1 million distributors on their books) wrote an article in the popular industry journal, *Chuanxiao Yanjiu* (Direct Selling Review), in an attempt to clarify the personal attributes of the MLM marketer.

> Chuanxiao people are those who "deeply love" this profession. They show loving concern for their colleagues, give their hearts in exchange for others' sincerity, and tenaciously endure misunderstanding and attack. . . . They should be (1) leaders in the social environment, (2) protectors of professional morality, (3) students of open-mindedness, (4) predictors of industry development, (5) models of perfect character, (6) organizers of group affinity, (7) heart to heart communicators, (8) producers of satisfied desires, (9) managers who create efficiency, and (10) leaders who steer things in the right direction. (Ai 1997; my translation)

Chinese MLM required the creation and maintenance of a new individual, one who nevertheless shared many qualities with the ideal socialist models of an older era: honesty, patience, morality, leadership, and, above all else, tenacious diligence and a constantly evaluated self.[20] The project to create a new individual, as well as some of the defining characteristics of that individual, draw in part on discourses of the "new socialist man" in Maoist theory and policy.[21] The *model self* of earlier consciousness-altering projects therefore may have discursively enabled its modern MLM counterpart, the duplicable self. Chuanxiao was constructed as a civilizing practice that brought health (through products), wealth, and happiness and raised the moral quality (*suzhi*) of the nation. One successful woman announced happily to an enthusiastic crowd, "What we are selling is not product but character!" And the best-selling character was the one that most closely matched the "mold" created by those above.

Making for the Margins From the point of view of those already included in multilevel marketing networks, network edges were the really important places to be—in the sense of having access to them. Profits were determined by the number of recruits below, who brought material gain and status. The people at the edges were the raw material waiting to be developed through the technology of duplication; they were always represented as limitless (though, realistically, marketing networks do reach their limits when they run out of people to recruit) and were always courted vigorously. From the point of view of those on the edge, of course, the middle was the place to be. By "duplicating" those above, one could begin the transformation of the self, but it was only through recruiting those below that one could leave the margins, construct one's own network, and thus complete the transformation. Duplication produced MLM's most compelling product—the formerly marginal individual, now increased in social and economic value and included in a global network. In this way, the spatial location of individuals within the world, the network, and the country was given a monetary value. As every Chinese practitioner will tell you, MLM was invented in the United States. It traveled to Japan, from there to Taiwan, and then on to China. In a very real way, proximity to the "top" of the line determined financial reward, with foreign MLM companies at the peak and Chinese rural residents at the bottom. The concept of a network that stretched in many cases "back" to the company in the United States, Taiwan, or Japan positioned Chinese individuals as the last to get in on the act, residing at the bottom of lines charted as "generations" of kin.

As Rofel argues, an entire and huge category of people—workers (*gongren*)—now appears "both outside of and as a hindrance to a reconstituted imaginary of modernity (1999: 96). Especially for those constructed as peripheral in terms of the ability to create and participate in various kinds of modern images within their own society, the opportunity to refashion themselves as possessors of cosmopolitan knowledge is a powerful incentive to join chuanxiao. Those farthest away from the "top" have the longest distance to traverse—and have to try the hardest with the fewest resources. But of course it is more complicated than this. It took only a few years for Chinese in the chuanxiao industry to begin constructing a specifically "Chinese" MLM corporate philosophy and practice. In order to challenge the "proximity to the foreign" as commodity, MLM companies owned by mainland Chinese sprang up, many of which used nationalism as a sharp marketing tool.[22] And in order to challenge the "proximity to the urban" as commodity, a few entrepreneurs started chuanxiao companies in small rural cities and inner provinces such as Ningxia and Xinjiang.

Through duplication and inclusion, MLM contained the possibility of upsetting typical Chinese urban/rural and current class power dynamics, by privileging newly imagined locations within the network over former visions of the local. It was possible for articulate, savvy ruralites and urban working class people to be at the top of huge networks, and a few became extremely rich, famous, and powerful in the chuanxiao world. They served as models for their former peers as well as tributes to the supposed equal opportunities of the network. Since MLM profit was mainly dependent upon recruitment and everyone—women, men, ethnic minorities, retirees, and the disabled—had "potential," marketing networks constituted a novel spatial trope and practice that could significantly destabilize hierarchical spatialized geographic, class, gender, state, and ethnic categories, although they could never be completely independent of them. Conventional Chinese spatial distinctions between urban/rural, center/periphery and inside/outside as spaces of relative privilege and poverty were overlaid by the network, which spread weblike across the country and indeed the world.[23] With their nodes of concentrated power linked horizontally by "rank" in the company and integrated vertically by financial control and "generation," Chinese MLM may have capitalized on a structure that looked very much like the structure of the CCP. Chuanxiao mobilized and literally traded on not only the familiarity of this morphology of human links but also the rhetoric, narrative form, and propagating techniques of the party. We must understand MLM narratives, like all market narratives in the PRC, as profiting from but also constrained to some extent within past and present state narratives, as they construct their own allure.

Erasure: The Demise of Chinese MLM for Now   The MLM network carved out a self-contained yet supposedly limitless sphere that placed participants in a transnational community, an economic sphere based on personal relationships that existed somehow *outside* the state economic system and *inside* a transnational economic one. Although chuanxiao's reliance on building personal relations into pyramids in order to turn a profit was the subject of years of sustained state media condemnation and general public distrust, MLM narratives and practices did echo larger discourses on the civilizing potential of the market. Its proponents claimed it capable of transforming the most recalcitrant laggards into upstanding individuals; its critics called it "murdering the ones closest to you." While chuanxiao traversed the far edge of appropriate economic and social behavior, it was not actually deemed illegal until state officials began to understand the incendiary power of its central processes. Industry training sessions focused first on the destruction of inhibitions against the desire for financial success and, second, on the encouragement of unflagging ambition. This had one meaning within the transnational MLM corporate network (namely, that one joined a wider community of like-minded, extraordinarily motivated people) but quite another when it was applied to mainland Chinese society more generally. There it only highlighted people's frustrations and anger at the government's failure to include them in modernization projects.

It is no wonder that the state first pathologized chuanxiao and then moved to criminalize it. What is curious and disturbing, however, is the reasoning offered by the state in its ban on MLM in April of 1998. Almost apologetically, the problem was said to lie not with the industry but with the Chinese people, who did not have a "mature" mentality, and with the state itself, whose "regulatory system was backward." The "low level of development of the market" meant that the Chinese were not ready for multilevel marketing. As the keeper of the market, the government found itself unable to launch a full-scale critique of the conditions leading to the wildfire growth of an industry that instilled dreams of getting rich quickly, left a wake of frustrated, angry consumers, and caused more than its share of violence. Instead, it spoke within what Anagnost writes about as "a discourse of lack, referring to the failure of the Chinese people to embody international standards of modernity, civility and discipline" (1997: 76). As MLM shows, there is a struggle over what kinds of sociospatial practices count as the enactment of these standards, to whom and where allegiances will be owed, and through whose bodies they will be made manifest.

Notes

I would like to thank the Wenner-Gren Foundation and the Fulbright-Hays Doctoral Dissertation Abroad program for funding my research from 1995 through 1997. This chapter initially benefited from substantive comments from participants at the Ethnographies of the Urban conference in 1997, particularly Professor Mayfair Yang. In the years since then it has undergone extensive revision, fueled by invaluable assistance from my coeditors, Nancy Chen, Connie Clark, and Suzanne Gottschang, as well as Cheryl Barkey, Jay Dautcher, Gail Hershatter, and Lisa Rofel.

1 Technically, multilevel marketing is part of a larger industry called direct selling. Direct selling is defined as the marketing of products outside of a fixed retail location, in other words, in homes, offices, schools, and so on. Multilevel marketing is perhaps best known to Americans through companies such as Amway and Mary Kay.

2 These estimates were provided by economists Li Shaohua and Yang Qian, deputy editor and chief editor, respectively, of the Beijing Commercial Management Cadre Institute's *Direct Selling Review.*

3 A detailed discussion of the notion of guanxi and the implications for and of chuanxiao is beyond the focus of this chapter. See Yang 1994; Kipnis 1997; and Yan 1996.

4 In the late 1990s, the Chinese identity with the most "rights" (*quanyi* or *quanli*) was that of the consumer, hands down. The Chinese government has put considerable effort into constructing a consumer identity "with Chinese characteristics" through the propagation of consumer protection rights and selective media coverage of those who harm them. In this way, the state attempts to dominate several troublesome discourses: that of rights, that of the proper agent of the socialist market economy, and the relationship between the two. International Consumer Protection Day, March 15, has become an official extravaganza along the lines of International

Workers Day. This includes a Spring-Festival-type television variety show and a three-day media blitz. China Central TV (CCTV) broadcasts programs in which uniformed members of the Ministry of Industry and Commerce staff tables around China's cities, fielding questions and complaints from consumers. The TV show follows a typical format of singing, dancing, and humorous skits but adds in exposés of faulty products and dramatic replays of human tragedies caused by manufacturers' neglect. See also Anagnost 1997 and the chapters by Gottschang and Chen in this volume.

5   In 1997, most urbanites had at least heard of chuanxiao, and many had friends or family who had tried it if they had not done so themselves. Very few who had tried it felt it was immoral, only that they were not suited for it. More often it was those who had never been tempted who felt most indignant.

6   Here I draw on Stuart Hall's use of a theory of articulation, which he developed from Laclau. In this sense, MLM, as a transnational capitalist practice, is linked with the other ideologies in culturally and historically embedded ways, but it does not inherently *belong* to any of them (Morley and Chen 1996). Indeed, one of anthropology's main strengths is the specification of why and how certain social forces articulate to others in a given cultural framework.

7   What MLM proponents often fail to mention is that, simple as it sounds, most networks do not develop this easily and quickly. Networks are actually sophisticated numbers games that accrue the most benefits for those at the top.

8   Contrary to what MLM practitioners imply during sales pitches, distributors never make huge profits for very long before they're forced to recruit new members. In other words, the dream that somehow one can find a few people below to do all the work (leaving one with plenty of money and leisure time) is a false one. Were this the case, marketers would have no incentive to keep working for the company. In fact, high-level distributors had to work even harder to maintain their income flow since bonus systems that often rewarded handsomely at lower levels (in order to attract newer recruits) later diminished considerably.

9   One such economist is Li Shaohua (see n. 2).

10   An exception might be the opium industry. More recently, in the 1980s, there were chain-letter-type scams, which were deemed illegal, but nothing so organized and sophisticated as commercial MLM.

11   The performance of such narratives is a common feature of MLM activities worldwide (Biggart 1989). In China, it incorporates older public speech practices such as *suku*, or "speaking bitterness" (Rofel 1999; Anagnost 1997).

12   See Yang 1997 on the TV drama *Beijing Sojourners in New York*, as well as Chen Xiaomei 1995 on novels such as *Manhattan Chinese Woman*, for commentary and examples of some of the cruder visions of capitalist culture propagated widely in China. To be fair, the direct selling industry in the United States uses equally raw appeals to the desire for material goods and the equation of money with happiness and goodness.

13   American MLM narratives rely heavily on this tactic for their recruiting. Many

advertisements reach out to those who are "angry about working for Uncle Sam," "tired of making your boss rich," and so on. Alternatively, MLM is said to be suitable for women, who may have difficulty in more conventional business dealings.

14 See Hoffman's essay in this volume for another instance in which college graduates found this phrase particularly meaningful.

15 See my dissertation, "Selling Selves: The Cultural Construction of a Market in the PRC," University of California, Santa Cruz, 2000, for an in-depth discussion of the narratives and practices of "potential" (*qianneng*).

16 See Hoffman in this volume for another instance of the notion of packaging people.

17 See Susan Brownell's *Training the Body for China: Sports in the Moral Order of the People's Republic* (1995) for more on bodies and nationalism.

18 This phrase was used often in training. Note, however, that it stood for handshaking and embracing, not the European kissing greeting or Japanese bowing.

19 I often wondered at how "business" had become "traditional" so quickly in only twenty years of economic reforms.

20 These qualities also bear the influence of concepts of self-cultivation and rectification, central in Confucian ethics for more than two thousand years. However, a sustained analysis of the intersection of Confucian philosophy with MLM and Maoist socialist ideals is beyond the scope of this chapter.

21 See Meisner 1982 and Rickett and Rickett 1957 for interesting perspectives on the earlier project.

22 As companies often tended to reproduce each other's products, recruitment techniques, and bonus systems, the owners' nationality was extremely important. While many companies sold their American, Japanese, or Taiwanese status as an asset, mainland firms often used strongly nationalist arguments to critique foreign firms for taking their profits out of China, for not understanding local conditions, for imposing high prices, and so on. A few companies in the South tried to blend "traditional Chinese culture" with chuanxiao but with unconvincing results in terms of sales and recruits.

23 See Lida Junghans' chapter in this volume for an extended discussion of the inside/outside binary in particular.

Lisa Hoffman Guiding College Graduates to Work:
Social Constructions of Labor Markets in Dalian

Q: What do you think is most important in a job?
A: Training, development, and salary, in that order.—graduating senior
at Dalian University of Technology, male, May 1996

On the fourth floor of the main building at Dalian University of Technology (DUT), directly behind a grand statue of Mao, sits the graduate employment office. It was a cold December morning in 1995 when I walked there to discuss the changing role of universities in job placement, as the state phased out direct assignments (*fenpei*) in favor of job fairs, "mutual choice," and recommendations. Through the cigarette smoke, I listened to Director Xie explain that his office now engaged in "service work" instead of the implementation of central government plans. "Our work is now about graduates' careers and helping them with professional planning—not about assignments," he said. "The system we use now is called guidance (*zhidao*) rather than the mandatory plan." The onset of guidance indicated that important changes had taken place in the role of universities as young people, like the man quoted in the epigraph, entered the working world for the first time.

While a move away from direct job assignments certainly indicated a change in how the state engaged the process, it did not signify the end of governmental concern with where the future professionals took their educated labor power. Universities no longer participated in a system of central bureaucratic allocation, but they continued to receive directives from central and local authorities on where graduates *should go*. This meant that school administrators needed to convince graduates to work in certain industries and locations. In fact, at DUT, a technical university under the jurisdiction of the State Education Commission, a significant majority of the graduates in 1996 and 1997 entered state-affiliated units—without being directly assigned to them.[1] Thus, the story told here is not necessarily about how young professionals turned away from the state and the state economy but rather about how their entry into the labor force through the medium of guidance was a cultural and political experience.

Pressure on universities to produce the kind of patriotic professionals desired by the state often led to tensions with what students desired and what employers demanded. State-run enterprises, for example, increasingly made their own decisions about who to hire and when to hire them, while struggling units found it extremely difficult to hire educated workers at all. At the same time, private and foreign companies legally employed their workers, a distinctive shift from earlier Maoist campaigns against capitalists. Embedded in these hiring decisions were cultural notions of competence and quality as well as social networks and connections.

Young people's attitudes changed along with the role of universities and the labor acquisition methods of units. Students entering college in the 1990s knew they would not be assigned to a workplace for life, unlike the previous cohort of workers, who received the "iron rice bowl" of a set salary, housing, medical coverage, and other benefits.[2] Instead, armed with the knowledge that they were the most highly educated workers in China and supported by a modernization strategy that relied on professional and technical labor power, they expected some kind of capital accumulation from their educational credentials.[3] "Mutual choice," a system in which both graduates and employers could choose one another, presented these young people with possibilities for social and professional mobility quite different from those of the assignment system. Thus, as young people entered the working world for the first time, they had to maneuver among university implementation of state policies, employers' hiring practices, and their own ideas about a successful future. Expectations were high and disappointments common. In the following pages, I describe a small part of this complicated story.

Geographic Hierarchies and Urban Desires Exploring the ways in which young professionals first experienced labor exchanges and understood their labor power is an important aspect of practices of the urban in China. Labor markets aimed at graduates of higher education were concentrated in urban areas, and most of the educated elite who frequented them were urban citizens.[4] In the 1990s, both popular culture and official discourses associated social mobility with personal career selection and educational credentials, albeit not exclusively.[5] In turn, this association was closely tied to urban-rural dichotomies. Aspirations to find a "city job," meant both figuratively and literally, worked within what I call a hierarchy of desire, which cut the national space into places that were developed and undeveloped, modern and backward, convenient and bitter. Social imaginaries, discussed by Louisa Schein in this volume, linked urban landscapes to cultural ideals of civility, progress, and opportunity—culminating in the comparatively booming coastal centers. These cultural hierarchies of opportunity and stagnation were laid across structural divisions between urban and rural areas that have been institutionalized in the household registration system (*hukou*) and the traditional socialist welfare package for state workers.[6]

In this sense, the desires of graduates to have certain kinds of jobs, to live in particular places, and to consume distinctive products were "urban" desires and their experiences of labor markets were urban as well. In striving for lives they thought of as promising, stable, and successful, the majority of graduates shunned positions in remote districts and tried to stay in larger cities, gravitating in particular to major metropolitan coastal areas. Obtaining a Shanghai or Beijing registration, many students commented, could justify a poorly paid and uninteresting state job for several years. Yet, while graduates and their families strategized about how to live in a place identified with recurring opportunities, central and local governments struggled over how to retain some control of the distribution process. The government pressed universities, for example, to help develop remote areas and to support "key" industries such as agriculture, communications, and defense production.[7]

Managing Labor Flows in the 1990s   Although some Maoist techniques continued to be used in the mid-1990s to fill certain jobs (e.g., hukou and university admissions) and to encourage patriotic professionalism (e.g., moral education), significant changes did occur. The techniques of power used under the planned economic system helped produce a citizen appropriate for that society. Mayfair Yang has argued that through practices of the redistributive economy—"differential distribution, political campaigns, and education"—the state was able to order, regulate, and discipline its subjects (1988: 413; see also Foucault 1980b). In other words, through direct allocation of job assignments, housing, medical care, and even permission to have a child, the state rewarded certain behaviors and penalized others and in the process normalized society. The dossier (*dang'an*), a file with information about an individual and his or her political behavior, became a powerful mechanism for regulating the populace, particularly when all assignments and promotions were controlled by the government and the Party.[8] "Normalized behavior [was] ensured by the general anxiety of not knowing what [had] been written and what could be written in one's dossier, and what future disciplinary use could be made of the dossier records" (Yang 1988: 413). Such techniques were intended to produce motivated socialist citizens for a planned economy of unequal job assignments and distribution of benefits.

In conjunction with reforms in the job placement system, however, Maoist techniques such as the dang'an lost some of their effectiveness. Dossiers still existed in the mid-1990s, but reforms had reduced their ability to determine one's professional life. Some young people I met had abandoned their dossiers and moved to another city and job without official permission, and some companies consulted dossiers only to verify graduation certificates and legal papers, not to investigate an applicant's political behavior. This loss of effectiveness raises serious questions about how the state managed and regulated its political and economic subjects (see below) and how various factors influenced the social, political, and economic circulation of these educated and skilled workers in the 1990s.

It is tempting to regard mutual choice and guidance as the "freeing" of educated labor, particularly since rhetoric about "choice" and "emancipation" of the marketplace increased. Yet I want to emphasize that while the state did retreat from many aspects of citizens' lives the introduction of reforms in the assignment system did not signify the end of state involvement in the labor allocation process. Thus, rather than trumpeting the end of state power, I wish to follow Foucault's arguments about subjectification and governmentality (and likewise aspects of Yang's) and argue that in the mid-1990s new professionals in China were produced *in relation to* modes of governing, not outside of them (Foucault 1979, 1991).[9] These modes of governing refer to the art of managing populations through such practices as disciplinary regulations, political education, and market rationalities. The disappearance of direct state job assignments in the 1990s signified a change in the management of the educated population, but it did not signify the end of governmental concern with who these young professionals would be and where they would take their educated labor power. Yet the process of subject formation always is a course of give and take. Young people had visions of success in the working world, for instance, which did not necessarily coincide with university policies encouraging graduates to return home or with employer definitions of quality and assets. In negotiating these tensions, educated youths came to understand and establish the norm of the new professional, which incorporated state demands for social stability and patriotic sacrifice, employers' standards of cultural competence, and the graduates' own ideas of success and ways to achieve it.

The Reform Era and a Turn to Talent   Before turning to the details of these demands and negotiations of them, it is necessary to put this phenomenon in its larger political, economic, and social contexts. In 1984, the government designated Dalian, a large port city in northeastern China, as one of fourteen "coastal cities," which made it subject to special economic and self-management policies (see Yeung and Hu 1992). A year later, work began on the Economic and Technical Development Zone (hereafter the Zone), an area similar to Pudong in Shanghai, where master plans leveled farmers' fields and constructed a "new city area." While the Northeast historically relied on large, state-run, heavy industries such as power generation, industrial chemicals, and machinery manufacturing, recent investments have focused on food exports, textiles, and pharmaceuticals. Moreover, in the past ten years numerous Japanese companies have invested in the Zone, opening a new chapter in the relationship between Dalian and its neighbors. Japanese forces had entered Dalian and the greater northeast area in 1905, after defeating Russia in the Russo-Japanese War and inheriting its twenty-five year leasehold on the Liaodong peninsula (formerly Kwantung Leased Territory). This colonial administration remained in Northeast China until 1945 when

Communist forces liberated the region. During those forty years, Japan declared Dalian a free port, greatly expanded the city, completed the wharves and railroads begun by the Russians, and developed heavy industry across the northeastern area. Today the city still reflects the Japanese presence, with functioning trolley cars and individual houses, as well as monumental architectural structures such as the former Yokohama Bank building in Zhongshan Square, which currently houses the Bank of China.

Although the international presence in Dalian waned during the Maoist years, recent development plans have included attracting foreign capital and management. To reinternationalize the city, Mayor Bo Xilai pursued an urbanization vision based on a Hong Kong model and named Dalian the Hong Kong of the North. In competition with other coastal cities for limited foreign capital, the city government advertised Dalian as a place with an abundance of educated and talented labor, a diversifying economy, and a state of the art deepwater port. The highly educated and cultured workers would not only help the foreign investor the official discourse argued but would learn management and technological skills from their companies as well, enabling the country to ultimately rely less on these outsiders and more on itself.

In addition to what was done locally, national policies launched during the reform era recast the role of educated labor power through a shift in emphasis from politically reliable and "red" cadres to expertise and talent. New reforms supported a return to college entrance exams, the elimination of class labels in personnel and educational decisions, and the identification of intellectuals as part of the working class. Moreover, reformers pushed for enterprise management by professionals rather than Party Secretaries and the expansion of contract labor and privately owned enterprises.[10] Previously considered a bourgeois subject by the government, management was called a "science" by Deng Xiaoping in a 1980 interview, opening it up as a new industry and coveted social position (1994: 351). In addition, in the early 1980s the term *rencai* (talented personnel) was more prominent in the official press and was promoted as a resource necessary for the nation's modernization. This is in sharp contrast to the more ambivalent and even negative portrayals of the largely uneducated and semiskilled "surplus" labor from bankrupt factories and rural areas.

Reforms in the job assignment system corresponded with government objectives to develop and manage "talent" as well as with wider trends toward contract labor and flexible accumulation. Global economic changes fueled the demand for employees with higher education and technological knowledge as well.[11] Initial foreign investments in China focused on its cheap labor and resources, but these projects began to require educated employees. Factory floors needed local managers, representative offices needed office workers, and trading companies needed salespeople. Support industries such as freight forwarding, consulting, service work, real estate, and advertising grew up around the new foreign investments, creating new ways for college graduates to gain prestige and wealth. Government narratives also suggested that since college graduates had new types of knowledge-based skills they had the potential for upward mobility as sought-after professionals. Such possibilities could invigorate youth to work for the country, exemplified in the slogan "Talent is our hope," which was emblazoned on the wall at a Shanghai jobs fair. Policies such as these create what Aihwa Ong has called "a system of variegated citizenship in which populations subjected to different regimes of value enjoy different kinds of rights, discipline, caring, and security" (1999: 217). Household registration policies, for example, which distinguished between educated professionals and migrant laborers, exhibited this "unequal biopolitical investment in different categories of the population" by the state and private enterprises interested in competing in the global economy (Ong 1999: 216).[12] It was in such a landscape—officially and popularly defined as developing, open, urban, and international—that I went to Director Xie's office to discuss labor allocation reforms.

A Generational Change: From Assignments (fenpei) to Guidance (zhidao)

To understand the significance of these changes, it is important to have sense of what existed prior to the reforms. One summer evening, the parents of an engaging twenty-four-year-old-woman, Song Yan, explained this practice by telling me about their job assignment experience. In line with state plans and the fenpei system, which was established in the 1950s, they were sent to a small town several hours by train from Dalian. Central planners had moved technical and industrial development out of coastal cities by this time in a bid to make interior regions more self-sufficient and key industrial sites less vulnerable to Soviet- or American-backed

Taiwanese attack (see Naughton 1988). Thus, assignments fulfilled central government plans and sent educated people to areas where they would not have gone voluntarily. For someone like Mr. Song, labor was conceived as a national resource and part of the means of production owned by the state (Bian 1994), not an individual resource to be developed for personal growth. Units treated employment as an assignment, a part of the socialist welfare system, rather than "a problem of efficient use of labor inputs" (Davis 1990: 87).

The combination of the hukou and fenpei systems enabled the government to use geographic distribution as a form of social control and sometimes as a kind of punishment. Forced assignments and geographic penalties permitted Party officials to incorporate politics and class background into the allocation process as well, relying on information accumulated in the individual's dossier.[13] In addition, it served as a method to prohibit pre-1949 elites from maintaining their hold on power. For Mr. Song, the forced move to a nonurban area far from Dalian was personally upsetting and depressing. While he assured me that both he and his wife felt dedicated to the country and their scientific work, they desperately wanted to return the family to the city. He used every possible method to get their assignments and hukou transferred back to Dalian, yet he also remained conflicted about these actions. As young people who had pronounced their commitment to the new society, he felt they should have accepted their assignments with pleasure. Instead, he managed to get them both assignments back in Dalian, unlike many families who were torn apart by this system.

A number of factors and new ways of thinking stemming from the economic reforms challenged this assignment system. For example, reforms that expanded ownership to private, joint venture, and foreign-owned enterprises confronted the state's monopoly on educated workers. The nonstate sector of the economy grew, and investments demanded more highly trained workers who could move from job to job and city to city. At the same time, what is now called the "poor utilization" of graduates in state units, or the "mismatch" of graduates and positions, also put pressure on the assignment system. Official narratives identified fenpei, which was heavily embedded in the planned economy rationality, as ridden with contradictions and inefficiencies. In Director Xie's words, units were to blame because they "did not use talent well. . . . these workers were not respected for their value and were wasted." Schools, too, "did not think about what kinds of students and what level students society needed; they just trained them." And students had "no pressure of competition," which made them "passive and not willing to study." Markets, real and imagined, became the saviors in this logic, forms of rationalization for a contradictory and inefficient system. "The school's goal now," Xie continued, "is to let the market help solve these problems." In job fairs in 1996, for example, employers faced accusations of waste head on by advertising themselves to prospective employees as "knowing how to use" rencai (talent).

Reforms in the assignment system were not meant, however, to eradicate the regulation of educated bodies; it was a *rationalization* rather than an elimination of the process (Agelasto 1998: 264; Paine 1994: 130). Students still needed to be guided and molded into responsible and patriotic citizens. During the dinner with Song Yan's family, her father said that his daughter's generation "liked a lot more adventure and risk" and that they had "less sense of responsibility to the government for training them." It was difficult for this man, who grew up in an era of direct assignments and virtually no job mobility, to understand how his twenty-four-year-old daughter could go through five positions in one year, finally settling on a foreign company. She stayed at this company for a number of years but felt no particular loyalty to it and left after she married and a better opportunity arose.

The patriotic obligation Mr. Song felt as a young man beginning his socialist career—and the personal conflict associated with his move back to Dalian—was in marked contrast to the seemingly carefree mobility and independence of his daughter. The younger generation, he was telling me, had a different sense of responsibility and even of patriotic duty than did his. Several weeks after this dinner, Song Yan confessed that she and her father often had small arguments when they talked about such things. Our dinner together gave him a unique opportunity to express his feelings and tell his daughter what he thought of her actions without risking a fight. He included messages of responsibility for one's training and loyalty to one's employer, hoping that his daughter would also feel loyalty to something greater than herself and have a sense of responsibility and obligation to the country. While Song Yan's family was not representative of all families with young educated workers, her story showed how cohorts differed, and how seriously the question of loyalty and patriotism was taken by individual citizens as well as those teaching patriotism on campuses. Ultimately, university administrators had to negotiate between these different degrees of loyalty in order to get their graduates into available jobs without directly assigning them.

Choice, Restrictions, & Macro Adjustments: "Balancing" Market Exchanges Beginning in the 1980s, the job assignment system went through a series of slow and incremental reforms, leading to guidance and mutual choice. Important directives in 1985, 1989, and 1993 structured the shift from what Mr. Song experienced to what his daughter did.[14] The early days of assignment reforms were quite controversial on campuses. Parents worried about their children's security as graduates began to make decisions about what kinds of positions were most suitable for them personally. Contradictions, which still existed in the system in the mid-1990s, emerged between graduates' expectations and society's offerings. Universities claimed that students were to blame for feelings of dissatisfaction because their expectations were too high—the same language that was used almost ten years later (Pepper 1995: chap. 18, 31).[15]

To facilitate expansion of the mutual choice system, although always "within a definite scope," universities held job fairs and cities established talent markets (*rencai shichang*) where municipal fairs could take place.[16] Talent markets were places where those with higher education and special skills could gather information, meet with employers, and sign contracts. My first experience of such an event was at Dalian City's Talent Market in 1993. People looking to change their workplace or find work for the first time stood with small notepads, eyes fixed on wall postings of job openings. Company representatives sat at desks with descriptions of the kind of employees they wanted hanging on the wall behind them, while job seekers approached for face-to-face interviews. Typically, these postings advertised how many people the company needed, position titles, and the required education level, knowledge base, and experience. Some companies even specified age, gender, and height. This was especially common in public relations, which aimed to employ attractive, tall, young women.[17] As at campus fairs, a job seeker filled out a standard application form with his or her name, address, age, schooling level, major, job experience, and so on and submitted a recent photo. On this day in 1993 and at many future events, I met parents who wanted to help their children, retired workers looking for second jobs, and dissatisfied workers seeking higher salaries, better benefits, and the chance for personal development.[18] In contrast to assignments, at job fairs like this, "employees" and "employers" tried to sell themselves to each other.

At the same time these markets were opened and mutual choice was promoted, detailed restrictions on where new graduates could go remained. Under a policy of macroadjustment, universities and municipal personnel bureaus intervened in market processes in the name of national development and fairness. For example, DUT instituted strict rules about hukou transfers to Beijing and Dalian in order to ensure that graduates would not congregate in these cities, which would have made DUT's distribution of its students "irrational." Fees associated with a lower number of scholarship points made hukou transfers to these cities expensive, which was intended to create an incentive for graduates to return home.[19] The vice director of the employment office explained that the State Education Commission monitored where each university's graduates went. As a school drawing on a national population, DUT was required to send its graduates across the nation in a "reasonable" manner similar to earlier state plans of geographic distribution.

Administrators at Dalian's Personnel Bureau also worried about the "unbalanced development" of the market and the lack of fair competition, which justified another form of macrolevel government action. For instance, statistics showed that female graduates, "common students" (children from families with no "good" connections), and students with certain majors were not able to find work easily. If the government threw them into the market carelessly, the bureau argued, "it would not be good and would damage the reputation of the Party, advantages of socialism, and the safety of society" (Dalian Personnel Bureau n.d.: 4). To remedy the negative effects of what they identified as the "immature" aspects of markets in China, local personnel bureaus provided assignments to students "in the plan" who had not found work by the end of the year in which they graduated. Students, however, often rejected such assignments in their hometowns because they assumed that these were dead-end positions. Dalian responded with a guarantee that posts would match the student's major and would not be in unprofitable units.[20]

Students complained especially about the rampant use of social connections (*guanxi*) to secure coveted positions in stable and profitable state units. "Getting a good job in a good state-run unit is about 70 percent luck [connections or being at the right place at the right time] and 30 percent ability," lamented a student who claimed he had no profitable family connections. Another young man introduced himself to me as someone "without a good background," referring directly to his family's lack of helpful political or economic connections in urban areas. New graduates with rural sensibilities and few family connections found it difficult to find their first job, as they had no work experience to bolster their "poor" family backgrounds. Policies during the Cultural Revolution had tried to counter this kind of class (re)production by promoting those with worker and peasant backgrounds and denying former elites access to universities and thus coveted government positions.[21] College entrance exams and practices of mutual choice reframed these same issues and raised important questions about who would become the new power and prestige holders in China. Despite the efforts of universities and local governments to minimize the use of guanxi and to "rationalize" mutual choice, they could not change the family from which a student came.[22]

Practicing Guidance: Tensions in the New System   By the time I arrived in the mid-1990s, universities in Dalian had had numerous years of reform experience. They continued to be in difficult positions, however, as they had to produce a supply of both the educated professionals desired by the "market" and the patriotic economic subjects desired by the state. In addition, student expectations remained high as they listened to rhetoric about how the nation needed talent to modernize, and frustrations developed as they watched others with less education establish careers and accumulate wealth and prestige. Universities implemented a variety of measures to meet the sometimes conflicting demands placed on them and to make sure that students signed contracts by the time they graduated. At DUT, for example, administrators held on-campus job fairs, created data base systems, published job search newspapers and guides, collected information from various employers, recommended students for "appropriate" positions, and engaged in curriculum reforms.[23] DUT also sent their officials directly to workplaces to ask what kinds of personnel they wanted—a further important distinction from the bureaucratic distribution of labor. A discussion of some of these methods and how students reacted to them will help clarify the ways in which young people came to understand what it meant to be an urban educated worker in the 1990s.

The normalization of potential professionals included lectures on appropriate expectations as well as suggestions on how to write letters and act at interviews. Handwritten characters in a letter, for example, expressed the student's ability much better than typed ones, Director Xie assured me. DUT administrators helped students with the letters, telling them what to put in each and explaining that the content should be different for the different units. Before the campus jobs fair, students were reminded not to ask about salaries or benefits "because units were opposed to that." In addition, administrators instructed them on how to dress and act as they thought cultured, socially responsible, educated professionals should. Women were cautioned not to wear makeup, and young men were instructed not to smoke or act too informal, which included getting their hair cut and not wearing flip-flops. A recent publication available at the Shanghai Talent Market offered advice to job seekers on how to prepare for interviews, including a reminder to go to the washroom and check one's physical appearance one last time (Shanghaishi gaoxiao biyesheng jiuye zhidao zhongxin 1998 [Shanghai higher education graduates' career guidance center]). Bodily practices were enmeshed in the ability to conduct oneself as a proper urban professional, an increasingly desired sensibility.

Since the government no longer used direct assignments, methods of persuasion and guidance, and thus moral education in general, took on a new kind of market-oriented role. Reminiscent of conversations during the Maoist era, official discourses inserted patriotic comments about modernization, development, and political duty into debates about graduates' participation in markets. Messages of sacrifice and national loyalty continued to be important, echoing Song Yan's father's comments. Wen Fuxiang, director of the Higher Education Research Institute of Huazhong University of Science and Technology, for example, has called for educational reforms that would allow students to develop their "special talents" and "realize their individual potential while not promoting selfishness or egoism" (Wen 1996: 217). "We should establish the relationship on the basis of the development of individuality with appropriate guidance," he wrote, "so that individuals are able to be aware of their social responsibilities as they learn to know themselves" (276). Powerful discourses of patriotism, based largely on the nation as a global ethnic body, were used by DUT to establish the boundaries of what was a morally acceptable career choice. The use of patriotic duty as an incentive to do certain kinds of work was not new, but the fact that choices were available was.

Narratives acquiescing to the needs and offerings of society, however, did not always mesh with competing narratives of happy modern consumers who had plenty of disposable income and time to take advantage of the new products and experiences available in the urban arena. Social debates on these points were common. When graduates' expectations and desires were too high in comparison with their actual abilities, people used the expression *yan gao shou di,* which meant literally that "the eyes were high and the hands were low." A personnel director at a large joint venture explained that "the ones who just graduated don't understand society well enough. They think they have a lot of ability and can find satisfying work. That is a mistaken thought. They have some culture and knowledge, but they are not necessarily good workers. Their cultural or educational level (*wenhua*) might be high, but perhaps they are not good workers. . . . We need to see if their wenhua can become profitable, but they don't understand this." This enterprise translated the competence of the employee into the ability to make money for the company: one form of capital could be turned into another. On their own, cultural assets had no particular value, this woman argued; only if educational credentials led to economic profits for the employer would there be the opportunity for further accumulation of status and wealth for the worker.

College students, however, assumed that their educational credentials would be immediately convertible into other forms of capital. Higher education bred higher expectations, which were supported by a tradition of Confucian scholar-officials, the previous socialist guarantee of employment, and contemporary policies of "variegated citizenship" (Ong 1999).[24] Expectations that did not coincide with opportunities caused students to feel anxious and criticize what was available. Outside the campus job fair in 1996, for instance, I overheard a group of young men grumbling about what was offered—the fair had too many unprofitable state-run companies, only a few famous units, and not enough companies from Dalian city that could help them transfer their hukou. "Every year the same enterprises and units come to our school," a chemical engineering student complained to me.

> I am used to seeing the enterprises and companies who aren't very profitable or vital. Even though many enterprises just fired a lot of workers they come here to hire more graduates. So I am really confused. This is really bad for students, and the school pays almost no attention to this situation. It does harm to the students. They should tell the students the facts—these units cannot offer sufficient money or decent job environments. They don't provide us with this information.

One woman even said that the DUT fair was useless to her. "This university is not the best in China," she explained

> so only those units that find it difficult to find workers come here. No one finds work here. In Dalian city's Talent Market there are more opportunities. . . . If a job is available in the talent market then you have a fair chance, but most of the best jobs are not in the market. My classmates find the better jobs through their parents or friends [which I won't do] because then others will look down on me if I use guanxi and they will say I got the job because of my father. I think I can work hard and in the future I can be more successful than those others [who used connections].

Her comments about the use of guanxi highlighted an important dimension of her frustrations and of broader issues of social mobility. While the use of connections to secure a job was a common occurrence, there was also a desire to find a position on one's own, prompted by both a lack of useful connections and an urge to prove that individual hard work mattered. Relying on herself, as this woman hoped to do, not only would prove that she was valuable to employers but also would help her to avoid the complicated networks of obligation and jealousy instigated by use of "the back door." By starting out on her own, she hoped to avoid the potentially difficult interpersonal relations and gossip often associated with older state-run units. While in the Maoist era self-reliance referred to a national goal of political and economic self-sufficiency, in the 1990s it referred to an emphasis on *individual* ability and independence.

In addition to being tangled in notions of success and ability, graduates' critiques were enmeshed in tangible issues of their future lives. Settling their hukou in a desirable location was particularly important since it made them feel as if they "belonged" in the city and were proper, legal residents. According to one woman, Zhou Gaolin, who did not want to return home as she should have, settling her hukou in Shanghai was the most important issue. She did not approach foreign companies or joint ventures since they would not have been able to transfer her registration.

> If I go back to Wuhan, life will be just the same as before I went to college. I want to go to a new place so I can start from a new point and not just follow my old life. . . . This idea is different from [those of] my parents. My parents are over fifty, and they don't want more change. They want a stable life, but I think their salary is too low. I am twenty-two. I should take the opportunity to use my youth, my advantages, and try as many new experiences as possible. Even if I fail in my new life, it will still be worth it. I can think of my experiences. I want to exert myself to the utmost. Maybe I won't be successful, but [I'll know] I did it, unlike my parents.

Ms. Zhou, a 1996 DUT graduate, linked the urban arena in which she wanted to live with opportunity and potential success. Her hierarchy of desire identified Wuhan as a stagnant urban area that would limit her growth while Shanghai offered a new life and the chance to exert herself "to the utmost." These dreams of success also were in contrast to perceptions of her parents' experiences and the lack of professional growth afforded their cohort. She focused on the conservatism of her parents' more traditional socialist lifestyle and compared it to her own dreams of individual hard work and future success in a cosmopolitan city.

The idea that hard work and ability justified the social stratification of the mid-1990s was quite widespread and coincided with other comments I heard about the "naturalness" of contemporary distinctions based on merit. As educated and talented employees, college graduates hoped for a future that offered such naturalized success. One DUT graduate explained that before the reforms began "we just earned fixed and low salaries from the government and did fixed things, and people were very satisfied at that time. Now people are practical. They face the reality that they have to join in the competition. We have to earn our bread by our own struggle, but material things and money are limited. If you want to earn more, you must work harder than others. That is fair. Most people have realized it. It is common sense now."

Students told me that if they could "practice" themselves, develop themselves as individuals, and find opportunities to bring their abilities into full play, perhaps they would see the material fruits of their talented and cultured laboring selves.[25] Comments by young people about the growing rationalization of social divisions were always in contrast to the "imposed" social structure of the Maoist era. Reforms in the assignment system, they felt, allowed those with *real* talent and ability to have the opportunity to get ahead, just as other segments of the population such as farmers and the urban unemployed had taken advantage of government policies to accumulate capital earlier in the reform era. Social prestige, many claimed, had begun to align itself more *naturally* with merit and education-based criteria in recent years.[26]

Commodities and Quality   As Song Yan's father expressed it, the 1990s focus on the individual and his or her career contradicted traditional Maoist ideas about labor power and national duty. In a similar way, language usage indicated a possible shift in ideas about the commodification of labor. In interviews as well as printed materials, terms such as *chanpin* (product) and *zhiliang* (quality, a word usually used for objects) were used to describe college graduates, highlighting the tensions between traditional socialist notions of exploitation and contemporary views of labor market exchanges. To expalin why universities continually experimented with majors and curriculum reforms, a young woman working in Finance University's student recruitment office proclaimed that "students are now more like products (chanpin)," which was quickly followed by a comment from a professor: "and they need to be packaged a bit."[27] Packaging these budding professionals meant regulating their desires as well as making them desirable to prospective employers.

At the DUT job fair, when I asked a representative from a large, state-run unit about mutual choice, he said: "This system is much better [than assignments]; we can meet them, talk to them, interview them, and understand the student better. . . . We hired everyone we needed at this fair; a lot of students came here. . . . Their level (*suzhi*) is higher here; their quality (zhiliang) and ability are better, so more units are willing to come to this school." Both *suzhi* and *zhiliang* mean "quality" and both words have gained prominence in the reform era, but there is an important distinction between them. *Suzhi* usually referred to a *person's* quality or level of achievement (e.g., in character, morals, education, or ability), while *zhiliang* referred to those of a product (e.g., design, durability, technological level, or quality of materials).[28] One DUT publication also used this term, stating that units had higher quality (zhiliang) requirements for workers now, particularly in foreign language ability, practical experience, and political quality (suzhi). Use of *zhiliang* to describe graduates was noteworthy both because of its "improper" use and because it signified the possibility that students were being objectified by employers and universities. Maurice Meisner reminds us that "what distinguishes wage labor in a capitalist economy is that human labor-power is a commodity, to be freely bought and sold much in the fashion that the products laborers create are bought and sold on the market" (1996: 290). By the mid-1990s, reforms in the assignment system had markedly altered the manner in which graduates experienced their labor power, to a certain extent transforming them into objects, commodities that needed quality control and packaging.

The story of how college graduates found their first full-time jobs in the mid-1990s is complex. Guidance and mutual choice framed their experiences as they negotiated their way through state interests, employers' hiring practices, and their own dreams for the future. In doing so, they made decisions about what it meant to be an educated worker and how they would relate to their labor power. Changes in the job assignment system altered the way in which the state was involved in this subject formation process, but they did not eliminate its presence. Universities, as governmental institutions, wanted to both instill feelings of patriotic professionalism in their graduates and support important state industries. Often in conflict with university regulations, young people's own desires were closely connected to geographic hierarchies that associated success, opportunity, and urbanity. While universities tried to temper their desires with appeals to nationalism, notions of marketability, and tips on how to succeed in interviews, graduates still critiqued the choices, contesting government representations of the rationalizing power of the patriotic market. Rather, like other "market" exchanges, the practice of mutual choice for labor allocation was a cultural and social process that existed in the tension between those involved and in relation to governmental objectives to produce high-quality talent (rencai) to help China prosper in the twenty-first century.

Notes

The research for this chapter would not have been possible without the generous support of my dissertation fieldwork by the Foreign Language and Area Studies Fellowship, the Committee on Scholarly Communication with China, and the Center for Studies in Higher Education at the University of California, Berkeley. Prof. Liu Zhongquan of Dalian University of Technology and all the students, employees, and administrators with whom I talked deserve thanks as well. I also wish to thank Jennifer Hubbert, Janis Mimura, Aihwa Ong, Suzanne Pepper, Hai Ren, and the editors of this volume for their helpful comments on earlier drafts of this chapter. I, of course, take full responsibility for the failings of this piece. Research was conducted in August 1999, for six months in 1997–98, twelve months in 1995–96, and the summers of 1993 and 1994. All names have been changed, including those with official titles.

1   In 1996, more than 80 percent of the graduates went into state-affiliated units, and in 1997 about 70 percent did. In 1996, 23 percent went into the civil service, research institutes, and educational facilities, and 61 percent went into factories or enterprises. In the summer of 1999, the vice director of DUT's employment office said that this number continued to decline, due to both a change in "market needs" and a change in students' willingness to go to private and community-run companies.

2   Here I follow Lisa Rofel's (1999) use of cohorts in order to incorporate ideas of identity and political experience into the notion of different laboring generations. The young people I researched graduated from the late 1980s on, primarily went into contract-based positions, and came of age politically during the reform era. In this chapter, I focus more specifically on 1996 graduates of Dalian University of Technology and the Northeast Economic and Finance University (Finance University).

3   Here I draw on Bourdieu's discussion of cultural, symbolic, and economic capital and the ways in which they can be converted into one another (1984). For example, these young graduates wanted to turn their educational credentials into both economic and social capital.

4   While official statistics claimed that the majority of students entering college in the early 1990s had rural origins, they also claimed that the number of urbanites with a college education far exceeded the number in rural areas. For example, 60 percent of those taking the entrance exam in 1992 were rural students, a figure that rose to 61 percent in 1993. In terms of enrollment, in 1993 the ratio was 53 percent from rural areas and 46 percent from cities and towns (SEC 1992: 156; 1993: 112, 113). Yet according to 1997 population statistics 92 percent of all college educated people lived in urban areas, suggesting an urban concentration of the educated elite (CSBP 1997). In response to State Education Commission claims of high numbers of rural students, Suzanne Pepper wrote, "One possible explanation is that the students are from

county seats and small towns . . . which are often referred to in categoric fashion as 'rural.' In this blanket use of the term, it extends to everyone living in such towns and their rural hinterlands, without distinguishing town dwellers from farmers, much less the diffuse category of registered rural residents (*nongye hukou*). But that even the latter, registered rural residents, could account for so large a percentage of college candidates seems unlikely—without major changes in rural school patterns, the key-point school establishment, and college entrance requirements" (1995: 18.35). See also Pepper 1984, chap. 6; and Orleans 1987. On the issue historically, see Pepper 1996, chap. 13. For more on urban citizenship, see Clark, this volume; Solinger 1999; and note 6 below.

5   Higher education was not a guarantee of social mobility, as money and connections were important factors in social and economic capital accumulation. Yet it certainly offered the prospect of mobility to many. See Delany and Paine 1991 and Paine 1994 on the notion that studying did not matter. For a discussion of how education, unequal development, and social mobility are related both in China and in the education and development literature in general, see Pepper 1996, chap. 1.

6   See the introduction to this volume for a discussion of the household registration system (*hukou*). In recent years, cities have allowed people to buy residency if they did not have a work unit that would provide one. In Dalian in 1995–96, an administrator at the Personnel Bureau stated that legal registration for those with bachelor's degrees cost 50,000 renminbi (RMB). Alternatively, one could provide a minimum investment or housing purchase of 120,000 RMB. In terms of housing, by 1999 permanent legal residency required a purchase totaling 700,000 RMB. (U.S. $1 = approximately 8.3 RMB).

7   For example, students at DUT were offered reductions in their loan payments and scholarship awards (2,000 to 5,000 RMB) if they agreed to go to remote areas that needed their talent. Dalian city also loosened hukou restrictions in order to fill difficult (*jianku*) posts (DRJ n.d.: 5). Another important method for developing rural areas was through locally committed enrollment (*dingxiang*), which emerged in the 1980s. See note 16 for more on enrollments.

8   Schools and workplaces monitored an individual's behavior and noted any offenses or political deviations in the dossier. Black marks in the file could have made one a future political target and certainly would have affected promotions. Generally, dossiers contain information on background, appraisals, assessments, punishments, work history, rewards, rank, and party status (Dutton 1992, chap. 6; see also Whyte and Parish 1984, chap. 9).

9   Lisa Rofel stated this well, writing that "power exists not merely 'out there' in macroinstitutions but in the very formation of bodies and desires. . . . Modern disciplinary power, then, operates most effectively when self-interested, individuated subjects believe they are most free, and thus it confounds the emancipatory premises of modernity. Put another way, actions we take in the name of individual freedom are figured by and within, rather than externally to, regimes of power" (1999: 11).

10 These kinds of reforms led Martin Whyte to argue that significant political changes

occurred during the Deng Xiaoping era, even though researchers have commonly focused only on economic reforms. Party power was undermined, he argued, as "Promotion more by 'expert' than 'red' criteria produces individuals in influential positions who feel they have some basis for making independent judgments about their society's problems, rather than people willing to rely entirely on Party and leader dictates" (1993: 530). The literature on reforms in the 1980s and 1990s is vast; see, for example, Solinger 1993 and Naughton 1996. On college entrance exams, see Pepper 1984. On the political dimensions of the emergence of China's "technocratic movement," see Li and White 1991. On the Factory Director Responsibility System, see Chevrier 1991; Naughton 1996; and Chamberlain 1987. On the development of contract labor, see, for example, White 1987 and Sensenbrenner 1996. And on management reforms more specifically, see Chevrier 1991 and Child 1994.

11 Economists studying the industrial growth of Asia point to the improvement in the "stock and quality of human resources" in the newly industrializing economies (NIES) as a sign of how governments prepared the labor force for a certain kind of engagement with the global economy (Chowdhury and Islam 1993: 19 and chap. 9; Xiao and Tsang 1999; Siu and Lau 1998). For a discussion of how China proposed to have education respond to the new socialist commodity economy, see, for example, Paine 1994 and Rai 1991.

12 One finds this situation in what Ong calls postdevelopmental states, which "focus more on producing and managing populations that are attractive to global capital," (1999: 216) such that not all segments of the population (e.g., those with gender or skill differences) are regulated or valued equally.

13 The Anti-Rightist campaign in the late 1950s, for instance, expelled more than 300,000 intellectuals and cadres from their posts, many to the countryside, and policies of the Cultural Revolution sent more than 16 million urban youths to learn from the peasants (Spence 1990: 638). Even during the 1960s, negative views of the countryside were reinforced "by treating the countryside as a dumping ground for urban rejects. . . . A rural work assignment had become a form of class retribution and carried the stigma of failure with the urban hierarchy of status and achievement" (Pepper 1996: 350).

14 The literature on educational reforms is extensive. For information on these directives, see, for example, Hayhoe 1989; Hayhoe 1993; Hayhoe 1996: chap. 4; Pepper 1984; Pepper 1990: chap. 7; Pepper 1995; Rai 1991; Agelasto and Adamson 1998; and Li 1999. The earliest reforms in the fenpei system began in 1983 with experiments at Shanghai Jiaotong University, Xi'an Jiaotong University, Shandong Marine University, and Qinghua University (Agelasto 1998).

15 Until the mid-1980s, college graduates were quite satisfied with their job assignments, as the Cultural Revolution had left many openings in the civil service, research institutes, and other desirable posts. After those were filled, however, especially at the state and provincial levels, job dissatisfaction increased and overstaffing became even more serious (Hayhoe 1996: 119–20, 174–81).

16 The practice of mutual choice "within a definite scope" referred to several restric-

tions. Students should have returned to their hometowns, gone to key state units in need, abided by school deadlines for the job search, and taken jobs that matched their majors. Schools could reject any position students found on their own if they did not meet these terms. Participation in mutual choice also was related to one's type of enrollment. Locally committed students (*dingxiang*), for instance, agreed to study a certain subject and return to their hometowns upon graduation in exchange for university admissions. Many of these students came from smaller cities and remote areas. Their scores were not high enough for state sponsorship, and their families did not have the resources for self-paying enrollment. Self-paying (*zifei*) students covered their own expenses, chose their own majors, and found work by themselves upon graduation since schools considered them "outside of the plan." Their scores on the national entrance exam were too low for state sponsorship. Unit-sponsored students (*weituo peiyang*) were more like the committed students and had their expenses paid by an enterprise, to which they returned after graduating. State sponsorship (*gongfei*) was the traditional form of enrollment, but even these students paid partial tuition by the 1990s. The breakdown at DUT for 1995 graduates, for example, was 2,027 state sponsored and 107 self-paying, for a total of 2,134 graduates. Within the state-sponsored category, 459 were unit sponsored and 59 were locally committed (Dalian University of Technology 1995a). Through a policy of "merging tracks" (*binggui*), distinctions between state-sponsored and self-paying students disappeared with 1997 admissions, however, when all students began paying a regulated fee. To keep higher education affordable, fees were not to exceed 25 percent of actual education costs and schools offered more loans. At DUT and Finance University, this meant that yearly fees for 1997–98 ranged from 2,000 to 2,700 RMB, depending on one's major. The more popular majors were more expensive.

It is important to note that graduates in the fields of agriculture, teaching, and medicine faced many more restrictions in the job search than did graduates of DUT or Finance University. There was no open mutual choice at schools in those fields. Since 1993, graduates of Liaoning Teacher's University in Dalian had been allowed to seek units on their own, but they had to work for the government, not a private or foreign company. The school considered some students so difficult to place, such as those majoring in history, that they allowed them to look for jobs outside of teaching. The only way to get around the commitment to work for the government was to pay the school a "training fee." A young woman in Dalian paid 10,000 RMB to avoid taking up her assigned teaching position upon graduation, money she had saved while working part time in college.

17 Gender was a pervasive form of cultural evaluation in these labor exchanges (see Hoffman 1997).

18 A popular subject for commentary in journals and newspapers was the reasons why people changed jobs. Articles often divided these into "good" categories (e.g., further study and development) and "bad" ones (e.g., higher salaries and perpetual dissatisfaction).

19 To avoid additional fees for the hukou transfer to Dalian or Beijing, DUT graduates

in 1996 had to have a minimum of six academic scholarship points. Each semester students could earn these points based on their class ranking (first place = five points, second place = three points, third place = two points). Points were awarded in each major according to academic accomplishments (80 percent) and behavior (20 percent, based on teachers' recommendations). The restrictions once covered fourteen major urban centers, but DUT reduced them to just Beijing and Dalian. If the students lacked points, they had to pay 1,000 RMB for each missing point, going no higher than 6,000 for the six points required, a sum that was prohibitively expensive for many students. See also Dalian University of Technology 1995b.

20 Dalian city's bureau assigned 180 people in 1993, 250 in 1994, and 300 in 1995. According to its statistics, 80 percent of these students "happily" took the positions (Dalian Personnel Bureau n.d.: 8).

21 During the Cultural Revolution, educational institutions worked to increase the number of worker and peasant children who attended college. At this time, recommendations and politics took the place of exams as admissions criteria. Despite such attempts "to mask the essentially elitist nature of higher education," a college education remained coveted, as those wishing to go far exceeded the number of enrolled students (Hawkins 1982: 420). For more on origins, education enrollments, and the Cultural Revolution, see Unger 1982; Pepper 1984, 1996; Rai 1991: chap. 6; Adams 1970: chap. 4; M. Zhang 1998; and Seeberg 1998.

22 Besides the use of guanxi in the job search process, the graduate's "family environment" (*jiating huanjing*) was important to employers. Numerous personnel directors distinguished between potential workers on the basis of what their parents did for a living. For example, children of professors and doctors were expected to have "higher levels" of culture and civility and be able to speak and think well as employees.

23 Campus fairs differed from municipal fairs in that they were run by a specific university, open only to that university's students, and, in the case of DUT, drew units from across the country. These units were predominantly large state-run enterprises that used to receive DUT graduates through assignments. Citywide fairs, described above, were organized by the Personnel Bureau, open to anyone, and drew units from Dalian city, surrounding counties, and the Zone. In terms of texts, in 1992 DUT published a small paperback entitled *Helping with Your Career* (Dalian University of Technology 1992). Related volumes in the campus bookstore were entitled *Xin jiuye shidai* (The new employment era) and *Xue shenme zhuanye hao* (How to pick a major). In addition to national publications, DUT published its own monthly employment newspaper with articles about specific restrictions, letters from graduates with advice for their schoolmates (e.g., go to the small towns), and updates on campus visits by companies. See, for example, Dalian University of Technology 1995a, 1995b.

Curriculum reforms were ratified in the 1985 education reform document (Communist Party of China), which allowed schools to move away from the unified curriculum. Such reforms reflect the increased flexibility of major educational institutions in urban China. The reduction or advancement of certain majors in the name of enhancing a graduate's competitive edge illustrated China's involvement in transnational economic practices and flexible production. Curriculum changes represented the ways in which universities responded to perceptions of market needs in ways that paralleled production processes the world over. For more on curriculum reforms, see Hayhoe 1987, 1993; and Pepper 1990, chap. 7.

24 Another important issue related to expectations was the background of the student. Young people from elite urban families were simply not willing to take certain jobs.

25 An intriguing parallel is found in Nicolas Rose's discussion of "advanced liberalism," where self-fulfillment and actualization are highlighted in a "respecification of the ethics of personhood" (1996: 60). He argued that an emphasis on the client as customer "specifies the subjects of rule in a new way: as active individuals seeking to 'enterprise themselves,' to maximize their quality of life through acts of choice, according their life a meaning and value to the extent that it can be rationalized as the outcome of choices made or choices to be made" (57).

26 Similar arguments claim that the reforms have created more room for identity construction related to one's professional and economic activities than was allowed during the Maoist era of strict class identifications and severe control by units (see Lu 1997). An important part of this argument is that the new social structure emerging with economic reforms is *reasonable and natural*. My argument here, however, is that labor market exchanges and the social distinctions emerging at this time are political and cultural practices and not a liberalization or rationalization of irrational systems. Meisner's past argument still seems relevant in that "those portions of the Chinese economy that now appear to function in a capitalist fashion reflect neither the 'natural' processes of economic development favored by most Western observers nor the workings of the 'objective economic laws' proclaimed by Chinese Marxist ideologists. Rather, the economic changes are the products of decisions made by a small group of state and party leaders in Peking designed to serve the goals of national wealth and power" (1986: 482). On the naturalization of gender differences in "postsocialist" China, see Rofel 1999, especially chap. 7.

27 See Jeffery in this volume for another use of the concept of "packaging" people.

28 I wish to thank Connie Clark for raising questions on this point and pushing me to explain these differences more clearly.

Robert Efird Rock in a Hard Place:

Music and the Market in Nineties Beijing

More than an hour before the concert, people began to mass in front of the giant dance hall in northwestern Beijing's university district. One among the flurry of "megadiscos" that debuted in Beijing during the mid-1990s, the club usually drew nighttime revelers with the throb of imported techno. This afternoon's crowd had come for something different, however: four Chinese "rock" bands performing live, original music. My three Chinese bandmates and I were slated to open the show.

This would be our band's fortieth concert in Beijing; in nearly two years of practicing and performing together, we had played a range of venues, including bars, nightclubs, a beer festival—even the U.S. Embassy's annual Fourth of July event. But this was our biggest audience by far: the concert organizers printed two thousand tickets, and all were gone by the day of the show, largely due to the marketing efforts of student associations from nearby universities.[1] Student leaders agreed to sell the tickets on their campuses in return for having the names of their respective student associations included on the concert posters, of which more than five thousand were printed at considerable cost.

The glossy, oversized posters featured a dynamic concert photo of two anonymous—but obviously Caucasian—rock guitarists. Nobody seemed to find this incongruous, despite the fact that I was the only Caucasian to play (and I play drums). The posters also featured a map marking the concert's venue and, even more prominently, the location of a nearby bar. Not surprisingly, the concert's organizers also managed the bar, and the concert was in fact a means to celebrate—and publicize—the bar's opening.

As showtime neared, the crowd outside thickened and began to squeeze up against the disco's glass facade. Preparations inside the disco took longer than anticipated, and the crowd's impatience mounted. Finally, just minutes before the concert was scheduled to begin, the staff opened the doors. It was like opening a floodgate: the tightly packed crowd burst into the disco, shattering a glass door and two massive planters and scattering glass and pottery fragments throughout the lobby. When truncheon-wielding security guards finally staunched the flow, only a hundred or so people remained outside. Furious at the damage, the disco's manager refused them admission.[2]

Inside the disco's cavernous belly, however, over fifteen hundred concertgoers—mostly Chinese college students—filled the floor and flanking balconies and crushed up against the stage. As we played through our set, I could see and almost feel the rapt attentiveness and barely suppressed excitement in the faces beyond the stage, an intense silence rent by intermittent roars of "Hao!" (Yeah!) when some riff or lyric hit home.

> Living in this space / A narrow crack / This feeling of being in darkness suffocates me / Having no choice to choose / Is the reality of my life / Who can give me a compass / So I won't lose myself again? / Let me out! / Let me out! / Let me leave this place / Let me out / I don't want to wait / Let me out! / Out! / Out! (from "Fengxi" [Crack])[3]

Taking Place   A large body of recent social science scholarship has been devoted to the definition and discussion of "globalization" and "transnationalism," concepts that sacrifice analytical value in order to achieve a hollow, universalizing descriptiveness. The attempt to simultaneously explain both the universal and the particular (or "global" and "local") leads many models of globalization—of global "flows" (Appadurai 1990), for example—to risk overly abstracting cultural processes from the places in which they occur, even as they assert the importance of "locality" and the imaginative (re)constructions that result when ideas, products, and language are deterritorialized.[4] A further problem with globalization models is their frequent failure to adequately differentiate between consumption and production. After all, it is one thing to consume a Big Mac in China, say, and quite another to produce and market an indigenous alternative. An approach that seeks to redress these shortcomings would therefore do two things. First, it would rigorously attend to the particularities of local life in order to document how products and practices "take place," that is, necessitate specific environments for their existence. Second, it would pay close attention to the widely shared medium by which transnational exchange—both production and consumption—is broadly structured: the capitalist market economy.

The development of *yaogun*, as "rock and roll" has been rendered into Chinese,[5] demonstrates the importance of an analysis grounded in the gritty and often prosaic necessities of everyday life and the political and economic forces by which local lives are mediated. Music is not created in a vacuum: it is laboriously crafted by musicians who need time and places to practice and perform; money for food, housing, and instruments; and opportunities to record and promote their music. This chapter is an attempt to illustrate how yaogun production "takes place" in Beijing through a complex negotiation of state intervention and private initiative wherein foreign and local concerns strive to cultivate preference and capture market share. Publicity, or *xuanchuan* (see also Ballew, this volume) is integral to this place taking and the development of yaogun as a product in China's diversifying market economy.

"Place" in China is increasingly a privatized, market-structured milieu in which Chinese musicians are active as both producers and consumers. The evolution of China's market economy—and its concomitant black market economy—presents these musicians with both opportunities and challenges. Take the role of pirate recordings, for example. On the one hand, Chinese rock icon Cui Jian recently asserted that his access to pirate recordings of Western music significantly contributed to his education and development as a rock musician in China. On the other hand, the profits of Chinese rock musicians (and Cui Jian in particular) also seriously suffer from the rampant pirating that immediately follows their albums' commercial success.

The dramatic and hotly contested privatization of both physical and virtual spaces in contemporary China is also an ambivalent development for musicians. The ongoing privatization of heretofore state-owned housing and industry and the disappearance of subsidies for firms that are still nominally state controlled have sent highly publicized shock waves throughout Chinese society and resulted in an efflorescence of entrepreneurship. The proliferation of new commercial ventures has exposed Chinese musicians to a host of opportunities for performance and employment and an improved prospect of exposure via privately owned record companies and radio stations. Many musicians argue, however, that the quality of Chinese rock music has suffered from the growing preoccupation with profit and loss and the need to please a mass market. In any event, it is essential to bear in mind that recordings and radio appearances are generally the visible and audible culmination of a lengthy and arduous process of rehearsal, performance, and self-promotion under straitened economic circumstances.

Emphasizing yaogun's commodity qualities is not to deny the importance of state regulation in shaping its performance and propagation. Recordings, radio and television broadcasts, and large-scale performances (particularly in Beijing) are all subject to varying degrees of official scrutiny and repression. But Western journalistic exaggerations of Chinese rock's underground, dissident character ignore the economic factors that have transformed the space musicians occupy from a "crack" into a market niche. Moreover, they ignore the ways in which state efforts to contain and constrain yaogun may occur not outside but through the market, by setting the price of tapes and thereby restricting musicians' profits from their recordings, for example.

In placing yaogun, I have focused upon Beijing. Rock performance and production in China are distinctly urban phenomena; bands have existed in most, if not all, of China's large metropolitan centers since at least the early 1990s.[6] Among these, Beijing is widely acknowledged among Chinese musicians, producers, and fans as the center of China's rock world.[7] Yaogun's development in Beijing has been privileged by a felicitous combination of three factors: (1) China's largest concentration of foreigners, particularly foreign students; (2) a relative abundance of performance places where bands can find work and a receptive audience for their music; and (3) the highest concentration of recording opportunities for rock musicians, comprising both foreign and domestic record companies and producers. Thus, much of the musical product that appears in the mass media's "virtual spaces" of cassettes, music videos, and radio traces its origins back to Beijing. Moreover, Beijing is a magnet for provincial artists wishing to record, learn an instrument, or just find a more sympathetic audience. Indeed, the formation of a number of these bands was influenced by seeing Beijing-based bands on tour in the provinces.[8]

Taking place involves taking time. Although space-time compression (Harvey 1989) may uproot products from their historical contexts, history returns in the act of reception. Chinese receptions of yaogun (and they vary) are strongly colored both by an awareness of rock's history in the West as well as a sense of yaogun's separate but related trajectory in China. Thus, in order to understand the ways in which yaogun is understood in the 1990s, we must first return to its emergence as a genre in the 1980s.

Yaogun Generation Indigenous conceptions of yaogun[9] in the 1990s refer to both a foreign and a Chinese history. As the aforementioned poster photo demonstrates, Chinese in the People's Republic (PRC) routinely associate the practice of yaogun with images of Western rock. These associations range from the superficial (electric guitars and long hair) to the extremely nuanced understandings many musicians possess of such Western rock subgenres as grunge, punk, and several types of "metal." These understandings of Western rock are complemented by varying degrees of familiarity with yaogun's "local," Chinese history, a history of performance and recording that stretches back to the mid-1980s, when a number of Chinese artists—notably Cui Jian—began producing original, Chinese-language music in a Western rock idiom.

The emergence of local yaogun music was preceded and precipitated by a cascade of imported foreign music from both the West and Asia following Deng's market reforms in the late 1970s. Returning travelers and foreign visitors brought the light pop tunes from Taiwan and Hong Kong known as "gangtai" and a broad variety of recorded Western popular music.[10] This was supplemented by radio broadcasts of Anglo-American pop and folk music, initially on Voice Of America and stations based in Taiwan and Hong Kong.[11] When radio and cassette technology rapidly spread throughout China in the early 1980s, both foreign imports and local products found a dramatically enlarged audience.[12] Mainland radio also played a major role in exposing Chinese to the latest popular music from the West. In the mid- to late 1980s, international stars such as Michael Jackson and Madonna became widely popular in the PRC via radio broadcasts on state-owned stations.

Live performances quickly followed the recorded imports. In 1985, the British pop group Wham! performed in Beijing.[13] The next year, following a spate of multistar concerts in the West and Taiwan, two Chinese music companies organized a massive televised concert of one hundred Chinese pop musicians entitled Let the World Be Filled with Love. This 1986 concert "heralded the birth of rock and roll on the mainland" when Cui Jian broke ranks with the gangtai-style singers and belted out an original song entitled "Yiwusuoyou" (I have nothing).

Ethnomusicologist H. Stith Bennett has observed that "labels for types of popular music represent sales categories for recordings to a far greater extent than they represent distinguishable music cultures or even styles within a single music culture" (1980: xi). Yaogun's history also demonstrates recording's role in defining genre: although "Yiwusuoyou" is now widely regarded as China's first yaogun song, it was not immediately identified as such by many Chinese listeners until Cui Jian made its genre explicit with his 1988 album *Rock 'n Roll on the New Long March*. Cui's album is significant not because it acquainted Chinese listeners with the Western genre of "rock" but because it concretely defined a Chinese-language, original musical expression by means of the Western rock tradition. The bewildering variety of musical inspirations and affiliations that have blossomed in 1990s China render the term *yaogun* as vague as the term *rock* has become in the Anglo-American musical lexicon. Musicians in particular bridle at the term's imprecision. Since the music in question is often defined in opposition to the gangtai-style pop tunes that dominate the domestic market, the term *alternative* (*linglei* or *feizhuliu*, literally "nonmainstream") might be more appropriate. But the broad designation of this music as yaogun—a convention that is in any case followed by many of the musicians and their listeners—not only conveys the music's differentiation from mainstream pop but calls attention to the Western musical heritage to which all of the artists claim at least partial allegiance. Both characteristics—its "Westernness" and its distinction from pop—are crucial to the ways in which yaogun takes place in the market.

Showcases and Market Places   In the late 1980s and early 1990s, rock performance in Beijing was defined by the two poles of large concerts and small parties (the English term *parties* was used). The former were often staged in concert halls or athletic arenas and frequently featured several bands or highlighted a single performer. Parties were loosely—and often covertly—organized and staged on university campuses or in a handful of restaurants frequented or owned by foreigners (Jones 1992a: 107–8). As Andrew Jones writes in his seminal study of yaogun and "popular" (tongsu) music in the 1980s and early 1990s, "because rock parties in Chinese-owned venues have been subject to police harassment, musicians have increasingly been compelled to hold events in foreign-run restaurants in Beijing, where there is some measure of 'extra-territoriality.'" "The spaces that result from this exclusivity," he asserts, "are clearly spaces apart, both literally and metaphorically, from the everyday life of the city" (97, 108).

By the mid-1990s, however, yaogun had spread from the periphery to the vibrant, emerging foci of cosmopolitan consumption. Bands in Beijing began to find work in the growing number of Western-style cafe/ bars, restaurants, and nightclubs that catered to Beijing's large expatriate population as well as its burgeoning group of young, urban, professional Chinese with expendable income and cosmopolitan tastes. Many of these establishments had small stages and experimented with musical performances as a means of drawing customers. A number of foreign and domestic companies also began to use yaogun performances in their promotional events, and some sponsored concerts by well-known artists as a vehicle for publicity.

Image and Volume: Yaogun as Western Spectacle   Beginning in 1994, the embassy section of eastern Beijing known as Sanlitun experienced a phenomenal proliferation of Western-style bars, restaurants, and cafes.[14] Unlike the foreign-owned bars and restaurants of the 1980s and early 1990s, the owners of these establishments were often young or middle-aged Chinese who had spent time abroad and were sensitive to the aesthetic and culinary tastes of the expatriate crowd. Some featured dartboards or pool tables, and almost all embellished their interiors with advertisements for foreign alcohol and tobacco products. Although these establishments were initially targeted at the large foreign population in the area—including businesspeople, embassy employees, and their families—they also drew large numbers of foreign students from the many universities throughout Beijing and a growing number of local Chinese ranging from businessmen to artists. Many of these establishments experimented with live music performance in 1994–1996. Cover charges for shows were rare, so admission was relatively open. Pay for the bands varied widely, from several hundred to 2,000 RMB (approximately U.S.$240) per night. Owners generally viewed bands as complementary to their establishments' Western themes and congenial to their clientele's Western tastes. Since the bottom line was increased customer flow, there was considerable tolerance of different musical styles as long as they brought people in the door. By the same token, pressure on the bands to bring guests and publicize their own shows was high.

Our band performed in one of the Sanlitun restaurant/bar establishments. The stylishly appointed, plant- and wood-accented interior featured both a dartboard and a pool table, and the walls were festooned with an astonishing variety of promotional media for Western tobacco and alcohol. On the wall behind the stage, for example, a large Jack Daniels banner, an electric Marlboro sign, and a Budweiser poster with three Asian women in bathing suits competed with our performances for the clientele's attention. Most of the restaurant's employees were clean-cut, plaid-shirted, Chinese college students who had some command of English, and the Chinese owner had lived in Australia for a number of years. The customers were largely a mix of Chinese and foreign businesspeople and embassy personnel. The owners cared little about the style or quality of our music. They were concerned with cultivating a Western image and increasing customer volume, with the idea that the former would help achieve the latter. These priorities were succinctly demonstrated when the bar commissioned a professional video of one of our performances there. The cameraman appeared unannounced one evening to film the last half of our performance, including extended footage of the mostly foreign crowd that was dancing to our music. The video was then used on the bar's TV monitors for its visual appeal alone, the original soundtrack having been replaced with recorded Western pop music. As such, the video also served as a form of advertisement for the restaurant's band nights, when customers could presumably see this spectacle in the flesh.

Advertisement of bands was a major concern of club owners and many musicians. Club owners would often put out a signboard advertising that week's or evening's performances, and some printed flyers or even monthly schedules. Since their continued employment heavily depended upon customer volume, bands might put up posters (our band did a lot of postering in university dorms) or hand out leaflets. However, the single most influential means of publicity was a calendar of events printed in a biweekly English-language newspaper distributed free of charge to hotels, restaurants, clubs, and schools in Beijing. The paper was established in 1994, just as the boom in cafe/bars was beginning, and expatriates in particular relied upon it when selecting their evening activities. Although the paper itself survived largely on advertising revenue, the calendar of events was free. In order to benefit from this free publicity, however, an establishment had to have an event to list. Thus, the paper not only helped draw customers to music performances, but it also constituted something of a rationale for having performances in the first place.

A second type of yaogun performance space to emerge in the mid-1990s was the commercial event. In this context, rock bands served as an accessory to the marketing of a consumer product or pastime, which often had explicit Western associations. As with the foregoing cafe/bar and restaurant scene, the employer was generally concerned with spectacle over (or as) substance. Our band's first taste of such events was in fact our first paid performance: an international mountain bike race on October 1, 1994, China's National Day. While large-scale celebrations took place in Tiananmen Square to mark the country's forty-fifth anniversary, my band members and I were on the outskirts of Beijing playing covers of the Beatles and Nirvana for a race-going crowd that for their part showed little interest. The Hong Kong–based organizers of the event told us to simply provide background noise for atmosphere between races. Exactly what sort of atmosphere the organizers were looking for is suggested by the race program, in which we were cavalierly identified as the American Band. By contrast, our next commercial event performance was arranged by an international advertising firm seeking an authentically "local" Chinese band to represent their client—Budweiser—at the annual beer festival in Beijing's Asian Games Village. The American advertising executive in charge of the account mentioned that Budweiser sponsors bands all over the world to promote their beer and we shouldn't feel that we were compromising our artistic integrity since "even Mick Jagger" helped market Bud. As it turned out, most of the foreign and domestic beer companies at the festival erected stages and hired rock bands to draw and entertain crowds. Festival organizers initially asked us to submit song lyrics for inspection, but we didn't bother and nobody objected. Although we refrained from playing our original Chinese-language songs, other local bands working the festival performed originals without incident.

Our band was hardly alone in taking advantage of these emerging opportunities for employment promoting transnational firms and commodities. Commercial events and Westernized cafe/bars and restaurants opened up important new moneymaking spaces for a host of Beijing's rock musicians, particularly those who were still "underground" (*dixia*).[15] Moreover, performances were largely open and free from official intervention.[16] Nevertheless, few if any yaogun musicians were able to survive solely on their music. In this sense, Beijing bands resembled the local American bands profiled by Bennett:

> Whether or not it is so conceptualized by the musicians, a local group is a transitory phenomenon that exists by virtue of a local demand for rock events which require only a small investment on the part of a casual employer. In this way the local market provides an experimental training experience . . . for the career of becoming a popular musician; but it does not provide a place for full-time employment as a professional popular musician. (1980: 97)

Given that most Beijing bar bands earned less than a thousand RMB (around U.S.$120) per show and were lucky to find one paying gig a week, musicians had to rely upon side jobs and/or parental support for survival. While this side work might involve playing music (as a studio musician, acoustic performer, or backing musician for a pop singer), it rarely allowed for the creation and performance of original songs. Moreover, since many restaurant and cafe/bar owners saw yaogun bands as generic accessories to a Western "atmosphere," these bands could be dropped in favor of other types of performance that brought in guests by satisfying the same criteria. This is indeed what happened in many Sanlitun cafe/bars and restaurants: after a period of experimentation with loud yaogun bands whose original music was often unevenly executed and in Chinese, several establishments in the area switched to acoustic duos, foreign (often Filipino) bands, and/or jazz bands that played polished, English-language, cover songs that owners regarded as less intrusive and more varied.[17]

In contrast to the establishments and events that employed musicians as little more than a marketing gimmick, a small number of clubs, bars, and periodic musical events constituted places where musicians, organizers (often musical or visual artists themselves), and most if not all of the audience shared an artistic interest in the performance of original rock music. Such bars frequently became gathering places for the loose "circle" of Beijing musicians and their group of fans and friends, and performances often featured jam sessions in which musicians from the audience switched and mixed with those on stage. As sites for spontaneous musical exchange, experimentation, and collaboration (both on and off the stage), these establishments served an extremely important role in local musical development. There were also infrequent multiband musical events, such as the one that opened this chapter, in which the music was foregrounded. Beijing disc jockey Zhang Youdai has organized a number of such shows, including annual musical observances of the date of grunge rock artist Kurt Cobain's suicide, rock awards events, and a series of free concerts at several Beijing universities. At one such concert, staged in 1996, musicians performed for free and the sound equipment was donated by a local entrepreneur who garnered publicity through the event. A spate of multiband Chinese punk shows was organized and executed during 1996–97 by an American musician living in Beijing, drawing audiences of several dozen to approximately two hundred fans. Local music producers have been able to secure performance opportunities for their artists through a variety of indirect methods, such as holding album release press conferences featuring performances or securing sponsorship from a major international beer company and staging shows that simultaneously promote both the band and the beer.

Despite their importance in giving artists exposure and performance experience (not to mention enjoyment), such concerts and club performances did not represent significant sources of income for owners, organizers, or musicians. This is largely because rock's audience is composed primarily of young Chinese (often college students) who have relatively little expendable income. A second issue is one of scale: although Beijing venues ranging from bars to large discos may hold rock events with relative impunity and arena shows have been held in large provincial cities, arena-sized yaogun shows in Beijing—particularly those by Cui Jian—have not been permitted by local authorities. Thus, even well-known bands find it difficult to make money in China's capital.

In order to escape the financial dead end of the local bar and event scene, Beijing rock bands must seek recording opportunities with local and foreign record producers. Recording marks the first step away from the physical spaces of Beijing's bars and restaurants to the virtual spaces of tape, radio, and even television. On the strength of their exposure in these media, bands can negotiate new and larger performance opportunities beyond the Beijing scene.

Marketing the Musical Product "We're determined to find a Chinese Bob Dylan," announced a senior vice president of MCA Music Entertainment International, Ltd., whose company opened a Hong Kong office in April 1995.[18] Yet two years later MCA had not signed a single mainland artist and the executive in question had returned to the United States after making only a single trip to Beijing. With the exception of Cui Jian's early collaboration with another large company, EMI, multinational record companies have been conspicuous in their absence from the mainland rock recording scene. During the 1990s, the majority of rock recording on the mainland was conducted by two Beijing-based independent producers and two small Asia-based companies—Red Star (Hong xing) and China Fire (Zhongguo huo)[19]—with offices in Beijing. The debut albums of major artists such as Dou Wei (1994) and Tang Dynasty (1992) were both released by China Fire's parent company, the independent Taiwanese label Rock Records. These have proved to be moderately successful, selling a combined total of more than 1.5 million compact discs and cassettes as of May 1995.[20] Independent producers (such as Lao Ge, producer of the Yaogun Beijing series) seem to focus on the recording of compilation albums, which represent the first shot at recording for many bands and may serve as a stepping stone to the release of their own albums. However, a band's immediate financial return from a compilation is generally negligible; in return for one song, a group often makes little more than the average price of one night's performance.[21]

If official intervention in small-scale rock performance is the exception rather than the rule, the influence of the state is considerably more pervasive in the process of recording and marketing a musical product. Before an album can be released on the mainland, it must first pass inspection by a government examination committee that reviews the music's lyrical content. According to one producer, if an artist fails to pass on the first try, subsequent submissions will likely fail as well, since the committee will be suspicious of the artist's sincerity. Since all music and printed matter in China must also be published and distributed by state firms, a producer may first consult a publishing company, which will review the material and later act as the producer's proxy with the committee. Some producers may also take the risky step of disguising a potentially offensive lyric by changing its written form to an inoffensive homophone, leaving the original recording as is and hoping the committee will fail to notice the discrepancy. Although scrutiny of song content was apparently rather lax and disorganized in the early 1990s, it reportedly grew more stringent toward the end of the decade. "You can't even say that society is bad or that the city is chaotic or ugly," complained one producer. Such words are described as "too sentimental, too gloomy." For example, on one recent release a group had to change the word *death* in a song title to *life*.[22] Images on lyric sheets or record jackets that are deemed offensive may be blotted out, as in the case of another recent release that contained pictures of Chairman Mao. In addition to these overt instances of censorship and government control of publishing and distribution, some artists and producers also describe the government-mandated price of music cassettes (10 RMB, approximately $1.20) as an attempt to control the profits of bands and producers. The latter keep less than 20 percent of each cassette's price, leaving the lion's share for the state-owned publisher and distributor. In order to turn a profit, the band must therefore sell an enormous number of albums.[23] Rampant pirating also cuts into producers' and artists' profits—as in a case in which one successful album by a Red Star artist spawned six different pirate editions.

Following an album's production and acceptance by the censorship committee, the work of promotion begins. In general, a single will be released to radio stations nationwide a month or two in advance of the album's release. In order to get the album played, disc jockeys may be treated to meals or given gifts, or the promoter may take out an advertisement with the station in exchange for airtime for the music that they are promoting. Promoters may also pay journalists from local newspapers and nationally distributed trade publications such as *Yinyue shenghuo bao* (Musical life) to write an article on the band or album; the journalist may be paid 300 to 500 RMB ($36 to $60) for each piece. Radio interviews may also be arranged, and some producers organize local performances to showcase their artists.

According to a number of producers in Beijing, yaogun records rarely make money. When they do, however, their profitability appears to be closely related to exposure in the mass media of radio and television. This basic principle is perhaps best illustrated by the commercial success of pop rock singer Zheng Jun's 1994 Red Star album entitled *Chi luoluo* (Stark naked).[24] The album's hit single, "Huidao Lasa" (Return to Lhasa), a saccharine ode to the beauties of an exoticized Tibet, incorporates heavy-metal-style electric guitar and a female accompanying vocal that seems designed to evoke "Tibetan" singing. Red Star spent an unusually large amount of money on the promotion, which included nationwide broadcast of "Huidao Lasa"'s video on China Central Television (CCTV). It apparently required a great deal of financial persuasion to secure official permission for long-haired Zheng Jun to appear on TV, but the investment paid off handsomely for the record company. Earnings would have been far greater if not for the serious problem of pirated cassettes, which immediately appeared in response to the album's popularity.

The ability to broadcast Chinese rock music on state-owned television and radio unquestionably reflects the latter's increasing dependence on advertising revenue in order to turn a profit.[25] But it would be incorrect to assume that money can buy airtime irrespective of content. Zheng Jun might be described as a crossover musician: although his long hair and occasional incorporation of a heavy drum and electric guitar sound led many Chinese to identify him as a yaogun musician, most of the album differed little from mainstream pop music. His incorporation—some would argue appropriation—of ethnic motifs and voices lends Zheng's music a certain novelty. But it also harmonizes nicely with a government effort to downplay ethnic conflict by celebrating ethnic exoticism: Tibet as tourist destination, for example.

Since all music is scrutinized before release, the presence of content offensive to the government is unlikely in any event. Yet selective sensitivity may persist. One group's song, "Good Night, Beijing," featured a line bidding "goodnight to all the sleepless people" (*wan'an suoyou weimian de renmin*). Because it was suspected that this referred to the massacred souls of June 4, 1989, the song was allowed to be broadcast and sold in Beijing but was not allowed to appear on the Beijing musical charts published in the trade journal *Yinyue shenghuo bao* (Musical life).[26]

Once yaogun artists can claim name recognition through recordings and commercial airplay, they are more capable of securing performance opportunities, in particular, shows at large-scale venues in the provinces. These shows might be sponsored by companies that seek to promote themselves through association with the artist and hopefully turn a profit at the same time. Given his almost iconic status as China's biggest rock musician, Cui Jian is the definitive example of such a "name" artist. The value of his name is suggested by a 1996 front-page article in *Musical Life,* which describes a Cui Jian concert in the northern city of Harbin. While criticizing the promotional disorganization that led to a dramatic short-fall in the concert's attendance and an enormous loss of money on the part of the promoters, the article closes by noting that the promoters were "still satisfied, since their original intention was publicity, and they were able to make themselves more widely known through Cui Jian's name."[27] But Cui Jian also best illustrates the limits of fame. While free to play large cities outside of Beijing and abroad, Cui—who lives, practices, and records in Beijing—cannot play large-scale concerts there, and his attempts to play smaller venues have often been thwarted by the police.

Feichang Zhongguo: Unusual China/Unusually Chinese   The double entendre of the phrase meanings Feichang zhongguo—title of cable music Channel V's program on mainland Chinese rock—neatly summarizes the native-other tension in much recent yaogun. The proper interpretation depends on the terms of comparison. While foreigners and Chinese alike may view yaogun as unusual or even deviant in comparison with Chinese mainstream pop, yaogun's language and sociocultural referents mark it as "unusually Chinese" with respect to the Anglo-American artists who dominate rock's international market.

Beyond the simple (but salient) fact that yaogun music is largely sung in Mandarin Chinese, testimonies to yaogun's "Chineseness" on the part of foreign journalists and record company public relations men often simply reflect an attempt to exoticize it for non-Chinese consumption. By contrast, Chinese audiences often focus upon its "Westernness." In a 1996 interview in *Musical Life,* Cui Jian was asked whether, given rock music's origins in the West, there was such a thing as a rock music that "truly belonged to us Chinese" (*zhenzheng shuyu women minzu de*). The interviewer, a Chinese poet, felt that in the context of the Chinese mainland both orchestral music and rock carried a sense of "colonial culture," a certain "invasiveness." Instead of immediately addressing the interviewer's question, Cui engaged in a devastating condemnation of Chinese who use racial pride and the achievements of their ancestors as a means of compensating for their own lack of self-respect. "Having said this," Cui continued,

> I can now give a more profound response to this question of yours. Rock music isn't some kind of colonial culture; it's not some sort of invasion. Rock music is individuality. Only if you are capable of understanding this are you a true rock musician. . . . The expression "colonial culture" is deeply colored by politics; there's the issue of ethnic face involved. There's no way to resolve this issue. As long as you're still debating "colonial" and "ethnicity," well, then you're not doing rock music. I feel true rock music goes beyond these sorts of things; it's neutral.[28]

What is in fact remarkable about 1990s yaogun is not some unifying Chinese or Western essence but the profound stylistic diversification that has occurred over the past decade. For example, one 1997 mainland Chinese journal defines a so-called Post–Cui Jian group of contemporary bands as "orphans" with respect to their predecessors, those pioneering musicians of the 1980s. The lead singer of one contemporary group put the difference this way: "Today's young people are different from Cui Jian and those guys; we could care less about politics and society and all that. We don't have any tragic qualities; all our anguish is fake. I chose this decadent art (*tuifei yishu*), this interconnection of English punk and Seattle grunge, because serious China doesn't have this kind of culture."[29] Other artists refer to changes in China's economy when distinguishing themselves from the "I Have Nothing" (Cui Jian's "Yiwusuoyou") generation. The young lead singer of a well-known Beijing punk band asserted that the relative prosperity and depoliticized atmosphere of the 1990s were responsible for major differences between his generation and the Chinese rock singers of a decade earlier. In the 1980s, he said, it was easy to identify the sources of suffering and oppression. Now things are less clear; the causes are deeper, more complex.[30]

While yaogun music may lack a common chord, most musicians still broadly share a common economic environment, which is structured by market demands, foreign and domestic entrepreneurship, and state regulation. Cui Jian once described yaogun as not representing rebellious-ness but a spirit of no compromise; yet yaogun almost invariably "takes place" in a context of compromise between often conflicting goals (politi-cal, aesthetic, and economic) and agents (government censors, musi-cians, producers, club owners, journalists, disc jockeys, and fans).

Cui Jian's own recent experience demonstrates that many of the op-portunities and obstacles outlined in this chapter still exist. His latest album, "Wuneng de liliang" (The Power of the Powerless), was released in May 1998 and singlehandedly injected life into a sagging domestic record market. Almost immediately thereafter, however, profits suffered seri-ously when a host of copies and pirated editions began to appear in stores. An investigative report published in the *Beijing Evening News* reported no less than nine illicit editions discovered in a brief survey of Beijing record shops. Noting the devastating effect this was having on both record companies and the cultivation of promising new artists and music, the article ends with the lament that "perhaps there will come a day when we no longer have any music of our own to hear."[31] Moreover, despite his ability to openly market his music and perform large shows in the provinces and abroad, Cui continues to face official opposition in Beijing. In the summer of 1998, the authorities enforced a last-minute ban on a huge, multiband, outdoor concert in the Beijing suburbs partly due to Cui Jian's scheduled participation.

Although such dramatic interventions suggest a continued role for the state in determining how yaogun is produced and performed, the pri-mary contention of this chapter has been that the influence of the market will prove decisive in determining yaogun's future in China. Consumers—not bureaucrats—determine profit and loss in the market economy. And recent history clearly demonstrates that there are many in the mass media and music industry who are willing to contravene state policy in order to satisfy a desire (or need) for profit. If we acknowledge that consumer taste in China is not simply dictated by some "culture industry" (much less state ideology), then a potential market for independent, creative expres-sion will continue to exist. Moreover, increasingly widespread personal technologies of musical production, performance, and replication (such as musical instruments, tape recorders, and the Internet) ensure that even commercially nonviable music has the opportunity to circulate.

To end this discussion of yaogun on an up beat, however, risks trivializing the difficulties and reversals musicians in China continue to face in their efforts to be heard. Cash-strapped creative artists will always be marginalized in a profit-maximizing economy wherein the physical and virtual spaces of musical performance and dissemination are owned by others. Out of respect for the predicament of Chinese musicians and the capricious political and economic environment in which they live, I have tried to document how below the kaleidoscopic, facile flow of borderless goods, images, and ideas that globalization theorists hold dear the precarious work of creation and performance continues to take place.

Struggling / In the darkness / I want to live. / In the netherworld / Awaiting / I seem to hear a sound. . . . (from "Fengxi" [Crack])

Notes

This essay is based on two years (1994–96) and a summer (1997) of research, practice, performance, and recording in Beijing. I wish to thank the Blakemore Foundation for generously funding my initial year under an Asian Language Training Fellowship and the University of Washington Department of Anthropology for helping to support my summer 1997 research. In Beijing, I am deeply grateful for the support of Chris Millward and Rob Cliver. I also thank the many fellow musicians in China who shared their time and thoughts. I am further indebted to Dennis Rea and Andrew Jones for advice, editorial assistance, and materials. Finally, and most importantly, this chapter and so much more would not have been possible without the friendship and patience of my band members (and teachers) Zhang Jianpu, Fu Ning, and Qin Jiye.

1 Tickets were priced affordably at 12 renminbi (RMB) each, approximately $1.50 (in 1996, U.S.$1 = approximately 8.3 RMB). By comparison, a typical disco entrance fee ranged from 50 to 60 RMB ($6.00 to $7.00). The two thousand tickets included a small percentage of "giveaways" (*zeng piao*) that were allotted to band members, organizers, and others.

2 Following the incident, members of the Public Security Bureau arrived with a top official from the municipal Bureau of Culture. Although the performance was allowed to continue, both the disco and the bands were cited for lacking the proper performance permits. The disco was fined the amount it had earned from renting out the space for the afternoon (3,000 RMB) and was ordered to close for four days. The company that organized the performance faced a fine that, according to regulations, could have ranged from 9,000 to 30,000 RMB. It responded by spending 10,000 RMB to entertain an individual with close ties to the authorities; the fines were subsequently dropped.

3 Lyrics by Zhang Jianpu, music by the MoHe band.

4   See Ong and Nonini (1997: 13) for a critique of the "American cultural studies approach that treats transnationalism as a set of abstracted, dematerialized cultural flows, giving scant attention to the concrete, everyday changes in peoples' lives or to the structural reconfigurations that accompany global capitalism."

5   *Yaogun* is a compound of the verbs *yao* (to rock/shake/sway) and *gun* (to roll). This literal translation does not imply a direct semantic correspondence.

6   A producer with one of the major foreign record labels in Beijing told me that he has received bands' demo tapes from every region of China. With the exception of *Yaogun Beijing,* most compilation albums contain a few songs by bands that are specifically identified as coming from beyond Beijing. One recent compilation (entitled *Yaogun: linglei pinpan* [Rock and roll: Alternative assortment] with the English title *Alternative in China*) includes a song each by bands from Yunnan, Xinjiang, Shenyang, Shanghai, Dongbei, Sichuan, and Mongolia (Menggu), with only three songs by Beijing bands. See Rea 1993 for a description of local rock scenes in Chengdu, Guangzhou, and Kunming during the early 1990s.

7   This opinion is widely held by both Beijing residents and musicians who have come to Beijing from the provinces. For example, see Jaivin 1995: 102.

8   For example, Rea mentions that a number of Chengdu bands had "sprung up in the wake of Cui Jian's 1990 Chengdu concerts" (1993: 50).

9   The history of yaogun's development in the 1980s is a complex one warranting its own extended treatment. See Brace 1991; Friedlander 1991; and Hamm 1991. Andrew Jones (1992a) sketches the development of Chinese popular music from the 1920s to the 1980s, with special attention to the relationship between *tongsu yinyue* (popular music) and yaogun in the latter decade. Peter Micic (1995) discusses the various new musical genres that appeared in the 1980s and speculates on the reasons behind their emergence. Gold 1993 is useful for his description of *gangtai* pop's penetration of the mainland. For an excellent Chinese discussion of this history and yaogun's relationship with pop music (*liuxing yinyue*), see Jin Zhaojun 1993, 1994. A more theoretical Chinese-language treatment of yaogun's history may be found in He Li 1997. Dennis Rea's "A Western Musician's View of China's Pop and Rock Scene" (1993) is essential for its depictions of rock performances and "scenes" in several parts of China during 1989–92.

10 *Gang* refers to *Xianggang* (Hong Kong) and *tai* to Taiwan. This style is also variously termed Cantopop (reflecting the Cantonese in which most Hong Kong tunes are sung) and Pacific Pop, suggesting its stylistic affinity with the light pop music consumed throughout East and Southeast Asia (see Hamm 1991: 17).

11 Friedlander 1991: 68–69; Jin 1993: 6.

12 Brace 1991: 45–46; Gold 1993: 916.

13 Twelve thousand fans were in attendance, and the concert was reportedly a catalyst for some Chinese musicians. See Micic 1995: 86; and Jaivin 1995: 100.

14 In less than two years more than forty establishments were said to have opened in this area. See Sugawara 1997; and Hong Tian 1997. David Armstrong's "The Chuppies Are Coming" (1997) conveys the ambiance of two of these cafe/bars and profiles

some of the Chinese who patronize them. Nightclubs and bars featuring live music opened in other parts of the city as well, particularly in areas adjacent to universities in Beijing's western and northern quarters.

15 The term *dixia* was used by Chinese to describe a band that had yet to make a name for itself or record; it did not necessarily imply persecution by, or opposition to, the authorities.

16 Police intervention occasionally occurred because of excess noise, overcrowding, or failure on the part of the owner to establish good relations with the local authorities. Most club owners I spoke with sidestepped the official requirement of performance permits by averring that the musicians were simply friends playing for fun and not compensation.

17 Bennett 1980: 97.

18 *Asiaweek,* May 19, 1995, 40.

19 Red Star is a subsidiary of the Hong Kong–based company Kinns Music, Ltd. China Fire is a division of Taiwan's Magic Stone, Ltd.

20 *Asiaweek,* May 19, 1995, 43. Of this total, 1.4 million represent mainland sales. Hong Kong and Taiwan sales numbered over 100,000, with the remaining (some 30,000) sold largely in Singapore, Malaysia, and Japan. U.S. sales totaled 5,500. It is important to note that these sales were undercut by widespread pirating, and the artists' profits are negligible compared to those of Western rock stars.

21 For instance, we were offered 1,000 RMB per band member for a song that was included on a Yaogun Beijing compilation.

22 Personal communication, Beijing, 14 July 1997.

23 An executive with Red Star told me that they generally need to sell 250,000 cassettes to make a profit; only two of their albums have managed to do this.

24 The first of a four-album contract, the album has sold between 500,000 and 600,000 copies, according to a Red Star representative. Zheng Jun broke his contract after the first album's success, and Red Star has taken him to court.

25 See Yang 1997: 299 for a description of how stations will even break government regulations to attract advertisers. See also Ikels (1996), who reports that operating budgets for TV stations are 90 percent dependent upon advertising (236): "Advertising had become the most significant source of revenue for papers and broadcasting stations by the early 90s" (ibid.).

26 *Musical Life* publishes top ten charts for the nation's major radio stations every week.

27 "Cui Jian xianqi Haerbin xiaji yaogunfeng" 1996: 1.

28 Ma Yongbo 1996: 3.

29 He Li 1997: 84. The band in question has a Japanese bassist and guitarist. It released its first album in Taiwan.

30 Personal communication, Beijing. July 1997. See Jones 1994 for a discussion of continuities and differences in pre- and post-Tiananmen Chinese rock, the latter including what he terms "commodity nativism."

31 *Beijing wanbao* (Beijing evening news), July 17, 1998, 9.

Part Two Gender, Bodies, and Consumer Culture

Suzanne Z. Gottschang The Consuming Mother:
Infant Feeding and the Feminine Body in Urban China

There is no finer investment for any community than putting milk into babies—Winston Churchill, 1943

In spite of supportive policies implemented prior to the economic reforms in the 1980s and the relatively late appearance of foreign breast milk substitutes in the market, China has experienced a marked decline in the rate of breast-feeding in urban areas.[1] For example, the number of urban mothers who breast-fed declined from 81% of mothers who breast-fed their infants for six months in 1950 to less than 11% who breast-fed for six months in 1992 (Ministry of Public Health Statistics, cited in *China Daily*, August 8, 1992). In response to this decline, in collaboration with the World Health Organization (WHO) and the United Nations Children's Fund (UNICEF) the Chinese government developed policies and laws to increase the rate of breast-feeding as part of an overall program to improve child health by the year 2000 (Xinhua News Agency in FBIS, April 13, 1996).[2] To this end, a dramatic reorganization of hospital routines and spaces in maternity wards and obstetrics clinics is occurring to conform to the ideals and regulations of the "Baby-Friendly" Hospital as defined by U.N. agencies and the Chinese government.

In addition to these health-focused policies, Chinese women are also encountering heightened expectations of femininity and sexuality as they make decisions about feeding their infants.[3] Indeed, the importance of sexuality and interest in bodily appearance are increasingly a concern that urban Chinese women must contend with as a part of their identity. Evans argues that "the public focus on female appearance in the past fifteen years has inscribed the female body with metaphors of self-control and surveillance which are quite different from those of the former period. Practices of body management, long and obsessively publicized in Western societies, are now prominent in the Chinese media. How to cultivate beautiful pale skin, exercise to keep the body slim and supple, and massage to keep breasts in shape are all familiar topics in women's magazines" (1997: 140). The physical changes women experience throughout the pre- and postnatal periods do not mesh well with the bodily imperatives of consumer culture as promoted by advertising. Ironically, in the hospital the idealized trim and sexual female body is communicated in both state-produced images and messages that endorse breast-feeding in international formula manufacturers' promotional literature.

In this chapter, I examine how the hospital, as an urban location, promotes ideals of motherhood that embody these conflicting norms for women. On the one hand, women are encouraged to maintain well-nourished bodies and to breast-feed their infants in compliance with larger state policies and goals to produce a healthy population. However, they simultaneously confront sexualized conceptions of a slim, feminine body in the context of the hospital's promotion of breast-feeding. Paradoxically, the increasing presence of foreign formula companies' advertisements in the hospital setting advertises sexualized images of the mother in their attempts to ally their products with the cachet of modernity and cosmopolitanism and a subjectivity based on consumerism.

In the case of decisions about using either breast milk or infant formula, urban Chinese women also function in a larger social context that extends beyond their bodily concerns and experiences. For example, the one-child policy has placed a premium on the health and well being of the child for both the family and the future of a modern nation (Anagnost 1995).[4] At the same time, they participate in a cultural and economic milieu that marks individuals as participants in a world where the ability to consume "scientific" products signifies one as modern. This is not to say that women's decisions to use one feeding method over another result from a utilitarian rationality created by the contexts of the one-child policy and consumer culture in urban China. Rather, I explore how conflicting ideals of motherhood are promulgated in an urban hospital at a moment in women's lives when bodily changes related to childbirth and infant feeding are the focus of "interpretive activities through which fundamental dimensions of reality are confronted, experienced and elaborated" (Good 1994: 69). In the following analysis, I highlight moments in the prenatal health care process when women confronted the importance of infant feeding in relation to concerns about maternal body image and sexuality through the hospital's advertising, which promoted breast-feeding and foreign infant formula promotional pamphlets that were disseminated during these classes.

Urban Hospitals and Infant Feeding   My research, conducted between 1994 and 1996, focused on following thirty women during the course of their pregnancy, birth, and postpartum periods.[5] By locating my research in one hospital, I was able to document the representations of ideal motherhood as they were presented to women in their classes on breast-feeding, their prenatal checkups, and eventually their births. As a result, I witnessed their reactions as they were presented with texts, images, and other information about infant feeding and motherhood. These moments presented opportunities to discuss what these women thought about the ways in which the hospital environment was shaping ideals of motherhood.

In addition to the opportunity to observe and discuss women's reactions to images of mothering, locating my analysis in the hospital served another purpose. In the case of infant feeding practices, studies by more public-health-oriented research suggest that the urban hospital is an important location for influencing women's decisions about breast-feeding (Popkin et al. 1983). Jelliffe and Jelliffe (1981) suggest that hospitals are centers conveying powerful representations of what is modern and scientific for urban and rural society, especially in the realm of promoting infant formula products to new mothers. While these observations indicate the power of the hospital to affect women's decisions about infant feeding, in this chapter I am not interested in confirming or disproving this point. Rather, I would like to shift the focus and ask different questions with regard to the Chinese hospital.

Ong's (1997a) suggestion that we rethink our conceptions of modernity and Chinese culture as either a project of national cultivation of productive citizens or the explosion of entrepreneurial capitalism and flexible, self-defined subjects is apt when we consider the promotion of infant feeding and maternal health.[6] She suggests that a dynamic tension exists between the Chinese state's interest in maintaining a stable collective of citizens and an increasingly powerful capitalist economy that emphasizes individuality and flux. As a result, the rhetoric of a uniquely Chinese modernity has focused on the adoption of Confucian values emphasizing stability, collectivity, and patriarchal authority. Ong argues that this move serves to counter Western capitalist and liberal notions of modernity as China marks its political and economic place in the global hierarchy and at the same time offers a culturally legitimate form of control in the national realm (358). In this chapter, I want to expand on this argument and examine how an urban Chinese hospital is situated in relation to the state's imperative to produce healthy citizens and the forces of capitalism that valorize individuality and choice. Indeed, the Chinese hospital, in its role implementing state policies to produce healthy urban citizens and its more recent adoption of health promotion activities that emphasize individual behavior, encompasses aspects of the tension between the collective and individualism in China. However, I demonstrate that in the midst of this tension the state and multinational and local infant formula companies co-opt the rhetoric and ideals associated with the other in order to "sell" individual women on the idea of breast-feeding or using infant formula. Thus, the state uses images and ideals associated with consumerism and individualism to influence women's decisions to breast-feed their infants and companies marketing their formula products employ the state's rhetoric and ideals about producing a healthy future generation. This case suggests that the dynamic described by Ong becomes more complex when it is examined beyond national and regional levels of discourse. Moreover, the urban Chinese hospital presents an instance where notions of modernity are not fixed but rather represent a blurring of boundaries between the state imperative to produce national subjects and citizens and the flexibility accorded to individual women through their participation in more transnational economies of capitalism.

Nationalism, represented by the resurgence of Confucian values in China, on the surface appears to embody a reaction to the lack of fixity in the process of globalizing capitalism. Yet, as Massey demonstrates, what gives a place its specificity is not some long internalized history, but the fact that it is constructed out of a particular constellation of relations, articulated at a particular locus. . . . The uniqueness of a place, or a locality, in other words, is constructed out of particular interactions and mutual articulations of social relations, processes, experiences and understandings, in a situation of co-presence, but where a large proportion of those relations, experiences and understandings are actually constructed on a far larger scale than what we happen to define for that moment as the place itself, whether it be a street, a region, or even a continent." (1993: 66)

Massey's conception of place is a reaction to those who view the postmodern world as one in which the ever increasing pace of time and movement, driven by capitalism, is eliminating the importance of space and place (see, e.g., Harvey 1989 on time-space compression). She argues that relying on a dichotomy of time and space fixes locations with a static and frequently undifferentiated nature (1993: 67). Moreover, if places are a constellation of relations, they are also likely to be locations of internal conflict and differences. In the urban Chinese hospital, conflicts surrounding the broader discourse of the Chinese conception of modernity and nation can in fact be viewed as a configuration of social relations that not only are imbued with difference and conflict but are often melded in combinations that appear contradictory. The multitude of local, national, and transnational representations and practices that result from these relations in turn shape women's bodies and experiences in contradictory ways as they participate in pre- and postnatal health care and make decisions about how to feed their infants.

Marketing Health and Body Image in the Hospital In order to better understand the hospital as a location where state policies and the realm of transnational consumer culture coexist in the promotion of breast-feeding, infant formula, and idealized feminine body images, let me describe some of the ways the hospital is organized as a "baby-friendly" institution. The Number 385 Hospital, where I conducted much of my fieldwork, is a small three-hundred-bed institution located in southwestern Beijing.[7] It is a neighborhood hospital primarily serving local residents and a few large work units in the area. When I arrived to begin my research, it had recently achieved certification as a "Baby-Friendly" Hospital by UNICEF and the Chinese Ministry of Health. Becoming a baby-friendly hospital involves a dramatic reorganization of maternity wards to create private rooms for mothers and eliminate the practice of keeping all infants in a nursery. Today, babies are roomed with their mothers throughout their hospital stay. In addition, all women who receive prenatal care in the hospital's obstetrics clinic are required to attend three classes taught by a specially trained nurse. The certification process required that at least one obstetrics nurse, physician, and pediatrician attend special training seminars organized by UNICEF on breast-feeding. These staff members were charged with facilitating breast-feeding among new mothers and educating pregnant women about the benefits of and techniques necessary for successful breast-feeding.

The ultimate goal of the "Baby-Friendly" Hospital is to promote the growth and development of healthy babies who will become China's future citizens. As such, the breast-feeding policy meshes well with the one-child policy's goal to produce a healthy population (Anagnost 1995). Indeed, the hospital is an important institution in the promotion of the one-child policy. From my research, it seems that once women are pregnant bearing an intelligent, healthy, future citizen and worker is emphasized in numerous ways. In addition to the literature they receive from family-planning workers, women were often reminded during their checkups and breast-feeding classes and at other times of the importance of producing a healthy child. For example, the nurses in the Number 385 Hospital would often tell a woman who was not gaining enough weight during her pregnancy that poor nutrition would affect the baby's brain and might result in a less intelligent child. The infant formula industry also incorporated the Chinese government's rhetoric about producing the perfect baby in advertising literature intended to sell nutritional drinks to pregnant women. As one advertisement graphically demonstrates with a picture of an infant's brain, using the company's product during pregnancy would ensure the future intelligence of the child. Thus, the imperatives of state policies that promote breast-feeding and maternal health operate as important components of the one-child policy, whose ultimate goal is to "raise the quality of the population" (Anagnost 1995). Here we see an instance where multinational corporations, as they seek consumers of infant formula, play on the state's concerns with producing healthy children. However, as we will see below, the mothers responsible for these healthy infants are also expected to maintain their slim bodies and sexuality.

At the same time that the Number 385 Hospital was reorganizing itself to conform to governmental policies that promote breast-feeding, foreign infant formula and other companies were making their presence known in the hospital setting through the promotion of products such as maternal nutritional supplements. Interestingly, a kind of co-optation of similar imagery and ideals was used by both the state and the companies to promote their individual products and the idea that breast-feeding is best for infants. For example, posters advertising one consumer product for maternal nutrition use the image of a breast-feeding woman. In the same vein, posters in the obstetrics clinic use photographs of well-groomed Caucasian women to promote breast-feeding as the ideal form of infant nutrition. The use of what is termed "social marketing" in the public health field is clearly at work in advertisements that use full-color images of attractive women engaged in breast-feeding. Indeed, the goal of social marketing for health is to "apply advertising and marketing principles to the popularization of positive health behavior" (Wallack 1990: 149). In other words, social marketing seeks to create messages that certain behaviors are easy and to make them appear attractive. In the case of infant feeding, breast-feeding is promoted in a way that implies that a woman can be sexually available, well groomed, and rested and can still successfully breast-feed. In this instance, the state is appealing to women's ideals of femininity in its attempt to present breast-feeding as compatible with a lifestyle shaped by consumerism and hence individual self-realization.

In addition to the advertisements women encounter in the form of posters in the hallways and rooms of the obstetrics clinic, during the first breast-feeding education class Nurse Bai, the educator, routinely hands out information about breast-feeding and maternal nutrition. Paradoxically, she uses pamphlets produced by foreign formula companies. When I asked her why she used their materials, she told me that the hospital did not have any of its own materials and that these pamphlets provided useful information to pregnant women. She also said, "They are a small gift for attending class." The glossy pamphlets are like small books (one in particular contained twenty pages) with their full-color images of women breast-feeding and provide a range of data on nutrition during pregnancy as well as information about breast-feeding. However, it is impossible to forget that these pamphlets are also designed to market their products. Moreover, Nurse Bai, as she distributed these pamphlets in her role as a nurse-educator, was actively participating in the crosscutting of state and corporate interests.

All women participating in my study during their prenatal care in the hospital had received pamphlets produced by foreign companies promoting their infant formulas, and these colorful, glossy advertisements indeed may have induced women to use their products. For, as Van Esterick (1989: 175) notes: "Feeding bottles are not simply used to feed infants, they are also used as part of a broader semiotic or sign system to communicate something about the user." At the time these women were exposed to the advertising campaigns of foreign formula companies, however, they were also receiving their pre- and postnatal care in a baby-friendly hospital where the message that breast-feeding was "scientific" and "modern" was being conveyed in mandatory classes, videos, promotional materials, and hospital routines.

The regulation of the bodies of pregnant women I observed in the hospital presents an excellent opportunity to explore how bodies are habituated not simply through ideology but through the organization of time, space, and movements in daily life (Foucault 1994; Bourdieu 1977). I want to spend the remainder of this chapter examining how the constellation of relations I have described operated in a breast-feeding education class and constituted ideal representations of women as mothers through the information and knowledge that is imparted in these texts. Breast-feeding, postpartum exercise, and diet regimes all represent ways female bodies in urban China are increasingly "bodies whose forces and energies are habituated to external regulation, subjection, transformation, 'improvement'" (Bordo 1993: 91). However, it is not simply my intention to demonstrate the ways in which bodies are "made." Rather I also wish to explore women's narratives as they experienced these disciplinary forces. Ultimately, this process will contribute to an understanding of new mothers' self-making in the constellation of relations that make up the world of the hospital.

As I mentioned earlier, the hospital environment, in its use of visual media to promote breast-feeding, also ironically promotes sexualized images of women and consumerism. Glossy images of sexually attractive breast-feeding mothers in pearls and makeup mesh closely with the images found in contexts that advertise and promote consumer goods in Chinese society. As women wait in the hallway seats for their physical exams, they face a wall lined with posters promoting breast-feeding. These posters contain slogans such as "breast-feeding is the best" and "help mothers achieve breast-feeding" (*bangzhu muqin shixian muru weiyang*). The rhetoric of these posters clearly mirrors other forms of government propaganda. However, the presentation and images extend beyond the state's interest in a healthy citizen (infant and mother) and present a sexualized and consumer-oriented mother. One poster in particular shows a serene-looking Asian woman, wearing a lacy nightgown and a strand of pearls, breast-feeding her infant while a nurse in a crisp white uniform stands with one hand on the mother's shoulder and the other moving the mother's arm into position. The image was drawn to my attention by Wang Li Qing, one of the women in my study. As we were walking out of the clinic, she pointed at the poster and laughingly said "That is a mistress (*xiaomi*) breast-feeding, not an ordinary mother." Defining the woman pictured in the poster as a mistress rather than an "ordinary mother," this woman highlighted the sexual nature of the poster in her comment to me. Her comment calls attention to the way the poster presents the breast-feeding mother as still sexually attractive and presumably available to her husband. Indeed, the poster presents an ideal image of the breast-feeding mother who is still a sexually attractive woman. As I discuss later, the expectations of most women that they can maintain these dual identities caused conflict in terms of their definitions of self and their relationships with husbands and other family members. It is important to point out that the state's goal of developing healthy children through the behavior of good mothers mingles with the individual flexibility accorded to capitalism. Moreover, the image represents the capital goods of the consumer body, in other words, that one is able to achieve social prestige or social opportunities through bodily management, adornment, and presentation. In this case, women can, if they embody the poster woman's style, dress, and comportment, add the sexually attractive, breast-feeding mother to their self-identity. The pearl necklace and lacy nightgown, in particular, project a more consumer-oriented woman. Both items are identifiable luxury goods and as such add a note to the viewer of the importance of consumerism in conjunction with mothering and infant feeding. When Wang Li Qing described the breast-feeding mother in the poster as a mistress, she was articulating her apprehension of the sexual message of the image, and her laugh and tone of incredulity indicated how incompatible breast-feeding and sexuality were. Indeed, as we continued our conversation after her comment, she told me that the image represented something out of reach for an ordinary woman like her. When I asked how she felt about that, she said "my husband would like it, but it is not me."

While posters promoting breast-feeding formed a fixed aspect of the hospital environment, the formula company pamphlets distributed by Nurse Bai during the breast-feeding classes were portable and were taken home and ultimately read in more detail by women. The pamphlets offer a different type of authority of knowledge than the poster advertisements, which in most cases are associated with the hospital. These texts use scientific and medical language to justify the achievement of a healthy body during pregnancy (presumably assisted by use of their products). Yet in many ways they also reinforced the concern with beauty and attractiveness. For example, a pamphlet produced for Mead-Johnson's maternal supplement MaMa Sustagen includes a series of exercises for the prenatal and postpartum periods and shows a slim, leotard-clad woman performing the exercises. The information provided in the text outlines the importance of maternal nutrition for the healthy development of the fetus. The photographic images of the woman and the accompanying text tell the reader that performing the postnatal exercises will help her return to her prepregnancy shape and help heal the perineal area and prevent prolapsing of the uterus. Interestingly, the exercises targeted to prevent these medical problems consist of situps. What is more important is that the text articulates concern for regaining body shape and preventing postpartum health problems. The feminine body, not the pregnant body, must be restored as soon as possible after birth. And, if one doesn't find this compelling enough, the text raises the subject of medical conditions that reinforce the importance of exercise. Whether the exercises work or not, the ultimate message is that bodily discipline is necessary not simply for beauty reasons but for health in a medical sense. Here we again see the blurring of the state project of producing healthy citizens and the more individualized ideals of bodily control in advertising from a Western company.

The glossy, slim woman in the photo also presents an ideal body, one that differs dramatically from the pregnant woman, who is experiencing a larger body. Motherhood, it is implied, is not simply a matter of a healthy birth but rather requires a body that can quickly return to a prepregnancy state of slimness. Out of the thirty women I followed in my study, only five ever exercised prenatally. In fact, when I asked women what they thought about the exercises described in these pamphlets, many of them laughed. Often they told me "I have no time, it is not for me" or, as Han Aihua stated, "If I had a body like that I wouldn't have to exercise." However, their lack of interest in exercise did not reflect their lack of concern for their body shape. Most women mentioned that they were concerned with their shape, weight, and muscle firmness at various times during the perinatal period.

The visual representations and ideals about body and sexuality were also present in the breast-feeding class video. Once again, conflicting messages were presented about the maternal body in relation to mothering, sexuality, and self-presentation. Specifically, one of the benefits of breast-feeding described by the narrator, as a slim, contented-looking woman strolls with her husband and baby in the park, is that breast-feeding promotes postpartum weight loss. Additionally, the video at a later point reminds women that they must eat more food while breast-feeding to ensure adequate nutrition for both the mother and her infant. It graphically represents the increase in calories needed by the mother's body to produce breast milk. The narrator states that it is harmful to the mother and baby if the mother eats poorly or does not eat a wide variety of foods. One image in the video during this message shows a husband and wife sitting at the table in their apartment with an array of eight different dishes (Shanghai Jiaoyu Dianshitai 1994). When I asked women how many dishes they ate during an "average" dinner, most told me two dishes with rice and sometimes three. They thought the food scene presented in the video was excessive and unrealistic. During the prenatal period, most women were not concerned about regaining their prepregnancy body shape, as they all believed it would happen naturally without the need for exercise or dieting (twenty-seven out of thirty women). In fact, ten women (one-third of my sample) told me that breast-feeding makes one gain weight, and they were concerned about this dilemma. Zhou Li An, a twenty-four-year-old middle school teacher, asked me: "How can I breast-feed and lose weight?" When I pointed out that the video they had watched claimed that breast-feeding contributed to weight loss, several women told me that this was not true from what they knew about their friends' or relatives' experiences. In fact, Zhou Li An responded that "My sister never lost weight while she breast-fed her child, [but] once she stopped she was able to lose weight!" The video, as part of the hospital's program to promote breast-feeding, presents conflicting messages about women's health and body image. The claims made by the narrator suggesting that breast-feeding may aid in weight loss were clearly added in response to women's concerns with their body shape after birth, but the video also conveys the importance of eating (an excessive amount according to these women) to maintain the health of mother and infant while breast-feeding.

Sexuality was never broached in the video, but one sequence of scenes indicated that breast-feeding and sleeping in the same bed with a husband were incompatible.[8] As the narrator describes strategies for feeding on demand, the images shift to the bedroom, where we see a woman with her newborn infant preparing for sleep. The husband is absent, as the narrator suggests that mothers who sleep with their babies can conveniently breast-feed while in bed and thus suffer less disruption to their sleep during the night. The final shot in the sequence shows a woman on a double bed with her infant sleeping next to her (Shanghai Jiaoyu Dianshitai 1994). Presumably, the husband is sleeping on the couch. When I asked pregnant women what they thought about this message, they all agreed that the infant should sleep with the mother and if the bed was small it would be best if the husband slept elsewhere at least for the first month. After the first month, when many women anticipated completing the ritual seclusion of "doing the month" (*zuo yuezi*), they thought the baby could be moved to a crib or basket near the bed and that the husband should sleep with them (see Pillsbury 1978). The majority of women were not concerned with the timing or necessity of resuming sexual relations with their husbands during the prenatal portion of my research. Five women, however, specifically talked about the fact that pregnancy had interfered with their husbands' sexual needs. These women expressed fear or concern that their husbands would seek sex with a prostitute or might even fall in love with someone else while their wives were pregnant and breast-feeding. The concern with sexual relations increased during the postpartum period, as I will discuss in more detail below.

In terms of the content of Nurse Bai's lectures on breast-feeding, in all the sessions I documented she never mentioned the mother's body shape or weight or sexual issues. She focused only on the psychological and physical benefits of breast-feeding for the infant. In fact, at one point I asked her whether the training she received at UNICEF/WHO workshops had ever raised this issue. She told me that it had never come up and in her opinion this issue was an individual woman's own business. Then she pulled out the training manuals she had received at the workshop and told me to note that there was no information on sexual relations and breast-feeding. She did acknowledge that there were "traditional" beliefs about the appropriate time to resume sexual relations and that for some people this meant waiting until "the month" had been completed. Medically, she said, doctors in the hospital recommended that women wait at least until their six-week checkup before resuming sexual intercourse.

Constellations of Modernity, Consumerism, and Mothers' Bodies To move away from outlining the ways in which the hospital promoted images of women's bodies and infant feeding practices, I want to give some examples of how the women in my study responded to these messages. During pregnancy, I asked all thirty women, after their first and third breast-feeding classes, whether they planned to breast-feed. All of them told me they would try it. Some were enthusiastic, and others pessimistic about whether they would continue for longer than a few weeks. They knew the health benefits of breast-feeding for the child but were concerned that it might not be practical, that it might make them fat, that their breasts would sag, that it was too messy, or that it would tie them too closely to the baby and not allow other family members to help care for the child. I interviewed these women at a number of intervals after their births, and eighteen had switched to bottle-feeding after a few weeks. Most of these women found breast-feeding too difficult, feeling that they did not have enough milk and the procedure was too messy. Four women told me that they were very concerned that they were not losing the weight they had gained during pregnancy. Ah Qiao, a twenty-three-year-old factory worker, told me that she was still too fat and asked on a number of occasions how long it would be before she returned to her prepregnancy weight. Another woman told me that her husband would not sleep with her or engage in sexual relations while she was breast-feeding and so she started bottle feeding.

By contrast, twelve women in my sample continued to breast-feed for up to four months (the state's recommended interval) and reported that they felt they were being good mothers by doing so. Chen Lihong, a twenty-four-year-old seamstress, said that "to be a good mother, I must give my son the best I can. Breast-feeding is the only way to protect and nurture him. If I didn't care about my child I would just give him a bottle." This woman and the others who chose to breast-feed emphasized that this was something that good mothers should want to do. All the women in my study stated on numerous occasions that they wanted to raise healthy children. The decisions made by these women indicate that the ultimate goal of raising a healthy child meshes with the Chinese state's goal of creating a healthier population. However, the women in my study believe that a variety of means may be used to do so. Some women's decisions to breast-feed accommodate and mirror the policies of the state; for others, the decision to bottle feed may be a response to other pressures deemed more important in their lives.

Conclusion   Throughout this chapter, I have discussed the ways in which women respond to the sexualized conception of the ideal feminine body as they become mothers and renegotiate their identities. Indeed, pregnancy and the postpartum period are times of heightened body awareness, when women's bodies do not conform to the slender, sexy images prevalent throughout urban China. The hospital as a location where women are confronted with these images reflects the larger changes occurring in Chinese society, where capitalism and modernization have reshaped the social, symbolic, and experienced female body. Concomitant with these changes, the Chinese government through its reproductive policies is seeking to redefine and prioritize motherhood to create a healthy population. The state-produced and transnational capitalist images create pervasive norms for pregnant and postnatal women's bodies. On the one hand, women should maintain well-nourished bodies during pregnancy and breast-feed their infants, but popular culture demands that they maintain slim, sexually available bodies even as they breast-feed. While many other factors affect women's creation of self-identity, the inherent contradiction between these two norms provoked women in my study to raise these issues in our conversations over the course of my research. The ways in which different women resolved this conflict in their lives indicate the complexity and variety of ways of being female and especially a mother in contemporary urban China.

Notes

1 China, unlike many developing nations where rates of breast-feeding are declining in urban areas, presents an interesting case for developing a more nuanced understanding of how women make infant feeding decisions. In particular, China is one of a few countries that have formulated policies designed to promote breast-feeding in urban areas. For example, prior to 1978 urban women workers were provided with nursing breaks, infant day care at the workplace, and longer maternity leaves to help establish and maintain breast-feeding (Pasternak and Wang 1985). This chapter derives from my dissertation research and responds to Pasternak and Wang's suggestion that our analysis of breast-feeding declines in urban areas of developing countries requires a more powerful theoretical framework, one that accounts for factors beyond socioeconomic indicators such as education level, age, and wage employment. See also Harrell 1981 for a discussion of the complex nature of breast-feeding from physiological and cultural perspectives.

2 China passed the Law on the Health Protection of Mothers and Infants in 1992.

3 See Honig and Hershatter 1988 for discussions of adornment and sexuality in 1980s China.

4 This topic demands much more attention than the space here allows and has been addressed more fully by Anagnost (1995) and Ong (1996). See Brownell 1995 for extended discussions of the state's project of modernity in relation to gender in the realm of sports.

5 Twelve factory workers, nine white collar office workers, and nine women working in small family enterprises (*ge ti hu*) formed the sample for this study. This research was conducted with funding from the Committee on Scholarly Communications with China from 1994 to 1996.

6 See also Dirlik 1997; Greenhalgh 1994; and Duara 1995.

7 "Number 385 Hospital" is a pseudonym, as are names of all individuals.

8 See Furth 1987 for an extended discussion of historical beliefs about the taboo of intercourse during pregnancy and the postpartum period. Pillsbury (1978) describes these proscriptions in contemporary Taiwan and China.

Constance D. Clark Foreign Marriage, "Tradition," and the Politics of Border Crossings

Zuo sanci hongniang keyi cheng xian (Do matchmaking three times and become an immortal).—male manager of the Good Fortune Comes marriage introduction agency

I can never get a Shenzhen residence permit. My best chance of marriage is to find a foreigner.—female receptionist, Shenzhen, May 1995

This chapter explores marriage expectations and possibilities for young women in Shenzhen who consider foreign marriage. Marriage to a foreigner (*shewai*) or the securing of a Shenzhen permanent residence permit are two avenues of social mobility through which many women attempt to realize their personal goals. Based on a study of thirteen marriage introduction agencies and on interviews with women clients and agency staff, the chapter places foreign marriage within a context of China's Asian regional development status, Shenzhen's cosmopolitan lifestyle, and many young women's raised expectations of self, marriage, and life.

In this chapter, I borrow geographer Doreen Massey's notion of "power geometry" to describe relations of power involved in the movement of potential brides and grooms between countries in East Asia. Massey used the term to introduce complexity to the ways in which time, space, and mobility are experienced in the current phase of global capitalism, which she does by introducing dimensions of class, ethnicity, and gender. She writes that "different social groups have distinct relationships to this anyway-differentiated mobility; some are more in charge of it than others; some initiate flows and movement, others don't; some are more on the receiving end of it than others; some are effectively imprisoned by it" (1993: 61). This point about mobility is well illustrated by the ease with which Asian men pass through international borders in search of brides, while Chinese women, to use Massey's words, are "more on the receiving end" of the mobility.

The politics of border crossing therefore—who, why, when, and where—depends on a complex of factors, including gender, age, skill, and nationality. The differentials of power that Massey examines in global flows of people are clearly evident in the regional marriage arrangements I present here.

Media portrayals of Chinese women as "gold diggers" searching for foreign "airplane tickets" (*feiji piao*) (*Sunday Morning Post*, October 4, 1992) present only a partial view of a complicated story that does not end with brides boarding planes for their host countries. The story continues, with no follow-up by the agencies, as many Chinese women settle into Japanese farms and become less visible subjects of the celebrated Chinese diaspora (cf. Nonini 1997).

This chapter also emphasizes that the local/global may not be the most salient dynamic that engages people in everyday life. Women reworking their identities as "traditional" Chinese women in Shenzhen's marriage introduction agencies are sought after by men in Asian countries such as Singapore and Japan. As many societies in Asia (including China's) undergo profound transformations in gender roles and marriage, some Asian men are looking to China for brides. In the bridal context, *tradition* conventionally means qualities of support and nurturing (for men) that women elsewhere seemingly no longer possess. Yet more broadly *tradition* here can also stand for poverty and underdevelopment, as though there is some kind of popular evolutionary equivalence between the level of national development and the location of female "tradition." The representation by Chinese female bodies of China's modernization vis-à-vis the West throughout the twentieth century has received much scholarly attention (Barlow 1994; Chow 1991). Within East and Southeast Asia, however, a modernization hierarchy among countries ranks China near the lower rungs and Chinese women, along with their Thai and Filipina sisters, as keepers of vaguely defined traditional gender and marital ideals. This phenomenon occurring within Asia points out a need to consider the regional level, as it may have more significance than the global level in shaping identities and individual decision making (cf. Ong 1997b). In this chapter, I examine how issues of power, nationality, age, and tradition are central to Japanese and Singaporean men's bridal searches, and how the pendulum of power shifts as the marital process nears completion in China.

Immigrant Dreams   A constant theme in young men's and women's stories of migration to Shenzhen is that of the regenerative nature of the city. The city is often seen as an anonymous space with myriad possibilities for the re-creation of self and for making a "second start" in life (*chongxin kaishi*). The first special economic zone permitted to experiment with capitalist economic practices, Shenzhen rapidly became a magnet for youth from across China. Although its reputation as a new urban "paradise" (*tiantang*) where jobs were plentiful and where people made fortunes overnight didn't hold up for most of the newly arrived, young people still wanted to try their luck (*shiyishi*). Their understanding and visions of Shenzhen were shaped through returning migrants' narratives of the city, print media, and television, now widespread in many regions. Many likened the migration to Shenzhen itself to a "small going abroad" (*xiao chuguo*), as the city was full of people from nearly every province in China. Their visions of what urban life could offer centered on making money and experiencing adventure, love, and freedom. In Shenzhen today, many young female and male immigrants have the freedom to explore their identities and sexuality away from the watchful eyes of family and to take control over decision making regarding their future (cf. Croll 1995). Through wage earning, hometown and workplace relations, and leisure activities, single women accumulate the skills and metropolitan knowledge required to navigate city life. Ideals of independence and gender equality, still shifting in their meanings and practices and now sought by many women, may sometimes result in choosing singlehood over a potentially unsatisfactory marriage. For other women, marital decision making may take them beyond China's borders to distant destinations such as Japan, Singapore, and America.

Mobility in Reform China   Here I briefly summarize the household registration system (*hukou*), which, although attenuated today in China, still affects people's lives in terms of marriage and raising children in a location other than their place of household registration. Hukou was a system of social control created by the Communist Party, which segregated the entire Chinese population into a two-tiered rural-urban ranking of privilege. Statuses of "agricultural" or "nonagricultural" meant that a person born into an agricultural family had no opportunity to convert to nonagricultural status and was therefore denied benefits allocated to those in the cities such as housing, medical insurance, food allotments, and pensions (Cohen 1994; Potter and Potter 1990). In many ways, the package of urban welfare came to be understood as socioeconomic rights that were the property of urbanites. Unequal access to these goods has long divided the Chinese population into two kinds of citizens (cf. Solinger 1999).

Economic reform in China has required a freer flow of labor than was allowed during the socialist era. Migration has undermined somewhat the effectiveness of the household registration system, yet in some spheres of private life the system still holds sway, particularly with regard to housing and marriage registration. Transferring household registration from one's hometown to Shenzhen is nearly impossible for most temporary residents, who constitute 67 percent of the population of 3.69 million (Lin 1997). Purchasing a permit is prohibitive, as a Shenzhen permit sells for around 40,000 renminbi (RMB) (U.S.$4,700).

In Shenzhen, women's possession of the urban residence permit may override criteria still considered critical by some men for marriage, in particular chastity. That a young woman could tell me, "It's okay if a woman is not a virgin as long as she has a Shenzhen residence card" illustrates the transformation of the permit into a highly valued commodity, providing a marital substitute for "damaged goods" sexual status or nonvirginity. In my study of the marriage introduction agencies, possession of a Shenzhen residence permit is still one of the most important marriage requirements listed by men and women (cf. Pang 1993). The household registration permit has become a marker of urban citizenship that differentiates social groups and determines access to limited social and economic opportunities and goods. Given this state stricture, what are the marital possibilities for many of Shenzhen's young women and men?

Imagining Foreign Marriage Young women, with or without a Shenzhen residence permit, experience difficulties in finding a suitable marriage partner. The reasons given by many women varied widely, from the dearth of social venues, the gender imbalance, and the lack of the Shenzhen residence permit to the qualities of Chinese men (practical and not romantic), the male preoccupation with female youth and beauty, and the idea that men come to Shenzhen and "turn bad," meaning that they cannot be trusted. Those who contemplated foreign marriage did so for widely divergent reasons. Many searched for adventure, economic mobility, romance, or the fulfillment of personal goals such as higher education or building a family of more than one child. Although work opportunities for many women have expanded in the reform era (and declined for others), Chinese women are largely socially defined by marriage and family, and it is often through marriage that women improve their economic and social position (cf. Lavely 1991). By their midtwenties, women are under pressure from family, colleagues, and themselves to find a partner and marry (cf. Croll 1995: 158). The normalizing results of marriage are particularly clear for women, as unmarried women in their thirties are said to become "abnormal" (*biantai*) or are thought strange, as if they have an illness. In a newly emergent immigrant city like Shenzhen, where a significant number of people are young and single, the dilemmas of finding a spouse are amplified. These dilemmas of marriage are illustrated in the following story about A'Mei, a receptionist in a Chinese communications company.

Eating lunch with A'Mei, whom I had met in 1994 in a marriage introduction agency, she pulled out a letter and photos from a friend who several years earlier had married a Japanese man and moved to Tokyo. Her friend knew of two Japanese men interested in marriage and hoped to convince A'Mei to seriously consider the men's proposals. Since our acquaintance A'Mei had been searching for a partner, for at thirty she is part of a growing sector in China termed "aging youth" (*daling qingnian*), single men and women whose chances of marriage have diminished as they have aged. That this category of people is called "youth" regardless of their age reflects the social importance attached to marriage as a defining moment in the transition to adult status. The term includes women and men, yet men are given several more years' grace period.[1] A'Mei, a temporary worker from Jiangsu Province, was not able to transfer her household registration to Shenzhen and didn't have the resources to buy one on the black market. She had arrived in Shenzhen with a border pass three years earlier and did not see bright prospects for her future in either career or personal life. A high school graduate, she had planned to enroll in evening computer classes, a popular educational choice, but her dormitory was located too far outside Shenzhen for her to feel safe returning from classes alone late at night.

Her age, temporary residential status, and some would say her dark skin color made her a less than desirable candidate for marriage to Chinese men. Men with the coveted Shenzhen household registration look for women of the same status, for reasons with far-reaching implications. The couple cannot purchase subsidized housing if one person is a temporary resident, and they must pay additional tuition to send their child to primary and secondary schools. Most significantly, as the registration is inherited through the mother (Cohen 1994; Potter and Potter 1990), having a mother without permanent urban residency means that the child will not have access to the material and social rights granted to Shenzhen urbanites. Many women in A'Mei's predicament, caught between desires for social mobility and state residence restrictions, regard foreign marriage among their options.

Media reports of women searching for foreign airplane tickets often present only one side of a multifaceted situation, which belies the complexity, hardship, and dangers inherent in "stranger marriages." How did A'Mei imagine a future married life in Tokyo? She pondered the potential of love in a marriage to a sixty-year-old man in the hope of material security and greater educational opportunities. Her married friend in Tokyo was doing well, according to her letters. What about the stories in circulation about Filipina and Chinese women who end up virtual prisoners in the Japanese countryside? She believed she could avoid this situation and retain a modicum of control by going through her friend instead of an agency. Moreover, both suitors lived in Tokyo, allowing her more possibilities to develop a social circle outside the household than if she were confined in the countryside. Last, she would make the opportunity to attend a university a requirement of marriage, explaining this as part of an equal marital exchange.

Remaining in Shenzhen was her ideal choice, so as to be near her sister. However, given her educational ambitions, absence of permanent residence rights, and few interested suitors, A'Mei believed foreign marriage was one of her best options. That the man is Japanese will create a family controversy. "My parents don't like Japanese people. They remember the war; they cannot accept this. My generation doesn't think about the war, but my parents do." She asks me which man I would choose. I avoid a direct answer by inquiring specifically about each man and what she likes about them. Picking at her rice, she replies that they are both "okay" (*hai keyi*).

A'Mei was one of three informants I met at various marriage introduction agencies. She had applied and checked over the applicants for a six-month period but then withdrew her application, claiming the impossibility of finding a good, trustworthy man through an agency and deciding that a safer avenue was through personal recommendations, such as that of her friend in Tokyo.

Imagining oneself in a foreign marriage is a process into which one grows and with which one eventually becomes comfortable. The young women in my study arrived in Shenzhen, usually through the efforts of a relative or hometown friend, expecting to find work, adventure, and love. Many had never considered the idea of leaving China. Some had relatives or hometown friends in Shenzhen or had gradually built up a social circle through work and other venues such as hobby clubs. Yet the lifestyle many young women grew to expect was beyond their financial reach. Low-level office workers earning a monthly salary of 1,200 RMB ($140) had difficulty making ends meet while occasionally remitting money to their natal families. Over a period of several years, female informants found themselves still single, struggling financially, living in dormitories, and nearing the end of the culturally acceptable marriageable years. The cost of purchasing or renting a flat is prohibitive, and most women with temporary residential status remain in company or work unit dormitories until they marry. However, an official recognition of the shifting social demographics is occurring in Shenzhen. Single permanent residents, male and female, who reach the age of thirty-five are now able to move out of the dormitory rooms into private ones provided by their work unit (Chen Li Peng, personal communication, 1996).

University-educated women concurred with the difficulty of maintaining a desired standard of living, noting that they understood how even a university graduate could marry a wealthy Japanese farmer. They believed that life in Japan would be easier than in Shenzhen and that women there wouldn't have to struggle to attain the level of material comfort they had expected to acquire over time.

State residence restrictions act as barriers to many temporary workers' wishes for marriage, residence, and family in Shenzhen, excepting those who can afford unsubsidized housing and school fees. The Shenzhen municipal authorities hope that temporary workers will eventually return to their hometowns. However, becoming an urbanite is an intellectual, psychological, and bodily process that is not reversed with ease. Having grown accustomed to Shenzhen's cosmopolitanism, with its variety of people, lively nightlife, career possibilities, and access to Hong Kong and global TV, many women (and men) do not regard return to one's seemingly dull hometown to be an option. Moreover, the scarcity of work opportunities originally drove many away from their hometowns. How would they use their skills at home? How could they marry somebody who had not "seen the world"? Other women in my study had given up on the idea of marriage, as, according to them, finding a good partner was almost impossible. Many had grown tired of the rituals of dating, which one woman likened to an interview about her family responsibilities, work, salary, and residence status.

Several other women searching for a partner had set their sights on a transnational life. This informal process of locating foreign spouses through friends, preferred by many young women contemplating marriage, has been institutionalized in introduction agencies specializing in foreign marriage. I now describe the explosion of marriage introduction agencies in Shenzhen and look at how women are packaged by men as brides for not so distant destinations.

The Business of Marriage   A phenomenon that began in the 1980s and has mushroomed in China's southern cities is the marriage introduction agency (*hunyin jieshaosuo*). These private and state-run agencies are venues where women and men register their marital criteria for a fee and have access to the agency's data base of clients. Marriage introduction agencies were first established in conjunction with a state agency such as the All China Women's Federation or a trade union and were present in China's major cities and several smaller ones by the end of 1980 (Honig and Hershatter 1988: 85).

In Shenzhen, the role of matchmaking, long a Chinese cultural institution, took new shape in marriage introduction agencies and expanded into television dating programs (*China Daily,* May 13, 1991). During the early to mid-1990s, marriage introduction agencies sprang up in Shenzhen at the rate of two and three per week, many specializing in foreign clients. Most were privately owned, either wholly by mainland companies or through a joint venture with a foreign firm. In my survey, eleven agencies were private and two were state operated. Three catered to overseas Chinese and foreign men. Physically, the agencies ranged from tiny rooms sharing space with another small business to spacious, well-designed offices with several rooms for social activities. Researching marriage introduction agencies was somewhat like investigative journalism, as I never quite knew where my research with one agency would take me. Many brokers were unscrupulous, falsely advertising the "quality" of their foreign connections (*South China Morning Post,* January 11, 1994). Some agencies operated without proper permits or duped people into believing that they offered legitimate introduction services. A common strategy was to open a domestic service agency and then venture into marriage brokering on the side without obtaining proper clearances. The first marriage introduction agency I visited had closed by my third visit for doing business without a license. A few weeks later, some of the same people, minus the former manager, opened another agency about six blocks from the first one. Three of the marriage introduction agencies that I surveyed were shut down over an eighteen-month period, leaving me to return to the newspaper ads to locate new ones.

Seeing a foreign woman enter the agency doors invoked one of three responses by the staff: fear that I was a reporter hoping to expose fraudulent practices, interest in opening a joint venture whereby I would supply American grooms for Chinese brides, and disbelief that I would be interested in such a topic. I had several business propositions from these agencies during my time in Shenzhen.

I frequently visited the Shenzhen Marriage Introduction Agency, the oldest in Shenzhen. It opened in 1984, sponsored by the municipal trade unions and the All China Women's Federation. The assistant director of this agency noted: "Many of these agencies were set up to solve the problem of the *daling qingnian,* the older youth who were sent down to the countryside [in the 1960s]. They spent their marriageable years in the rural areas, and when they returned to the cities it was very difficult for them to find a spouse. So the government set up these agencies to help them" (interview, March 1994). This agency initially handled only domestic marriages, yet by the mid-1990s it also was facilitating a small number of foreign marriages.

The most common reasons offered by social workers and marriage introduction agency staff for this flurry of new matchmaking activity are Shenzhen's gender imbalance, the lack of leisure time to spend locating a spouse, and the fact that Shenzhen is an immigrant city where people have difficulty meeting prospective partners or even friends. Staff members at two agencies specializing in Hong Kong marriages gave the lack of a Shenzhen residence card as a reason for women to marry Hong Kong men. Commented one at the Heaven and Earth marriage agency:

> Many of the male customers are from Hong Kong, lots of taxi drivers. They have worked for fifteen or twenty years to buy a home, so they now are in their late thirties or early forties. They come here because of the ratio imbalance. If they can find a wife in Shenzhen, the cost is lower. It is easier for a Hong Kong man to support a wife here for the time he must wait to get clearance from Hong Kong to bring her over the border. The Hong Kong government has a quota of people allowed in from each province. For instance, if the woman is from Guangdong the wait could be as long as seven years. If the woman is from Zhejiang, the wait is much shorter, maybe one year. The women customers are mostly over twenty-seven years old; they are from the inner land and have no Shenzhen hukou. They have worked here several years and have missed the chance to marry at home. They have broadened their minds and think there is a better world outside. So they come here. (interview, June 1995)

"Border crossing" in the Hong Kong case is much more uncertain and complicated than the state arrangement with Japan, due to not only the large number of applicants but also to the mistress/second wife phenomenon that occurs between Hong Kong men and mainland women (see Shih 1999).

Video Brides Upscale marriage introduction agencies have utilized video technology to improve upon the concept of the picture bride catalog (cf. Wilson 1988). In the following story, at an agency where I was invited to view some of the video clips, I describe the construction/production of a "traditional" woman whose goal was marriage to a Singaporean man.

Mr. Wu ushered my companion and me into the back office of the joint venture marriage introduction agency. We were to view videotapes of prospective brides that his company produces for male clients in Hong Kong, Singapore, Japan, and America. A joint venture between Hong Kong and Shenzhen firms, the company was called an "international marriage service center" specializing in foreign marriage. This company had branch offices in several Southeast Asian countries. All of their domestic clients were Chinese women with some secondary and university education, ranging in age from their mid-twenties to late forties and searching for a foreign partner.

This was my third interview with Mr. Wu, a young Cantonese man who managed the office and produced the videos with a staff member. His office was in the fashionable Forum Hotel near the Luohu train station in downtown Shenzhen, occupying bright spacious rooms with a view toward the New Territories of Hong Kong. Of the thirteen marriage introduction agencies in my survey, Mr. Wu's was the most sophisticated in presentation, advertising, and video technology.[2] In the process of video production, members of the staff offered clients advice about attire, makeup, and behavior, such as dressing modestly and walking unhurriedly. They also provided knowledge about cuisine and protocol, especially for those women going to Japan, where they faced not only cultural but linguistic differences. Many Chinese women and Japanese men registered at the agencies did not speak English, and their means of communication initially consisted of Chinese characters, phrase books, and electronic translating machines (*Sunday Morning Post*, March 21, 1993). Marriage to a Singaporean man presented fewer problems in cultural styles and language. According to Mr. Wu, Chinese women preferred a Singaporean spouse and skilled women have greater opportunities to work in Singapore than in Japan. However, more of the agency's male clientele came from Japan. Mr. Wu remarked about the clients: "Singapore men are the most popular among women here, but the Japanese men are our biggest customers. There are all kinds of men from Japan; however, many are farmers or villagers. Their quality is not high, but they are wealthy. Women who go to Singapore are very competitive in the labor market. Chinese women are more accustomed to struggle, they can endure more than Singaporean women" (interview, May 1995).

This discourse of endurance and struggle following mainland Chinese brides is similar to what Brownell found in her research with Chinese female athletes. In the Chinese world of sports, women in general, but especially those from the countryside, are considered to have the ability to endure and "eat bitterness" (1995: 228 and in this volume). Brownell suggests that these ideas about Chinese women have become common-place in the social body through a socialist ideology that exalted rural labor and made politically visible the long-standing suffering of rural women (ibid.).

Returning to the videos, the camera's emphasis (Mr. Wu's eye) is on the silent female body, framing it in its entirety, dissecting it, lingering on the face, hand movements, and the walk. The tape opens to soft music and a woman in motion, as she gracefully descends on the hotel's escalator, eyes downcast or looking out, and steps onto the lobby floor (frontal view). Next the audience views her strolling leisurely through the lobby and garden, head turned and smiling slightly (back view). Then we see her seated at a desk, chatting softly on a portable phone (closeup facial view). The work the women are portrayed as doing is feminized, usually typing or selling beauty products. The tape ends with the woman walking toward and entering the elevator, turning and pausing to wave or say a few parting words such as "bye-bye."

On the tape, each woman gives her name, age, hometown, hobbies, and marital requirements, providing scant personal information but al-lowing male clients a sense of her tone of voice. Some women may say something more intimate about themselves and their desires such as "I'm looking for a warm-hearted man" or "I am looking for a family to belong to." From a video shoot of ten minutes, the tape is edited to three min-utes, during which the women speak for about twenty or thirty seconds. The remainder of the time is spent watching the women walking, sitting, talking, and smiling. Clearly, the video production favors a male, here Asian, gaze. The visual construction of the woman through the editing process is left entirely to Mr. Wu and a male friend familiar with video technology, which raises questions of agency and the influence of Mr. Wu's own ideas of gender upon the production.

Through this video technology, female bodies travel twice to their destinations, first as packaged commodities for male consumption and later as embodied brides. Women receive no such tape of prospective mates; the male clients have the power to do the initial and final choosing. In fact, only when a woman has been selected as a potential bride does she see a photo or receive information about the man.

Mr. Wu and the staff match couples based on marital requirements, family background, and personality. Male clients first receive biographical information and photographs of several women from the marriage service branch office in their country. From a selection of five, a man can choose at most two women. Once this selection is made, he is sent the women's individual videotapes by the Shenzhen agency. He then makes his final decision and, if the chosen woman agrees, arranges to travel to China to meet her and finalize the exit documents. The entire process is completed in about three months, at which time the bride can leave China. The time frame itself is remarkable and underscores the differentiated mobility of social groups that Massey has discussed in relation to global capitalism.

I asked Mr. Wu why Japanese and Singaporean men go to China in search of brides. He replied: "Japanese men come to China because Japanese women's demands are too high. High salary, high education, and the man's height are important [to Japanese women]. Also, the male-female ratio there is out of balance, like in Chinese counties. The men come here with individual demands, but most want a young, beautiful wife, younger by about ten years, who can take care of the home. The men like traditional women" (interview, December 1994).

From Mr. Wu's account, it seems there are few available "traditional" women in Japan. In news reports, the marital pool imbalance in Japan is presented as a problem residing with Japanese women (*Sunday Morning Post*, March 21, 1993). Many Japanese women don't want to lead a rural life and often leave their hometowns for the cities. In one district of Yamagata Prefecture, the population of single males is two thousand, while that of single females is two hundred (ibid.). In their own search for a more gender-equitable partnership, some women are also less willing to put up with the conventional demands of marriage and are either choosing to marry at a later age or opting out of marriage.

The unhindered flow of brides between Japan and countries such as

China and Thailand indicates that states often facilitate national border crossings at particular times to allow for the movement of certain kinds of people (*Sunday Morning Post*, October 4, 1992). Whether there is a demographic imbalance in Japan or a shortage of brides due to disinterest among Japanese women, the Japanese government imposes no restrictions on the immigration of foreign brides. On the Japanese side, since the 1980s as many as five thousand agencies have opened to introduce Japanese bachelor farmers to both Japanese and Asian women (Iwao 1993: 66). I learned of this firsthand through a chance encounter at the Shenzhen State Marriage agency with a Chinese marriage consultant who lived in Tokyo and was in Shenzhen assisting two Japanese farmers in their quest for a Chinese bride. Municipal governments in Japan are involved in the search for brides and host welcome ceremonies for the incoming brides and their new spouses. Mr. Wei, the marriage consultant, showed me pictures of the bridal ceremonies, which he had brought along to show to potential Chinese brides. Looking through them, I saw women standing on a stage in frilly white dresses with a large banner behind them in Chinese characters welcoming (*huanying*) the women into Japan and the particular district of their husband's family. Some were smiling, while others seemed in a state of shock. Mr. Wei's clients did not speak English or Chinese; they nodded my way while continuing their examination of the registration booklets, calling him over when they had located several women to their liking. As I observed their interactions with Mr. Wei, who spoke fluent Japanese, I had difficulty imagining my women informants as wives of Mr. Wei's clients. Mentally and bodily comfortable with an urban environment, how would they adjust to the farming life etched into these men's wide, roughened hands and coarse skin? I next look at the Chinese side and the involvement of local authorities in marriage transactions.

Border Crossings   Both the Chinese and Japanese states have eased procedures involved in crossing national borders to assist in the transnational mobility of women (*Sunday Morning Post*, March 21, 1993). As both Mr. Wu and Mr. Wei attested, the process is uneventful and is completed in a short period of time, in contrast to the interminable wait and bureaucratic intricacies many Chinese endure to be able to leave China.

In many major Chinese cities, state officials also have a hand in the transnational dimensions of foreign marriage. In Guangzhou, where four hundred matchmakers had set up shop by the early 1990s, the state-run *Yangcheng Evening News* listed several benefits of such cross-cultural unions, including improved business and investment contacts, increased foreign exchange, and enhanced diplomacy (referred to in *Sunday Morning Post,* October 4, 1992). Provincial governments benefit greatly from the revenues accruing from the taxation of hundreds of marriage introduction agencies and the foreign currency earned. Many individual officials also line their pockets with the proceeds of foreign marriages. For example, for a Japanese man, the total cost of marrying a Chinese woman, excluding the wedding ceremony and the honeymoon, is between U.S.$14,000 and $19,000, about two-thirds of which goes to the Japanese and Chinese brokers. Roughly $4,250 of that total is supposed to be given to the family of the bride, yet people involved in the process suspect that most of this ends up in officials' pockets (*Sunday Morning Post,* March 21, 1993). Clearly, in China's spiraling market economy Chinese women and their bodies have been commodified and represent exchange value to the nation (cf. Schein 1996a).

Tactics of "Traditionalism"   Chinese women, through their bodies, appearances, and thinking, are imagined and imagine themselves as representing a kind of generic and gendered "tradition" by Japanese and Singaporean men. But what does *tradition* mean in the contexts of marriage, generation, and China? That a woman defers to her husband? That she can cook and do laundry? I mention cooking because many single and married women in Shenzhen prefer to eat out and enjoy nightlife. Cooking is a skill that many single women do not develop, as the majority live in dormitories and eat meals either in a restaurant or a company canteen. Many married women have domestic helpers and don't take an interest in or have the time for such domestic tasks.

According to interviews with many employees at marriage introduction agencies, among their male clients the meaning of *traditional* encompasses appearance and attitudes. I sat with Mr. Wu looking at photo albums as he pointed out pretty women who looked refined and demure and would be good matches for his clients. Slender attractive women, with seemingly reserved manners and appearance, stared at me from the photos. A woman I inquired about, wearing her hair short with a perky hat and forthright smile, was, according to Mr. Wu, not acceptable to his male clients and was not one of the agency's success stories.

As female clients' expectations are that most of the male clients look for reserved women, they acted appropriately on the videotapes. In addition to their own sense of presentation of self, the women were given some coaching by agency staff in comportment, attire, and speech. Yet, as Mr. Wu said, he and the female staff were only lightly involved in the coaching, as it was more important for the woman's personality to fully come through on film.

I argue that in Shenzhen many Chinese women interested in foreign marriage engage in practices that are "self-orientalizing," as Ong has described Chinese capitalists (1996: 195), emphasizing the role of individual agency at work in manipulating essentialized constructs to one's advantage. Understanding that some Asian men search for "tradition" in a Chinese mate, women act out *tradition* on the videotapes, to the point of making comments such as "I am a very traditional woman." Women who marry "out" are not without power; they manipulate received notions of gender and use them to their benefit, thus maintaining a modicum of control over the process. In marriage negotiations, women use what power they have to shape the decision-making process to their advantage, yet once they depart the country the power balance shifts, as they then are "guests" of the Japanese government without permanent residence rights separate from marriage. Divorce is not a practical option for a Chinese woman brought into Japan through marriage, for if divorced she must return to China.

Popular news accounts attest to the potential risks involved in these marriages, for many women end up spending their days in isolated rural regions under the control of their mothers-in-law (*Sunday Morning Post*, March 21, 1993). The agencies do not follow up on their female clients, making it difficult to learn the outcomes of these marriages. Mr. Wu had declined my request to interview women preparing to go to Japan. The next time I attempted to reach him I learned that the marriage agency had closed (summer 1996). This was due to a clampdown on foreign marriage agencies by the local government.

In this context of marriage between Asians, Singaporean and Japanese men uphold essentialist notions of Chinese women in their search for marriage partners in China. Chinese women are considered to be more "pure" (*chun*) and able to endure hardship, similar to the way Chinese urbanites view rural Chinese women, as Brownell points out in her chapter. Yet how do Chinese youth in Shenzhen define a traditional woman? According to both male and female informants, a traditional woman is a good wife and mother. Several women invoked an old Chinese expression (*xianqi liangmu*) about women whose main tasks are to attend to the household, the husband and his career, and the child's education, subordinating her life to her family (interviews, summer 1996). Many women and men were convinced that Japanese men were more controlling than Chinese men, forbidding their wives to work outside the home, and they often let loose comments about Japanese male chauvinism. University-educated women described for me the character of a traditional Chinese woman, using such terms as *reserved, shy,* and *submissive,* in their words a typical "Eastern" (*dongfang*) woman (interviews, July 1995).

I did not meet these kinds of women during my two years of research in Shenzhen, working and living among immigrant youth of all classes as they sought employment, made friends, and searched for marriage partners. Nor did the women define themselves as traditional. The women in my study worked full time, some held two jobs, and all were on their own in Shenzhen, managing their lives independent of family and boyfriends. Young women whose subject positions included financial manager, employee, girlfriend, and night student would find it difficult to adjust to the stresses of a less cosmopolitan lifestyle and a Japanese mother-in-law. At a time in China when some women's paid labor allows them relative independence and the ability to make modest contributions to their families, raising their status somewhat (cf. Davin 1999), marriage to a rural Japanese man and his family would likely result in a decline in status and power.

I thought of A'Mei, in the midst of a foreign marriage negotiation, who fit the traditional picture only by being attractive and having an ability to cook Jiangsu cuisine. Yet she had two suitors waiting for a reply. She was willing to put aside her sense of independence in order to obtain a middle-class lifestyle and gain educational opportunities, viewing foreign marriage as an avenue to the upward social mobility she had been unable to achieve independently.

Conclusion   As stated earlier, the regional may have as much significance as the global or East-West dynamics in influencing identities, modernities, and major life decisions. In the realms of gender and marriage, male-female relations in some Asian countries have shifted such that mainland Chinese women are considered bearers of a kind of tradition seemingly lacking among other Asian women.

For many Chinese women, foreign marriage as a means of achieving social and economic mobility is worth the risk and the requirement that one reinvent the self.

The gendered power embedded in the politics of border crossings allows Chinese women to easily gain the exit visas and passports that most ordinary Chinese spend years waiting for, or never obtain, being repeatedly denied by foreign bureaucrats in consulates around the world. In the new economic exchanges occurring in Southeast and East Asia, states often view women as resources; however, the women themselves capitalize on their sexuality through tactics of "traditionalism" to improve their present and future positioning. Yet in the marriage introduction process women are positioned passively, as it is men overseas who initiate courtship through their positionality and privilege of movement. In the power geometry of foreign marriage within Asia, women must wait, illustrating Massey's concerns about the linkage between control over movement and power (1993: 61).

Who actually is demanding "traditional" Chinese women as brides is not so clear. Are Japanese and Singaporean men given glimpses of what young Cantonese men editing video productions imagine a Chinese bride should be like, based on their own constructions of Chinese women and China? Or is it more likely that a seemingly cultural notion of tradition bumps up against persistent structural ideas about the status of women held by men from countries where many women have made strides in public and economic life? The notion of tradition that many Asian men search for in women sounds uncomfortably familiar, characterized by a predominance of attention to domestic and reproductive life and little attention given to women's self-development outside the home.

Economic reform and individual mobility have raised life expectations for a generation of women. Many, unable to fulfill lifestyle expectations in Shenzhen and unwilling to contemplate a return to their home-towns, imagine a better life as a transnational. Women who wish to settle permanently in Japan are restricted by residence laws similar to those they faced in China; if divorce were to occur, their residential and work rights in Japan would be revoked. Transnational privileges of mobility, facilitated by state-to-state compliance, are more accessible to some Chinese women than access to the rights of permanent urban residence. For many temporary workers, young and old, male and female, China's cities, as material spaces and "imagined environments" (Donald 1997), remain objects of desire and frustration.

Notes

I would like to thank Zhao Wei Jie of the Shenzhen Social Science Research Center for her assistance during the research period, the staff at the marriage introduction agencies, and most of all the young women who shared a critical stage of their lives with me. Many thanks to the UC Santa Cruz workshop participants for a stimulating weekend and to the discussants, in particular Aihwa Ong and Lisa Rofel. I thank Andrea Louie and Susan Brownell for reading an earlier draft. I am grateful to the anonymous reviewers for Duke University Press for their valuable comments and to the editors of the volume.

1   During the research period, the term was used frequently by female informants and marriage introduction agency staff members to refer mainly to single women. Young women would sometimes call themselves daling qingnian, yet young men rarely used the phrase either to refer to themselves or to other single men and women.

2   Mr. Wu took pride in his video production, as he had designed the program. He also was the only male staff member I met at any of the agencies. The majority of staff I interviewed were young women in their twenties and early thirties.

Susan Brownell Making Dream Bodies in Beijing:
Athletes, Fashion Models, and Urban Mystique in China

Body Culture and Urban Spaces   In recent years in China, rural-urban migration, particularly in the form of the migrant, unskilled wage laborers known as the "floating population," has increased dramatically, attracting the attention of many scholars, including authors of chapters in this book. This chapter concerns another kind of rural-urban migration, which has also increased dramatically in recent years—the migration of those who participate in the production of the elite culture that emanates from urban centers. In her contribution to this volume, Louisa Schein observes that urbanity has become an object of popular cultural production and consumption in post-Mao China. Her chapter focuses on how images of the urban are consumed by Miao villagers in the Chinese hinterlands; I focus on people living the urban dream—or trying to—at the metropolitan center. I describe star athletes and fashion models as two kinds of professionals involved in occupations that produce images of bodies for popular consumption and emulation. When images of athletes and models are used to sell products, normative notions of femininity and masculinity are sold at the same time, so that urban centers become sites for the dissemination of new technologies of gender. One of the main ways in which the images of athletes and models are promoted is through large-scale public events that are widely reported in the media. I discuss two events held in Beijing in which the bodily images that were presented were also linked with the image of the city: in the case of athletes, the 1990 Asian Games; in the case of models, the 1995 Supermodel Contest. Through events such as these, urban metaphors and myths are promulgated that in turn seduce more would-be athletes and models with images of the good life and the beautiful body in Beijing. As a research method, analyzing such public performances and technologies of the body in an urban setting is especially illuminating because of the way they are located at the intersection of the strands of transnational, national, urban, and local forces, which converge at such sites with a special clarity and intensity.

In what follows, I have tried to construct a conceptual framework out of theories and concepts from anthropology, cultural studies, and feminist studies, which brings into view an image of a China enmeshed in the late twentieth century. I have chosen to focus on bodily practices, and in making conceptual sense of them I have utilized the notion of "body culture." I define *body culture* as a broad term that includes daily practices of health, hygiene, fitness, beauty, dress, and decoration as well as gestures, postures, manners, ways of speaking and eating, and so on. It also includes the way these practices are trained into the body, the way the body is publicly displayed, and the lifestyle that is expressed in that display (Brownell 1995: 10–11). This focus on the body gives us insight into how an orientation toward the world becomes habitual because the body as a mnemonic device reinforces it. In studying body culture, it is important to look at both mundane, everyday behaviors and at cultural performances in which the "legitimate body" is publicly displayed. Body culture also includes an important performative dimension. Inspired by the ideas of Victor Turner, I am particularly interested in the conflicts over body culture that are evident in public performances.

For reasons that are important, the bodies under discussion here are located in cities. As representatives of the nation, and as subjects of the party-state, it is important that top athletes have as their home base Beijing—the nation's capital and the site of the National Team Center and the State Sports Commission. The National Sports Games have been held only in Beijing, Shanghai, and Guangzhou because only these cities have the necessary infrastructure, which includes a large stadium able to seat sixty thousand or more spectators. For similar reasons, fashion models and major fashion shows are also located in major cities, with Beijing offering the most opportunities, followed by Shanghai and then other cities.

This brand of "urban anthropology," then, is not a brand that specializes in urban settings and can be applied only in them. My own work, for example, has not made a problem out of the urban, which is to say it has not focused on specifically urban problems such as rural migration, anomie, and so on. The theories about cultural performances and body culture that I employ could be used to describe research in a village setting as well. I focus on Beijing because the bodies that I discuss are important to the party-state, and the party-state has strategically decided to pour resources into developing these professions in Beijing.

The Revival of the Urban Mystique in the Post-Mao Era In the last five years or so, the mystification of the urban has gained momentum in China. Until the end of the Maoist era, the party-state's emphasis on a uniform and unified national culture suppressed attempts to celebrate any kind of difference, whether of gender, ethnicity, region, or urban identity. More than other representations, the sole urban image constantly reinforced in the Maoist era was that of Beijing as the center of state power and authority, "civilization," and social order; as I discuss below, this effort continues. Perhaps the main way in which particular cities were experienced was through the foods unique to certain cities: thus, Tianjin is known for its "*baozi* that the dog ignores" (*gou buli baozi*), Beijing for its fried pancakes (*laobing*), and Shanghai for its "little basket baozi" (*xiaolongbao*). Discussions of travel to cities by Chinese people invariably touch upon experiences of the "local flavor" (*fengweir* in Beijing dialect). The bodily experience of the Chinese city begins with the stomach. Although these kinds of urban experience were not highlighted in the Maoist era, they were never totally forgotten and have begun to emerge with greater force under the reforms as *fengweir* are commercialized for the tourist industry and popular consumption. In addition, other urban identities have begun to reemerge: Beijing as a center of education and intellectual activity, Shanghai as a center of finance, and Guangzhou as an open economic and cultural frontier. For cultural and historical reasons, the marking and marketing of urban identities are very recent in China, and the producers of culture are grappling with how to do it in today's postmodern world.

Even the vocabulary of urbanity is somewhat undeveloped compared to, say, English or French.[1] *A Contemporary English-Chinese Chinese-English Dictionary* (1986) defines *urbane* as "well mannered" (*you lima-ode*) or "cultured" (*wenyade*), thus ridding it of its association with city life. *Wenyade* is often used by models to describe the appeal of their profession. The word *cosmopolitan* is somewhat awkwardly translated as "worldly" (*shijiexingde*). *Metropolitan* is equally awkwardly translated as "of the big city" (*da chengshide*). Even the Chinese word for *civilization* (*wenming*), which has figured so prominently in the party-state's promotion of an image of Beijing, does not connote city life as does the English, which shares with *city* the same Latin root (*civis* 'citizen').[2] None of these Chinese words captures the mystique of urban life that accompanies the English (which in turn is derived from the French). In recent years, Chinese neologisms have appeared, often translated from the English, which function as much to call categories into existence as they do to label existing categories. Thus, *dushi* is frequently used to imply "urban" in the Western sense, as in the "urban white collar" (*dushi bailing*). *Yapi* is a phonetic approximation of *yuppie*. As these labels become widespread, young professionals begin to use them to label themselves, in the process associating themselves with the Western white collar classes that they perceive as exemplars of modernity. The particular appeal of the "urban white collar" identity is indicated by a survey of readers of the popular, Beijing-based magazine *Shishang* (Trends), which showed that the regular feature most popular with its readers was the one entitled "Urban White Collar" (*Shishang* 1995: 65).

Despite the relative weakness of notions of urbanity in their own backgrounds, the producers of elite and popular culture in China are very aware of the importance of these notions globally, and they are seizing upon them in their effort to present China as a nation taking its place on the cutting edge of global culture and style. In the summer of 1995, I noticed a magazine at a newsstand in Beijing with the English subtitle "Metropolitan" under the Chinese characters for "city person" (*chengshi ren*). Small characters at the top of the cover were translated as "The successful light of metropolitan, the leading lamp of countryman" (*chengshi ren chengshide guang, xiangxia ren ru chengde deng*). The covers of the April and June issues featured young, white, female models—one of them showing a good bit of cleavage—in the foreground and vistas of Chinese high-rise buildings in the background. Thinking that the magazine might offer insights into emerging notions of urbanity in China, I bought the two issues available. As it turned out, the magazine was published in Tianjin, not Beijing. I have sometimes felt that, perhaps due to its treaty-port history, Tianjin's residents possess a greater consciousness of cosmopolitanism. The content of the magazines themselves, however, proved disappointing. There were almost no articles on particular urban lifestyles (such as features on local restaurants, nightspots, or fashion), nor did the articles address any general urban lifestyle. An ongoing segment on the "Twelve Urban Classes" seemed like a likely place for vignettes of city life, but the urban class under discussion in April was "cadres," and in June it was "children," and the content was no different from the usual discussions of the hard lives and sacrifices of cadres and the importance of children for the future. One article that showed promise was "The Self-Told Story of an Old Taxi Driver," but it concentrated on the driver's finances, not his experiences of urban life. The one article that offered a somewhat insightful commentary on city life was "A Bold Outline of China's First Generation of White Collars" (Li Jianjun 1995: 20–21). However, this article, by a member of the Liaoning University Center for Research on Social Problems, took a definite page from the Marxist tradition in criticizing the new white collar worker for pursuing ever higher salaries without regard for company loyalty, for consuming extravagantly, and for aspiring to unreasonable standards of taste. Of course, *Metropolitan* was a cheap (1.80 yuan) magazine that can hardly be taken as the last word on concepts of urbanity in China, but that is my point: like so many popular periodicals of the moment, it used a trendy concept on its cover to sell a magazine, but the publishers had only a superficial notion of what the concept included. The most concrete notions of urbanity that emerged out of the magazine were those related to the formation of new social classes and the nitty gritty of earning money in the city. As I will argue, these are very much the central issues for athletes and models who migrate from the periphery to Beijing while the mystique of city life takes a back seat. The cultural producers who must figure out how to produce urban images have to mystify this reality such that they promote a "misrecognition" of the lived experiences of city life in the sense discussed by Pierre Bourdieu. By this I mean that the objective truth of unequal urban-rural power relations is concealed by legitimating myths that portray the social importance of cities as emanating from some mysterious quality of urban life and not from real class structures, government policies, and so on (see Bourdieu and Passeron 1990: 4–5, 12–15, 177–78).

Representing Beijing   When I represented Beijing city as an athlete in the 1986 National College Games, it was evident that representing Beijing had significance to everyone on the team, but at that time the meaning of this representation was quite different from the kind of urban identity I was accustomed to in the United States. More than anything else, Beijing was supposed to provide an example of the correct implementation of state policy. Our duty to represent Beijing with style received its importance from the construction of state power in China: Beijing, regarded as the civilizing center, should exercise a civilizing influence upon the periphery. We, as representatives of Beijing, were to lead the civilizing process by the force of example. This was similar to what Geertz calls the "doctrine of the exemplary center" in his description of nineteenth-century Bali: "the theory that the court-and-capital is at once a microcosm of the supernatural order . . . and the material embodiment of political order" (1980: 13). The Party was supposed to be the moral exemplar of Communist ideology in practice. This was part of the party-state's efforts to construct "spiritual civilization." In the guidelines given out to the team for study and discussion at team meetings, there was a section entitled "The Cultivation and Construction of Spiritual Civilization." It pointed out that "The athlete's construction of spiritual civilization is a strict requirement that is important in everyday life. . . . The concrete demand to set an example (*biaoshuai*) is put upon party and youth group members" (Beijing daxuesheng daibiaotuan mishuzu [Beijing College Team Secretariat] 1986: 6). Thus, in the 1980s it seemed that being an exemplary Beijinger meant that one must have the self-control necessary to obey party-dictated principles and lead by example. This was the conception promoted by the Party and also perhaps the most important element in Beijingers' conception of their city. Almost any Beijinger would tell you that the "social order" in Beijing was better than elsewhere in the country because government policies were obeyed more closely there than elsewhere. During a trip to Tianjin in 1995, for example, my host asked me how I could be sure I was not being cheated by taxi drivers. I told him that I asked for a receipt. These receipts detailed the points of origin and destination and the fare and thus were proof of gouging. Most drivers were afraid to trick passengers who asked for a receipt. My host sighed and said, "In Beijing they obey the policies. Here it doesn't make any difference." When crime and disorder began to increase in the 1990s,

Beijing residents blamed it on the "outsiders" who were migrating to the city in search of prosperity. In 1996, official publications devoted great attention to Beijing's promulgation of a revision of its Civilization Code (*wenming gongyue*). First issued in 1984, the code was designed to improve public etiquette and morals (Xu 1996).

One of the occupations that moved people to Beijing from outlying areas was sports. The state-supported sports system is structured so that talented athletes move from the grassroots level to provincial teams and ultimately to the national team headquartered in Beijing near the Temple of Heaven. Since the mid-1980s, increasing numbers of these athletes have come from peasant backgrounds. This is because sports are a path of mobility for peasant athletes who hope for the chance to obtain urban residence permits and enter physical education institutes or colleges for higher education. I was told that peasants are envious of athletes because their physiques are strong and healthy and they are issued sweatsuits that look very nice. After athletes have been in the city for a while, they start dressing up more, and when they go back to their homes it is as if they are foreign. This is reflected in a rhyme that was said to apply to peasant athletes: "One year later rustic, two years later foreign, three years later won't acknowledge Dad and Mom" (*yinian tu, ernian yang, sannian buren die he niang*). Peasant sports cadres told me that television had stimulated the desire of peasants to see the world and that a strong motivation of peasant athletes is to go abroad. "When I was at the spare-time sports school," wrote weightlifter He Zhuoqiang, who came from a peasant background, "I heard that if you practiced hard you could travel around the world, see the wide world, and I secretly vowed to train until I achieved something" (He 1988).

Sports cadres contrast peasant parents with urban parents, who are reluctant to allow pampered only children to engage in hard training. "The cities have more only children who don't want to participate in sports as a career," noted one peasant cadre. "For peasants, sports are a way out: they can test into a college, get a higher education. The countryside has talent. They can eat bitterness because their economic situation is poor. They have the chance to change their residence permits to the city. . . . The future of Chinese sports lies in the countryside. They are the bulk of China's population." Peasant enthusiasm for sports is said to derive from several factors. One is that peasants are acutely aware that they are to a large degree excluded from the dominant, "legitimate" culture, but they are eager to take part in it and emulate it. Second, they eagerly exploit opportunities to leave the countryside to take part in urban culture. A third reason is that people from the countryside are accustomed to hard labor and do not feel that sports are beneath them, an attitude said to characterize urban white collar workers.

Because state-supported athletes are still very much a part of the party-state's efforts to produce a homogeneous nationalism, the images of athletes promoted in the media reveal few of the gender norms that characterize fashion models. This is changing somewhat with the growth of corporate sponsorship and product endorsements, but it is still not typical of sportswomen featured in advertisements to wear heavy makeup, for example, or assume stereotypical female poses. These athletes are the products of a sports system that deliberately erases gender differences. Removed from their families and put into sports boarding schools, their bodies are trained with military-style discipline from a young age. Sports teams have rules against fraternizing with the opposite sex, wearing long hair loose, and marrying while still in training. Several famous male coaches also forbid their athletes to wear face cream, makeup, or high heels. These rules have loosened somewhat in recent years, but an athlete who draws attention to her femininity is considered to lack a properly serious attitude. By the mid-1990s, the market reforms had begun to create an occupational niche in Beijing for female fashion and print models trading on their appearances, but change was much slower to come to sports teams than to society at large. The female athletes who represented Beijing were still, more than anything else, representatives of the civilizing center of the entire nation—not of a single city with its own unique characteristics. One might contrast this, for example, with the structure of men's professional sports in the United States, which pit cities against each other and trade on urban stereotypes and the loyalty of city residents. With the formation of men's professional soccer and basketball teams in China in the mid-1990s, most of which are associated with particular cities, the foundation has been laid for urban rivalries and expressions of identity.

As runway modeling began to develop as a profession, many if not most of China's runway models were former athletes who had been selected for sports participation because they were tall. The militaristic body culture of sports was blamed for the bodily awkwardness of Chinese fashion models. Several described to me a kind of awakening that occurred as they learned to imagine themselves as models rather than athletes.

Images of Beijing in the 1990 Asian Games　The 1990 Asian Games presented the first opportunity in the post-Mao era for the promotion of an image of Beijing to a large international audience. These games were to be a stepping stone to Beijing's hosting of the 2000 Olympics, which would have promoted the city to an even larger audience if the Olympic bid in 1993 had been successful. These games built on the experience of the seven National Games held in China between 1959 and 1987. The opening and closing ceremonies are the main occasion for representing the host city to its audience. From 1959 to 1979, the ceremonies had utilized mass calisthenics to represent a homogeneous national culture to a national audience in line with the homogenizing nationalism promoted by the party-state in these years. Ethnic, regional, gender, and urban identities were minimal in the ceremonies of the first games and were totally absent in the games surrounding the Cultural Revolution (1965 and 1975). Liu Xiyu, who was one of a national team of choreographers for the 1975 games and the subsequent National and Asian Games, discussed with me the team's growing concern with moving beyond these displays of homogeneous nationalism. After 1975, the choreographers began to think about the issue of local culture, in part as a reaction against the erasure of difference in the 1975 ceremonies, in which the student performers were dressed up like soldiers, workers, and peasants and used slogans like "Learn from Dazhai." As Liu Xiyu put it, "If you invite a guest to your house to eat, you'll offer local delicacies that he can't eat outside. You do not offer him food that he can eat every day in his own home. Mass calisthenics are the same. You invite guests to your city and show them things they cannot find elsewhere. You show them local culture and traditions." All of the PRC National Games were held in Beijing until the 1983 games in Shanghai and the 1987 games in Guangzhou, where the choreographers began to experiment with representations of local culture. For the 1990 Asian Games in Beijing, they moved on to consideration of how to represent Chinese culture to a foreign audience and, in Liu Xiyu's evaluation, carried their representation of local, folk traditions to new extremes. In 1990, in addition to elements that represented the "Chinese" heritage to a foreign audience—such as a panda bear mascot, rural drum dances, lotus flowers, and martial arts—there was an effort to display the best of Beijing culture. This included imagery from Beijing's imperial past, such as huge drums and racks of bells reminiscent of the ritual paraphernalia of the imperial court, and placard sections depicting the Summer Palace, the Great Wall, dragons, and horses. Beijing as a contemporary ritual center had been symbolized by Premier Li Peng's lighting of the torch at the base of the Heroes Monument in Tiananmen Square, which was replayed at the beginning of the television broadcast of the ceremonies. The opening ceremonies also featured a solo by a singer from the China Song and Dance Troupe and aerobic dancing by female students from Beijing colleges. The closing ceremonies showcased the city's elite culture even more, with a finale featuring ballerinas, a grand piano and symphony, and a duet by male and female opera singers, all from national groups headquartered in Beijing.

These choices reflect practices that have become common in Olympic Games opening ceremonies since the Los Angeles Games in 1984; the ceremonies have been used as stages to display achievements in the globally recognized forms of elite culture: ballet, symphony orchestra music, opera, and in the unusual case of the 1992 Barcelona Olympics, high fashion. These particular performance genres demonstrate a city's participation in global high culture, thus symbolizing its modernity and cosmopolitanism. In 1990, Beijing first presented itself as a member of the elite cities of the world, and this effort intensified over the next three years as part of its unsuccessful Olympic bid. I find two things especially interesting about the dilemmas of the choreographers for the Asian Games: the first is that the whole notion of representing the unique characteristics of a city was relatively recent to them; the second is that in their representation they drew mainly upon imperial symbols and contemporary transnational practices. The Maoist era was a poor inspiration for symbols of Beijing that would have international appeal.

Fashion Models and the Metropole In 1992, the *San Francisco Chronicle* observed that the party-state had promoted high fashion as a major area of economic growth since China's first post-Mao fashion show, staged by

Pierre Cardin in 1979; at the same time, it has carried on a long-term campaign to win international recognition for Chinese models. It noted that the medals for the 1992 Supermodel Competition were presented by Vice Premier Tian Jiyun and National People's Congress Vice Chair Chen Muhua, thought to be the highest-ranking woman in the government (Price 1992: 2). The promotion of fashion modeling is closely linked with the promotion of the textile industry in China, and many modeling teams are attached to garment industry organizations. One of the most influential nationwide and in Beijing is the China International Clothing and Accessories Fair (CHIC), under the China Garment Industry General Committee (*Zhongguo fuzhuang gongye zong gongsi*). CHIC was the organization that worked with Pierre Cardin in his fashion shows. These organizations recognize that fashion models perform two functions: they signify China as a player in the fashion world, and they sell clothes.

Nevertheless, despite the passing of two decades, astronomical growth in the Chinese garment industry, and official attention lavished upon models, runway models can make a living only in large cities, and most of them either come from Beijing or move there. Beijing offers more opportunities than other cities. This is evident in the fact that, according to the program descriptions of the forty-seven contestants in the 1995 Supermodel Contest, fourteen were from Beijing; five from Shanghai; four each from Dalian and Nanjing; three each from Hangzhou and Tianjin; two each from Jiangsu, Shandong, Shenzhen, and Xiamen; and one each from Chengdu, Guizhou, Jilin, Kunming, Shanxi, and Xian. Many of the models who were labeled as Beijingers in fact had moved there to pursue modeling, and some of the models from elsewhere had moved there just before the contest for the same reason. Beijing is in fact the fashion center of China, although the popular conception is that Shanghai occupies that role. I asked many of the young women I encountered in Beijing whether they found that Beijingers dressed fashionably. Most replied that Beijingers were very practical and not very fashionable; if they were from other cities, they usually stated that women dressed more fashionably in their hometowns. They also seemed to possess a stereotype that Shanghai was the center of China's fashion industry. Leaders in Shanghai's fashion industry reminded their audience that Shanghai was once known as the Paris of the East, a title they now sought to regain (see the congratulatory letter by the vice mayor of Shanghai in the magazine *Fengcai* [Beauty],

March–April 1995, 10). Actually, Beijing was the site of most of the shows staged by major foreign designers, and this was because of CHIC's location there—which, in turn, resulted from the fact that CHIC was part of a chain of command in the state-controlled textile industry that ultimately harkened back to the central government in Beijing. And so haute couture, that symbol of global capitalist elites, was in China still inextricably linked to the old state-controlled socialist economy. Even in Beijing, major fashion shows are still relatively rare, and those staged by foreign designers constitute the major opportunities for Chinese models. Chinese name designers are still few and far between. And even in Beijing, there are only a handful of models who can make a living working full time at runway modeling, the most rarefied form of modeling. There are considerably more opportunities in print and electronic modeling, but those who aspire to be top runway models feel that too much of this kind of exposure may damage their reputations; in addition, they are not often in demand for this kind of modeling since advertisements usually feature more everyday-looking people. Many of the runway models lounge around in their agencies day after day with little to do between fashion shows. So far, no Chinese models have succeeded in establishing regular international employment relationships, for reasons outlined below. At best, groups of models have been invited by a few name designers—in particular Pierre Cardin—to participate in fashion shows in Europe for a short time.

In point of fact, the image of Beijing as a cosmopolitan center of elite culture is still more fantasy than reality. Most models supplement their incomes with regular jobs such as secretarial work or teaching school. Two of the more enterprising models were involved in designing clothes for Valentino and putting together a feature on models for *Yanyiquan* (Entertainment and Arts Circles) magazine (which styled itself "The Urban Entertainment Illustrated" [*dushi yule huakan*]).

Other models earned some money doing fashion shows for *nouveau riche* (*baofa hu*) at karaoke clubs. One model's distaste for karaoke club modeling revealed the mystique that had attracted her to the profession in the first place.

I got into fashion modeling because I thought it should be a kind of aesthetic appreciation (*yishu xiangshou*), it should be cultured (*wenya*). But these people [the nouveau riche in the club] gave me a lower-class feeling. They sat there smoking their cigarettes and watching. Also, the clothes are very simple. The broker (*xuetou*) [literally "cave head"] makes them by herself or buys cheap clothes. Not like the international designers whose clothes, I have heard, sell for up to several tens of thousands of yuan for one item. I didn't like it, and I won't do it again.

Models who move from the periphery to Beijing may soon find that they need to search out other ways of making money. Agencies are reluctant to hire them, since they cannot provide housing and a guaranteed wage. One older model with a college degree from a physical education university told me the story of a young woman who came to Beijing from Henan Province and managed to sign a contract with an agency. She didn't get enough work to support herself, and soon her savings ran out. She scraped along for several months by hanging around the agency and asking others for money for food. Finally, a friend introduced her to a Taiwanese businessman who wanted a companion when he was in town. She was told that all she had to do was to eat and drink with him—no sex was expected. Eventually, she disappeared, and my informant did not know if she was now living in a hotel with the businessman. She noted that sometimes it will happen that a model moves into a hotel with a businessman—especially a Taiwanese, who like tall women. She said that this young woman wanted to be a model because "she didn't want to study. She didn't want to work either. She wanted to be beautiful, march around the stage, and not have to work." Another former model was hired as a "secretary" by the son of a high official. She accompanied him to social functions, where her only noticeable purpose was to present his business cards to new acquaintances when asked and to provide a subject of conversation between him and other men ("She was a model? With all those freckles?"). I was told that this was not a sexual relationship—though I was never sure—but it certainly was a form of status display on his part.

The urbanization process is gendered in significant ways; Greg Guldin reminds us that the density of sex workers can be read as a measure of development and urbanization (1996: 282, n. 9). Although the models I talked to all insisted that there is a vast difference between a fashion model and a prostitute and that most people understand that models are a part of refined culture and prostitutes are not, these conceptual categories were not always so clear in practice. Professionals in television and advertising who had to deal with models criticized them for their failure to develop themselves, describing them as people who don't want to work hard or cultivate their minds but just want to rely on their appearance to "eat the food of youth" (*chi qingchun fan*). They recognized, as older models quickly found out, that even the best careers only last a few years in Beijing. One major reason for this is that the height of models has increased rapidly, so that the 1.70 m (5'7") model who was successful five years ago is already too short for the foreign designers, who are now demanding models 1.80 m (5'11") and up.

Despite the lack of full-time employment for runway models in Beijing, the forces that drive the urban dream machine move on. This was evident in the 1995 Supermodel Competition in Beijing. The guiding assumptions of the contest were that the Chinese fashion industry was in a position to produce models who could compete with foreigners and that the production of world-class models would signify China's position as an important player in the realm of elite transnational culture.

The Supermodel Contest   The First Chinese Supermodel Contest was held in 1991, the year after the 1990 Asian Games. Although it was a different kind of public display, in many ways it continued the thematic development outlined above. On June 16–17, 1995, the preliminaries and finals for the Fourth Chinese Supermodel Competition were held at the International Conference Center, part of the Asian Games Village built for the 1990 games. (That these sites for large public displays are built with central government funds is another example of their dependence on the state-controlled economy.) The competition had begun months before when more than two hundred applicants from fashion show teams and modeling agencies from twenty-three provinces around the country submitted applications, which were narrowed down to a total of forty-seven participants on the final two nights. The winner of the Chinese competition would represent China in the world finals in South Korea two months later. Elite Hong Kong Model Management Ltd. produced the Beijing contest. Elite is one of the largest international modeling agencies, and the Elite Model Look world contest is one of the most im-

The 1995 Chinese Supermodel Contest, Beijing. Photo by Susan Brownell.

portant international modeling competitions. It should be noted, however, that "supermodels" do not generally emerge on the international scene through such competitions—rather, they are carefully cultivated by their agencies over time. Nevertheless, the explicit purpose of the Supermodel Competition was to promote Chinese fashion models on the international scene.

Therefore, as with sportswomen, the main issue was not urban identity—which was almost totally absent—but national identity. The key question was: what kind of beautiful woman was most representative of China and therefore most suitable to promote Chinese culture on the world stage? Should she be a "traditional oriental" beauty, a sophisticated cosmopolitan citizen of the world, or some combination of the two? The ways in which these qualities were to be symbolized were fairly simple. Chiefly, short hair, a direct glance, and energetic movements signified Westernization; long hair, an averted glance, and restrained movements represented a traditional beauty. These qualities were associated with complex technologies of gender. As it was explained to me by several people involved in the modeling industry and beauty contests, runway models are recognized as representatives of a Western feminine tradition that is perceived to be different from the Chinese feminine tradition—in particular in the assertiveness, openness, and exuberance of the models' body movements and emotional expressions. Within this form, however, it is possible for a Chinese model to represent either the "traditional oriental" (*dongfang chuantong*) woman or the "Western" woman. The traditional oriental beauty is characterized by an air of melancholy that is reminiscent of paintings of concubines staring sadly into space because they have been neglected. I would suggest that this represents her resignation to her position in the patriarchal system; because her spirit has been broken, she is nonthreatening to men. The modern, Westernized woman is exuberant, expressive, and threatening to men. In some ways, then, the selection made at the supermodel contest would make a contribution to nationwide norms of femininity radiating out from Beijing via the mass media.

The supermodel contest was not, however, a strict beauty contest. The models competed in swimsuit, leisure wear, and evening wear categories and were judged by the prevailing trends in runway modeling. This form of modeling, of course, has rather unique standards for age, height, body shape, and a host of other attributes. The models were judged on their walk, movements, agility, coordination, level of ease, aesthetic appeal, musicality, awareness of the camera lens, and harmony of appearance. Personality and English skills were also important, as the judges spent quite a bit of time getting to know the models outside the contest. And so the issues of identity were highly constrained by the global market for fashion models.

Further, a Chinese model must appeal to European designers and customers in order to be employed in international fashion shows. The model who is considered most "representative" of Chinese beauty will not necessarily appeal to European eyes. The organizers of the competition, based on previous failures to produce a Chinese supermodel, had concluded that Chinese people do not have the same ideals as Europeans. Therefore, the judges included five Westerners along with two Hong Kongese, two Chinese, and one Thai. This balance of five Westerners and five Asians was to ensure that the eventual winners would have pan-global appeal. Through a process of self-orientalizing, the organizers utilized a non-Chinese gaze to choose a representative of the Chinese nation as seen through non-Chinese eyes.

One of the Chinese judges, Chen Fuli, did not agree with this balance of power, however. He told *Zhongguo Shangbao* (China trade news) that he felt the number of foreign judges was too many and that this competition basically was decided according to Western standards of beauty (*Zhongguo shangbao* 1995a).

The similarity between the nationalist rhetoric surrounding international sports and that heard in this contest was remarkable. Chinese models were compared to foreign ones and found deficient, although much improved from previous years. In an onstage interview, one of the emcees asked Stefano Ricci, one of the judges, whether Chinese models had what it took to succeed on the world stage. He emphasized that models aren't born but made and they had to work hard and with dedication to be successful. The emcee, struggling to do his own simultaneous interpretation into Chinese, concluded with a formula that is very common in sports: "There will come a day when they will advance on the world" (*zou xiang shijie*)! The Chinese representative of Pierre Cardin in China, Song Huaigui, told *China Trade News,* "The level of the models, from one aspect, reflects the level of cultural attainment of a nation's people" (*Zhongguo shangbao* 1995a). The same statement is made about Chinese athletes.

In the end, the top three places went to nineteen-year-old, 5′10″ Xie Dongna from Shanghai; twenty-year-old, 6-foot Luo Jinting from Xian; and twenty-one-year-old, 5′11.5″ Guo Hua from Beijing. Although roughly half of the participants had very short or above the shoulder hair, the first two winners had long hair, suggestive of "traditional oriental" beauty. The second and third places went to two of the tallest women in the contest. There was confusion among the Chinese audience about why Xie Dongna had won. As the models lined up for the awards ceremony, the young woman sitting next to me turned to her friend and asked, "What's so good looking about her?" Onstage, Stefano Ricci stood at Xie's side, kissed her, and looked up at her with an expression like that of a proud father, at which the young woman concluded, "Oh, the foreigner (*laowai*) likes her." After the awards ceremony, the emcee announced that Ricci had offered her a contract to do some fashion shows in Italy.

To me, the first- and second-place finishers seemed to have a more "oriental" look according to the Western stereotype; they had oval faces, arched eyebrows, and long hair. All three winners had a quiet, demure manner and downcast eyes. The fourth place went to sixteen-year-old Yu

Ya'nan, who had short, spiked hair and a style that was more vivacious and sassy than anyone else's. She later became successful modeling domestically in China.

The head judge, Paoletti, revealed his own stereotypes of Asia and the West in an interview with *Zhongguo shangbao* (1995b)—translated into Chinese for the newspaper, and here translated back into English by me. The way that his discussion of the Asian image segues into the logic of the market shows how the two are intertwined in his view of the world.

> REPORTER ASKS: In recent years, more and more Asians have felt that making a living as a model entails many inherent obstacles, is this so or not?
>
> PAOLETTI: Asians and Europeans have many inborn (*xiantian*) differences, but Asian girls' eyes are softer; faces are also softer. For a female, this easy to approach (*pingyi jinren*) temperament is very good; being easy to approach is the strength of Asian girls. For a model, it is important to be good looking, but it is also important to continuously change your image. Chinese models should be confident. This is 50 percent of success; the other 50 percent is the opportunities for development planned by the agent. In addition, Chinese models should study other nations' cultures, and it is necessary for them to master English.

In an on-site interview after the competition, a reporter from an English-speaking TV station asked Paoletti if there would be a market for these models. He replied that they would encounter "the same problems as a black girl. But fashion is so big and wide that there won't be a problem. Europe's oriental population is not that big, but we do appreciate them." He observed that there is a growing market in Asia because lots of clothes are made in China. There is also a large Asian population in the United States. Paoletti assumed that Chinese models would primarily be used to sell clothing to Asian customers and that crossover appeal is difficult to achieve.

Afterthoughts A larger point is that these debates were carried out in Beijing, which for many reasons was positioned at the center of the web of global, regional, and national networks involved in this public event. And in occupying this position Beijing can also be identified as a site where gendered technologies of the body are disseminated, not just nationally but internationally—for instance, among the Asian diasporas, which were regarded as the potential markets for the clothing promoted by these models. Will Asian women in the diaspora get to see melancholy "oriental beauties" or sassy, expressive, Chinese models in their fashion shows and photo layouts?

In many ways, the concept of body culture could have been applied to bodies located elsewhere, and that is because these bodies are nodes in a nexus of the kind of modern polymorphous power structures that can now exercise their force almost anywhere in space, thanks to the power of television and other means of space-time compression. But star athletes and runway models subsist only in large cities because they participate in certain kinds of cultural performances that require vast spaces, media coverage, and audiences of a size and character found only in densely populated urban areas with some degree of cultural sophistication. And they are participating in a process of symbolic elaboration of the urban, the "metropolitan," that is occurring in the post-Mao era—and which in Bourdieu's sense is part of the misrecognition of growing class divisions in Chinese society.

At the same time, the accounts that I have related show that the urban image still takes a backseat to the national image in most of the intentional image-making that is going on in Chinese popular culture. Ultimately, the newborn Beijing cosmopolitanism was put into the service of Chinese nationalism, and this was in large part because the urban dream machines described here were funded by the state. Yet this is not exactly the same nationalism as that of the Maoist era: this process of image-making is simultaneously linked with the revived interest in local culture that has accompanied economic decentralization and with transnational cultural flows, which are particularly evident in prominent realms of global culture such as Olympic sports and high fashion. Nevertheless, at least in the moments described here, these potentially centrifugal forces did not seem to exert their decentralizing potential.

Notes

The research on sports was supported by the Committee on Scholarly Communication with the People's Republic of China, funded by the U.S. Information Agency. The research on fashion models was funded by a University of Missouri, St. Louis,

Research Award and a University of Missouri Research Board Award. I would like to thank Nancy Chen and the organizers for inviting me to the original conference and Suzanne Gottschang for comments on earlier drafts of the manuscript.

1   I would like to thank Liu Xin for elucidating some of these points in a discussion at the conference in Santa Cruz.

2   Thanks to Steve Harrell for pointing this out in his review of the manuscript.

Sandra Teresa Hyde Sex Tourism Practices
on the Periphery: Eroticizing Ethnicity and
Pathologizing Sex on the Lancang

From looking at a map,
China is only a floating island,
and its people a floating body,
fluttering toward their eternal destiny.
—Wang Anyi

On a sweltering afternoon, so hot you can almost hear the sidewalks
sizzle, grandmothers fan sleeping grandsons under the palm trees that
line South Nationality Road. Fat black pigs rest on the dusty tarmac,
while chain-smoking hooligans (*liumang*) laugh, joke, and watch plumes
of blue smoke rise. Under the afternoon sun, Jinghong is a sleepy town,
but at night it comes alive with the fastest nightlife this side of the Lao
border. As night falls, quietude disappears and motorcycles and red
taxis filled with finely dressed tourists race to discos and bars blaring
Japanese karaoke and American rock and roll. In this liminal time, subtle
changes are taking place in terms of who occupies the streets. By day,
locals go about their daily affairs; at night the 1.5 million tourists, who
flock to Xishuangbanna every year, emerge from their air-conditioned
hotel rooms, bringing with them a taste for a blend of commerce, capital,
and commodity fetishism.

The Disappearing Village This chapter considers the borders of an
urban/rural space, Xishuangbanna Dai Nationality Autonomous Prefecture in southern Yunnan, as a window of understanding onto the urban

in 1990s China. If we wish to make sense of the city in China, it is important to explore what Anthony King calls the "discourses, symbols, and fantasies" through which people ascribe meaning to the experience of urban living (cf. King 1996b). King (1996b) argues that it was Foucault who problematized the relationship between "the real city, the discursive city, and the disappearing city," but what concerns me in contemporary China is the disappearing village. How has the socialist development project transformed the rural villages of Xishuangbanna into the urban space of Jinghong? This urban space bears a particular resonance in China as a place where the fantasies of sex, travel, and minority ethnicity come together.

The development project in "Banna" is the story of how a small town on the Lancang River (the local name for the Mekong) became a city of sex tourism. Jinghong is a city of prostitution (*piaocheng*) according to the local folklore and, more importantly, in terms of the local economy: it provides Han Chinese male tourists with a lucrative sex tourist destination. What the male tourists come to Jinghong to consume are Tai women. However, the majority of prostitutes are not Tai but women from Sichuan and Guizhou dressed in Tai clothing to attract Han male customers. They, just like the men who solicit them, provide an allure that is marketed in tourist brochures. Prostitution practices within a Chinese-governed Tai autonomous region constitute what Manderson and Jolly call a "site of desire." This term captures the confluences of cultures with "the smaller eddies of sexual contact and erotic imaginings created between cultures" (1997: 1) that happen in this case on the borders of China. This site of desire encompasses what is uniquely urban about China and what is unique about Chinese ethnic boundaries in Xishuangbanna.

Writing about urban prostitution in early-twentieth-century Shanghai, Gail Hershatter suggests that prostitution can be read as both an occupation for urban women and a metaphor for how Chinese urbanites discuss their fears about the future. She says: "Prostitution was not only a changing site of work for women but also a metaphor, a medium of articulation in which the city's changing elites and emerging middle classes discussed their problems, fears, agendas, and visions. . . . prostitution was understood as a source of urbanized pleasures, a profession full of unscrupulous and greedy schemers, a site of moral danger and physical disease" (1997: 4). Informed by Hershatter's notion of prostitution as a source of urbanized pleasures, studying prostitution in Jinghong highlights a series of overlapping and interlocking dichotomies: urban/rural, pleasure/danger, polluted bodies/clean bodies, Han/non-Han bodies, illegitimate space/legitimate space, and public/private. While a full discussion of these far-ranging dichotomies is beyond the scope of this essay, what is instructive is to organize these binary oppositions with the notion of an urban/rural divide. However, there is no static divide between the urban and the rural. Both shift and evolve as swiftly as the changing Chinese notions of what is urban and what is rural. Like the Chinese symbol for yin and yang, the urban can be found in the rural and the rural resides in the urban. Thus, while the border region of Banna reflects a rural social imaginary for Han Chinese from northern China, simultaneously the border region functions to reinscribe an urban morality on the rural. By marketing rural authentic Taineess, urban residents from China's hinterland come to Jinghong, and it is they who transform the villages in the rural jungles of Banna. Furthermore, it is through the performance of sex and the eroticization of ethnicity that Xishuangbanna becomes representative of Chinese modernity and urbanity (Gilmartin et al. 1994; Parker 1992; Ong and Nonini 1997).[1]

Constructing this cosmopolitan out of the rural jungles of Banna involves conceptualizing an urban journey into a place that is idealized as both a tropical paradise and an exotic home of an ethnic erotic. In order to market Banna to greater China and Han Chinese, the notions of a peripheral space, a space outside of the norms of urban living in Shanghai, Guangzhou, Nanning, or even Kunming, must be maintained. Banna is marketed as a rural paradise complete with an urban center that coordinates, manages, and filters such rural pleasures as elephant riding and Tai women bathing. Jinghong, like many global tourist destinations, holds a fantasy world for those embarking on a journey there, while at the same time it presents a possibility of urban modernity for China. This notion of modernity embraces sexual desire and pleasure as legitimate while it simultaneously castigates the purveyors of prostitution as dangerous, polluting "others."

During sixteen months of ethnographic fieldwork in 1996 and 1997 on a larger project on the emergence of the HIV/AIDS epidemic in Southwest China, I conducted twenty interviews with men and women of diverse occupations, including prostitutes and their clients in Jinghong.[2] The first part of the chapter provides a social history of Xishuangbanna and the city of Jinghong because in order to understand why Banna is now marketed as a sexy tourist destination one must know its history. The second analyzes China's changing sexual morality and some of the practices that mark sexuality as intrinsic to the urban and modern in Jinghong. The third explores how exoticism in Banna is marked by celebrating an ethnic erotic that is practiced by Han women performing and playing on the cultural characteristics of Tai-Lue ethnicity (Schein 1996). In other words, I explore how fantasies of the exotic Tai are experimented with and fulfilled through prostitution with Han women and how in turn Han women imagine and construct fantasies for male tourists through their practices. I discuss this eroticization through my ethnography of two people who are integrally connected to the New Wind Hair Salon: one, the madam, owns the salon; the other, a businessman, is a customer.

A Recent Social History of Xishuangbanna Sipsongpanna (in Tai it means "twelve rice-growing counties") was once an independent kingdom of Thailand called Lan Na Thai. It was renamed the Xishuangbanna Tai Nationality Autonomous Prefecture of Yunnan Province under the Chinese state in January 1953 (Hsieh 1995). Muangjinghung was the capital of the Sipsongpanna kingdom for more than eight hundred years and is now the prefectural capital of Jinghong. It borders the Shan States of Myanmar (Burma) to the southwest, the northern tip of Laos to the southeast, and Simao County in Yunnan Province to the north.[3] Jinghong has an official population of 140,000, but this statistic does not include the large numbers of migrants who work there. As Li Zhang points out in this volume, China's large floating population (*liudong renkou*) migrates across the country in search of work. However, it is not only migrant workers who uproot themselves. With increasing mobility and disposable income, Han Chinese tourists also travel to Banna to escape their workaday lives in the metropolises of Shanghai, Nanjing, and Kunming. While 90 percent of Banna's tourists are mainland Chinese, the immigrants are drawn from the wider Asian diaspora: the Singaporean who cuts hair in a salon owned by someone from Macao and the Pakistani who travels from Myanmar to sell jade. Migrating Chinese workers, for example, come from Sichuan to drive cabs, from Hunan to sell imported Korean clothing, and from Guizhou to run beauty salons-cum-brothels (*meirong ting*).

Historically, Banna was not a Han tourist destination. The Han Chinese came to Banna in three distinct waves of migration: in the 1950s to plant rubber, during the Cultural Revolution (1966 to 1977) as educated youth "sent down" (*xiaxiang*) to serve the poor minorities, and, finally, in recent years to develop the local resources by planting rubber trees (now the largest cash crop in the region) and mining manganese. As Grant Evans (2000) points out, from 1949 until 1978 there was almost no significant foreign trade with Yunnan Province, and Banna lived up to its name as a "mysterious land south of the clouds." In the late 1980s and early 1990s, several Tai villages south of Jinghong were transformed in the process of building a new economic development zone for joint venture hotels, restaurants, and tourist parks. According to local rumors, little or no compensation was given to village leaders for repossession of their lands.

Under provincial policies in the 1980s, Jinghong authorities opened trade routes into the golden quadrangle of Laos, northern Thailand, Myanmar, and southwestern China, creating pathways for the future transnational flows and migrations of people. Banna was viewed by the central Beijing government as a critical path into Southeast Asia for trade, goods, and tourists. Therefore, Han Chinese came in the early 1990s to develop Banna and open a gateway to Southeast Asia. Opening this gateway also meant marketing the region through tourism. Xishuangbanna was the launching point for ethnic tourism into the rain forests, Buddhist temples, and Tai cultural areas in the mid-1980s. By the early 1990s, Xishuangbanna had become a honeymoon spot for Han couples, a place of rest and relaxation for businessmen, and a prime destination for government-sponsored, all expenses paid, work unit meetings (*danwei kaocha*). By the mid-1990s, a very different kind of tourist arrived in Jinghong, the middle-aged male with money to spend on brothels, dancing girls, and gambling. In Jinghong, sex tourism is practiced under the guise of new occupations in karaoke bars, hair salons, barbershops, massage parlors, saunas, and bars, where services extend beyond the karaoke mike and the blow dryer. Massage parlors not only provide massages but have on-site escort services where men may be entertained by young women in the privacy of hotel rooms.

In 1995, more than 1.5 million tourists came to Banna, of which more than 90 percent were newly prosperous Han Chinese from greater China (Qing 1995). The majority of these tourists are indigenous middle class Han Chinese who come to Banna for rest and relaxation at the end of their Kunming-based business meetings. Jinghong is a forty-five-minute flight, or a twenty-four-hour bus ride, from Kunming. Several informants explained that the reward for attending a work meeting is one of these three- to four-day trips to Xishuangbanna, the tropical paradise of southwestern Yunnan. The regional development office now paints what Evans calls a "Disney Worldesque" picture of the future, capturing the world beyond China's very real and enforced borders (Evans 2000; Anagnost 1989, 1997). Banna provides a unique case, for, although few Chinese can get passports to travel overseas, they can go on excursions to Chinese-controlled border towns in both Myanmar and Laos.[4] Once there, tourists can spend yuan in the Chinese-run businesses in town, thus benefiting the Chinese on both sides of the border. The local development office now plans to "renovate" the old Tai temple torn down during the Cultural Revolution and bring Southeast Asia to the relatively closed borders of China in a theme park (Evans 2000). Li, a young man of twenty-nine who works for the *Sheng gonganju* (Provincial public security bureau), pointed out that key leaders of the local police went to a conference in Las Vegas in 1995 and returned with visions in their heads of turning Banna into the Las Vegas of China.

As economic development under Deng's dictum "to get rich is glorious" took root, the state appropriated collective farmland and redistributed it for private redevelopment. As four-star international hotels (built by Thai-Chinese, Taiwanese-Chinese, and Shanghainese developers) emerged from these fields, rice cultivation in the two adjacent Tai villages of Manjinglan and Manting was destroyed.[5] While many Tai were critical of this appropriation, most local Han understood it in terms of progress and development. Wu,[6] a Han woman of twenty-five born and raised in Jinghong, a teacher by profession and a tour guide and secretary on the side, told me this story:

> Jinghong was very poor prior to economic reforms; everyone was treated the same and served the same, respected everybody's spirit (*women fengxian jingshen*). When I was growing up in Jinghong, the

only large buildings were the prefecture's Communist Party headquarters. The site of the Banna hotel was a Tai village called Manyun. Now the Tai villagers are landlords, they have become rich subdividing the bottom dirt floors of their houses into rooms for let. Before, the peasant's trade market was just vegetable fields; the road to the Teacher Training School was just dirt. Everything changed with the airport, with planes came new businesses, with new businesses came the *heishehui* [the underworld or Chinese Mafia]—prostitution in 1992 and gambling in 1994. Jinghong is definitely now a town dependent on the tourism industry (*luyouye*) . . . we have moved from an idealistic to a realistic society.

For Wu, China under socialism was very idealistic but under Deng's neocapitalism it had become more realistic, realistic in providing jobs outside the work unit (*danwei*) system as well as permitting the growth of newfound leisure activities. No informant, including Wu, could give me an exact genealogy of prostitution; however, many stated that it "came with the airport," as if flights and sex went together. These newfound pleasures and entertainments are what I term "icons of modern Chinese sexual morality."

Sexual Morality and Notions of Modernity   In Jinghong, sexuality has emerged as one face of modernity. Here I suggest there are three modern moral codes at play, which are mapped onto different ethnic groups and more broadly onto people in particular locations in the local Jinghong social hierarchy. A *libertine* moral code promotes modern, adventurous, and consumptive sexuality, which includes prostitution, multiple lovers, and unprotected sex. A *parochial* moral code operates not only to limit certain behaviors, especially among sex workers and intravenous drug users, but to hide the prevalence of the commercial sex industry entirely. The third, the *urban* moral code, stigmatizes one ethnic minority group, the Tai-Lue, as sexually promiscuous and licentious. What is most striking is the internecine battles between these moral codes, which each seeks to legitimize a unique moral universe under the modern Chinese state. The urban moral code stigmatizes the Tai-Lue while it also permits the marketing of leisure activities that build on ideas about post-Mao sexuality. Myriad sexual practices create pleasure through the purchase of services such as sexual entertainment. Here modernity in Jinghong develops through the Han, who perform sexual activities (visiting prostitutes) in a non-Han space (Tai country).

Previous studies on prostitution tend to create an unproblematized binary between the exploited (prostitutes) and the exploiters (customers). One way of reading this is to borrow from Mascia-Lees and Sharpe's (1992) work, where Han Chinese women may be read as the "epitome of civilization" against the "sepulchre" of ethnic minority women, who are labeled as both uncivilized and the source of forbidden pleasure. But such static binary oppositions cannot fully address a more nuanced reading of ethnicity in Banna. We have not just two groups, the exploited and exploiters, but in fact several groups. If we only read "Han wives" (the ones living in China's hinterland) as virtuous and "Tai girls" as uncivilized in their rural paradise, we miss the fact that there are also Han women who are prostitutes (the unvirtuous) and Han men who are buying sex (another unvirtuous category). While I do not intend to completely throw out the concept of exploitation in prostitution, it needs to be teased out in an examination of who is exploiting whom, at what time and in what place, and perhaps even by what ethnicity. As Virginia Cornue (1997) demonstrates, new forms of urban life emerge that touch on personal ambivalences toward sexual behavior and arise from following multiple moral codes as well as from claiming new identities. Many female informants who did not work as prostitutes felt ambivalent toward the practice of exchanging sex for money as well as the role of Han migrant women within cosmopolitan Jinghong.

The renaissance in prostitution is only one facet of the rise of the multiplication of sites wherein a new modern sexuality seeks expression. In Jinghong, I heard many of my informants (both Han and Tai) fervently say that they, unlike promiscuous Westerners, are very cautious and conservative in the ways of sex. Yet at other times I saw them engage in all kinds of sexual activities that completely contradict the way they talk about themselves. Here sex and the sex industry are not about Han repression and Tai promiscuity but about how sex as a commodity is circulated. Representations of sex are everywhere in a plethora of sex toy advertisements, condom packages, videos and films, anti-HIV/AIDS campaigns, hair salons, sexy clothing, and even stories about sex in the news. As a result, the desire to consume newfangled leisure amusements among tourists and locals alike includes the consumption of sexual commodities.

In terms of the parochial and urban moral codes of behavior, what is important for a tourist "site of desire" is to manage the image of the place rather than develop strict moral imperatives regarding sex. Often in Jinghong what does get repressed is the circulation or will to know, to openly acknowledge what is being practiced (Foucault 1980a). One friend in her thirties, in speaking about taboo acts, said: "In China, we just do . . . we act. We never speak about what we have done." Thus, in almost every Chinese city one sees street posters advertising fly-by-night doctors who claim to be able to cure sexually transmitted diseases and AIDS, yet such cures are not openly discussed. In Jinghong, these posters are prominent only in the alleyways where locals venture; they are torn down where tourists are apt to view them. The idea that dangerous sex must be concealed in order to promote tourism fits with the notion of competing moral universes: a modern sexual morality promotes sex tourism while a parochial one hides the consequences of unprotected sex. Underlying all of these practices are these three conflicting moral codes—three competing discourses—which often simultaneously challenge and embrace Confucian notions of Chinese sexual behavior (Dikotter 1995; Zito 1994; Ruan 1991).

If the contemporary sex industry signifies a kind of liberation of sexuality (the rise of post-Mao urban pleasures) wherein market forces revolutionize certain social practices, I would further suggest that the sex industry has revolutionized sexuality in Banna. The forces for moral order and their representatives in the state view the sex industry in Banna as symbolic of the rise of urban moral decay and crime. Nonetheless, several female informants alluded to their sex work as a part of modern China, which embraces sexual liberation and thus provides them with the freedom to capitalize on their sexuality. Wu, the young woman quoted earlier, explained prostitution this way:

> Prostitutes make quick money. . . . They think about the impressions of marriage and the lights of the city. . . . Most are from the countryside and outside the province, and it [sex] is just a fashion for society. . . . There are so many single women in Jinghong, the women who make up the sex industry are in highly paid occupations, and that

is why prostitutes are plentiful. There is a saying in Jinghong, *yang xiao bai lian*, which means to raise a small group of young handsome men. If women can keep a gaggle of handsome men around and just work [exchanging sex for money] . . . cultivate this group . . . just take care of these elegant boys, the boys will take care of their girl-friends in return. . . . To have a nice looking man to look at and take care of you while you provide the money is pleasing.

For local women like Wu, prostitution signifies the numerous opportunities women have to make money and become wealthy. But it also signifies the possibility of taking care of a small army of young men. This is clearly a usurpation of traditional gender roles. Here the practice of sexuality, the selling of one's body for money, completely transgresses older notions of proper Confucian behavior. Sexuality in 1990s China both shapes and is shaped by the dynamics of human social life that bring the rural Banna into the city of Jinghong (representations of Tai culture) and the urban cosmopolitan into rural Banna (via the sex trade). What these competing sexual morals pivot around is the eroticization of the Tai, for what the entire sex tourism industry in Banna survives (or depends) on is this eroticization. It is to this idea that I now turn.

Performance and the Eroticization of Ethnicity   Several sinologists have argued for a more nuanced reading of Chinese ethnicity, one that views ethnic categories as fluid and socially constructed through both time and space (Gladney 1991, 1994; Harrell 1995; Honig 1992b; Schein 1997a, 1997). In exploring the social construction of ethnicity in Banna, it is important to recognize the distinction between social representations of the Tai and actual Tai cultural practices.[7] In Jinghong, because Han migrants and tourists both claim to appropriate authentic images of Tai culture, ethnicity becomes an especially malleable category. However, even the fluidity of ethnic boundaries has its limits. For example, Dru Gladney, among others, has noted that the Han often construct the non-Han as feminized minority others, and in Banna this is evident in the local market economy for sex tourism. Consumers, Han men, are driving the market for ethnic women, who are in fact Han women who mimic Tai culture for profit. But money is not the only desired profit here; what these Han women can do away from home, away from watchful eyes, is also important. Over and over again, people remarked that Banna is the land of freedom, unbounded cultural limits, and promiscuous sex. It is also important to note that ethnic boundaries in Banna are very much shaped by its recent history in what we could perhaps call a colonizing process—or what Stevan Harrell calls a "civilizing progress" (1995). In an effort to understand local representations of the Tai in Banna, here I present a few of the images of minorities.

A contemporary belief among other ethnic groups in Banna is that the Tai are the most intelligent, clever, and enterprising of the minority ethnic groups. They have culture (*tamen you wenhua*), unlike the Bulang or the Lahu, because the Tai possess a written language based on ancient Pali-Hindu texts and are practicing Theravada Buddhists who train young males in the old traditions.[8] These beliefs are mitigated by the influence of Chinese (Han) entrepreneurs, who remark on how "the locals" (an epithet for the Tai) are stupid because they do not have a clue about how to run a business: "Locals don't know how to eat bitterness" (*bendi ren bu hui chi ku*). The concept of eating bitterness begs further explanation. To eat bitterness in China has multiple meanings, but here it means that one must work hard and suffer in order to reap the benefits of one's labors at a later time. When outsiders say the locals don't know how to eat bitterness, they mean that they do not know how to delay gratification.

The Tai have in fact become economically and socially marginalized in urban Jinghong because of their absence from one of the main businesses, that of selling sex. Local Tais explained their absence in the sex industry as linked to their strength in maintaining cultural values and traditions. Here the local Tai read themselves as superior to the Han, who have forgotten traditional Confucian notions of fidelity. But, while in the Tai villages people upheld notions of traditional culture that read against images of sexual promiscuity, in the city of Jinghong local Tais often internalized their inferiority. Many local Tai entrepreneurs who were engaged in business similarly mentioned how their friends and family members didn't like or know how to work hard. When I asked Ai Yang, the young owner of an appliance store, how he could call his Tai compatriots "lazy, unable to eat bitterness" when he was successful, he shrugged his shoulders and said, "I am different, not like other Tai."

In Jinghong, Tai villagers no longer grow as much sticky rice as they once did because they have become landlords for the local Han immigrants, who live beneath Tai homes in the spaces formerly reserved for farm machinery and pigs. While locals joke about Han living in spaces formerly reserved for the pigs, the situation of the locals is very precarious because the government may crack down on illegally registered tenants at any time (Evans 1996). These tenants are often immigrant youths who migrate to Jinghong from China's hinterland in search of employment and the good life. Another consequence of the Hanification of Xishuangbanna is that Tai businesses are being replaced with Han ones. In 1994, on Manting Street there were three or four restaurants run by local Tais, but by 1996 there were no Tai businesses. Most of the Tai-owned restaurants had been bought by Han businessmen, who then turned them into clubs replete with pseudo-Tai dancing, dinner table massages, and pseudo-Tai food.

One local teacher, Ai Lao, a young man of thirty-four, complained bitterly that the breakdown in Tai culture has been detrimental not only to Tai farming methods but to traditional cultural practices. Ai Lao was involved in several projects intended to revive Tai culture: playing in a local, all-Tai, popular music band; teaching at the local temple school; and organizing cross-border exchanges with Tai-Lue in Myanmar, Laos, and Thailand. For Lao Yang and Lao Ai, the city of Jinghong embraces both the promotion of Tai culture (since it brings in money and capital) and revulsion against and destruction of that culture (by sanitizing Tai practices; refusing to promote Tai language, culture, and religion within the city; and eliminating village farm plots). The consequences of this production and destruction of Tai culture are that several Banna Tai are looking to the former borders of the Tai nation for support and capital for such endeavors as training young monks and investment in Jinghong businesses (Hsieh 1995).[9]

Although the Han eroticization of Tai ethnicity has eroded Tai identity, it is precisely this Han representation of Tai women as beautiful, sexualized, and at home in their tropical paradise that makes Banna a desirable travel location. When the Han Chinese majority in Banna configure the Tai in their own imaginations as licentious, free, and lazy, the Tai are conceptualized as weak, eroticized subjects for people in greater China. Here the logic of internal colonialism takes root because the Tai are constructed as an other and as sexualized in the Han imagination. As Louisa Schein (1994) points out, in China desire has been fused with both *writing material used one or more times after earlier writing has been erased.*

the sexual and the political. The eroticism of the Tai body has been written over by what Schein calls "a palimpsest of other meanings" inclusive of freedom, individualism, progress, a critique of morality, and nonconformism (144). In Banna, the Han represent and perform Tainess for a Han audience in order to achieve secondary gains in their own economic status, personal freedoms, desires, and amusements.

In Jinghong, what is Tai sells. One merely becomes Tai in order to profit. This applies most readily to Han women who dress in Tai clothing to attract Han male customers. Local Han prostitutes dress in Tai ethnic clothing, which is a close-fitting, floor-length sarong and a short-cropped, long-sleeved top. However, other women—tour guides, restaurant servers, and dancers—also dress in Tai ethnic clothing and mimic Tai hairstyles. Since Han Chinese women from Sichuan and Guizhou who work in the brothels, nightclubs, and karaoke bars all dress in the traditional clothing of the Tai minority, they are often perceived as local Tai by Han tourists. All one has to do is speak with these women to know they are not from Jinghong, for their accents immediately give them away. To clarify how this performance of ethnicity operates in one place where fantasies of the erotic are located, I turn now to my description of a hair salon/brothel.

Female Fantasies of Work: Madam Liu's Hair Salon Madam Liu operates a hair salon that is also a brothel.[10] Her story provides an ethnographic canvas on which to sketch the larger issues of how tourism in a border region actually instantiates the social imaginary that tourism aims to provide. As I mentioned previously, prostitution temporarily functions as a quasi-legal business under the gaze of the state. I am defining it as quasi-legal because prostitution functions under the guise of barbers and hair stylists. Whereas the salon is legal, the back rooms are illegal. The local policemen warn some of their favorite brothel owners when a nationwide government anticrime campaign (*yanda*) begins. There is definitely a complicated but often cohesive and cordial relationship between legitimate businesses, businesses on the periphery such as hair salons that are also brothels, and the local police, who represent the Chinese state. All the activities associated with what I dub sex tourism are not legally sanctioned by the state but are allowed to function in certain guises. The sex industry masks itself under certain types of hair salons that are spatially divided by task: the outer storefronts are hair salons; the middle rooms are massage parlors; and the inner sanctums, small rooms with beds, are brothels.

Liu, a Rubenesque Han woman in her late thirties, is divorced from her husband, who lives in Guiyang with their eight-year-old daughter. Liu has been a resident of Jinghong since 1994. She and her lover Wang, a tour bus driver, own the New Wind Hair Salon. In our conversations, Liu said she was extremely glad when she came to Banna; it meant an escape from drudgery and her miserable marriage. She regularly works from one o'clock in the afternoon to one in the morning, beginning with haircuts in the afternoon and at night dispatching her staff out on calls. The majority of the sex conducted through the salon consists of hand jobs, or what Liu calls "massages," given in the back room. Sex acts that require condoms are only conducted on out-calls. Men negotiate these encounters by driving up to the salon and discussing the price and place with Liu. She then yells to a woman to come over and accompany the man to his hotel. When I met Liu, she had four women working in her salon—Zhu and Yue from Ruili, a border town in northwestern Yunnan, and Zhang and Zhou from rural villages upriver from Luzhou in Sichuan—all ethnically Han.

When I first met Yue she was twenty-three years old. She had come to Jinghong from Ruili only one month earlier because work opportunities were better. She said: "In Ruili the hair salons employing prostitutes only operate for local businessmen, not tourists. You cannot make as much money. Local businessmen are not interested in paying local women for their services, but in Banna you become something special." Zhu, also twenty-three and from Ruili, came to Banna to visit her sister, who worked in one of the gambling salons. Her sister made really good money. Although Zhu wasn't making as much as her sister, she preferred Jinghong to Ruili. Yue, Zhu, Zhou, and Zhang all said they made from 300 to 600 yuan per day, 70 percent of which they give to Liu. Most days they take home 100 yuan, meaning that they clear on average 3,000 to 4,000 yuan a month—six to ten times what shop assistants or restaurant workers make. While Yue and her sister spend most of their earnings on themselves, on fancy clothing, perfumes, and jewelry, Zhang, a twenty-seven-year-old married woman from Sichuan, sends a portion home to her family. Zhang told me that her parents are peasants and she has not told them what kind of work she does in Jinghong. Her biggest frustration is that she misses her six-year-old son terribly. She only gets to see him at Spring Festival (Chunjie). But there is no work in Luzhou.

Liu liked to discuss female body types and joke about sex with analogies through eating and food. She often teased me by insisting: "How can you know China, without tasting Chinese men . . . ?" She explained: "In Banna, men taste like sticky rice (*nomifan*), in Thailand like pineapple rice (*boluofan*), and in Guizhou like plain white rice (*bai fan*)." Zhu and Yue were the most popular women in the salon, perhaps because they often dressed in Tai clothing, beautiful batiks that were closely cropped to fit their figures. Regarding her dress, Yue explained that the men who come to Banna really like the Tai look and to attract customers and keep Liu happy she often dressed that way. While she laughed at the idea that anyone could mistake her for a Tai woman, she said that Tai clothes are so beautiful that men come in just to look. That brings more customers into the salon.

There are more than a hundred hair salons throughout Jinghong that resemble Liu's. Some are genuine beauty salons that only cut hair, others cut hair and conduct a prostitution business on the side (like Liu's), and still others are complete facades. For Liu, Yue, and Zhu, Banna is the land of opportunity but an opportunity that has to be masked—they cannot share their professions with their families in their natal homes. Because the use of hair salons as fronts for prostitution is so widespread, even mentioning that they work in one could be dangerous. Zhang would have preferred to stay on her family's land in Sichuan, for working the fields would have maintained her sense of family and a grounding in what she called her roots in the soil. Just as prostitution has to be hidden behind the facades of beauty parlors, so, too, these women had to lie to their families about what they do.

Several informants countered the view, espoused by several members of the Women's Federation, that "women are just being exploited again. . . . we are back to preliberation China. . . . and what have we gained? . . . one step forward and two steps back." What appears as a marker of difference between the preliberation sex industry and its contemporary renaissance is the fact that a number of young women consider prostitution to be a viable occupation rather than a form of ostracized servitude. Other informants remarked that "it is much easier to get a job, a good job, as a female than a male . . . there are many more opportunities." When asked about the vast differences in salary between prostitutes and female tour guides (the key tour guides are all young women under the age of thirty), one informant explained it this way: "While there is a big monetary difference, prostitutes don't get to admire their work." As a prostitute, one makes a minimum of 100 yuan (U.S.$13) per job, and some women make more than 6,000 yuan ($750) per month, but then one must pay for clothing, makeup, and other things. As a tour guide, one makes around 1,000 to 3,000 yuan a month ($130 to $400) and everything is yours to keep. Even uniforms are provided by the tour company.

As mentioned earlier, to understand Banna one must look to tourism as creating an experience outside the mundane; tourism and tourist practices build on the fantasies through which people ascribe meaning to urban living (King 1996a). To travel to Banna is to move from the profane to the sacred, to move outside of our everyday lives into fantasies marketed by re-creating authentic Tainess. Banna is that fantasy, and sex with Han women who look like beautiful Tai women is one of the pleasures it provides. However, prostitution is not a monolithic enterprise; its myriad forms are expressed in different ways at different times and in different geographic locations.

I turn now to a tale of the many diverse male fantasies of Banna. While women prostitutes capitalize on their beauty and mimic Tai ethnicity, it is men who consume such images by consuming these women. If women come to Banna for money, profit, and freedom, the question remains, why are men coming?

Male Fantasies of Place: Manager Zhou Conducting head counts on each flight from which I disembarked in Banna revealed that most planes were full of men. On some flights of two hundred passengers, I was one of only two or three females. A few times, all-female work unit tour groups skewed the balance to around 60 percent males and 40 percent females. Borrowing from Appadurai's (1996) work on transnational flows and consumption, I argue that Chinese male tourists come to Banna to chase young Tai women as markers of modern urban consumption practices. Several informants mentioned a saying in Banna that in literal translation means "eating spring rice" (*chi qingchun fan*). It is a metaphor for young girls living off youth and beauty that will not last forever.[11]

As China enters international markets, new products must be consumed to denote the increasing prosperity of its citizenry. Therefore, sexual products and the consumption of sex (the exchange of money for sexual favors) become part of what it means to have a modern sexual identity in northern cities. Wealthy men consume bottles of XO cognac, fancy hotel rooms, and dinners as well as these fantasy women in Jinghong. Banna's sexual pleasures carry connotations far beyond intrinsic physical satisfaction to cultural capital. In Banna, it is precisely these nouveau riche male tourists who come to consume sex and women. While the Yunnan government condones neither prostitution nor gambling, several informants described Jinghong as one of the most popular places in China to seek both (for other locales, see Allison 1994 and McClintock 1995).[12] A wealthy Hong Kong businessman sitting in a friend's cafe asked a local businessman in what he should invest. He was told by the local man: "Why, prostitution and gambling, that is where the money is." While workers like Liu, Zhang, and Zhu have varied relationships with the city of Jinghong, the tourists are the ones who ultimately drive the images of eroticization. Their relationship with the place provides another picture of Jinghong. In illustrating this drive to eroticize place, I turn to Zhou, an assistant manager of a trading company in Jiangxi, who was in Banna for an extended business meeting and vacation.

After numerous requests from Liu's customers to join them in the nightclubs, one night I acquiesced and went on a date with Manager Zhou, who frequented the hair salon for massages. I decided it would be an ethnographic exchange: he wanted to discuss American politics as we gambled and danced, and I wanted to find out why he came to Banna. After several hours of gambling at the New Elephant Hotel, I finally asked him about Liu. He told me: "Of course, you know she is not a hairdresser?" I replied that I did. When I asked him how he and his colleagues came to engage in massages, he laughed: "I'm on vacation, away from my wife. Of course, I want some relaxation accompanied by beautiful women." One friend distinguished his feelings about infidelity this way: "Sex is like eating. . . . If I eat cabbage [*baicai*] every day, I may want some fancy seafood [*haiwei*] once in a while. If you eat haiwei every day, you want baicai . . . [for] one cannot live by eating the same thing all the time. . . . It gets boring!"

Manager Zhou did not discuss his trips to Banna with his wife but said that going there was a frequent treat for him. He didn't consider gambling out of the ordinary, and he told me that the slot machines in Banna were rigged. The owners of the hotels were not honest gamblers; they cheated him. For Manager Zhou, Banna was a place of not only fantasies come true but a break in his routine, a chance to both work and play in a freer environment. He repeated, like a mantra, that in Banna the women are more open because of the influences of Tai culture and their openness about sexual promiscuity (*luanjiao*) made this place desirable to him.

Conclusion Xishuangbanna offers the escapist pleasures of an exotic location and the comforts of an urban setting. Han migration and China's state tourism policies have transformed a series of large Tai villages into the cosmopolitan city of Jinghong—a city that caters to Han tourists seeking an escape from Han China. As an escape that remains within China's geographic and linguistic borders, Jinghong is titillating yet not threatening. Xishuangbanna itself provides an instructive example of China's ethnic quilt. The place demonstrates the notion that minorities are cousins, but Han are the oldest (*laoda*). The older and wiser Han must teach their younger cousins, the Tai.[13]

The infelicitous coupling of market reform and sexuality within the context of modernity has transformed China, resulting in the proliferation of people living, working, and traveling in this borderland. Newly blossoming occupations encompass employees in both legal and semilegal endeavors, including women who cut hair, own beauty salons, work as prostitutes, and serve as tour guides. All of these people create a modern vision of Banna that bolsters its reputation as a fantasy land. Other locals, such as the police, have developed even grander visions of Banna, beyond its Disneyesque Tai pleasure ground, based on their own transnational crossings.

Banna is marked as a key site in the Han imaginary, a place of desire: the desire to work and tour and the desire to consume and produce images of the exotic. It is quintessentially what Schein (1999) dubs an "imagined cosmopolitan" of late capitalist consumption because people consume not only products but practices and moral codes. Understanding how travelers, migrants, and locals negotiate the ruptures between imagining Banna and living there every day enriches our understanding of the urban as a site of desire in 1990s China.

Notes

My greatest thanks go to those who offered me their hospitality, generosity, and assistance in Yunnan. My fieldwork in Southwest China on the HIV/AIDS epidemic was generously supported by a Fulbright-Hays Doctoral Dissertation Fellowship (1995–96), the Wenner-Gren Foundation (1996), the Center for AIDS Prevention Studies at UC San Francisco (1994), and UC Berkeley's Anthropology Department's Lowie Fund (1997). Lisa Rofel, Aihwa Ong, Virginia Cornue, Lisa Hoffman, Liz Herskovits, Tim Kingston, Matthew Rudolph, and the members of Stanley Brandes's and Sharon Kaufman's dissertation writing seminars all kindly commented on earlier drafts. Finally, I am extremely grateful for the incisive comments from the two anonymous reviewers for Duke University Press and especially the editors of this volume.

1   First let me note that in Xishuangbanna a popular folk notion classifies the Tai into three subgroups: the floral Tai, the water Tai, and the black Tai. Prof. Gao Lishi, a Tai linguist at Yunnan Minorities Institute, in an interview in January 1996, said that ethnologists classify the Tai into ten groups that speak at least three mutually unintelligible languages.

2   My original dissertation research focused on the proliferation of AIDS and sexually transmitted diseases in Yunnan. Jinghong was selected as my field site precisely because of this sex industry, one that many doctors, bureaucrats, and officials in Kunming characterized as symptomatic of Tai-Lue cultural values. The underlying assumption was that the Tai are a loose, sexually uninhibited people (*xingluan*), and my role, according to several individuals in the provincial medical community, was to find the cultural clues linking the Tai to risky sexual practices that predisposed them to HIV/AIDS.

3   Xishuangbanna has a land base of 19,000 square kilometers, is situated on the Yunnan Plateau, and is divided by the Lancang River. It has over 1 million people and is divided into three counties and three main cities: Menghai to the southwest, Mengla to the southeast, and Jinghong close to the center.

4   There are currently twelve travel tours available around Xishuangbanna, including excursions into the border regions in Myanmar and Laos and further south into northern Thailand (Qing 1995).

5   Sara Davis (1999) notes that the contemporary Mandarin term *Man* is an inaccurate translation of the Tai term Ban, which in Tai would be Banjinglan and Banting, the old township names.

6   These names are pseudonyms, and to further protect them I have only given them one name instead of the usual two metonyms used to denote respect in China.

7   Historians note that this southern frontier was long perceived as a desolate waste-land of malarial and leprosy-infested jungles. The perception today is that malaria and leprosy have only recently been eradicated—and not entirely from Xishuang-banna. See Wang Lianfang 1993 and Yin Shaoting 1986.

8   The Tai language has undergone changes similar to Kazak in Xinjiang. There, as in Banna, three generations often cannot communicate through one writing system because of policies that aimed to simplify China's minority languages in the name of literacy. In Banna, what is called *lao Tai wen*, or old Tai, is now the official language. However, from 1961 to 1986 a script called *xin Tai wen*, or new Tai, was used in the schools, the media, and official documents. This renaissance in Tai culture can be attributed to links with Southeast Asia, where several other countries' minority groups use old script. China is unique in having raised only a generation or two on new Tai. However, unlike the efforts to romanize ancient Arabic script in Xinjiang, old and new Tai are not mutually unintelligible (interview with Tai linguist Gao Lishi at the Yunnan Minzu Xueyuan, January 1996).

9   Simultaneously, many Tai have resigned themselves to what they deem the final stage in the complete destruction of the Tai-Lue that liberation and the Cultural Revolution began. Other Scholars such as Shihchung Hsieh believe that the closer the Tai are to northern Thailand, the more dangerous the reaction of the central Chinese government might be (Hsieh 1995: 328). I should also note that while Tai women were noticeably absent from the sex industry in Banna one woman who owned a brothel was Tai.

10 Prostitution is often a symbolically gendered category, as the majority of sex workers are females; however, not all of them are female. This ethnography privileges the female sex worker because that is the one to whom I had access. There were rumors about the presence of gigolos (*mianshou*) in Jinghong, but I did not come into con-tact with any of them.

11 I would like to thank Mayfair Yang for pointing this out in her commentary at the Ethnographies of the Urban in Contemporary China workshop in September 1997 at UC Santa Cruz.

12 Brothel owning is one of the crimes punishable by death under China's legal code.

13 I want to thank Melissa Brown for reminding me of this notion of ethnicity in China.

Part Three Negotiating Urban Spaces

Nancy N. Chen Health, Wealth, and the Good Life

"The streets are much more lively (*renao*) than before." Ah Deng, a photographer in his late forties, continued to elaborate over coffee as we sat in a cybercafe of a newly opened bookstore in Dongsi, one of Beijing's busiest commercial areas. "Now you can find anything you want nearby instead of having to bike across town looking for just one thing. Even on weeknights you can go strolling and check out the stores. If you don't want to shop, you can just check out all the new performances on the street." Similar pronouncements about the quickened tempo and transformed material life in the Deng reform urban context were made to me by numerous friends and colleagues when I returned to China in 1995. In contrast to the pronounced silence and intense control of the streets in the immediate post-Tiananmen years, the economic transformations and construction boom of the mid-1990s had literally reconfigured the urban landscape. In the process of market revitalization, health-seeking practices had also changed as consumers renegotiated shifting boundaries and meanings of medical care.

This chapter is concerned with how meanings of health and well-being become reconfigured as biomedical technologies and transnational pharmaceuticals become widely available and as Chinese medicines also continue to undergo vast changes in mainland China. My analysis addresses the transformation of national programs of health care from socialist communal care to individual consumption. Shifts in state health care policies during the post-Mao period, from guaranteed medical care to more complex combinations of reimbursement and self-payment, have meant that individuals are ever more responsible for health care costs. There is an increasing everyday sense that well-being and the pursuit of health require more personal wealth in an era of commodified medicine.

Health and wealth have always been intertwined as ideals in Chinese culture. In imperial China, health consisted of a regimen with specific dietary and seasonal prescriptions. Ancient medical texts promoted longevity and vitality as equally precious as any form of wealth. The concept of health as wealth was also asserted in the early decades of socialism to counter the prior experiences of floods, earthquakes, famine, and disease over the past century, when "the sick man of Asia" was often invoked to describe China's perceived place in the world. Mao believed that a large population of healthy bodies represented individual well-being as well as the power of the nation. Early socialist public health initiatives under Mao thus promoted healthy subjects as the wealth of the nation. In the early years of socialism, national programs were devoted to eradicating infectious diseases, developing mental health care programs, and encouraging exercise activities in all institutions. In the current reconfiguration of health care, health is less a marker of the wealth of the nation than of the wealth of individuals. New economies of bodies in the 1990s were no longer determined by rural-urban distinctions but by more complex lines of wealth and access in a market economy. One must possess many resources and much capital to have access to medicine and health. What follows is the suggestion that late-twentieth-century health pursuits have simultaneously changed people's experiences with their bodies and the urban. Following Sennett's analysis of cities and bodies (1994), in which bodies reflect metropolitan dynamics and spatial relations, my discussion will explore how once familiar categories of urbanity and ruralness have shifted in these changing health regimes.

Sensibilities about health and the good life are profoundly experienced through the body and increasingly shaped by consumer culture. Bodies can be viewed as key sites that document the social and political changes that have taken place over the past decade in China. Bryan Turner notes that in late capitalism "the body is indeed the principal topic of civilization in a somatic regime" (1996: 34). Chinese socialist discourses have consistently framed bodies in disciplinary terms of civilization and *suzhi* or "essence" (Anagnost 1995). In the Chinese urban context, bodies and embodiment practices are often structured in dialogic relation to the state. My research with health practitioners and social healing groups indicates that the strict delineation between urban cosmopolitan and rural peasant bodies has shifted as consumption practices have relocated geographies of distinction through the movement of goods and ideologies. Brownell's notion of body culture also provides a useful framework in which to situate body practices and microtechniques of discipline, or "training the body," that have shaped the bodies of athletes and ordinary Chinese citizens (1995). As I will address in the following section, *qigong* and *yangge* were two distinct body practices that surfaced in 1990s urban China that seemed to emphasize social aspects of healing as well as individual physical regimens. The two forms are examples of a body culture that offered communal alternatives to the trend of intensified individual consumption and unequal access to health.

Bodily regimens have been transformed as daily life has become saturated with material goods such as vitamin supplements, health aids, brand label exercise clothing, and beauty products. New meanings of well-being and the good life are promoted through individual consumption of medicinal products and beauty aids. Although the association of the good life with material goods and well-being is not a new concept in socialist China, with the expansion of materialism there are more elaborate systems of classification. During the 1970s, there was a familiar saying about three main items that everyone ought to acquire: a watch, a radio, and a bicycle. This list was revised in the 1980s to include a washing machine, a color television, and a refrigerator. In the 1990s, the list of desirable consumer goods has expanded considerably beyond three items and is distinguishable according to age, gender, region, and occupation. Such popular sayings indicate that Chinese consumers are familiar with the world of goods, however limited or expansive. In the 1990s, specific health practices and commodities such as pharmaceuticals reflected highly differentiated and gendered meanings of the good life and access to health. As Brownell's and Gottschang's chapters in this volume also suggest, such gendered concepts of beauty and well-being present new options through which urban residents are choosing to represent themselves. To be healthy these days means that one is pursuing a lifestyle in which one is externally marked and engaged in consumer culture. In contrast to more traditional forms of social healing, in which phenomenological experiences simultaneously embody self and others, these new forms of medicine indicate that new regimes of health care based on participation in circuits of consumption and what Farquhar has referred to as "the radical valorization of the personal" are under way (1996: 240).

Bodily experiences are profoundly shaped by the urban context as well as revealing of social orders introduced by new markets, body regimens, and gendered technologies (Sennett 1994; Balsamo 1995; Bray 1997). Sennett's analysis of European cities in specific historical moments addressed the extensive impact of urban material forms such as streets, public spaces, and architecture on the spatial relations and ordering of bodies as well as the formation of civic subjectivities. Similarly, in the cities of Beijing and Shanghai, where I conducted most of the ethnographic research for this chapter, daily life in the 1990s has been filled with breathtaking changes that have great impact on people's lived experiences of city life (Guldin 1996). In spite of early socialist comparisons between the rural and urban that sketched city life as pathological—filled with crowds, pollution, and corruption—the urban context is nonetheless a privileged site with regard to the infrastructure of health care and new drug markets. After discussing two notions of healing that emphasize communal forms of practice, I will turn to circulating urban ideals of health that are clearly based on having the means of access and wealth. Even as notions of well-being and health care become more commodified, there are multiple notions of health circulating in urban regions that draw significantly upon the rural as well as the transnational.

Into the Streets   At twilight, several dozen women and a few men in their midforties to sixties gather to practice an assembly of folk dances to the accompaniment of loud drumming. Most dancers wear colorful clothing, have silk flowers or combs in their hair, and carry large fans. Some women even paint their faces with bright rouge and lipstick. The usually male drummer and sometimes accompanying horn and cymbal players tie turbans or place towels on their heads in a distinctive peasant look. The music is loud and lively, easily drawing crowds that look on as the yangge dance troupe practices. As the epitome of liveliness (*renao*), the colorful gatherings extend into the night, illuminating streets filled with construction.

In the 1990s, urban spaces were key sites of popular communal healing practices in mainland China. Numerous qigong practitioners and masters literally took to the streets, as well as occupying other major venues such as parks, work units, and stadiums, to participate in group sessions. Healing in this way was simultaneously a group experience and a means of experiencing one's own body. Taking up qigong in the urban context meant that a practitioner could encounter diverse groups and other practitioners from all walks of life, whether in packed stadiums, in auditoriums, or on the street. Intense visualization of one's inner body in order to cultivate the life energy (qi) of the body was a crucial component of qigong practices. Both male and female practitioners of all ages participated in qigong sessions. Ironically, even as most qigong practice took place throughout the cities of China, it was primarily in the parks, among the trees and open spaces, that practitioners could escape the pressures of urban life—crowds, tight living conditions, and ever-present pollution. Parks contained elements of the rural within the urban and provided refuge from everyday city life.

Instead of seeking a quiet respite from city life at dawn before other city dwellers stirred, yangge dancers were very much part of the city scene, located primarily on street corners and under noisy highway overpasses. Every evening at dusk one could hear drumming and reed instruments and see older women dressed in brightly colored clothes and waving fans while taking elaborate steps. Crowds of a few dozen or even several hundred formed each night to watch the dancers practice. The street corners quickly turned into impromptu street fairs as vendors hawked their refreshments. Despite the fact that these troupes seemed to provide a bright oasis of color in the grayness of Beijing traffic, as well as a spectacle of free entertainment each night, many neighbors complained about the noise and the garbage generated by onlookers. Other city residents made rude comments about the appearance of the dancers, remarking how inappropriately dressed the older women were. On a taxi ride over the Third Ring Road, which circles Beijing, Xiao Tang, a young woman in her twenties, wrinkled her nose as we passed a yangge gathering. She quickly remarked how garish it was for older women to wear heavy makeup and parade around each night. While qigong practitioners in the late 1980s and 1990s enjoyed their practices in privacy in city parks and popular discourses focused on the phenomenological, even magical, the yangge troupes of the early to mid-1990s were subject to public discourses about age and beauty.

By 1995, each neighborhood in Beijing had semiorganized dance troupes of older women ranging from their mid-forties to their seventies. When interviewed, most women explained that they had previously practiced other forms of exercise such as morning calisthenics, disco dancing, qigong, and taiji (a slow, meditative martial art often referred to as tai chi outside of China). The women now preferred yangge as a form of healing for their ailments, such as rheumatism, as well as for the social support this activity generated. Lin, in her sixties and an avid organizer in her neighborhood, praised at length the health benefits of yangge to me. When asked about her previous health pursuits and regimens, she replied, "I've done them all—taiji, qigong, dancing—at home, at work, in the park. But yangge is best because it's more lively and we get to move around more, all over the city in fact." In contrast to earlier state discourses calling for the regulation of qigong, most official media portrayed yangge as a way for older women to enjoy more youthful activities rather than a potentially subversive activity.

Even though yangge initially emerged in the urban landscape as a predominately women's leisure activity and therefore harmless, as with qigong, the municipal government quickly began to regulate the activity, requiring each troupe to register for a formal permit to practice on street corners. The impromptu crowds of up to several hundred people that gathered to watch in the evenings were too much of a distraction for city authorities and often obstructed traffic. With such a formal structure however, it became possible for yangge troupes to compete with each other. They became official representatives of civic neighborhoods at sporting events, even dancing in the opening ceremonies. During the Midautumn Festival of 1995, I followed one troupe to Beijing's Haidian Stadium, where more than twenty different troupes had gathered to perform. As each troupe walked into the stadium, the front line carried bright flags announcing the district they represented while members of the audience roared and cheered. Yangge thus initially occupied spaces within neighborhoods and on street corners, but it soon created a social world for health-seeking activities, performance, and social engagement that the state recognized and eventually regulated. Regulation by municipal authorities indicated that, while people might continue to gather spontaneously, there was concern for the potential disruptions that could erupt on the streets. The collective response to lively activities in public could still slip too easily into chaos (*luan*), which resonated with deeply felt memories of the Tiananmen demonstrations only five years before. Renegotiating and claiming urban spaces on the part of social groups, however benign, still required a complex process of recognition by authorities.

The two examples above illustrate how healing can be simultaneously an individual experience and a social practice. These healing activities in an urban context were also unique, as both qigong and yangge were derived from indigenous styles that were common in nonurban sites such as the mountain temple or countryside. The practices emphasized communal bodies that were integrated at multiple levels with one's own body, the local group, and even larger neighborhood associations aligned by popular interests that did not necessarily originate with state institutions such as the work unit or municipal authorities. Most practitioners in both of these forms talked about how the collective energies or spirit of the group were a primary part of the experience and enhanced one's own practice. As a qigong practitioner at the Temple of Heaven noted, "The *qi* of the group can be invigorating and is quite different from the qi of one person." Yangge troupe members also remarked on how it was the collective music, movements, and energies generated during a performance that made this activity so engaging and productive for the individual. Healing the body communally thus provided an important context for attending to one's own health.

In the following section, I shift from popular healing practices such as qigong and yangge to consider the impact of the pharmaceutical industry on these and other health pursuits. The emergent pharmaceutical industry, like the related health and beauty products circulating in China, has begun to target a consumer-oriented body that is based on appearance and corporeal symptoms of illness rather than addressing the mind/body or inner being. Rather than focusing upon the social experience of healing, the emphasis of the drug companies has shifted to the commodification of health and well-being exemplified by the consumption of specific drugs and other products. These are processes that have intensified in the 1990s. A large number of my informants and close friends have taken up sideline employment as cosmetics representatives or multivitamin sales-persons and are usually staunch users of the latest over the counter (OTC) drugs from Europe or the United States. Patients were no longer ad-dressed as such by the drug industry and were referred to instead as clients and consumers. The new forms of health care and body regimens emphasized consumption, commodification, and above all the individu-alized body.

Remapping Health Care and Meanings of Place On the eve of the Cul-tural Revolution, in a 1965 "Directive on Public Health," Mao launched a tirade on rural and urban health care inequalities, beginning with the dramatic statement: "The Ministry of Public Health is not a Ministry of Public Health for the people, so why not change its name to the Ministry of Urban Health, the Ministry of Gentleman's Health, or even to the Min-istry of Urban Gentleman's Health?" Noting that the vast majority of the Chinese were peasants in rural areas, he urged the radical reformation of medical education and the distribution of care with the now famous state-ment "In medical and health care put the emphasis on the countryside."[1]

China's socialist health care system continues to be best known for the barefoot doctors, now referred to as rural doctors, who were sent to transform health care and public health in the countryside. Indeed, in the campaign against schistosomiasis and other infectious diseases, these workers were immensely effective. Yet, despite the barefoot doctors and other rural health care initiatives that greatly improved access to health care and prevention of epidemics, afflicted individuals and their families would still draw upon *guanxi* (local networks and social connections) and monetary resources to seek diagnoses and therapies from doctors with better reputations, most likely in the cities. The significance of the urban has particular resonance for health care in China. At the onset of the twentieth century, medical clinics and "modern" hospitals were pri-marily located in the major cities and provincial capitals. Concrete differ-ences between urban and rural hospitals could be located in a hierarchy that began with Beijing, Shanghai, and Guangzhou at the top. Better funding, staffing, and instruments would more likely be found in urban regions. In the 1950s and 1960s, many of the largest hospitals were built in provincial urban centers, while cities such as Beijing and Shanghai reno-vated already existing metropolitan hospitals. A handful of older institutions that were remnants of original missionary hospitals, such as that of the Peking Union Medical College or the Shanghai Psychiatric Hospital, were renamed and reorganized. Rural and urban inequalities in health care continued throughout the 1980s. Even at the onset of the 1990s rural and suburban residents interviewed in my early fieldwork drew an overwhelming picture of the disparity between rural and urban health care. In order to receive better diagnoses and care, regardless of whether they were in the form of traditional Chinese medicine (TCM) or biomedicine, residents believed it was worth the long train rides and other efforts to visit an urban clinic or hospital. In a visit to a rural Shandong hospital in 1991, there still seemed to be differences in equipment and staff training.

Despite Mao's rural health care campaign, the urban has always been the center of health care, in part to support the leaders of the country. In the best-selling and widely discussed memoir *The Private Life of Chairman Mao,* Mao Zedong's private physician, Dr. Li Zhisui, described the intense attention he had given to Mao's body as well as the regimen that had been needed to meet the national leader's corporeal and medical needs. Mao's body, like those of the emperors, was read as emblematic of the state such that the entirety of the country's needs would be fulfilled if his needs were met first. Such a prioritizing of needs and medical access is still present today, and special hospitals or wings of hospitals are reserved for cadres.

In recent years, two trends have made rural-urban differences in access to health care less distinct. First, as more outside funding from nongovernmental organizations (NGOs) and the World Health Organization (WHO) have targeted rural providers, certain biomedical technologies have been acquired by rural hospitals, making the trip to larger hospitals for tests unnecessary. The second trend that has shifted meanings of health and wealth is the burgeoning pharmaceutical industry. Rural consumers can readily visit entrepreneurial private doctors in the countryside to purchase pharmaceutical drugs that are produced there (Farquhar 1996). There has been a vast transformation in the notion of the good life in China such that one's spatial location in the rural or urban is not as important as one's ability to consume. As other authors in this volume suggest, the good life is not necessarily urban nor urban produced. Rather, the urban is a nexus or set of "social arenas" (Appadurai 1986) where people can seek a variety of commodities and opportunities. Instead of conceptualizing these social arenas solely in terms of location, it is also important to address how time, or specifically speed, is increasingly a crucial component of health care. The instantaneous and often spontaneous adoption of new health products or technology by consumers and larger institutions remains intimately tied to long-standing beliefs about health and the good life. Under present urbanization policies, rural and periurban regions have become increasingly urbanized and less peripheral to the flow of goods, technologies, and services. Similar patterns are also occurring with regard to health care. Distinctions once based on one's place of residence, and hence access, have given way to one's location as a player in the market economy and the ability to gain access to a healthy lifestyle as a consumer.

Consuming Medicine and Popular Culture In "Eating Chinese Medicine" Judith Farquhar points out that the lengthy process of preparing bitter-tasting herbal remedies is not only an expensive one but perhaps also belongs to a past generation, suggested by "Gourmet," by Lu Wenfu, who had the taste and sensibilities for traditional Chinese foods and medicines (1987). As the forms of "traditional" medicines are being re-packaged for convenience, faster consumption, and less pungent odors, place figures prominently in both their production and consumption. In traditional Chinese medicine, herbal medicines gathered nearby were viewed as most appropriate for one's constitution and most potent for treating ailments. In the Chinese pharmaceutical industry, place also matters immensely, as consumers pay attention to the site of production from whence a drug originates, despite how far it might travel to reach the local clinic. There is great concern for authenticity and reliability of drugs, particularly as pirate firms are believed to produce inferior and less efficacious drugs for much profit.

Consuming medicine does not merely refer to the ingestion of herbal medicine or pharmaceutical drugs by patients. The flows of biomedical technology and ideologies have contributed to a booming market in health goods and services, which are also transforming notions of health. Consuming medicine in China today is increasingly a marker of the significance of place and a person's location in the new economy of bodies. Place continues to be crucial as the state health care system is reconfigured relative to the emerging market in biomedical technologies and the pharmaceutical industry. The urban context continues to figure prominently in the center of the latest medical technologies and concentrated health services.

Since the 1980s, most major transnational pharmaceutical firms have established operations in China, often keeping representative offices in the metropolitan centers with assembly plants owned by overseas Chinese conveniently located in nearby towns or industrial parks. The firms capitalize on the fact that Chinese patients spend far more on prescriptions (60 percent of total health care expenditures) than their counterparts in the United States (8 percent) and Germany (12 percent).[2] Such differences can be ascribed to the fact that as Chinese hospitals receive less support from the state a sure way to increase their income is with prescriptions. The more expensive the medicine (i.e., imported drugs) the more revenue for hospitals. The lucrative market in pharmaceuticals thus boomed in the early 1990s. Local Chinese firms also joined the fray with state support, making the domestic market even more competitive and complex for new consumers, who must make difficult choices in deciding which drugs to purchase with limited resources.

In the 1990s, dozens of new advertisements for over the counter drugs for headaches, indigestion, and children's colds were televised, printed in newspapers and magazines, and displayed on billboards and windows. These nonprescription drugs were usually produced by a transnational company with the brand name translated for the local market. The commercials had vivid images of a Chinese person, usually male, suffering with a headache, heart pain, or indigestion and taking the drug for immediate relief. Other commercials portrayed family images in which the mother would administer over the counter drugs to her children or elderly parents. There were also many advertisements for Chinese medicines produced by local companies, and these sometimes used animals or images of plants to indicate the ingredient or symbol of power that the tonic or medicine would give to the consumer. While a rich tradition of medical advertising flourished at the turn of the nineteenth century and well into the Republican era, there were few advertisements for most personal goods during the early socialist period. Even in the 1980s, many displays in department stores and commercials on state television focused on heavy industrial goods or socialist morality campaigns such as "Learning from Lei Feng."[3] In stunning contrast, contemporary advertisements for medications in China display instead individual bodies and an array of goods to promote a better life, if not the good life of modernity, which can be instantly obtained with the purchase and consumption of new pharmaceuticals and health products. The revival of old medical ads and posters from the 1920s and 1930s drew upon the brand familiarity of now elderly consumers who grew up in the Republican era.

The carnival-like atmosphere on the streets and the spectacle of seeing other customers purchasing goods contributed significantly to creating new notions and aesthetics of medicine. Moreover, prominent window displays and drug advertisements on street corners situated drugstores as *the* site of health and good life rather than the hospital clinic. On visits to a number of local shops and pharmacies in Shanghai and Beijing, the vast array of shelves devoted to over the counter medicines included biomedical drugs, traditional Chinese medicines, other types of home health aids, and even contraceptive technology. The spatial arrangements of the medical goods next to bright visual displays of smiling faces or bold characters claiming "health for a lifetime!" and sales clerks ready to answer questions could not have been more different from the atmosphere in hospital pharmacies, which were poorly illuminated and chaotic as multiple hands of patients or family members sought to fill prescriptions through the same tiny window. During weekends, with newfound leisure time (more than two days rather than the former one-day weekends), the streets and department stores of most cities would fill with large crowds of consumers looking at the new goods, which were often accompanied by promotional deals. In contrast to yangge practitioners, who took over the streets with their music and dancing and ultimately became regulated by local authorities, the commercial utilization of urban spaces by proprietors was undertaken with the tacit support of the government. Most pharmacies and drugstores held impromptu shop-front clinics where patients could consult physicians about their ailments alongside graphic posters of various disorders. Representatives of local firms, dressed in white clinical coats, would stand by to offer samples and literature on new drugs or show off the latest medical technology that could give instant diagnoses. When I visited drugstores on a typical weekend in the summer of 1997, a representative offered to assess my health status using instant palm diagnosis. For twenty-five yuan, I placed my hand onto the machine and received a printout that gave detailed figures, allowing the salesperson to assess the state of my internal organs. Displays and everyday uses of goods in the pursuit of health thus promoted a specific lifestyle of convenience and engendered consumption.

With the turn to individual consumption, there were also distinct patterns based on gender. Local pharmacies already had an abundance of goods devoted to enhancing masculinity. These medicines and products ranged from traditional Chinese remedies such as ginseng to tonics using rare animal parts and even male-enhancing products such as creams to combat baldness or promote vitality. As with most over the counter products, the prices were considerably higher than hospital prescriptions, which were listed on state formularies that accounted for most patient medications. Rather than being subsidized by the state, patients and their families would have to pay out of pocket to obtain these new products. For instance, when Formula 101, an ointment meant to remedy male baldness, was introduced to the local markets, an 8 ounce bottle initially cost more than 300 yuan (about U.S.$40, nearly two weeks salary for a state factory worker in 1991). Such goods have been joined on the shelves by cosmetics and beauty aids for the face, skin, and body. Weight reduction pills and slimming teas have become popular items not just for women but for men and adolescents. As the market in pharmaceuticals and over the counter goods continues to expand, all ages have been targeted as potential clients.

The array of goods has introduced to Chinese consumers specific ideals of health, wealth, and happiness in the form of individual regimens that diverge greatly from early socialist ideals of social welfare. Appearance and the body are emphasized as sites of individual regimen and social order. Health products and beauty aids are often situated next to posters with "before" images of various afflictions and "after" images of the ideal life and well-being that could be had by using the goods. Mass consumption has provided new arenas for bodily regimens that emphasize products for one's social skin rather than healing through communal activities such as qigong. The urban spaces in which these health practices take place relate to markets and street pharmacies rather than the institutional spaces of hospitals or even the open spaces of parks. Such spatial reconfigurations also contribute to temporal transformations of patient-consumers' encounters with medicine. Rather than waiting in long lines at hospitals, waiting at home to finish boiling herbal concoctions, or waiting for the desired results, recent medications promise fast results and immediate availability. As a young Chinese doctor remarked with despair in 1997, "These days everyone wishes to take herbal medicines in pill form, which is completely different from the way in which the remedy was meant to work for the patient." While time was essential for Lu Wenfu's gourmet and the preparation of most traditional medicinal remedies, in the era of market medicine the speed of consumption was ever more critical for both consumers and producers in the late 1990s. As Farquhar has noted, very few families have the time or labor needed to cook herbal remedies, which can take a whole day to prepare (1994a). Instead of preparing herbal remedies at home, patients and their family members were drawn into a social world where personal hygiene and beauty were featured and promoted in place of the old-fashioned socialist public health initiatives of socialism.

Drug companies are fostering direct relations between the product and the client through the market rather than hospitals. The availability of new over the counter drugs for contemporary urban consumers removes the need to queue up in clinics and wait for prescriptions. One can self-diagnose the problem, attend to one's regimen, and even gain access to medicines not available in hospitals. In the present context, anyone can be a consumer if he or she has the money and sometimes the guanxi. In earlier times, one had to be part of the system, which provided tremendous health care to the masses. These days, as access to urban care has expanded due to new pricing structures, it is increasingly possible for people from rural areas with money rather than connections to bypass the old referral system from county to province to city hospital. This approach marks another form of health care consumption in China that is quite different from the socialist system. While present strategies by pharmaceutical and other biotech companies might promote better service to clients, access to biomedical drugs and services still remains stratified. Since not all drugs, especially over the counter ones from transnational firms, and diagnostic tests are included in state-subsidized health care (where the work unit covers the expense), only those with the additional means have access to treatments and newly circulating health practices and associated lifestyles.

What is at stake in these new forms of medical practice? Who benefits or is gaining wealth as a result of engaging with these new forms of technology and pharmaceuticals? As patients become transformed into consumers through the increased options that new drugs and tests offer, it is important to locate the flows of capital that are involved. Numerous representatives of transnational and local pharmaceutical firms whom I interviewed in 1997 referred to the "gold rush" mentality of the mid 1990s (Henderson 1998). Any drug introduced to the Chinese market during that time meant profits in millions of American dollars. The Chinese state clearly has a stake in regulating the burgeoning pharmaceutical, biotech, and medical technology industries so as to profit from them. In addition, the several hundred firms and hospitals that use these services also stand to benefit. Yet for individual patients and their families, who must travel further or dig deeper into pockets to pay for more expensive drugs and treatments, these new forms mean that well-being will inevitably require more wealth than before. The distinctions between urban and rural health care have become more blurred as contemporary marketing strategies have motivated people to consume in new ways and as wealth has more centrally determined health care choices. Even though the consumption of OTCs is not limited to urban clients (rural clients are also seen as a marketing niche), the commodification of drugs and the lifestyles associated with them originated in urban areas and have penetrated the countryside through concerted efforts of drug companies. As a regional director of the country's largest transnational pharmaceutical firm confirmed to me in 1997, "We have to move out to the rest of the country, *especially the rural areas,* in order to increase our sales in this next decade" (emphasis mine). Beyond the marketing strategies of pharmaceutical firms, the traffic of commodities in medicine and technology are further linked to social networks and flows of capital. Health fads such as multivitamins, special teas, and magnetic aids circulate between country and city as travelers bring along their goods and the social life associated with them. As Jeffery's discussion of multilevel marketing organizations indicates (this volume), marketers have joined the free-for-all ethos of the market in health by selling aids such as massage tools and nutritional supplements throughout the country as part of promotional pyramid schemes.

State hospitals and private companies are not the only entities that are accumulating wealth in the lucrative health care market. In addition, I suggest that individual healers, practitioners, and producers of other forms of traditional medicine (such as temples) also stand to gain. In response to the unruly and uncontainable production of drugs and medicinal goods, state bureaucrats have been engaged in setting standards for pharmaceuticals and regulating the market, including banning fake medicines. Numerous pharmaceutical companies or bandit factories have been manufacturing drugs that have not yet met licensing standards or have no proven effects. Yet personal testimony and anecdotal descriptive narratives of miracle cures continue to be invoked to create new clienteles and consumers. Charismatic healers such as qigong masters and famous doctors are able to generate tremendous followings (and incomes) as entrepreneurial agents in this new market of healing. Sometimes the perceived authenticity of a medicine increases as the cost to the consumer increases. This process of commodification has led to the fetishization of rare animal parts and herbs grown in special places as coveted items to obtain for consumption and even better health. Gifts of expensive medicinal goods remain prominent forms of reciprocity. In sum, the new ways of consuming medicine are the very embodiment of new notions of health and wealth.

The Good Life   Cities continue to be dynamic venues and settings for new practices of well-being. However, notions about the good life are increasingly based on consumer culture rather than just residing in Chinese cities. Notions of health in both rural and urban areas of China seem to overlap with the influx of new drugs and diagnostic practices. The "traditional" is still imbued with a sense of power such that it is not unusual for urban dwellers to leave the city to make a pilgrimage to the countryside or to seek special folk medicines from specific locations. More importantly, the former rural-urban diffusion model whereby technologies, practices, and commodities are slow to "trickle down" or may never reach rural areas has been transformed by the new means of travel and communication. Health as a lifestyle now comes in commodified packages ranging from multivitamins and OTCs to more complex body regimens such as cosmetic surgery and luxury health clubs.

The good life in China today includes health and wealth perhaps with transformed meanings of access. In market socialism, health and the good life have become commodities to which supposedly anyone can gain access. Even though notions of health and its pursuits are not necessarily limited to elites such as cadres or athletes and can also include ordinary citizens, distinctions of time and place are increasingly important. Wealth is increasingly imperative both in the speedy treatment of acute disorders and in overall health maintenance. As new commodities of drugs and services require additional means of payment, a patient now consumer needs to be wealthy in order have the means to achieve a healthy lifestyle. Such notions of the good life in a market economy are quite distinct from earlier socialist ideals in which addressing individual needs through the collective process of public health would ultimately mean the good life for all. The market economy, while opening new avenues of opportunity for those willing to take risks, has further deepened already harsh inequalities. As Richard Sennett observes for citizens in many urban contexts, "More and more fenced, gated, guarded, planned communities are sold to buyers as the good life" (1994: 19). While socialist and imperial Chinese cities already had significant numbers of gates and walls, the new divisions emerging in health care are determined by barriers of wealth and how much one is capable of consuming.[4] Health care is thus packaged for individuals rather than practiced as a communal goal. Dazzling new visions of health, vitality, and power afforded by the consumption of goods and services are creating a new economy of bodies and a social geography of health care for the twenty-first century.

Tracing the transformations of health practices and flows of medicine through new modes of consumption may shed light on what repercussions urban encounters with the global and rural may have for everyday life and experience in China. Particularly in the encounter between body culture and consumer cultures, the resulting forms of gendered consumption will continue to emphasize an individualized body subsumed by desires for health and wealth and the good life.

Notes

I am grateful to the Division of Social Sciences and the Committee on Research at UC Santa Cruz for supporting the research in Shanghai and Beijing. Special thanks go to Amy Stamm for her insightful comments on an earlier version of this chapter. Thanks also go to Lyn Jeffery and the two press reviewers for their helpful comments.

1　Schram 1974: 232.
2　I am grateful to Eric Karchmer for this information.
3　See Farquhar 1996: 239–57.
4　Steven Harrell contributed this observation in reviewing an earlier version of this chapter.

Lida Junghans Railway Workers between Plan and Market

The metaphors that have been used to describe the power of market forces over environments, such as "creative destruction" (Schumpeter [1942] 1962) and the "annihilation of space by time" (Harvey 1989, 1990) are useful in describing the transformations occurring in Chinese landscapes. Yet to apprehend and interpret the meanings of what is transpiring in the contemporary Chinese landscape, now "open" (*kaifang*) to the kinds of "progress" that markets engender, it is necessary to explore the processes that produced the present from which we begin (Moore 1987). In this chapter, I draw on experiences shared with me by railway workers in order to focus attention on the constructed nature of epochal time and national space as well as the effects these notions of time and space have in the production of local distinctions. Political and economic processes associated with China's planning era (1953–1978) created strong links between workers' locations—in both geographic and social-structural space—and notions of identity and status. The legacies of those linkages shape workers' experiences of the present and future.

Many historians and theorists of modernity have treated the railroad as the quintessential emblem of the modern industrial era. If the "logic of capital" mandates the elimination of spatial barriers that limit the circulation of capital, labor, and commodities and the acceleration of production, marketing, and capital turnover, then the railway fulfills this logic in material fashion. But during the planning era China's leadership actively rejected capitalism's logic and its social values. The PRC's version of modernity was not premised on the "time-space compression" that in capitalist economies sped up labor processes and overcame the "friction"

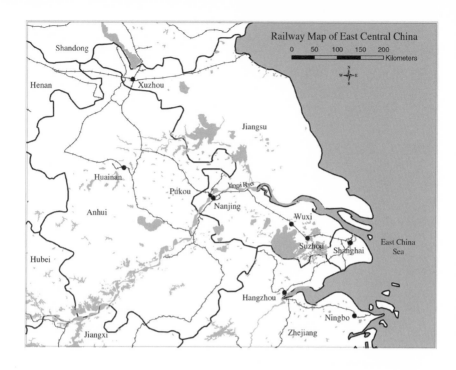

of geographic distances (Berman 1982; Harvey 1989, 1990). In socialist China, the railway was used less to foster trade and communication between regions than to integrate distant reaches of the nation for political and military goals. The friction of geographic distance was effectively maintained by means of legal and bureaucratic restrictions on the circulation of people, goods, and information. Centralized planning subordinated the projects and interests of individuals, as well as individual cities, towns, and regions, to the interests of the national whole.[1] China's planners seized the "chaotic," ambient, and self-interested time that paces lives by arresting it. Arrest occurred by "fixing" people in place and fixing places in gridlike frameworks of organization (cf. Mitchell 1991).[2] In this way, techniques for seizing time and governing space mutually reinforced each other. For people classified as urban, household registration and work unit (*danwei*) membership worked in tandem to render citizens "visible" to the state's local authorities.

China's socialist planners "spatialized" time. Citizens, economic enterprises, and whole regions were categorized according to hierarchical taxonomies that translated the fluid social processes that transpired across

China's landscape "before the revolution" into rigid classifications that placed people at greater or lesser distances from progressive virtue, conceived of in terms derived from a crudely apprehended Marxism. In those terms, coastal cities such as Shanghai were taken as ideologically subordinate to the towns and villages of the interior. China's planners denied coevalness to places and communities within their domain (cf. Fabian 1983). Categories of people and places were labeled as backward or advanced and invested in accordingly. A city like Shanghai may have been branded suspiciously "bourgeois" in terms of Maoist ideology, but in terms of material provisions Shanghai's residents and residents of any place classified as urban enjoyed benefits and provisions denied to people classified as nonurban.[3] In the marketizing era, neither the pull of ideological values nor the push of necessity draw Chinese citizens to China's less developed interior or its rural places.[4]

The landscape in the background of my presentation follows the railway tracks that lead from Shanghai to Nanjing, and beyond, across the Yangzi River Bridge to the northern Jiangsu town of Pukou (see map). In the foreground are the railway workers and cadres who organize and staff the stations, trains, and freight yards along this route. The landscape they live and work in is liminal, betwixt and between. Literally, their work links suppliers and demanders, producers and consumers. Their liminality is also figurative, meant to suggest the local categories that Chinese people use to talk about the ways space and time are organized in the People's Republic. These categories—backward and progressive (*luohou* and *xianjin*), work unit and local place (danwei and *difang*)—seem to pull ever farther apart in this liminal time, when China's institutions are making the transition between plan and market. What I have termed railway workers' *liminality* enables us to see with particular clarity the processes of creation and destruction that are occurring in China's marketizing landscape.

The terms *plan* and *market* do more than linguistically capture modes of economic coordination. In contemporary China, they also evoke distinctly temporal categories. And the epochs defined by these categories have, in turn, acquired certain qualitative, almost moral valences. The equation goes something like this: market economy succeeds planned economy, so market activities represent progress relative to the lack of progress that the plan produced. Market "places" and phenomena are now constructed as "progressive" in relation to purely planned places and the phenomena associated with them. But in an earlier era, the time of Mao, planning was seen as an advance over the unruly, unsavory, and unfair workings of feudalism, capitalism, and imperialism on the physical and human terrain.

Against this background, railway workers' experiences of their "place" in a restless landscape provide an extraordinary view of the many fractal planes that are emerging to distinguish people and places from each other in a landscape where unity and equality were once imagined as the highest good. Here I recount a few of the "spatial stories" told to me by people whose lives are situated at a very busy intersection in the Chinese landscape. The material and symbolic processes that are transforming the social and physical terrain of China show up in high relief from railway workers' perspectives.

Railway Places My primary research sites, railway danwei in Pukou, Nanjing, and Shanghai, are in a hierarchically nested relationship to each other according to the structure of power and authority in the organization of China's railroads. But, unlike the nested hierarchies first described by G. William Skinner (1977b), hierarchies whose interlocking hexagons followed the contours of local marketing and imperial administrative systems, the socialist hierarchy that orders this landscape follows patterns of its own making. The Shanghai Railway Bureau oversees a territory that encompasses Nanjing, one of six subbureaus. Nanjing, in turn, administers a domain that includes the Pukou stations and freight yards.[5]

Before we go to the railway stations in Pukou, Nanjing, and Shanghai, I want to stand back to give a panoramic view, so to speak, of the railway as a "place" in China's landscape. Railway workers I spoke with talked about two dimensions of this terrain: the abstract landscape of China's social structure and the physical landscape of Chinese terrain. In the era defined by "market socialism with Chinese characteristics," both of these spaces are being radically reconfigured. Identities and cultural meanings that had accrued to particular "places" in each of these landscapes have been destabilized.

The uniformity of the architecture of the nation's nearly six thousand stations, linked like a constellation, is a sign of the imagined community that is the nation. The train tracks connect disparate places to one circulatory system, one network of tracks, and one overarching hierarchy. These simple brick and concrete buildings bear a family resemblance to other structures built to shelter China's socialist bureaucracy. Thus, the railway itself is physically distinguished from the landscape over which it is built.

China's railway workers themselves also stand out from among their fellow workers. They were said to have had iron rice bowls long before the Chinese Communist Party created its version of that vessel. Four professions were especially envied in Republican China, and the envy is remembered in the language of rice bowls: customs officials had gold rice bowls, workers in banking had silver, workers in the Bureau of Posts and Communications had copper, and railway workers ate from bowls of iron.

Official histories of party and nation alike canonize the striking railway workers who were killed by the forces of warlord Wu Peifu in 1923. Their strike is taken as evidence of the awakening consciousness of China's working class. Close links with the Chinese military coupled with this illustrious revolutionary pedigree gave railway workers a prestigious place in the hierarchy of occupations. In addition to these symbolic distinctions, China's railway workers' salaries have been high compared to the salaries of workers in other industries. And for railway workers who staff the constellation of stations that stretches across the nation their salaries are determined by a uniform national standard, regardless of the economy of their surroundings. Distinctions that are both material, such as uniforms, benefits, and schooling, and symbolic, like work rhythms, familial and military patterns of relationships within the organization, combined to make work for the railway a specially entitled place to be when China's landscape was most powerfully shaped by the prerogatives of the plan. And, finally, the potential for physical mobility in a landscape where many were mandated to be static suggests that the railway has been a danwei with unusual advantages that distinguish it from work units tied to local bureaucratic organs. These are referred to in everyday speech as *difang,* or local, organizations.[6]

There are, of course, many categories and classifications of railway workers—they are not a unified group. But this sketch should suggest that for a working person the railway has historically been a very desirable place to be. The relationship between that "place" and the surrounding landscape is no longer as stable as it once was. The perception and experience of railway work as a uniquely privileged occupation have changed dramatically with the reforms. The powerful sense of railway workers' diminishing social status was foreshadowed to me by an old man who had retired from a railway career begun in the 1930s. When I encountered him in Beijing the year before I began my official research and told him why I was so happy to meet him, he looked at me, perplexed, and said: "Railway workers? Why are you interested in such a 'cold door' (*leng menr*)? It's the 'hot door' (*re menr*) topics like entrepreneurs (*getihu*) and county industries (*xiangzhen qiye*) that you should study."

His advice to me—that I turn my attention to another, more dynamic, sector of society, revealed the sense of relative stasis that aged industries in the state sector are thought to have in comparison with the smaller, leaner corporate entities sprouting up in China's marketizing environment. His dismissal of the railway for its "cold" stillness suggests that it is "behind" the times. The railway is cold in relation to sectors of the economy now hot with the kind of activity that generates progressive forward motion. His comment shows a significant dimension of the railway's contemporary liminality. Like many of China's gargantuan heavy industrial complexes, the railway bears the weight of an enormous dependent population. Generations of retired workers rely on the industry for pensions, hospital care, and the rest of life's necessities. Many of these industries have been allowed to go bankrupt, leaving permanent employees with small fractions of the pay they should receive. But the railway will not be allowed to go bankrupt. That much is certain to railway workers I spoke with throughout the national system. Instead, it straddles two epochs; the economically "irrational" legacies of the planning era and the current mandate to marketize and rationalize the organization of labor coexist in this single leviathan institution.

In what follows, vignettes from three railway towns show, in a kaleidoscopic way, how railway workers experience the changing relationships between social and geographic positions and the boundaries and horizons that limit and shape possible practices from them. The stories railway workers tell reveal the production of distinctions in the landscapes where they live and work.

Pukou   I met Zhou Shifu in a small two story office building in the riverside precinct that the Pukou rail freight workers share with the Pukou port authority. I'd asked the party secretary for permission to speak with workers of different generations, and Zhou was introduced to me as one of the oldest workers still employed. At fifty-five, he was five years away from retirement. Unlike many workers younger than himself, he had had no kin in the railway system when he tested into the service in 1958. The parents of the schoolmate he married had been ambivalent about his relationship with their daughter until he got his railway job. With that, they became enthusiastic. To be a railway worker at the Pukou station in the late 1950s was to be in a fortunate place—both in the hierarchy of occupations and in the hierarchy of places in the railway system. Everything and everyone who traveled overland between Shanghai and points north and west crossed the Yangzi on the ferries that linked Nanjing with Pukou. But in 1968 the construction of the Yangzi River Bridge coincided with the completion of a new station at Nanjing. The new station funneled rail traffic directly across the river, bypassing the Pukou station entirely. With that, the Pukou station lost its position as a major node in the national transportation infrastructure. It became a local freight depot and the terminus for a few passenger routes.

The decrease in traffic through the Pukou station didn't seem to affect Zhou's satisfaction with his career. Most of his comments about working at the Pukou railway station over his thirty-five-year career stressed the comparative advantages that he experienced as a member of the system compared to Pukou people "outside" the well-provisioned railway organization. But the image of an undifferentiated caste of workers whose privileges were insulated from changes in the physical environment (like the construction of the bridge and the rerouting of rail traffic away from the Pukou station) disappeared when I asked him how market economics was affecting work for the railroad.

He explained that cargo still moved according to plan but that the freight division had created a number of services to add convenience and save time for clients. When I asked what divisions of rail organization were best situated to benefit from the opportunities created by the trend toward "diversification" into profit-making ventures (*duozhong jingying*), he talked about which divisions were not: "Perhaps the worst off are the machinists. They spend all their time in the garage, repairing equipment. They seldom have the opportunity to interface with the public. And yet their workers have very valuable skills: bench work, fitting, lathe work, turning. . . . But they are going into the garment trade, hotels, construction. I think the machinists' team is running a hostel in the station district." Zhou Shifu summarized the unequal distribution of advantages among railway workers with a saying: "The ones with money are in freight. The ones with style are in passenger traffic. And the losers operate the machinery" (*You qiande shi huoyun, shenqide shi keyun, yunzhuande shi daomei*).

The days of celebrating work in the PRC with machine metaphors are clearly over. "Cogs in the wheel" are thought of as disadvantaged and behind the times. Being behind the times corresponds to being behind the scenes in rail stations and garages. In Zhou's saying, enviable positions are occupied by workers in the railway equivalent of stewardess professions and by traders who deal in the commodity of "space" in freight cars. Machine workers and engineers are invisible and so are far from the circuits where desirable goods and opportunities flow.

Zhou's narrative, much abbreviated here, shows the ways in which market values are creating very clear zones of distinction between workers positioned differently within the compass of one railway station. Yet from Zhou's perspective a bad position within the railway system is preferable to a good position outside it. This emerged when he discussed the railway job he had arranged for his youngest child. "No matter what changes will come, we have the guarantee of security. We can't go bankrupt. 'Outside' enterprises can always get liquidated. Not us. They have high salaries, but our lives are fixed and permanent."

Among the "outside" industries to which Zhou Shifu referred was the locally based Yangzi Yixi Corp., a petrochemical company with substantial backing from the multinational BASF. Many of Yangzi's employees are drawn from the local community and are renowned for the bounty of the benefits they enjoy. But while people speak admiringly of the largesse that an enterprise with foreign backing can afford to dispense to its workers, elder workers like Zhou Shifu seem almost to expect that such enterprises might very well be just a flash in the pan, destined to disappear with shifts in world markets or local political winds. Consequently, Zhou has cast his lot, and that of his son, with the railway—that most sturdy of iron rice bowls. Even though railway positions are increasingly stratified, and even though they might not compare so favorably with neighboring firms that are backed with foreign capital, they retain the mighty attraction of unbankruptability.

Two of his younger colleagues, a woman named Song Zhen and a man called Little Wang, expressed quite different perspectives on work and life for the railroad in Pukou. Although they both agreed with Zhou that what they valued most about their permanent positions in the railway system was the promise of security and stability in their working lives, neither of them were as satisfied as Zhou with where they were.

Song had heard most of what Zhou Shifu had had to say. She was more interested in discussing the concerns she had as the mother of a child in the first grade than in railway work per se. How worrisome that her young, naughty son could not attend the local school (*difang xue-xiao*). Because both of his parents were railway workers, he was required to attend the school provided by the railway for the children of its employees. She spoke matter-of-factly about the impossibility of her son ever testing into a good middle school if he were doomed to a Pukou railway elementary school education. Little Wang commiserated with Song about the stresses of contemporary parenthood. Although his small son was barely old enough to enter nursery school, he and his wife were already having major conflicts with his parents over school choice. The thrifty grandparents saw no reason to pay a high tuition to send their small heir to a private kindergarten when the railway provided one at negligible cost.

Wang at least had the luxury of such conflicts. As a young man in charge of allocating space in freight car containers, where demand for such space far outstrips supply, he was sought out by many supplicants needing to move their goods. In consequence, he was quite wealthy in terms of disposable income and the network of people from whom he could expect to receive favors.[7] Song Zhen's duties, on the other hand, did not tempt her clients to treat her to elaborate meals or to give her cash and other tokens of appreciation. Her job was to glue stamps to postcards notifying people, or more often factories, that their freight had arrived, then to collect storage fees from procurement agents when they came to claim their goods. She had no extraordinary power to do favors for anyone. Private schooling for her little boy was thus out of the question.

These exchanges in the Pukou station reveal an emergent pattern. The hierarchy in the relationship between workers "inside" railway danwei and workers "outside," employed by difang, has shifted. The advantages of being inside the railway system are no longer as apparent as they were in 1958, when Zhou tested in. Nevertheless, from the perspectives of Zhou, Song, and Wang, their Pukou railway danwei is a more desirable place to belong than any other option on the horizon. Within the Pukou railway hierarchy, they each enjoy relatively advantaged positions. The freight division has access to external money (*waikuai*) from customers and clients anxious to speed their goods on their way. Even though "cargo still moves according to plan," the plan does not dictate the order by which cargo moves. Some of the money that greases the wheels of commerce, even under the plan, trickles into freight workers' bonuses. But other workers at the Pukou station, those with technical skills who repair and maintain heavy equipment, for example, work in an environment that is impervious to external money. Their pay and bonuses are internally generated, and the engines that produce those benefits appear weak compared to income sources outside of the railway system.

Distinctions that pivot at a dividing line between inside and outside pattern these relationships. Danwei and difang are spatial markers that produce differences that are material and symbolic. While the relationship between the Pukou railway danwei and difang enterprises is being reversed and the contrast between them is sharpening, the relationships between the multiple danwei encompassed within the Pukou station are also becoming sharply stratified. Those danwei at the station in positions of relative exteriority—most clearly manifest by access to waikuai—benefit now from where they are. An expression that I heard frequently during my research year crystallizes the logic: "When on the mountain, eat the mountain. When at sea, eat the sea (*Zai shan chi shan; zai shui chi shui*). The sense is that you take what you can get, depending on where you are. The pattern that emerges is not unlike the image of nested hierarchies that G. William Skinner (1964–65) used to describe the spatial patterns of political, economic, and social relationships in late imperial China. Like fractals, the patterns that these nested hierarchies describe are chaotic (*luan*) compared to the structural regularities produced by planning logic, but they are chaotic in regular ways.

Shanghai　My story takes a leap to the east now, to the New Railway Station in Shanghai. There, in the summer of 1993, Yu Lin—a Shanghai sociologist and my research companion—and I visited the administrative offices of the team that staffs the short-distance train routes originating at the Shanghai station. This division, though housed in the precincts of Shanghai's New Station, was not under the same administration as the station. People who belonged to it considered themselves at a great disadvantage compared to their fellow railway workers who belonged to the station and at even more of a disadvantage in relation to the average worker in other Shanghai industries. The man who received us, Teamleader Li, spoke decisively when he said, "Local workplaces are better by far than the railroad. We're unable to attract workers like local industries can. Young people from Shanghai don't even consider working for the railways."

Until recently, many of Shanghai's railway workers lived in apartment buildings in the vicinity of the New Station. The commute from this quarter to the Zhabei station had been a quick one. With the construction of the New Station, the commute was virtually eliminated. But recently the land around the New Station had been sold to foreigners. Dwellings that had not already been demolished soon would be. Li himself had been forced to find temporary housing for his family since this railway work unit had not yet made arrangements to build housing for its staff. Li's commute took two hours each way by bicycle. The price of bus fare for the distance was prohibitive and provided negligible time savings. The pressure on Li, a man in a position of considerable responsibility, appeared both extraordinary and inevitable given the cosmopolitan destiny Shanghai seeks to fulfill, or recover, from the period of Maoist orthodoxy, during which time it appears to have stood still. He is one of countless numbers who have been displaced from homes on land being razed to make room for speculative, high-rent real estate.

Many railway workers who relied on their work units for housing were in similar straits. But railway workers who staffed the New Station didn't share these problems. The New Station's housing situation was "loose" (*bijiao song*) in comparison with the rest of the Shanghai railway's. The reason was quite simple: "Everyone in the city needs something from the station (*Dajia dou you qiu yu ta*). Our housing, on the other hand, is extremely tight. We merely work on the trains. We don't have the same power to bestow benefits that the station does. It's the station that sells tickets. We merely provide service during the time of travel."

The explanation for this difference between divisions of Shanghai railway workers related to the same notions of "natural" market advantage that gave certain positions in the division of labor at the Pukou station advantages over others. Within the same work unit, differences in gender, job position, and access to control over a scarce resource gave Little Wang, the allocator of container space, advantages over Song Zhen, the one who glued stamps. In Shanghai, another fractal pattern of distinctions emerges. From Li's perspective, difang enterprises in the metropolis of Shanghai have made far greater material progress in the market era. To him, the railway danwei appears to be a singularly backward place to be.

Li complained about the low regard in which the city holds its railroad and compared Shanghai's neglect with the strong support he said Suzhou and Wuxi gave to their railroad precincts and people. "Look at Wuxi station! All of the buildings in the area have been torn down, and zoning regulations put the interest of the station first. The *fengshui* of the stations in Suzhou and Wuxi is very impressive! And much more advantageous to those stations' benefits (*liyi*) than here in Shanghai. The Post and Telecommunications Hotel should never have been built so close to the Shanghai New Station Plaza." Finally, he lamented that the railroad would never catch up to other industries and professions. He said that working conditions were terrible. Workers who endure high temperatures, great stress, and considerable danger are not provided the rest and amenities prescribed for such positions. There aren't even mosquito nets in worker dormitories. And in the dormitories where out-of-town workers stay the night, only the noisiest rooms are retained for their rest. The others have been rented out for profit.

In team leader Li's reckoning, the railway's days are numbered. Whereas in Pukou an old worker like Zhou Shifu can still be glad that his own child will reproduce the labor force, Li claims that no self-respecting Shanghai youth would go willingly into the railroad now. He described the dismal place of the railway in Shanghai in terms of how it had lost in competition with market interests for space: space in the city for workers' homes; space in the New Station Plaza, where real estate values predominated over classical fengshui values; and space even within the railway's own buildings for worker welfare. Extrapolating from these spatial losses, Li forecast a dim future for the Chinese railway worker, linked, as that worker is, to the creaking and gargantuan machinery of the nation's infrastructure.

Shanghai's situation as a busy port city, a cosmopolitan center whose

leaders are bent on luring foreign investment to subsidize its modernization, renders its state-sector organizations behind the times. Workers for
railway danwei are disadvantaged compared to their neighbors, who
might belong to smaller, more nimble, local organizations better suited
to adapt to the market environment. Yet here, again, the relationship
between the railway work unit, or danwei, and local work organizations,
difang, is relative. The New Station and those railway workers who belong to it enjoy the benefits of a "natural" comparative advantage. But the
naturalness of the New Station's advantages masks a history of political
and economic decisions.

Nanjing My last vignette takes us back to Nanjing, where a discussion
with a pair of cadres showed that the distinctions emerging between the
railway and local places, and between railway workers themselves, do not
stem merely from abstract market forces. Their origins must be understood in terms of specific administrative logics, which operate on the
national scale.

The visit occurred upstairs in the West Nanjing railway station. My
companion, Su Hong, and I were entertained by the station's Communist
Party secretary, a man named Hu, who was dressed in a nice western-style
suit, and Wen Shifu, who held the title of director of passenger train
personnel (*chengwu zhuren*). Secretary Hu and Wen Shifu were each high
officials in the organization of the rail station who presided over different
realms of station work. Their clothing and the themes of their conversation seemed to recapitulate their realms of authority and expertise.

Wen, in ordinary work clothes, spoke first. As the cadre in charge of all
personnel who staff the passenger train routes originating from this station, he surveyed the fleet of trains for us. He explained that in this
network the routes to Beijing, Canton, and Xiamen had the heaviest
traffic. Each of those towns was a major center of industry and commerce, so for the sake of speed and efficiency express trains traveled to
those towns, omitting the small station stops. As a rule, the higher the
number, the slower the train, and the slower the train, the lower the
"quality" of equipment, service, and ridership.

In explaining the great differences in quality among railway lines,[8]
Wen Shifu emphasized that the line by line differences were inseparable
from the social conditions surrounding the lines themselves. He cited

essential local conditions as the primary explanation for the different evolutionary stages that staff and equipment of the various lines had achieved. These differences were in his view fundamental, but he went on to describe management techniques that worked to reinforce what were seen as qualitative, "natural" differences.[9]

Workers on the faster, more prestigious routes are better paid. More resources are invested in the outfitting and repair of those lines. Staff members themselves are chosen according to four criteria that distinguish them as more competent than workers on slower, more westerly routes: they are healthy and attractive, they have a high degree of "civilization," they are well educated, and they are young. All of these criteria were meant to suggest that such persons were hard workers and good learners. Wen Shifu described the objective differences among the work force he administered with evident pride in the high quality of the superior workers among them. Younger, more flexible, and able to change with the times, they are the breed of worker that should represent China's railways in the marketizing economy.

Throughout this survey of the routes originating from the Nanjing station and the cultural explanations given for their differences, Secretary Hu had remained silent. But when Wen Shifu paused in his presentation, the party secretary presented a sketch that followed different themes.

> There are three important traits that distinguish railway workers in general from ordinary workers. First, their discipline, organization, and enthusiasm. Second, their ability to endure hardships and hard work. And third, the extraordinary contribution they make to the construction of society and the development of the national economy. All of these characteristics combine to reveal their extraordinary willingness to make personal sacrifices for the benefit of economy and society.

Following his tribute to the virtues of railway workers, the party secretary went on to describe the buying power of contemporary railway workers. He listed the consumer durables that were increasingly common in the homes of ordinary folk and talked about how rapidly average standards of living had improved. To sum up the speed of progress, he noted, "Ten years ago, people wouldn't even have known what to do with a refrigerator!" His implication was that in 1990s Nanjing commodities that had just ten years before been considered unaffordable luxuries had become commonplace in railway workers' homes. Indeed, the refrigerator measure is often used in Communist Party discussions about how the nation must cultivate not only spiritual civilization (*jingshen wenming*) but material civilization (*wuzhi wenming*) (cf. Anagnost 1997: 75–97).

What struck me about this interview, though, was the "territorialization of virtue" revealed in Wen Shifu's account of his staffing criteria. Younger, more attractive, and better-educated people are assigned to speedier, newer trains, which travel rapidly to China's most modern and industrialized cities. Those deemed less handsome, less educated, and less "civilized" are shunted off to travel along the routes to "backward" places. From the Nanjing perspective, backwardness develops in the direction of Pukou and beyond. Over and over again, people talked about the Jiangxi-Anhui route. Stories usually followed themes such as "My child was offered a railway position, but she would have had to work on the Wangan line (as the route to the Southwest from Nanjing to Jiangxi and Anhui is called), so I would not agree to let her take the job."

I close with this vignette because in the most directly physical way it demonstrates how distinctions that stretch across space are now being "built on" and reinforced in material ways. The dichotomies I introduced at the beginning of this chapter—backward and progressive (luohou and xianjin), railway work unit and local place unit (danwei and difang)—define poles around which key cultural values have been organized. Culture and power converged during the time of the plan to produce a certain kind of social landscape, which, for persons situated in particular "places," engendered specific ways of practicing everyday life and understanding the boundaries and horizons of space.

Conclusion   Johannes Fabian (1983) criticized colonial era anthropologists for situating "the other" in culture gardens separate from and discontinuous with contemporary geopolitical realities. Fabian's ideas about anthropologists' ways of knowing and representing are useful in understanding the ways in which China's Communist bureaucratic administrators—its teleological planners—knew and represented Chinese railway workers' lives. And through these techniques of knowing and representing China's planners significantly shaped the possibilities of these workers' lives.

On the one hand, China's planners themselves insulated their nation from the time, space, and rhythm of the capitalist world system after 1949. For the planners, this was a strategic move, necessary in order to fulfill their vision of an alternative modernity. By closing China's borders—creating a "bamboo curtain"—China's leaders monopolized control over the flow of people, goods, and ideas that came and went from their domain. Only by carefully cultivating a culture garden on a tremendous scale could China's Communist Party leadership effectively prevent invasion by "poisonous weeds" that might threaten New China's potential to grow into a revolutionary utopia. Unlike the "denial of coevalness" for which Fabian indicts colonial era anthropologists, China's leaders denied that the PRC was coeval with the rest of the world, only to make the alternative claim that China had leapt ahead of the world beyond its borders.

As a whole, the nation was isolated from the economic and political time/space that had such transformative effects over the rest of the post–World War II world. In this way, China's planners effectively resisted coevalness with the capitalist world. They strategically crafted a time apart (or Fabian's "allochronism"). Within the nation, however, sectors of the economy, classes of people, and entire geographic regions were labeled so as to be known, represented, and reconstructed according to plan. These sectors, classes, and regions did not themselves inhabit a single time in the planners' eyes. Internally, sectors, classes, regions, and units—all parts of the whole—were also denied coevalness. Labels of "progressive" and "backward" were applied to collectives and individuals, indicating their economic and moral-ideological development.

It is tempting, in the late 1990s, to view these labeling practices and temporal ideologies as artifacts of a time past, one not directly relevant to China's present and future. Yet identifying an "end of ideology" in contemporary China overlooks the ideological premises of such a diagnosis.[10] Reform era China, where the economic system known as "Market Socialism with Chinese Characteristics" prevails, is often called postsocialist. But people who use that term bolster the illusion that "globalization and market trends are irresistible impersonal forces rather than products of willful political agendas; that any resistance to the prevailing Western model of scientific rationalism must be irrationalist fundamentalism; that competition promotes real diversity of products (instead of uniformity through pressured copying)" (Shusterman 1999: 26). Indeed, the denial of the continuing effects of China's socialist political system—the situational survivals from the Maoist era as well as the effects of the contemporary "market socialist" imaginary—contributes to the attitude identified as "capitalist triumphalism."[11]

The experiences gathered here point to the ways in which people have been situated in particular "places" to which there accrued particular meanings during the time of the plan. Places and persons were distinguished in ways that were sharp and symbolic. Yet the ideology of the plan also supported the vision that all were cogs in the same machine. Together, guided by the plan, the machine was making steady progress toward a revolutionary telos.

The embrace of the market has speeded up time. Places once temporally distant from each other in journey-time are now nearer. But symbolically the space between places grows. The space between railway workers on fast trains and slow trains, in garages or offices, and in Shanghai or Pukou has grown very wide. The pattern that I see emerging to describe these serial stratifications has the regularity of chaotic forms. Fractal planes are riven through the orderly grids that described the planned universe. The danger is that the distinctions being produced will be seen apart from the histories that produced them and the logics that perpetuate them.

Notes

This chapter is based on fieldwork conducted in 1992–1993 with the generous support of the Committee on Scholarly Communication with the People's Republic of China and the Wenner Gren Foundation for Anthropological Research. The Woodrow Wilson Foundation's Grants for Women's Studies program supported follow-up research in 1995. I am grateful to Nancy Chen, Connie Clark, Suzanne Gottschang, Lyn Jeffery, and Ellen Hertz for their valuable comments on earlier drafts of this chapter and to Ann Armbrecht, Julie Goldman, Michael Perrow, and James L. Watson for their sustained interest in the larger project of which this chapter is a part. I owe special thanks to Bonnie Burns of the Harvard Map Collection for the patient wizardry she used in creating the accompanying map.

1   On the imagery of the people-as-one in totalitarian ideology in general, and in PRC ideology in particular, see Lefort 1986 and Anagnost 1989, respectively.

2   Recent ethnographies by Rofel (1992) and Yang (1994) treat spatial disciplines and their transformations. Davis et al. 1995 treats many of the processes I outline here.

Verdery's analysis of the seizure of time in Ceausescu's Romania (1992) and Mueggler's work in Yunnan (1991, n.d.) also provide illuminating analyses of space, time, and meaning in socialist contexts.

3   Benefits enjoyed by China's urban citizens include easier access to superior schools, hospitals, and cultural institutions. But the most fundamental and profound difference between the lives of China's urban and rural residents during the planning era was the privilege urban residents had of eating grain and foodstuffs that they did not grow themselves. The rich social history of rationed consumption in the PRC remains to be written.

4   Rural places with historic or scenic resources with the potential for development as tourist destinations are a significant exception to this general rule.

5   China's twelve railway administrative regions accord more closely with its military regions than with provincial boundaries. Headquarters of the twelve regions are located in Harbin, Shenyang, Hohhot, Lanzhou, Urumqi, Beijing, Jinan, Zhengzhou, Shanghai, Chengdu, Liuzhou, and Guangzhou. The Shanghai Railway Bureau presides over six subbureaus located in Shanghai, Hangzhou, Fuzhou, Bengbu, Nanchang, and Nanjing. Nanjing's territory includes ninety-three stations and 783 kilometers of track.

6   In everyday speech, *danwei* means simply "work unit" and *difang* means "locale" or "local place." However, in the context of conversations with railway workers about their lot during the journey from plan to market, the two terms were used contrastively to mark the relative advantages of belonging to an organ of the central state versus belonging to a locally run unit.

7   On the economics of these sorts of connections, see Hertz, this volume; and Yang 1994.

8   Master Wen spoke about the "quality" of various railway lines' furnishings and equipment as *zhiliang*. Differences in the quality of inanimate matériel corresponded, in his presentation, with what he took as objective differences in the quality, or *suzhi*, of train crews and their passenger populations.

9   All of this is an interesting reversal of old wisdom. Fifty years ago, impact studies were conducted where railway tracks had been laid in an attempt to find an objective measure of the effect of railways on local economies. In this formulation, less developed places are themselves blamed for their lack of industry and commerce. Regional differences are thus naturalized.

10   As Daniel Bell did in his 1960 book. See Ehrenreich 1990.

11   In an article called "Clintonism, Welfare, and the Anti-social Wage: The Emergence of a Neoliberal Political Imaginary" (1993), Nancy Fraser provides a useful definition of the political and economic imaginary: "To analyze the political imaginary of social welfare is simultaneously to shed light on the construction of social identities. It is to examine the terms in which people formulate their sense of who they are, what they deserve, and what they hope for. These in turn are bound up with assumptions about identity and difference: who is like me and who is not? who is my ally and who is my enemy?" (9).

Li Zhang Contesting Crime, Order, and Migrant Spaces in Beijing

In November 1995, an order signed by Premier Li Peng was issued by the Beijing municipal government to "clean up and bring order back to" Zhejiangcun, the largest migrant settlement in Beijing. Under strong government pressure, about forty-eight housing compounds created by Wenzhou migrants were demolished by the government's yellow bulldozers. Shivering in December's chilly north wind, nearly forty thousand migrants in this community who had suddenly lost their homes were expelled from the city and went into hiding in Beijing's far-off rural counties and adjacent provinces.

This campaign to remove migrant housing was part of a fierce battle over power, space, and urban citizenship that ensued as millions of rural transients, known as the "floating population" (*liudong renkou*), streamed into Chinese cities.[1] The emergence of this large mobile population has challenged socialist state control of the population, which has been primarily based on the household registration system (*hukou*) and is reshaping state-society dynamics in an era of increasing mobility and marketization.[2] In particular, the "congregating zones of the floating population" (*liudong renkou jujudian*) that have mushroomed on the outskirts of Chinese cities are viewed as problematic by upper-level government officials due to migrants' relatively autonomous socioeconomic practices in these newly formed community spaces.

The contestation over migrant spaces in China is closely intertwined with the issue of crime and the power of representation. The "floating population" is often represented by the media and official discourse as an aimless, intractable, and menacing peril unleashed by the invisible hand of the free market. In the social imagination of the majority of urbanites, this floating population stands as a metaphor for uncertainty, insecurity, and instability brought by the post-Mao reforms.[3] Urban settlements created by rural migrants are imagined and represented as hotbeds of crime and disorder, eroding the existing urban social order and public security.

Yet what constitutes order, what kind of space comes to be marked as safe or unsafe, and what leads to increased crime in cities are highly contentious issues. In this study, space is not taken merely as a static background in which events and practices occur; rather, it is understood as a contested social process that is both shaped by and shapes human practices and power relations (cf. Agnew 1994; Harvey 1993; Massey 1993). Focusing on the politics of migrant space and representation, and the counterdiscourse provided by the migrants themselves, this chapter analyzes how the migrant population and their enclaves in the urban centers are differently conceived and how so-called migrant crime is interpreted by different social elements. I hope to provide what Moore has called "multiple visions of a passing historical moment, on variability, and on contestation" (1993: 4). And, more importantly, I argue that localizing migrants in specific spaces marked as dirty, chaotic, and dangerous through discursive practices is itself a form of ordering and is part of the larger schemes of power to turn people who are perceived as out of control into disciplinable subjects. At the heart of this discursive contestation over order and disorder is the production of knowledge/power central to ordering, normalizing, and regulating strategies (Foucault 1980b). Further, I maintain that these contesting ideological scenarios do not just reflect a reality but entail concrete social and political consequences as they encounter one another.

I first provide a brief account of Zhejiangcun's recent spatial and social transformations. I then analyze different social perceptions and understandings of what "order" is about, what kind of space is safe or dangerous, and who is responsible for Beijing's rising crime rate. After a brief examination of the effects of the government campaign against Zhejiangcun and relevant city politics, I suggest that a culturally mediated way of policing migrant communities is central to the reshaping of a dynamic state-society relationship in an era of increased spatial mobility.

Zhejiangcun and the Emergence of "Big Yards"   When one looks at a map of Beijing, Zhejiangcun does not appear on it. Yet in Beijing, although most people cannot point out its precise geographical location, almost everyone has heard of or claims to know something about Zhejiangcun. Indeed, the physical existence of this migrant community is far less important than its social presence in the popular imagination of Beijing people. The so-called Zhejiangcun (meaning "Zhejiang village") is neither an administratively defined village nor a squatter settlement exclusively occupied by migrants. It is a large migrant congregating zone embedded in a number of preexisting suburban communities in Nanyuan Township in the southern part of Beijing.[4] Because the majority of migrants in this area came from rural Wenzhou, Zhejiang Province, this settlement was named by Beijing residents after these migrants' provincial origin to demarcate a perceived "alien" social body from the established Beijing community.

Historically, Wenzhou merchants had traveled to many parts of China and to Europe for small family businesses and trade. Wenzhou migrants began to come to Beijing in the early 1980s as China's economic reforms began. As the nation's capital, Beijing was viewed by the migrant pioneers as a vast potential consumer market for emerging private businesses. With their special skills in tailoring and small capital raised from relatives and friends in their home villages, some Wenzhou migrants came to set up their family businesses in clothing production and trade. Through kin and native place networks, more and more Wenzhou migrants, as well as migrant workers from other provinces employed by Wenzhou households, poured into this area in the following years. By 1995, there were roughly one hundred thousand migrants working and living in this settlement. Using their settlement as the economic base, Wenzhou migrants' garment businesses soon came to dominate Beijing's informal clothing market. Their booming entrepreneurial activities have significantly transformed the physical and social landscape of the local community (Nanyuan) from a poor, bleak, and marginal suburban area into a wealthy and dynamic commercial zone. Most farmland was replaced with migrants' commercial buildings, marketplaces, and numerous private shops.[5] Such economic success, however, was overshadowed by the municipal government's concern with the subversive potential of migrant settlements with regard to political stability and social order in the city. Particularly, the controversial development of Wenzhou migrants' walled housing compounds intensified such political anxieties.

Under the household registration system, rural migrants are merely "outsiders" in the cities who do not have the formal membership (the urban hukou) or rights and benefits enjoyed by permanent residents. When Wenzhou migrants first arrived in Beijing, they rented rooms in local suburban farmers' private courtyards. Coming from the distant countryside and speaking a very different dialect, Wenzhou migrants were perceived as untrustworthy, dangerous, and uncivilized and were regarded as intruders and potential criminals by locals. Many farmers in the Nanyuan area refused to rent rooms to migrants. Gradually, local farmers came to realize that renting was an extremely lucrative way to generate cash. By renting one or two small rooms (for 400 to 500 yuan each, which roughly equals U.S.$50), a household could live a very comfortable life without working in the vegetable field or taking a second job. By 1995, over 90 percent of farmers' households in Nanyuan were renting two to four rooms to Wenzhou migrants. Renting gradually became the primary source of livelihood for local farmers.

With the increased migrant population pressure and fear of crime, sharing the locals' housing space became insufficient and unsatisfying for migrants. First, the overall living conditions for Wenzhou migrants worsened after large numbers of newcomers arrived. The average housing space was less than three square meters per person. In especially crowded villages, it was common to find eight to ten people crammed into a room of less than twenty square meters. A one-room apartment was usually crowded with bunk beds, sewing machines, raw materials, finished products, and cookware. Second, the fear of crime increased rapidly as robbery and extortion began to occur. Scattered in isolated individual courtyards, Wenzhou migrants found it very difficult to organize a crime watch and mutual protection among themselves. And robbers could easily escape and disappear in the crisscrossed, narrow, crooked alleyways.

It was in this context that the migrant residential compounds known as "big yards" (*dayuan*) came into being. Big yards were developed mainly by Wenzhou migrants who possessed money and social prestige. Due to their non-permanent-resident status in Beijing, migrants were prohibited from using land for housing construction. But migrant housing bosses were able to cut private deals with the local village authority for short-term land leases without reporting them to the district-level government. In the context of waning agricultural production, members of these suburban villages were interested in seeking alternative economic profits by cooperating with Wenzhou migrants even if this was officially considered illegal. Further, officials in local government agencies, who were bought off by big yard bosses with cash, banquets, and expensive goods, purposely overlooked the presence of these new compounds. They also offered migrants highly demanded resources such as water, gas, electricity, and sewage at a higher market price than what was charged to locals. Such commodified personal networks (*guanxi*), opened up new channels through which migrants without urban hukou could make use of the urban space and services monopolized by the state (cf. Pieke 1995; Yang 1989). The first Wenzhou migrants' big yard was constructed in 1992. In the following three years, over forty large and small private housing compounds were created in this area. Nearly half of the migrant households in the area moved into these walled residential compounds.

Surrounded by local farmers' houses inside the villages, big yards were less visible to officials and the urban public outside, yet they were highly visible to migrants and locals in the area. Constructed of cheap bricks with asbestos tile roofs, big yards were designed like military barracks to maximize the use of space and to reduce cost. The invisible locations and the temporary construction methods were concrete examples of migrants' marginal and liminal status in the city.[6] Big yards were welcomed by the majority of Wenzhou migrants, who needed housing space and longed for security and local protection. This new spatial organization served as a powerful basis on which migrants reordered their socio-economic lives. According to my informants, crime was reduced significantly within the big yards. But in the eyes of the district and city officials Wenzhou migrants' unauthorized appropriation of urban space for their own ends was a sign of danger and a source of alternative social power that might grow to compete with state domination in the socialist order.

Representing Migrant Spaces   The formation of migrant settlements in general and Wenzhou migrants' big yards in particular has both fascinated and daunted the social imagination of the Beijing public. Such new migrant spatial formations provoked heated debates about their social and political effect on the quality of life and the social order of the city. These ideological representations function as signifying practices that define the meaning of reality, structure people's experiences, and implement their own version of order (Hall 1985). At the heart of this spatial politics is a question posed by David Harvey: "In whose image and to whose benefit is space to be shaped?" (1989: 177). In what follows, I examine the perceptions and images of the migrant population and the cultural logic of migrant criminality presented by these hegemonic discourses. My analysis is based on a wide range of sources, including interviews, government reports, print media, reportage literature (*baogao wenxue*), and social science research. I then juxtapose these with alternative images and interpretations provided by some Chinese scholars, local Beijing farmers, and the Wenzhou migrants themselves.

In Beijing, official and urban public discourses share a great deal of commonality despite some subtle differences. They tend to regard "migrant congregating zones" and big yards as a crystallization of the "urban cancer" or "filth and mire" (Hao 1992) brought by free market forces. The popular perception that links migrants to crime and instability both draws from and is reflected in the press and media. Here are two typical examples that magnify one aspect of migrant settlements as their overall reality. A report by city officials delineates Zhejiangcun as a place that is dirty (*zang*), chaotic (*luan*), and miserable (*cha*): "Although they [migrants] have some positive influences on enlivening markets and making local people's lives more convenient, they have created a series of problems, including overpopulation, traffic jams, poor hygiene, disorder, crime, and other lawbreaking activities. All of these problems have seriously damaged the orderly regulation of the local government" (*Beijing Evening Daily,* November 28, 1995). Another article by four officials of the Beijing Municipal Planning Committee claims that "in recent years, the number of crime and lawbreaking cases among the incoming floating population has increased. . . . Especially in the congregating zones of the floating population, gambling, prostitution, drug use, and drug trafficking emerge like an endless stream, creating many new problems for government control of social order and security in Beijing" (Ji et al. 1995: 80). What typifies these official discourses is their unified and monolithic tone (cf. Yang 1994). The ultimate concern of officials is not just disorder within migrant settlements but more importantly their potential for jeopardizing state control and political stability.

In contrast, popular newspapers and magazines are more interested in spicy, exaggerated anecdotes about the crime, drugs, and prostitution associated with the floating population in order to attract more readers and make greater profits under increasing market competition. For instance, the *Beijing Evening Daily,* the most widely read newspaper in the city, recently created a special column entitled "People and Law" (*ren yu fa*) to cover the crimes and illegal activities of "outsiders" (*waidiren*), presumably migrants. Urban residents who retreat into their small, fortified homes tend to regard these social reports as a popular "window on society" (*shehui zhi chuang*) through which they can discern the social climate and problems of Beijing in order to ensure their personal safety. These images and the information produced by the popular press become the raw materials with which the urban public shapes its knowledge of, imagination of, and action toward the migrant population.

Rumors of gunfights, gang violence, and physical conflicts with the police in migrant communities widely circulate among Beijing residents. Most of these stories are re-created and distorted as they are passed from one person to another. I was warned by many friends and strangers not to enter Zhejiangcun, as if I would soon vanish into a dark cave. Taxi drivers, the informal social messengers of the city, told me what they regarded as the reality of Zhejiangcun: "They have formed their own little independent kingdom, with their own police, handcuffs, guns, and rules. Outsiders are not allowed to enter the tightly guarded, walled big yards. They run the place in their own ways. Some policemen who tried to step in were murdered." What ordinary Beijing residents are concerned with is not abstract political stability but their personal safety and security, which might be endangered by crime attributed to the migrant population and their new residential pattern.

Like a stream without a source, these images and anecdotes circulate through urban society, build on each other like a snowball, and eventually become elaborate urban myths that shape the popular imagination of Beijing residents. Through repetition, circulation, and expansion, these fantasies, desires, and facts mesh together to construct the "reality" of migrant communities. No longer appearing to be ideological, such representation becomes part of so-called common sense, a naturalized form of ideology, the validity of which people cease to question (cf. Gramsci 1971; Comaroff and Comaroff 1991; Hall 1985).

It is not my intention to suggest that official and urban public responses and perceptions about migrants and their communities are merely fantasies and paranoia without any social basis. Rather, my point is that crime and illegal activities attributed to the floating population are often exaggerated, statistically manipulated, and taken out of a broader context of changes occurring in Chinese society. First, the resurgence of urban crime in the post-Mao era is a nationwide phenomenon, which cannot be attributed to the migrant population only. Representations that solely focus on migrant crime divert public attention from other covert, serious crimes committed by officials and local residents. Because of their long-established social networks and connections with authority, the locals are less likely to be monitored, exposed, reported, or punished than migrant newcomers, who are used as the scapegoat for emerging urban ills. Urban officials tend to publicize migrant crime because they are less likely to be blamed for ineffective crime prevention since migrants are not considered to be official members of their districts. Second, statistics of migrant crime in official reports are largely inflated. For example, criminals who escape from jail are lumped into the category of waidiren.[7] Those who commit crimes but escape from the scene are also assumed to be floaters due to their nonlocal accents and rural, "outsiderlike" dress and demeanor. Third, since statistics on crime rates are not available to the public, the numbers provided by various writers are not verifiable. Contrary to most newspaper representations, I learned in a personal interview with a local police officer of the Fengtai District that according to police arrest records Wenzhou migrants are not a high-crime group. Instead, they are often the victims of robbery due to the high concentration of private wealth among them and the lack of government protection.

The Cultural Logic of Migrant Criminality The criminalization of the floating population is by no means a phenomenon unique to Chinese society. People who do not fit in the existing categorical order of things tend to be viewed by most societies as "out of place" and thus a source of danger and pollution (Douglas 1966). In other cultural contexts, scholars have analyzed similar processes in which displaced and marginalized groups—refugees, immigrants, blacks, gays, and the homeless poor—have become the subjects of criminalization and pathologization (see Gilroy 1991; Malkki 1992; Chavez 1992; Foucault 1980a; and Santiago-Irizarry 1996). In China, peasants who have left the farm and "float" in the cities are regarded as perilous and threatening because they do not occupy a proper structural position in the existing national order, which denounces spatial mobility.[8]

What is most problematic in the dominant discourse on crime in China is how so-called migrant criminality (*liudong renkou fanzui*) is interpreted. Here crime is viewed as a central expression of migrants' spatial mobility, displaced rurality, and craze for money.[9] First, this logic assumes that because of their mobile way of life migrants do not have moral accountability to urban communities. Some urbanites invoke an old Chinese saying to explain the problematic relationship between migrants and cities: "A rabbit never eats the grass around its own nest" (*tuzi buchi wobiancao*). It means that it is a natural tendency for people not to exploit their immediate interest groups or the environment in which they are situated. The implication is that migrants who are counted as outsiders in (i.e., not full or true members of) the city are most likely to act as criminals and take advantage of urban communities. For instance, as one urban resident explained it to me: "We locals do not commit crimes. Crimes in this city are mostly committed by the outsiders. They want to bring some money or nice gifts back to show off in front of their folks during the Spring Festival. When they cannot get money, they naturally go in for robbery and stealing. Since they do not live in the city permanently, they do not care about face (*mianzi*) and are not afraid of being captured." According to this reasoning, rootlessness will naturally lead to crime because it takes away one's concern for face (or moral constraints). Many urban residents believe that an important reason why migrants are more likely to engage in illegal activities is because they are not afraid of losing face outside their own local systems.[10] As "strangers" in the city, they are free from the moral constraints that they had in their hometowns. As a Beijing taxi driver explained it to me: "Nobody wants to do these dirty things in their own local areas because there are friends and acquaintances around. But at places other than their own locality, face is not much of a concern."

The demoralization of spatial mobility extends even further into the projection of political stability and order. The notion of *dongluan* in the Chinese political semantics readily links spatial mobility or movement to "chaos" and "disorder." As one writer claims: "Historically, those who lost the means of production and the basis for livelihood often became the floaters. They are the most unstable, destructive, and explosive social elements in Chinese history. . . . This kind of social force, which is mainly derived from rural surplus labor and unemployment, has become the major source of crime in China today (Ba and Ma 1989: 65). The underlying logic is that mobile workers do not have any long-term interest and benefits in any urban locality and they are more prone to perform the radical acts that lead to a fundamental reordering of society than are permanent residents.

Second, displaced rurality is viewed as a form of social pollution and another source of illegality. In the discourse on Chinese modernization, peasantry and the countryside are regarded as lagging behind in the nation's march to modernity. Negative images associated with peasantry such as "low class" (*cengci di*) "low quality" (*suzhi di*), "primitive" or "unenlightened" (*yumei*), "ignorant" (*wuzhi*), and "backward" (*luohou*) are transferred to the construction of the floating population (cf. Anagnost 1995). These residual qualities, presumably derived from the unpermeable, deep-rooted, "dark and poor dispositions" (*liegenxing*) of the peasantry, are considered to be incompatible with the official vision of Chinese modernity and civility. This is a typical official narrative about rural migrants: "These people's suzhi is generally lower. Their sole purpose in leaving home is to make a living by working in the city. Thus, money and wealth are their most direct and basic needs. . . . Some of them with low cengci take advantage of mobility to engage in illegal and criminal activities" (Zhang and Wang 1991: 32). The poor environmental conditions in migrant communities are also taken as an expression of low suzhi (Ji et al. 1995: 80). But migrants contend that the problem of hygiene is created by the local government, which charges them cleaning fees but does not assign anybody to do the work.

The notion of suzhi can be better understood in light of Bourdieu's "habitus" (1977). Like *habitus, suzhi* refers to one's disposition, abilities, and way of acting, which are formed through one's upbringing and cannot be changed overnight. At the same time, suzhi can also structure everyday practices. Who has the right to define *suzhi* has always been a contentious issue because it is both conditioned by and in turn reshapes power relations and social domination. Paradoxically, while the floating population is stigmatized as a group with poor suzhi, many of its members (especially migrant entrepreneurs) are capable, successful businesspeople who have gained remarkable economic capital and consumption power in the reform era. The urbanites' complaints of migrants' low suzhi partly reveal their own insecurity and jealousy, as they are being symbolically displaced by successful migrants and thus are failing to assume a prominent place in the post-Mao socioeconomic order, which upsets the old social stratification of people and the distribution of wealth.

Third, the dominant discourse construes crime as a result of migrants' greed for wealth, presumably unleashed by the market-oriented city experiences that promise too many unfulfilled dreams. Migrant workers are frequently depicted as ignorant, poverty driven, and jealous about the urban affluence they lack. As one article claimed, "Peasant workers who leave their homelands for survival cannot help but follow this crazy beast [money] and sell their lives and souls to this erratic 'devil'" (Zhang and Han 1993). Another city official concluded that "the contrast between city and countryside is difficult for peasants in the cities to adjust to; and from this huge contrast of material wealth ensues the unbalancing of their minds . . . leading to the path of reaping without sowing" (*bulao er huo,* implying "illegal ways of getting money") (*Beijing Evening Daily,* March 24, 1996).

Such cultural logic of migrant criminality as I have described basically functions through what Paul Gilroy (1991) has called "cultural absolutism," by which the problem of urban crime is mapped onto members of a particular marginal group and is explained in terms of their problematic culture. By essentializing "culture," the origin of crime is not sought in the broader social structure in transformation but is indiscriminately ascribed to the inferiority of migrants' suzhi or moral distance. Stereotyping migrants as a homogeneous low-suzhi group makes them appear to be alien to Beijing's presumably modern, sophisticated, cosmopolitan culture and high moral code. Such cultural and moral distance is then used to justify the argument that rural migrants are not suitable for the city and ought to return to their places of origin because their rural upbringing, spatial displacement, and low suzhi can lead to menacing psychological problems and submission to the devil of money.

Hegemony is never a complete and closed system of domination; instead, it is a fluid, shifting, and partially integrated social field open to contestation, as Comaroff and Comaroff (1991) have argued. Hegemonic discourses thus also presuppose a possibility of discord or the improvisation of subversion (Anagnost 1989; Borneman 1993). Although some Chinese social science discourses echo the hegemonic representation described earlier, there is a new segment clearly diverging from the largely negative view of the floating population. This new voice comes from scholars of the younger generation, who tend to assign positive values to the new dynamic flows of capital, commodities, and labor engendered by economic reforms.

Revalorizing migrant spaces and practices is best articulated by two young scholars, Xiang (1993, 1995) and Wang (1995), who have both conducted fieldwork in migrant communities in Beijing. While addressing the problem of crime and disorder in Zhejiangcun, they argue that crime should not be exaggerated so as to represent the entire social existence of migrants in this community. Their research convincingly shows that there is a great deal of order and productivity in this settlement. Crime emanates only from a small, specific segment of the migrants and thus should not be indiscriminately mapped onto the entire population. Wang (1995) located the origins of crime and disorder within the maladjusted social structure of the reform period, for example, the legacies of the old statist system, which impedes equal market competition; the erosion of the legal system through corruption; and local protectionism, which perpetuates unfair treatment of migrants. Xiang argues that Wenzhou migrant big yards created a better way to maintain local order and mediate the relationship between state control and migrants' self-regulation and that Wenzhou migrants as a whole constitute "a politically stable social group" (1995: 57). He provides convincing information about how the majority of Wenzhou migrants fight crime rather than commit it. This new liberal discourse, although still marginalized, has begun to reshape the popular imagination of the floating population through a different prism.

Local suburban farmers and residents who have personal interactions with migrants also tend to hold positive attitudes toward the migrants in their communities. For them, the economic prosperity brought by migrants is far more significant than the side effects, which they believe are exaggerated by the media. An old male landlord in Zhejiangcun said: "the situation is never as bad as what rumours paint. We have no reason to be afraid of them [migrants]. As long as you do not bother them, they usually will not bother you either. They are interested in their business, not in fighting." Therefore, in the past several government campaigns to clean out migrants, local farmers were generally sympathetic to migrants and expressed resentment toward the government officials.

Alternative Discourse: Relocating the Origin of Crime   While migrant communities are viewed as dirty and chaotic places that need to be eliminated or tightly controlled, these are precisely the places where migrants can find shelter and a sense of order and security. Outside the settlements, migrants are constantly driven by police and scorned by urbanites. For instance, those who try to stay at the Beijing train station over night are driven away by the police from place to place several times a night because of their unauthorized use of public space. Within Zhejiangcun, migrants felt safer in the big yards, which were better regulated and thus more orderly than on the outside. In a long interview with a middle-aged clothing stall owner, he expressed his and many migrants' experiences of big yards:

> Living in big yards is much better than living outside. Why? Because big yards adopt effective self-defense strategies. The backgrounds of renters are screened by the yard boss and they tend to be law-abiding businesspeople. Drug users and those without stable businesses are not accepted. More importantly, neighbors in the same yard interact and know each other well and can seek mutual help when needed. If we were dispersed in Beijingers' small, separate, private courtyards, we would not be able to identify who is who. When robbers attack, no one is there to help or is willing to be in charge.

The majority of Wenzhou migrant big yards had several private security guards on duty. These guards were mostly Shandong and Anhui migrants, employed and trained by newly emerged private security companies in Beijing. To motivate renters to collectively combat crime, some big yard bosses, for example, created a special fund of monies collected from each household. If a household was robbed and the family reported the case to the security team of the yard, the fund would pay for that household's loss in the robbery. But, if the victim did not report the case due to fear of revenge, he or she would not only receive no reimbursement but would be levied a heavy fine. Reporting criminal incidents made it possible for further investigation and prevention. Through the newly developed social networks of surveillance and mutual help, crime was significantly reduced within most big yards. Indeed, feeling safer was the most frequently cited reason given by renters for moving into the big yards. Using migrants' own words, "The development of big yards is a plausible way to restore order through self-development, self-regulation, and self-perfection."

This view of big yards as a place of order and security sharply contrasts with the official discourse, which denounces migrants' self-organization as a form of disorder. The discrepancy between migrants' experiences and the hegemonic representation suggests that an alternative form of ordering was in the process of formation, yet it conflicted with official regulation and thus could not be approved of by the scrutinizing power of the state.

The most critical alternative discourse was developed in the arena of contesting the origin of crime. Rather than limiting our gaze simply to the symptoms of crime, Wenzhou migrants insist that one must question under what social conditions criminal activities are able to reproduce. They argue that the problem of crime should be sought in the existing social structure, which perpetuates a particular form of criminal culture, instead of in migrant dispositions and spatial mobility. Notice how Chen, a Wenzhou migrant businessman, articulated this point:

Beijing people only know that Zhejiangcun is disorderly, but they do not ask why. And they do not know what the real origin of such disorder is. . . . I can assure you that the majority of us are good, law-abiding people. The emergence of crime is closely related to recent societal changes. The problem is more serious here because no one can do anything to stop it. With guanxi and bribery money, criminals can easily get out of the police station. This way, lawbreakers are not afraid of anybody and can assault people again and again. In my view, the real origin of crime is rooted in the corruption of the police as well as the entire legal system.

This narrative represents a widely shared view among migrants. First, they argue that one must differentiate criminals from victims and ask who commits crimes against whom rather than criminalizing the entire migrant group. In Zhejiangcun, robbery is mostly committed by a small group of migrants against the great majority. Criminals have learned that as long as they raid migrants only they are not likely to be arrested by the police, who are primarily interested in protecting the locals. As a result, the majority of Zhejiang migrants, like Chen, have no legal protection and become victims of crime rather than criminals themselves.

Second, Wenzhou migrants subvert the dominant discourse by relocating the origin of crime in the disorder of the state bureaucracy itself. In the eyes of many migrants, the post-Mao party-state, operating on the basis of the idiosyncratic power of officials (*quan*) rather than the rule of law (*fa*), is deeply corrupt. In the new era of marketization, local officials' formal incomes have declined relatively, which makes them more vulnerable to the temptations of bribes and payoffs from gangsters and criminals.[11] The corrupt nature of the government allows crime and disorder to proliferate and perpetuate. Local toughs and criminal groups that are directly or indirectly connected to local police and officials can bail their members out with large cash payments (as high as 10,000 yuan, or U.S.$1,250, for each case). As one migrant explained, "If two parties get into a fight and are taken into custody, both parties have to send money to the local authorities. The more you send, the lighter your punishment. Whoever sends the most money will get out first. If there is no fight and everything is orderly and peaceful, how will the officials make money?" Sometimes disorder is even desired by local police for such rhetorical and practical reasons as legitimating their presence and requesting more funding from upper-level authorities. Corruption sends out permissive signals to criminals. In many migrants' eyes, a police station is not the place where justice is done, but it is the place where criminals are recycled and money is extracted. By constructing the state as a regime of disorder, migrant discourses of corruption deconstruct the state's legitimacy and defend their own efforts to mobilize self-protection. Even though migrants' alternative discourse is largely articulated on the local level and is rarely reflected in the media due to their lack of access to the formal public sphere, it nevertheless has powerful effects on their everyday lives. This counterdiscourse plays a crucial role in helping migrants make sense of the world around them and prompting them to organize localized self-defense through their networks.[12]

The failure of governmental control over order in Zhejiangcun also reveals serious problems within the socialist system of regulation, which does not fit the new reality of a market-oriented society. In postrevolutionary China, state regulation in cities has been primarily based on vertical chains of hierarchical work units in the same system (*tiao*) and local government control of localities (*kuai*). Urban residents are simultaneously located and controlled by these two systems, namely, one's work unit and the local government of one's place of residence. Migrants in the cities, however, are not subject to either of these regulation systems because they do not belong to a work unit nor are they counted as full members of any urban community. Local officials are interested in charging migrants regulation fees, but they do not provide promised services or keep order. Meanwhile, because of frequent unfair treatment by the police, many migrants do not believe that justice can be served by them and have therefore formed an antagonistic attitude toward state intervention in policing. An alternative way to manage migrant spaces is through their own popular leadership (such as housing and market bosses), which mediates the relationship between the migrant group and the local government. Such an emerging leadership in the migrant community, however, is deemed by the government to be alien and dangerous.

Perceptions and representations of migrants and their social spaces often entail concrete material consequences "in so far as fantasies, desires, fears and longings are expressed in actual behavior" (Harvey 1993: 22). For example, since the migrant population is represented as a high-crime group, it is subject to arbitrary official cleansing and expulsion before and during important political events (e.g., the Asian Games, the World Women's Conference, and the 1989 student movement activities). The conflicting perceptions and interpretations of Wenzhou migrants' big yards and the origins of urban crime eventually led to a devastating political campaign that shattered thousands of migrants' lives.

Demolition as a Remedy for Disorder?   The campaign to "clean up and reorder" (*qingli zhengdun*) Zhejiangcun began in early December of 1995. A special governmental work team, consisting of two thousand local officials and cadres, was formed under the order of the Beijing municipal government and directly led by the Fengtai District government. Members of the work team went to Zhejiangcun daily to pressure migrants to give up their housing compounds and leave Beijing. Although many local officials were unwilling to carry out this task, since their own economic interests were tied to the informal migrant economy (e.g., through land leases, housing rentals, and taxes on migrants), refusal to participate in the campaign would jeopardize their political careers. Well aware of multiple-level hidden conflicts, the campaign headquarters constantly called for internal solidarity and urged local officials to give up factionalism and self-interest for the higher call of the central party-state. Meanwhile, five thousand armed policemen were called in, waiting for immediate deployment in case a migrant protest erupted.

Big yard bosses played a crucial role in mediating the relationship between ordinary migrants and the work team. They also mobilized their own regional governments in Zhejiang Province to negotiate with the city government of Beijing. Migrants confronted the work team by delaying their departure to support the negotiation. They criticized the city government's antimigrant sentiment as a typical expression of parochialism that opposed the fundamental principles of reform promised by former Chinese leader Deng Xiaoping. They also invoked the notion of equal citizenship to contest the unequal treatment they had received from the state.[13]

Despite pervasive popular resistance from migrants, local farmers, and local officials, the central and city governments decided to remove all the big yards by the end of 1995. The fact that Wenzhou migrants were able to mobilize support from their provincial and city governments and defy the order of the central state also upset some top officials and made them more determined than ever to destroy this growing nonstate power. Before the official destruction began, big yard owners were ordered to dismantle their compounds to avoid fines and other punishments. With tears and broken hearts, most of them removed parts of their roofs and walls in symbolic compliance. "It is no different than burning your own wealth or killing your own baby," many migrants told me. During the next several days, most compounds were dismantled, creating more than two thousand tons of debris. Thousands of migrants lost their homes and were driven out of Beijing.

Did the demolition campaign really improve social order and public security in the area? Throughout the campaign, it was the law-abiding, propertied, migrant households that were hurt most because they were least mobile and their production hinged upon direct access to Beijing's market. In contrast, those engaged in illegal activities were not seriously affected because they did not live in the big yards, the major targets of demolition. Instead, they took advantage of the disorderly situation created by the demolition to rob and loot even more. The policing of social order in Zhejiangcun was actually set back by this political cyclone. But in a few limited official reports, the narrative of the campaign presented an innocent story of the triumph of justice over evil, order over disorder.[14] These reports highlight the government's achievements in cleaning up the "dead corners" occupied by migrants and widening local streets by demolishing illegal housing. Not a single word was said about where the tens of thousands of displaced migrants went and how they coped with their shattered lives. An abstract notion of social order was claimed.

What is more troubling is the fact that after the campaign the majority of Beijing residents believed that Zhejiangcun no longer existed. This seeming disappearance was precisely what the city government wanted because the cleanup could help revalidate, to a certain degree, its lost accountability as a moral and caring patron by doing something good for its citizens, presumably Beijing residents only. In 1994, Mayor Chen Xitong and the vice mayor (who later committed suicide) were forced to step down after news of their involvement in serious corruption was released to the public. The municipal government was undergoing a profound power transformation and attempting to restore its legitimacy in the public mind. The new leadership, appointed by the central state, needed to differentiate itself from the former regime while constructing a new image and regaining the support of Beijing citizens. The attack on Zhejiangcun was one of the few promises that the new municipal government made to the Beijing public to improve security. The claimed achievement of cleaning up a "high-crime" place helped the city government to regain lost legitimacy and popular support among the permanent citizens of Beijing.

Further, the antimigrant sentiment and actions against this large migrant enclave are closely related to the image of Beijing and the crisis of its identity in a new social and economic era. In the eyes of its officials and residents, the crowded living conditions and poor hygiene in migrant enclaves damage the image of Beijing as the nation's political and cultural center as well as a major national and international tourist destination. The increased fear of crime, seemingly associated with migrants, can eventually reduce tourism and foreign investment. In sum, migrants are viewed as an obstacle to Beijing's beautification and civilizing projects. Migrants who bring with them diverse local cultural practices, including distinct dialects, foods, craft skills, and ways of life, are seen as incompatible with the vision of modernity inspired by some urban elites and upper-level officials. Meanwhile, the privileges and superior status once enjoyed by Beijing residents are eroding with the advent of rapid commodification (see Solinger 1994). Within such rapid social changes and cultural conflicts, what it means to be a Beijinger and what Beijing culture is all about need to be redefined. During the 1995 official campaign "Being Modern, Civil Beijingers" (*zuo xiandai wenming Beijingren*), the floating population was frequently used as the internal "other," an index to what Beijing culture and identity were *not* (cf. Honig 1992b).

Conclusion   Although the campaign to clean up Zhejiangcun was expressed in the language of combating illegal housing, its ultimate goal was to remove the spatial ground for the growth of an alternative social power outside state control. Thus, the campaign was not intended to reestablish legality within the migrant community per se but to restore another vision of order by dispersing and weakening the political energy of this migrant space. The results of the state intervention in Zhejiangcun show that the roots of crime and disorder were left largely intact; instead, migrants' efforts to establish a sense of order through a new form of residence (big yards) were halted.

In reality, Zhejiangcun did not disappear; neither did crime, drugs, and other problems. On the one hand, less than half of the migrants who lived in local farmers' houses managed to stay in the area. On the other, the majority of the displaced migrants eventually trickled back to Zhejiangcun only three months after the demolition. By the time I left this community in September 1996, the migrant garment economy was in the process of rapid recovery and the returned migrants had begun to rebuild their community. For instance, a number of disguised big yards had reappeared! These new housing compounds were not constructed by the Wenzhou migrants themselves but were preexisting sites of bankrupt or closed state-owned factories that were now rented to migrant entrepreneurs. The rent was used by the factories' leaders to support their unemployed workers. Wenzhou migrants believe more strongly than ever that self-policing is the most plausible way to fight crime given the anti-migrant sentiments in the city. Yet this self-empowerment is precisely what the government wants to eradicate.

From a structuralist point of view, a possible move beyond the current dilemma in managing the floating population is to nurture a social group that can mediate between the migrants and the local government. As Duara (1988) has pointed out elsewhere, if the state wants to successfully penetrate the local society it must work through the cultural nexus and reassert itself through commonly recognized symbols of power. Although the Chinese socialist state did just that by creating a grassroots cadre system in rural and urban society in the past, based on a relatively static population (Shue 1988; Siu 1989), it has not yet invented an efficient means of regulating the much more mobile and fluid social field created by the floating population. The new migrant social spaces that have (re)emerged outside the traditional gridlock of state regulation require new kinds of state-society dynamics, in which the modes of ordering and regulation need to be reimagined and renegotiated. Yet, if we look at this dilemma from a different perspective, we may arrive at the quite different conclusion that the reason why the reform era government has not invented a more efficient way to regulate the migrant population is because power needs a disordered social body to legitimize itself.

Notes

This chapter is based on my anthropological fieldwork (June 1995 to September 1996) on the "floating population" in Beijing. My project was supported by a Fulbright-Hays Doctoral Dissertation Research Abroad Fellowship and supplementary grants from the Committee of Scholarly Communication with China, the Wenner-Gren Anthropological Foundation, and the President's Council of Cornell Women. Cornell's East Asia Program, Center for International Studies, and Peace Studies Program made my preliminary research possible. I would like to thank

Aihwa Ong, Steve Sangran, Lisa Rofel, Dorothy Solinger, Ann Anagnost, John Bornemen, Stanley Brandes, Mark Miller, members of the dissertation-writing seminar at UC Berkeley, the editors of this volume, and the two anonymous reviewers who provided useful and insightful comments on the earlier versions of this chapter.

1 Elsewhere I argue that the floating population is a socially constructed category that has helped transform migrants with diverse experiences into a new kind of subject of the state during the very recent history of reform (Zhang forthcoming). This complex social group contains people with different class, occupational, gender, and native place backgrounds. The Wenzhou migrants I worked with are mainly middle class migrant entrepreneurs who operate family businesses rather than migrant workers who sell their labor.

2 The hukou law was enacted in 1958 and continues to be the primary method of regulating the population and policing public security and order in China. Under the hukou rules, every Chinese citizen is required to register at birth with the local authority as a member of the agricultural or urban population according to his or her mother's registration status and is assigned a fixed legal residence (see Cheng and Selden 1994; Christiansen 1990; Zhang 1988; and Chan 1996). Hukou has had profound effects on Chinese people's lives not only because it restricts spatial mobility but because it created two asymmetric forms of citizenship: the urban and the rural. People without the urban citizenship (such as migrants) are denied citizen rights, benefits, and formal residency in the cities (cf. Solinger 1999).

3 By "metaphor," I mean a powerful image whose form is concrete, specific, and tangible but whose meaning is condensed and widely applicable to a spectrum of social phenomena. It creates a new relationship between two seemingly different domains (cf. Fernandez 1991).

4 I was first introduced to a few key informants by Xiang Biao, a graduate student at Beijing University, who himself came from Wenzhou and did fieldwork in Zhejiangcun. Because of his shared local origin with these Wenzhou migrants and my friendship with him, I was able to gradually build up rapport with more migrants there through the snowball sampling method.

5 In China, almost all land is officially owned by the state. Yet, use rights to land are often distributed to work units and villages, which now enjoy some freedom to lease certain kinds of land to private entrepreneurs.

6 I follow Davis (1992) in viewing housing structure as a form of "archisemiotics" in order to unravel relations of domination inscribed in the built environment.

7 The terms *outsiders* and *floaters* (or *floating population*) refer to the same broad social group, but they carry slightly different social connotations. *Waidiren,* literally meaning "people from other places," emphasizes the outsideness, while *floaters* stresses the people's unstable relationship to places. They are culturally specific categories that emerged when the household registration system confronted these unceasing waves of migration.

8 This mode of national order is not unique to the socialist state but has deep roots in

the Confucian political ideology that attempted to adhere people to the moral order by tying them to the spatial order.

9   Perceptions of migrants as criminals are often magnified in the case of Uighur migrants in Beijing because ethnic Uighurs appear more "otherly" than Han migrants do.

10   For further discussions on the issue of face, see Hertz, this volume; and Yang 1994.

11   The regular salary of a local police officer or official is less than 800 yuan a month, while a middle-income Wenzhou migrant businessman can make more than ten times this amount on average. This striking difference in income distribution motivates local government agents to seek additional income by abusing their power.

12   Just because migrant discourse is not articulated in the urban public sphere (i.e., in the media), this does not mean that it has no real effect on their everyday lives. Precisely because migrant voices are not sufficiently heard by the urban public, I feel that it is imperative for me to bring such voices out through ethnographic writing.

13   The campaign was a complex event charged with tension and rife with conflicts among various social groups and state agencies. Space here is insufficient to elaborate on the complicated negotiations and political realliances. For a detailed account, see Zhang forthcoming.

14   The media were prohibited from reporting this event. Only four short articles in slightly different versions, drafted and sanctioned by the Beijing government, appeared in local newspapers such as the *Beijing Evening Daily* and *Beijing Youth Daily*.

Part Four Expressions of the Urban

Louisa Schein Urbanity, Cosmopolitanism, Consumption

Consumption Culture   This chapter presents urbanity as an artifact of popular cultural production and consumption in post-Mao China. That the city, however conceived, has become an object of increasingly intense desire in the era of reform is closely linked to a burgeoning consumerism. Cities, especially megalopolises such as Beijing, Shanghai, and Guang-zhou/Shenzhen, are widely viewed as glittering markets for a world of goods imported from the catalogs and store shelves of global modernity. Striving to become what Sassen has called "global cities" (1994: 18–24), they are the sites of intersection between China and the cosmopolitan affluence that continues to be emblematized by the West. Affluence, as indexed by the availability of myriad commodities and lifestyles, is coded as a modernity that, although still seen as "the most formidable achieve-ment of the West . . . remains a potent dreamland for the rest of the world" (Zhao 1997: 43).

"Dreamland" is a key image here, for the availability of goods is, of course, not paralleled by equal access to them. For much of the world, the modernity that goods signify is the stuff of unfulfilled longing. What cities have offered in the popular imagination of the postsocialist period is the potential for acquisition, not necessarily its actualization. For much of the Chinese populace, the higher prestige items, no longer restricted by state regulations, remain out of reach for reasons of economic limitation. Especially for rural folk, such goods and lifestyles might be encountered only by making visits to towns and cities, and then they often serve only as objects of a fascinated gaze, out of reach for purchase. But my starting point is that a general culture of consumption—an acute commodity desire linked to social status—has saturated all sectors of Chinese society, regardless of what specific changes in actual consumption patterns have taken place. This is a structure of feeling that is deeply implicated in what I call "imagined cosmopolitanism," for the visibility—or what Haug, following Marx, called the "flirtatious glances" (1986: 19)—of newly available commodities in turn has given even window shoppers a sense of participation in a global commodity culture.[1] Selves are crafted out of aspirations, as are hierarchized social distinctions.[2] What I will argue in the body of this chapter is that the making of these cosmopolitan, urbane, or "modern" selves involves highly performative practices that indicate struggles for relative prestige within the Chinese social order.

Indigenous culture is simultaneously implicated in these status negotiations. Even for those who have little access to the spoils of China's freshly imported modernity, cultural modalities that mark urbanity are tied to practices of consuming compartmentalized "traditional" culture. Henri Lefebvre has suggested that the expansion of cities both undermines and congeals the rural as oppositional noting that "the expanding city attacks the countryside, corrodes and dissolves it. This is not without . . . paradoxical effects. . . . Urban life penetrates peasant life, dispossessing it of its traditional features. . . . Villages become ruralized by losing their peasant specificity. They align themselves with the city but by resisting and sometimes by fiercely keeping themselves to themselves" (1996: 119–20). In post-Mao China, practices of nostalgia, revitalization, and reenchantment have taken up folk cultures from the countryside and worked them as malleable substances that can lend vitality and continuity in a swiftly changing, often disorienting, reform process. The rural, the folk, and the ethnic become codified and standardized as consumption objects of urbanites, losing, as Lefebvre suggests, their local idiosyncrasies. But such "internal orientalism" (see Schein 1997) has not been restricted to elite urbanites who long for the rural as the past. Those who themselves inhabit rural sites, whose daily routines are precisely those of the much-romanticized peasant, also rework cultural fragments in socially significant ways. Young people are particularly adept at recrafting, in *bricoleur* fashion, the elements they receive from both parental legacies and more cosmopolitan flows. The ethnography presented here suggests that cultural producers and consumers at multiple levels strive for positional superiority by situating themselves closer to urbanity/cosmopolitanism through their own refractions of "tradition." The urban, then, is also in a sense a workable substance rather than a static identity category.

Signifying the Urban Much has been done to characterize the late capitalist form of the city in terms of generalizable features. The city is seen as the apogee of commodity fetishism, where consumption rather than production shapes social life (Harvey 1990). Along with the workings of the fetish comes the emphasis on spectacle (Debord 1994), on surfaces and appearances. Patton (1995: 117) following Raban (1974) suggests that the anonymity of the city makes for a social milieu in which acting is the norm, in which the self is always being presented differently. By contrast, the rural, typically emerging as the dyadic complement of the city, is a place of stasis, of authenticity. It is cities that are portrayed as the settings where new states of mind could come into being.[3]

While such generalizations resonate strongly with the character of Chinese cities, it is important to keep in mind that we are dealing with a postsocialist setting in which state and economy have been closely linked in specific ways. Following Caroline Humphrey on Russians, ethnographies of consumption should look at locally particular "value-laden perceptions," which are "specific to recent historical time" (1995: 65). In China, as elsewhere, the rural has signified a kind of class position in relation to the urban. During the Maoist period, this became strictly formalized in the household registration system, which Potter (1983) has characterized as "caste-like" in its consignment of peasants to a geographic and social immobility. Rural classification, ostensibly valorized in the Maoist orthodoxy, nonetheless remained equated in the popular imagination with the lowest rung on China's social ladder. And, whereas the rural signified a homogeneous mass of manual laborers, the cities were internally differentiated, offering rare possibilities for mobility at least in lifestyle if not in vocation.

The inauguration of Dengist reforms after 1978 entailed a gradual unraveling of the castelike character of the rural-urban divide. Economic reforms returned agricultural production to households and promoted rural enterprise, creating conditions for the occasional amassing of unimaginable wealth in rural sectors that most urbanites witnessed with awe and envy. In the meantime, internal migration expanded with the lifting of state regulations on mobility and residence, intensifying an urbanizing trend that had begun with the industrialization of the 1950s.[4] Between 1949 and 1984, the percentage of the total population that was classified as urban increased from 10.6 to 31.9 percent (Chan 1992: 45). Likewise, in the first decade of reform (1978–87) the proportion of the Chinese working population that was involved in agricultural and related fields such as forestry decreased from 70.7 percent to 57 (Wang 1993: 156). Mobility was recast as that which punctured the barrier between the country and the city. In the contemporary period, then, social and economic mobility is thought to begin not within the metropolis but in the more spatialized move to it. This movement between what were once impenetrable sociospatial poles has, I will argue, also become the grist for cultural production. In the fluidity intimated by the accessibility of the urban lies the potential for other kinds of fluidity. It is not only that discrete persons will move from country to city but that persons, wherever located, are being refashioned in relation to urbanity.

Minorities and Social Positioning   As a demonstration of the extensive reach of ideologies of urbanity, I shift the focus away from the urban cultural centers so often analyzed in studies of China's contemporary change onto what is often characterized as the remote—the non-Han interior. While China's population as of the 1990 national census was 92 percent Han, it also includes the fifty-five minority nationalities heavily distributed across the border regions of the north, south, and west. With a high proportion of rural agriculturalists, minorities are often considered by urbanites to be culturally antithetical to progressive change. As an aggregate, they are regularly taken as emblems of earlier stages of social development in a classification system derived from Morgan and Engels and filtered through Stalinist and Maoist nationality theory. This social-evolutionist explanation of cultural difference has permeated popular understandings such that minorities have come to be aligned symbolically not only with tradition but with the past. Among these are the Miao, numbering 7.4 million and distributed over seven provinces in the southwest.[5] Known in Chinese popular lore, and more recently in commodified popular culture, for their polychromatic costumes, their songs, and their ritual practices (Diamond 1988, 1995; Schein 1996b, 1997), their own strivings for versions of modernity are commonly overlooked. Yet even Miao peasants cultivating rice, corn, and potatoes in rough mountains far from metropolitan hubs have been incorporated, through consuming the mass media and through their own limited travels, into the culture of desiring commodities. Only a few of them have become urban migrants, but post-Mao changes have given rise to myriad ways in which intraethnic social distinctions have been generated out of newer material and lifestyle pursuits.

This chapter, then, proceeds from the premise that studies of ethnicity in China, and elsewhere, need to be complicated by intersecting forms of difference. I particularly explore class, age, and rural/urban status in terms of how they fracture ethno-cultural milieus and forms of expression. As part of a larger project that examines cultural politics in the post-Mao era, I would like here to pursue the possibility that rapid change and the encounter with "modernity" may make discrete ethnicities less relevant, not by destroying "traditional" culture per se but by presenting both Han and minorities with similar cultural dilemmas of self-fashioning.

My analysis is based on ethnographic research carried out over the course of five trips to China in the 1980s and 1990s, including a year's residence in Xijiang, a Miao community in the mountains of Guizhou Province.[6] This was multisite research that also involved long-term residence at universities for minorities (*minzu xueyuan*) and short-term visits to multiple other sites of Miao cultural production. The remainder of this chapter offers ethnographic vignettes to show how the culture of consumption and the prestige of urbanity are worked in the production of status. My discussion proceeds through a comparative analysis of three iterations of urbanity/rurality involving young people, two situated among peasants in the countryside and one taking place in Beijing. One agenda of this juxtaposition is to present these disparate sites and levels as linked and interreferential. These types of social practice are equally important when it is urbanites engaged in the production of their own urbanity as well as the rurality from which they demarcate themselves.

Birthday Bountiful   It is 1993 and five years since I lived in the Miao mountain village of Xijiang in southeastern Guizhou Province. The community is a market hub in the region, and as it is a crossroads not only for visitors but for circulating goods residents pride themselves on their modern modalities and consumption styles. It is a site with a high concentration of salaried state employees and a small but growing number of entrepreneurial ventures. Flows of cash converge with displays of affluence, even though the majority of Xijiangers are still miserably poor by any national standards. Almost as if protesting too much, the announcement "things have changed" is proclaimed by Xijiang's tiny elite through the minutia of material trappings, interior ornamentation, and style choices.

It is in the enactments of fledgling domesticities, restructured according to revamped canons of gender, that some of the features of this strategizing around urbane status become most visible. A young woman I had known in 1988 to be still wary of the marriage market has now married and had a year-old son. The youthful parents have been busy fashioning themselves according to the markers that will index their accumulation of symbolic capital in China's national prestige economy. The husband has a coveted job—not only does he draw salary from the Forestry Department, but as a consequence they are entitled to reside in the newfangled concrete Forestry Building. The structure features a multi-storied collection of apartments free of the creaky stilts, mud-packed floors, and porous, breezy, wood-slat walls featured in local Miao architecture. Capitalizing on their privileged sense of opportunity, they have opened a tiny storefront-type concession out of a window on the building's first floor where they peddle cigarettes, matches, chewing gum, biscuits, and other sundries to whomever should pass by. No longer identified with agricultural personnel (*nongye renkou*), my female friend idly tends her baby at the storefront while her husband engages in lucrative forestry management. During the agricultural busy season (*nongmang*), they obligingly return to the nearby fields of the young woman's parents to help out.

Two reworkings of age and gender norms stand as emblems of their elevated status. Strictures of patrilocality have been suspended, for in this case it is in the bride's hometown that salary is to be earned. Although she has no motive to give up her land allocation, and although she lives in the immediate vicinity, she does not dirty her hands on a regular basis, preferring to let the peasant-identified members of her natal family till her state-designated parcel. It is as if the concrete of her apartment walls has become a class divide, giving the once-dutiful daughter a status only to be breached when her family gains the benefit of her geographic proximity at crunch times. And yet all approve of the arrangement, just as they accept the couple's gendered division of labor. For the daughter to be able to stay out of the fields, ensconcing herself in the commodity-identified space of domesticity and engaging in petty entrepreneurship on the side is the best thing she could be doing.

It has come time to design the ritual for the baby boy's first birthday. The codes for celebratory commemoration of birthdays were foreign imports that had become regularities in the urban China of the 1990s. In this family, the husband has a periodic practice of riding the long-distance bus to the nearby metropolis of Kaili to secure appropriate markers of consumption savvy. The birthday preparations will demand special attention to these choices. The big acquisition is a karaoke player, which will enable a simulation not only of pop music but of the mediated life of urban leisure activity. Karaoke has not really caught on in Xijiang, so this will lend its purchasers a kind of pioneer stature. Moreover, for Miao the practice of karaoke will have a special valence. Miao have spent decades offering up their local song traditions for processing in the slick and sometimes professional industry of manufacturing ethnic exotica for performance and sale. Now is not the moment for Miao melodies, how-ever, but for appropriating the music of the very centers that have made of the Miao a musical source. The significance of karaoke, as Adams has suggested for Tibet, is that for minorities whose performances of cultural "authenticity" have been subjected to diverse canons of representation it "takes as its reality principle the idea of role-playing, but creates a site where role-playing is itself satirized" (1996: 511).

All ironies aside, I never find out what kind of music will be lip-synched by these nouveaux consumers. The display of karaoke technol-ogy suffices for the evening, while the emphasis is instead on face-to-face socializing. Significantly, it is not the plentiful local members of the baby's extended family who are invited as the key guests, but rather myself, my partner, and my two-year-old daughter, American partici-pants who will lend instant cosmopolitanism to the event. A couple of neighbors also attend along with a couple of representatives from the mother's family. We gather in the concrete-walled living room for a home-cooked feast of many dishes. The children are goaded to play with one another and amuse the company. Finally, the moment has come, and the other key metropolitan purchase is presented. It is a fancifully iced birthday cake, handpicked from among the proliferation of decorated temptations that now dance in bakery windows all over Kaili, then tenderly transported on the long, steamy bus ride home. Pastel flowers and swirls adorn its surfaces. It is a few days old and not really to local tastes, but it is encrusted in a frosting so sugary and airtight that it remains edible even after its long journey. With considerable awkwardness, we sing "Happy Birthday to You" in Chinese and English; then we cheerily dig in. Elite distinction—coded in the commodities and the salary-derived cash it takes to acquire them—is celebrated right alongside the baby's first birthday.

Performing Hybridity   If karaoke was a strategy of urbane consumption, Xijiang locals also had modalities of cultural production that took up and staged local culture in styles that were decidedly self-aware. One was the midsummer "Festival of Eating the New Rice" (Chixinjie), a boisterous preharvest occasion for market gatherings, guesting and feasting for older generations, and late night promenading for young people looking for something more. At Chixinjie, the youth of the Xijiang region are most intensely engaged in courtship cruising. They pay the closest attention to grooming for marriageability, demonstrating their urbanity through careful style calibrations such as the use of Miao clothing made of artificial fibers, high heels, and Western-style shirts and blouses. Each must struggle with how s/he will participate in the after-midnight marriage market, deciding whether to sing the traditional antiphonal courtship songs, to listen on the sidelines and strike up conversations instead, or to flaunt flashy new technologies by recording the singing on big boom boxes.[7]

But other things have begun to take place at Chixinjie, activities that emblematize the negotiations over how Xijiang youth will position themselves in relation to "culture." Shortly before the festival, the young man who ran the local, state-funded Culture Station had proudly explained to me that he had been able to procure just enough funds to purchase prizes that would allow him to sponsor a youth performance. On a high festival afternoon, on the stage of the local movie house, groups of children and teenagers from all over the district would have a chance to give amateur performances. Each contestant, not only the winners, was to get a prize. The event was a homey imitation of professional song and dance troupe routines in which Miao in the Xijiang region join together to rehearse and consume changing cultural identities.

The structure of the event was established by the young man from the Culture Station. Spectators were sold tickets beforehand. Audience and performers were strictly separated by the spatial arrangement of Xijiang's movie house. Performers were framed as contestants and awarded their token prizes. Indeed, symptomatic of the rampant commodification of culture underway throughout China, the success of the event, its organizer stressed, was contingent upon the awarding of prizes to motivate the participants. Hence, he had approached six county-level offices for funds. None had granted him a cent, so he had only thirty or forty yuan with which to work. He regarded the prizes he was able to award—lipstick, handkerchiefs, and the like—as inconsequential. With more funds for better prizes, he claimed, they might have been able to stage a "real" competition.

There were seventeen numbers in the afternoon program. An emcee mediated the material, introducing all the elements of the program. A gong and drum signaled moments for applause. The audience comprised primarily children, with a few teenagers and adults. The ad hoc groups of performers came from far-flung villages, all within Xijiang District and all with a proud sense of representing their native place, which in some cases was signified by the production brigade (*dadui*) to which they had belonged before decollectivization. There were children and young adults performing. Four of the groups were nursery school classes.

Performers fashioned their renditions to demonstrate both their control of contemporary material and their fluency in Miao styles. Their media were song, dance, music, props, and costume. Flouncy pink skirts and skintight leggings mingled with People's Liberation Army (PLA) jackets. Performances spanned both the songs of Han popular culture and versions of the notorious Miao drinking songs (*jiuge*). Those who included Miao melodies in their medleys punctuated their endings with loud whoops, canonizing a custom associated with the rowdiness of social drinking. Some of the older performers flaunted their urbanity through the use of makeup, the microphone, or recorded Chinese popular music. Others choreographed dances intended to represent Miao styles. No ranking was imposed with regard to the indigenous or borrowed nature of the contestants' material. What was important here was that culture was an object of self-conscious display and hence control.

The performance amounted to a pageant in which Xijiang Miao demonstrated to themselves the shape and the viability of their contemporary hybridized culture. It was not publicized, and it was not directed at any outside audience. To the extent that it drew upon dominant styles, we may say that it represented a coming to terms with the outside. Mostly, it was a celebration of "culture," an objectified culture now loosed from its moorings in everyday or ritual life. As emblematized by the spatial polarization into stage and audience, the event asserted the ability of the participants to take hold of, contain, and manipulate "culture" employing "modern" formats. It identified them as producers. As members of a putatively backward minority group, commonly portrayed as unselfconscious and tradition bound, it marked them as active and aware, in charge of defining themselves, dominated neither by their weighty past nor by the subsuming mainstream. The sale of tickets and the fact that each performance was compensated with a token prize demonstrated participants' complicity with the growing market logic in which culture is broken up into little bits suitable for exchange.

Dancing the Past Away   By isolating and valorizing "culture" as something produced and consumed, the participants in the youth performance were enacting another "modern" practice, one in which lifeways were compartmentalized and associated with the domain of leisure. These themes were likewise poignantly dramatized in a Miao performance that took place in Beijing. The occasion was Siyueba, the April Eighth Festival, which Beijing Miao held annually on the campus of the Central Nationalities Institute. Throughout the Maoist period and beyond, nationalities institutes, colleges for the education of and research on minorities, have functioned as sites for the forging of permissible oppositional identities. Students and cadres-in-training learn to "be ethnic" within the parameters of state cultural policy. Siyueba drew together the nine-hundred-some Miao residents in Beijing (Xiong 1993: 259), including scholars and students as well as workers, cadres, and People's Liberation Army soldiers, and also served as an opportunity for Miao from the provinces to visit and perform their local cultural specialties. Orchestrated by the Beijing Miao intelligentsia, the event condensed many of the themes seen in the Xijiang youth performance. Among the numbers in an afternoon revue of performances of Miao song and dance—intercut with demonstrations of martial arts and of Han and Western music styles—was a solo dance by a young Miao woman.

The dancer entered the stage dressed conservatively in an urban-style pale pink shirt and black pants, her hair braided simply down her back. Her movements were graceful, controlled, dignified. After a few moments, she discovered in a heap some Miao silver jewelry and a flamered diaphanous skirt in a pattern evocative of the stereotypical Miao pleats. She approached tentatively and began to try on the jewelry. As she adorned herself, her enthusiasm seemed to grow, and she quickly donned the rest of the ornaments and pinned her hair up in characteristic Miao style. She danced with the skirt as a prop and then put it on, too. Now her movements became bold, flamboyant, confident. She seemed to have been somehow freed. The music picked up tempo. She smiled with an expression of childlike mischievousness. She twirled to make the skirt flare out triumphantly. Then, as if pulled by an inexorable force, her movements gradually slowed and she reluctantly began to shed her ethnic attire.[8] One by one, she removed the ethnic articles from her body, leaving only the generic urban garb. When her fanciful costume was returned to a heap on the floor and her hair again hung braided down her back, she brought her dance to a close by fleetingly covering her face with her hands.

Both the dancer and her product are suggestive of multiple themes. The dance was created by a young Miao woman whose own life trajectory had taken her out of peasant/ethnic status and placed her in her country's capital as an urbanite compelled to conform to the norms of Beijing's prestigious metropolitan-Chinese culture. An element of this cultural milieu was the nostalgia for the romanticized past that accompanies participation in "modern" urban life. In the case of this dancer, her own past, symbolized by ethnic dress, became the subject of romantic longing, even as it was inevitably renounced.

Renunciation, however, did not mean complete eradication, and in this light the dance enacted the recuperation of an underground sensibility. Reminiscent of the 1985 film *Qingchun Ji* (Sacrificed youth), in which a Han woman learns of feminine beauty and awakens to her sexuality when she is sent down to live with the Dai during the Cultural

Revolution, the dance encapsulated the tensions generated out of a cultural climate that valorizes the color and beauty of non-Han ways even as it condemns them as retrograde.[9] What was distinct about this creation, however, was that it was not about cultural interchange but the problematic articulation of the Miao self, a self even more fractionated by urbanity and its pained relation to the rough vitality of the countryside.

When I watched this performance, I saw the final gesture, in which the dancer covered her face with her hands, as an expression of shame, a retrospective condemnation of her momentary transgression. I interpreted it in a postmodern frame, assuming that what the dance enacted was a structure of feeling marked by ambivalence in which standards of beauty and contours of identity were unsettlingly shifting and indeterminate. A Miao scholar with whom I later discussed the dance read the message in terms of a more modernist teleology: her final gesture was one of mourning (*beixin, tongku*), expressive of the tragic but inevitable break (*tuoli*) with "traditional culture" entailed by the exigencies of progress. The interpretive disjuncture between my version and that of the Miao scholar suggests that ambiguity, as well as ambivalence, is the stuff of Miao youth culture.

Refracted through the lens of gender, this ambiguity can be seen in the way the dance both reproduced and ruptured conventional representations of the modernist trajectory. As suggested above, minority women are regularly consigned to the position of conservators of traditional culture, particularly traditional dress. Without a doubt, the dance worked within this paradigm in its emphasis on the central theme of costume. But, because the dancer as a woman portrayed herself as moving between the less ethnically marked, urban, more gender neutral positioning (pants, Western-style shirt, single braid down the back reminiscent of the Qing dynasty male queue as well as a ubiquitous women's style) and that of the typical colorfully dressed Miao woman, she in effect destabilized the prevailing binaries that placed minority women unilaterally in the rural/traditional category. The dance, then, substituted movement and flux for the static attributions of Miao character that was the staple of dominant cultural production. Indeed, the interpretation of the Miao scholar suggested a literal drama of movement symbolized by the change of clothing. In his view, the putting on of Miao attire signified the happy return of a college student to serve her country home (*gaoxingde wei jiaxiang fuwu*) as teacher, whereas the shedding of ethnic dress indicated her subsequent return to the city necessitated by her parents' concern for her personal advancement.

Youth, Mobility, and Cultural Struggle The post-Mao era has seen a marked shift in the character of sociogeographic movement brought about by the continuing development of market- and export-oriented economic reforms. Among college and technical/vocational school students with rural origins, fewer and fewer have returned to work in the countryside after graduation, favoring instead to exercise their option to seek employment themselves rather than having the state make their work assignment. Considerations of income level, lifestyle, and prestige encourage them to remain in the cities and even to migrate to Special Economic Zones in the Southeast (especially in Guangzhou and Shenzhen), where they find work in factories or fill the vacuum in the educational system created by educated Cantonese who choose business and entrepreneurial pursuits rather than teaching. One Miao intellectual estimated as early as 1992 that one hundred thousand persons had left Guizhou Province as labor migrants; among these, 40 percent were Miao and one-quarter of the Miao were women.

The shift toward a unidirectional movement out of rural villages and peasant status toward the promise of the metropolis took place throughout the 1980s and 1990s, burgeoning after the late 1980s change in policy that permitted high school and college graduates to look for work themselves.[10] Reduction in the numbers of actual rural returnees was correlated with a concomitant desire for a symbolic form of return and, as a consequence, a tremendous quantity of nostalgic cultural production. This diffuse nostalgic project was unified by its consistent quest to consume "traditional culture" in ways that affirmed the metropolitan sensibilities of the consumer.

Interpreting the vignettes offered here permits some generalization about how modernity was performed. To "be modern" was to consume or reproduce rather than produce, to perform rather than simply practice, to watch rather than do, to be urban rather than rural, to be masculine rather than feminine, to do things mechanically or with machines rather than with one's body, and to standardize or routinize rather than improvise. These valuations of the modern and nonmodern, however, were fraught with ambivalence. There was a continual renegotiation of boundaries as young people, both male and female, struggled for particular identities as well as a more universalized prestige whose indices were common throughout China. Thus emerged the kind of hybridized cultural practice that characterized events such as Xijiang's Chixinjie performance. Moreover, in certain domains of cultural production and at different historical junctures what constituted the modern mode was subject to what might be called turf contestation. Modernity and urbanity were not only statically distributed in fixed sites, but they could be generated and displayed as forms of symbolic capital. Thus, young people at Chixinjie and even at routine periodic markets paid great attention to appearances and practices.

The greater spatial mobility of Miao young people provides an apt metaphor for the increasingly fluid senses of selfhood that they were fashioning. It was not only those who moved who contributed to producing a more plural landscape for Miao youth. As the staging of the birthday party reveals, even rural young people were wielding fragments of urbanity to produce hierarchical distinctions among themselves. Such prestige struggles were, of course, endemic to the newly stratified social system ushered in by the features of reform that condoned heightened disparities of wealth and valorized cosmopolitan modernity for all. One of the ways in which Miao young people have dealt with their disparagement in the overall prestige structure is to become players in it themselves, even if their wealth and spatial/vocational mobility does not change. Their practices are part of an imagining of cosmopolitanism that excludes no social sector.

It is important, however, to keep firmly in mind that within the Chinese cultural scene Miao youth culture stands as multiply subordinate. As a minority culture, it is marginal in relation to that of the Han; as primarily rural-based, it is devalued in relation to the culture of the cities; and as a youth culture, it is struggling for legitimacy with that which older generations purvey. As Hall and Jefferson have suggested: "Groups or classes which do not stand at the apex of power, nevertheless find ways of expressing and realising in their culture their subordinate position and experiences" (1976: 12). Indeed, Miao young people seemed to work their subordination through their cultural practices both by performing it and by struggling over it. Achieving prestige by differentiating oneself from an objectified tradition was one of the ways in which Miao young people both reiterated and reworked a cultural hierarchy that ranked their rural ethnic practices near the bottom. On one hand, their struggle for prestige affirmed the China-wide hierarchy, but on the other hand it positioned them as players—or as climbers—in the general prestige structure rather than as immobile ethnic tokens. The stuff of their struggle was more often than not contested definitions of the modern versus the traditional played out through the mediums of class and gender. But their very playing with the adoption of more cosmopolitan roles attested to the ubiquity of the desire for the modern however constructed and regardless of their positioning within it. And the fact that increasing numbers among them had actually accessed these prized centers of urbanity via education, consumption, or employment made these symbolic moves even more freighted with significance. The Miao youth of the 1980s and 1990s came of age during the advent of Dengist reforms, cultural liberalization, and the massive importation of foreign consumer cultural forms. But the older among them had also lived through the demise of the era of the Maoist Cultural Revolution. Hence, it is not surprising that "tradition" would have appeared to them more as an object and less as something lived than it did to their parents. Nonetheless, it was not an object to be entirely disavowed. Even as they marked distinction from their parents by objectifying Miao culture, they marked their distinction from dominant and metropolitan cultures by retaining a modicum of ethnic alterity. The way they pulled this off was by creatively fusing disparate elements—Miao melodies, tape decks, high heels, embroidered costumes, and Han pop music. Similarly, their adoption of urban or imported aspects of style could be a double refusal. It resisted the strictures of ethnically marked local practice imposed by parents and the dominant culture alike and constituted "a subcultural gesture that refused to concede to the manners of subservience" (Cosgrove 1988: 4), to the inscription of the peasant stigma on their bodies. By both acting the ethnic and performing modernity Miao youth in the country and the city produced a form of culture that could encapsulate their somewhat anxious and ever-shifting selfhood, their sought-after urbanity, and their memorable past.

Ruminating on the relation between town and country, Henri Lefebvre has posed the question "Will the urban fabric, with its greater or lesser meshes, catch in its nets all the territory of industrialized countries? Is this how the old opposition between town and country is overcome?" (1996: 120). Certainly what I have been arguing regarding the incorporative, indeed transformative, character of urbanity, the saturation of all quarters of Chinese society with cosmopolitan consumer desire, and the assumption of metropolitan roles by rural as well as urban youth, would suggest a diminishing of the opposition between these two poles. But an ethnographic look at the specificities of cultural production, consumption, and struggle reveals that both the rural and the urban constitute important symbolic material. Indeed, Lefebvre's contradictory answer to his own question resonates strongly with the way in which this duality is retained by Miao youth at the level of meaning: "The 'urbanity-rurality' opposition is accentuated rather than dissipated, while the town and country opposition is lessened" (120). Even as they move—whether physically or symbolically—into a more urbane space, and even though such movement contributes to the diminishing of the gulf between these erstwhile sharply demarcated spaces, Miao cultural practitioners themselves transform the rural and the ethnic into something that will not be summarily obliterated by the advance of urbanity. And in so doing their practices continue to instantiate the urbanity-rurality opposition.

Notes

1   Haug's discussion intimately entangles commodity desire with that of sexuality:

> one category of powerful stimuli in the production of commodities for valorization is that of erotic attraction. Thus a whole range of commodities can be seen casting flirtatious glances at the buyers, in an exact imitation of or even surpassing the buyers' own glances, which they use in courting their human objects of affection. . . . commodities borrow their aesthetic language from human courtship; but then the relationship is reversed and people borrow their aesthetic expression from the world of the commodity . . . [and] powerful aesthetic stimulation, exchange-value and libido cling to one another like the folk in the tale of the Golden Goose. (1986: 19)

> I invoke Haug here to point to an acuteness of longing that, in the manner of erotic desire, is little diminished, or may even be intensified, by going unfulfilled.

2   My discussion here is indebted to social theorists such as Certeau (1984), who argued forcefully that consumption should be regarded as a productive practice, especially on the part of the relatively powerless, and to Bourdieu (1984), who delineated a

process whereby social distinctions were produced by means of consumption. In addition, theorists of global culture such as Jonathan Friedman (1990) and Arjun Appadurai (1996) have been instrumental in resisting notions of homogenization by detailing how transnational commodity culture is related to the formation of distinct local identities.

3   See the discussion by Peattie and Robbins (1984) of the image of the city in anthropological literature and, on this specific point, of Redfield's (1941; 1947; and with Singer 1954) characterization of cities in terms of the great tradition and the little tradition.

4   Chan (1992) shows that rates of rural to urban flow were comparable in the early Maoist industrializing years through the Great Leap Forward and in the post-Mao 1980s, with a sharp decline between 1961 and 1965 and a relatively constant situation in the late 1960s and 1970s. It is also important to note that the rural-urban flow in the post-Mao period was not only about permanent shifts in residence and official classification but also about a much more fluid mobility that characterized more temporary and unofficial types of labor migration (see Chan 1994).

5   Population figures are based on the 1990 national census in which the Miao constituted the fifth-largest ethnic group in China, after the Han, who number more than 1 billion, the Zhuang (15.5 million), the Manchu (9.8 million), and the Hui (8.6 million) (*Beijing Review,* December 24–30, 1990, 34). The Miao are concentrated in Guizhou, Yunnan, and Hunan provinces, with smaller numbers in Sichuan, Guangxi, Hubei, and Hainan Island.

6   For research support during these years, I would like to thank the Committee on Scholarly Communication with the People's Republic of China, the Fulbright-Hays Doctoral Dissertation Research Abroad Program, the Samuel T. Arnold Fellowship Program of Brown University, the University of California, Berkeley, and the Rutgers University Research Council as well as numerous institutions and individuals in China who sponsored or otherwise facilitated my research.

7   For an extended discussion and analysis of the scope of Chixinjie activities, see Schein 2000.

8   This may have represented growing up, conformity, modernity?

9   See Esther Yau (1989) for a provocative analysis of the introspective, post–Cultural Revolution *Qingchun Ji.*

10 On the social consequences of internal migration in China, see Davin 1999; Dutton 1998; Solinger 1999; and Zhang Li, this volume.

Tad Ballew Xiaxiang for the '90s: The Shanghai TV
Rural Channel & Post-Mao Urbanity amid Global Swirl

Social relations do not disappear in the "worldwide" framework. On the
contrary, they are reproduced at that level. Via all kinds of interactions,
the world market creates configurations and inscribes changing spaces
on the surface of the earth, spaces governed by conflicts and contradictions.—Henri Lefebvre, 1994

It is especially important to recognize the effects of the industrial revolution and the growing world market on peasant segments the world
over.—Eric R. Wolf, 1955

Shanghai is more beautiful than ever.—Shanghai Statistical Bureau Information Office, 1998

What happens to our dichotomies then?—Ann Anagnost, 1994

"Xiaosa yi dian . . . "
 The summer day in 1992 had begun more or less as usual. The three
offices of the new *Nongcun tai,* or Rural Channel, were bustling with
activity at Shanghai Television Station (STV) in one of its two main
production and office buildings. People were on phones, scanning the
papers for leads, carrying tapes to postproduction, arranging shoots,
brainstorming with colleagues, or just settling in to their new work
spaces. I'd filled the colorful thermoses with water from the boiler in the
air shaft downstairs and taken them up to the slender office of the Rural
Channel's Arts and Entertainment unit (A&E). Emptied Nescafe jars with

stout pinches of tea were filled with hot water and Kents and Marlboros were touched with tiny flames. The young migrant men from Subei regions of the lower Yangzi Delta, housed in makeshift semistructures recently tacked up just outside, had long since checked in with the power saws and drills and jackhammers from their various precarious perches upon the bamboo scaffolding, working away at the new office and production facility, with guest house, going up adjacent to this one, a shell of its former self, really, after first Italian then Singaporean monies had been pulled in the wake of the Tiananmen tragedies of 1989, putting punch in the "political" in global political economy for STV. All the din and hum and perpetual motion you come to expect in that "big giant construction site" (local parlance) that Shanghai has come to represent in the 1990s— or, rather, re-represent.

The Rural Channel was to go on the air in just a few weeks, beginning with a live opening ceremony prime-time variety show on the eighth day of the eighth month at eight o'clock—all very auspicious since *ba,* or "eight," rhymes with *fa,* "to get rich and prosper," making eights just generally good to have in Shanghai at the time in phone numbers, license plates, addresses, time slots[1]—and subsequently offering three and a half hours of programming each evening on one of the five existing channels then available in Shanghai. This first "narrowcasting" experiment in the annals of Chinese television had been launched through a joint initiative between STV, the Municipal Bureau of Radio and Television, and the Municipal Rural Work Committee. Its mandate was to offer news and entertainment programming for and about peasants (*nongmin*), especially the roughly five million living in the suburbs (*jiaoqu*), counties (*jiaoxian*), and villages (*nongcun*) within the Shanghai Municipality, with the express aim of playing "a powerful role in advancing (*tuidong*) the modernization of the Shanghai countryside."[2] Its staff of about sixty young educated Shanghainese had been culled primarily from within STV, but also included a few from radio and others selected through examinations. They were spread among the News unit and Special Topics unit in addition to A&E, each with its own tight office space abuzz with commotion these past weeks.

Soon an A&E crew was ready for one of its first forays into the Shanghai countryside for some on-location shooting. Chen Ming, the producer of a weekly show on Chinese opera that would be among the flagship A&E

offerings, had organized the group to compile the on-camera testimonials from a diverse demographic of ruralites to be aired as promotional bumpers during the *Opening Ceremony* variety show.[3] A delightfully bright and entertaining expert on Chinese opera in his late thirties, who had previously worked in radio and would occasionally and without warning launch into a few bars of "O Sole Mio" or something similar in a quite beautiful baritone, who was full of heartrending stories of familial history, and whose remarkable coiffure invited speculation on its authenticity, and occasionally its adhesiveness, Chen was in his more or less default sketched-out-inspired-genius mode: "Are we . . . did you . . . is there . . . have they . . . should I . . . ? Okay, 'Tsgo!" Set to go out with him were three of the other eight A&E members: Qu Tanrong, who had worked in security before broadcasting and had a manner of squinting-smiling-smoking strangely reminiscent of James Dean, would work the lights; Mu Zhenqing, a reserved young woman new to the business who kept broadcasting textbooks at her desk, would help with sound and the small playback monitor; and Mao Yinghua, the golden-hearted ever-dependable veteran, would come along to do the camera work and more or less anchor the group technically, since he alone had significant production experience. I rounded out the crew as VTR-toting production assistant lackey slash ethnographic fieldworker, just happy to be there.

We signed out the Sony-dominated equipment from the second-floor tech room, past the castaway domestic-brand equipment piled along the hallway attracting dust and snuffed-out cigarettes alike, then finally got away, fairly smoothly all in all, save for Qu Tanrong's burned ankle from an upended thermos and the more minor datum that we'd overshot our departure time by half an hour or so, a good mark actually.

Then off we drove for the ruralite soundbites, destination: Songjiang County, southeast of downtown Shanghai, one of nine within the Shanghai Municipality at the time and home to half a million people. The clogged city streets of Shanghai soon gave way abruptly, in part per the "garden city" urban design theories of Ebenezer Howard, to the vivid agricultural greenbelt immediately surrounding the city.[4] As cigarettes from around the world were tossed around the van, Qu explained that the giant satellite dishes and microwave tower lurking in the distance, looking urgent and about to exchange Cold War words across the Day-Glo green of freshly transplanted rice paddies, had been built expressly for the historic Nixon visit in 1972. The driver's protective Mao portrait with red tassel hung from the rearview mirror, bopping to the beat of potholes and a privatizing countryside, dodges and darts, stops and starts.[5] Chen Ming waxed epic on how "without Songjiang there'd be no Shanghai!" and offered a quick Berlitz of local history with characteristic narrative flair, as well as another brief on his own family's heritage in a better-known nearby town, including, wistfully, his proud if unconsummated kin relation (they'd never communicated, though he tried once) with an internationally famous architect now living in the West. Which he diagrammed nicely for me on his hand.

Fittingly in several respects, Chen Ming's opera show was called *Nanqiang Beidiao,* which means literally "southern accent, northern tone," but is also an idiom for "speaking with a mixed accent" according to the *Hanyu chengyu cidian* (1992). For this would prove to be a day positively brimming with admixtures of many kinds, linguistic and regional dialect-ical, for sure, but also politico-cultural, social, spatial, across all sorts of human regions, intersecting and blurring identities, much as the epigrams introducing this chapter variously suggest, and, indeed, as the history of dynamic Shanghai itself would suggest.

Any insights these episodes might offer on questions of "reconceiving the urban" or the old "urban-rural continuum" problem would thus have to do precisely with this interflowing complexity and blur as fundamental urban conditions.[6] As Vivienne Shue (1995: 90) evocatively put it recently, urban life in 1990s China presents "a jolting cacophony of possibilities and prospects . . . [where] truths are found everywhere . . . [amid a] jostle of options." Yet to lay stress in these directions is not to offer a reconceptualization at all, really, but rather a reminder of some anthropological ideas of considerable heritage about things like cities and urbanity, which nonetheless have much in common with more current ideas often termed "post-(something)." The stress on open-endedness, flux, urban blur that I want to extend here, however compatible with antiessentialist positions of late, turns out to have a long, rich history in anthropology, even if intoxication by the new often causes us to overlook it.

Of "Jolting Cacophonies" . . . First stop in Songjiang County was a dusty road at the edge of the county seat, Songjiang Township, population 91,000 (Fung 1996), 30 km from central Shanghai up the Huangpu River. Blurry urban interflow ratchets up a notch here already. Waiting roadside for our arrival was Li Mei, a forty-something woman in a black jumpsuit and serious hair wearing a watch ring and lots of perfume, whose husband, introduced as a writer but not joining us, had worked with Qu at STV Channel 2. Directed by Li Mei, we soon arrived at the Songjiang County Workers Club, where she introduced us to a trio of hosts with whom we sat sharing doilies, glass tabletops, tea, and cigarettes in a nice reception room. Our hosts were the Director of the Club, a smooth man in his midforties; the Vice Chairman of the Songjiang County General Workers Union, an amiable round man, fiftyish, who spoke with a slight lisp; and the pleasant woman representative of the Communist Party, similarly round and fiftyish, who would remain almost completely silent the entire time.

And you may ask yourself (with due apologies to David Byrne and Talking Heads of course): Where is the beautiful *nongcun* the Nongcun tai is supposed to be engaging? Where's the "rural" in the Rural Channel? Well . . .

The crew gave a general introduction to the new unit of STV. Chen Ming, animated as usual and oblivious to the very fine kinship diagram on his gesticulating hand, began by saying we had come to Songjiang largely because of Qu's acquaintance with Li Mei and her husband, reminding his hosts (as if!) how hard it is to get things done in "our China" (*women zhongguo*) without such links of *guanxi* (networks of relations, connections) and expressing his hope that this encounter would be the start of a fine and fruitful relationship.[7] He explained further that we were there also to elicit feedback from ruralites on the kinds of programming they would like to see and to videotape some of their statements. More specifically—and here his generalized preproduction anxiety began speaking—we had come especially to videotape people saying they'd like to see a particular kind of show like, well, *Nanqiang Beidiao.*

Mao Yinghua, the most seasoned and savvy of the group, soon interjected, with touching mercy for Chen Ming, to counteract his rather mercenary tone. He provided a more general and efficacious introduction, which emphasized how the Rural Channel aimed to redress STV's relative neglect of viewers in the Shanghai counties by producing programming directed explicitly at their tastes and interests, employing hosts, for example, fluent in local language usage, and giving voice to local concerns. "You've never had this stage before," he said. "Now you do. . . . Our target/object is you."[8]

The Vice Chairman politely began their response by corroborating the necessity of friends and good guanxi and then moved on to the familiar outline of the effects of post-Mao reform and openness (*gaige kaifang*) on the local community, namely, the rise in the standard of living—*shenghuo shuiping tigao le,* intoned with the usual raising of the hands from the belly upward and out, as if to express the viscerally, somatically sensed promise of and yearning for this particular social history—and the corresponding increase in consumption and spending on leisure and cultural activities such as those held at the Workers Club. Volleying back in what might be called the *keqi bisai,* or "contest of politeness," of *guanxi* practice in China, he insisted that the crew had spoken too kindly and it was they who stood to gain most from the work of the Rural Channel. The Club Director also chipped in on how economic development has led to increased demands for leisure and cultural activities in Songjiang and described the *redian,* or "hot spots," in local entertainments such as the twenty-odd performance/dance schools, the three 10-yuan Kala-OK (karaoke) houses (reflecting relatively high consumer spending), the Kala-OK nights many *danwei* (work units) host on occasion, and the various activities held at the club itself for its million annual visitors.

. . . But here: let's have some lunch.

We adjourned to a private dining room for many spectacularly tasty dishes and toasts to and fro. Conversation here was more informal and turned on some remarkable current event topics, such as the coincidental deaths of five STV workers under the age of forty in the past year, which you wouldn't expect to get outdone but very plainly was, hands-down, no contest, by their account of the young director of the local (retransmitter) TV station, who'd very recently tumbled off the top of the TV tower in broad daylight and of course died on the spot. To which, of course, our collective response could only have been, "Wow," or something very close to that.

Overall, it was quite a successful meet-and-greet, a good schmooze, productive networking. Chen Ming at one point was even moved to raise his glass to warmly toast the hosts and marvel, with perhaps a touch of hint dropping too, "Oh, we've gained so much already, and we haven't even started shooting!" It was now after one o'clock, and it's true we hadn't shot a frame.

But soon we were back in the reception room setting up a shot. After some cajoling, the Vice Chairman agreed to *shangjing*, or "get on the lens," and say a few words himself. He sat behind a table in front of the camera, crew, lights, and microphone, no hint now of his recent minor tipsiness. Chen Ming went over his lines about the level of local interest in *Nanqiang Beidiao* and the direction "they" would like to see it take in terms of content—nudging him to use the more colloquial *lanmu* (program) rather than the newsy, doctrinaire *zhuanti* (special subject/topic), to say, "I feel that" rather than the officialese "according to policy" and to plainly state what "people want to see," in addition to *Nanqiang Beidiao*, of course. The Vice Chairman lit a cigarette to take the edge off: long, deep, nervous drags, yes, that would do it.

Now the camera rolled, and the Vice Chairman was off, a pitch or so higher than at lunch but off nonetheless, delivering his lines without prompting in *putonghua* (Mandarin) through a thick local accent.[9] He was a bundle of self-conscious nerves despite the nicotine. Chen Ming was cheerful, encouraging, and patient. But after a few takes he felt compelled to go to the reluctant and increasingly tense Vice Chairman and awkwardly yet very skillfully first compliment him on his content, but add too with all the limited delicacy possible under the circumstances, "Um, perhaps . . . would you mind if we combed your hair?"

And another thing: "*Xiaosa yi dian.*" A touch more "urbanity," if you will, a notch more refined and relaxed. Even Li Mei, the liaison person, joined in on this, exhibiting clearly and multisensorily (clothing, accessories, perfume) that she'd long since fashioned a strong sense of what that meant for herself. "Sophisticate up," was the general direction the man was receiving from his unusual guests.[10]

The Vice Chairman did manage to get through it. When it was over, though, an off-camera scene captured some of the tensions of the episode. The Vice Chairman had come around to watch the playback on the small Sony monitor. Li Mei, the Club Director, and some other locals who'd amassed as an impromptu studio audience teased him good-naturedly, though it didn't loosen him up much. He was still self-conscious as could be. As he leaned over to watch himself on the screen, hands joined behind his back, he kept fidgeting with an object between a thumb and forefinger that he'd clearly been working over for some time and had by now rendered unrecognizable, at least for a few moments. Finally, I realized that it was the transmogrified remains of the filter of that tranquilizing cigarette. I wondered if he'd noticed putting the thing out bare-handed while the camera was rolling.

. . . and fuzzy dichotomies   Recognition challenges abounded, to be sure. Things were clearly fuzzy, distinctly blurred. Intertwining, usually contradictory, discourses and identities and practices were all around. This contingent of Rural Channel urbanites, for example, had come out to the hinterland as part of an official, state-mandated program to serve the countryside, primarily by giving it voice, by representing it. In this sense, they shared a similarity with the urban youth of the Mao-era *shangshan xiaxiang* movements, which sent in just the decade after 1968 some 17 million urban youth (including two of these Rural Channelers!) "up the mountains and down to the countryside."[11] They, too, had intended to serve the peasantry and by extension the entirety of the revolutionary Chinese body/subject, in their case by learning from them how to be properly revolutionary and identify with the masses and by helping communicate central policy to local level.[12]

Yet, in significant contrast to these earlier movements but also in contrast to the very rhetoric of their own newer project, these wielders of highly powerful technologies of representation "in the age of electronic reproduction" (cf. Benjamin [1936] 1969) and post-Mao sojourners *xiaxiang*—these people here were telling the locals in the hinterland specifically how to be, and that they should be, more urbane, sophisticated, and refined. They were effecting a powerful kind of ventriloquism, in Anagnost's (1994) insightful and evocative image—here is your voice, this is what to say—but, importantly, a ventriloquism no longer seeking to inscribe and speak unified revolutionary subjects but rather sophisticated, stylish, cosmopolitan ones. These were new "distinctions," that is, following Bourdieu (1984), new terms of and for "the judgment of taste" made on dramatically reconfigured fields. *Xiaxiang* in the 1990s isn't just not your grandfather's *xiaxiang*. It's not even your older sibling's *xiaxiang*. Or even that of your own youth.[13]

Such generalized ambivalence toward the rural, ranging from deep respect, albeit often condescending, to occasional contempt, was not uncommon among the urbanites at the Rural Channel. On the very first trip to the Shanghai countryside, some weeks previous, to meet with local leaders for introductions and feedback, and under the candied cadence of CantoPop radio in an air-conditioned bus, the young urban media professionals spoke of their understandings of the new Rural Channel's mission in terms that would recur throughout my work with them. Consistently underlying their accounts was a familiar syllogistic line of argument: China is predominantly rural; rural areas are "backward"; to make China modern, you need to address rural backwardness. "If you can't solve the rural problem you can't solve the China problem," one subunit leader explained. Another young man of twenty-one added that "150 years of post–Opium War tears and bitterness are enough to eat," and felt certain that ending that unsavory diet had to begin with improving life in the vast countryside. Others remarked on the need to urbanize the rural areas outside of Shanghai, pointing to satellite town development and the explosion of rural industry as steps in the right direction.[14] Another bright young producer said that he wanted to do a piece on rural housing construction, not to show new dwellings as enviable fruits of reform and progress but to reveal that "while they may look nice on the outside, inside they're really rustic and backward."

This kind of urban ambivalence has been noted in widely divergent contexts, from the contentious concepts of city and country during British industrialization examined by Raymond Williams (1973) to the "localist" and "cosmopolitan" images of rurality among workers on the Zambian Copperbelt illuminated by James Ferguson (1992). As noted, it has long been well remarked for China and repeats some of the tropes identified by Cohen through which urban elites have throughout the postimperial period, but particularly during the early twentieth century, constructed the peasantry "as a culturally distinct and alien 'other,' passive, helpless, unenlightened, in the grip of ugly and fundamentally useless customs, desperately in need of education and cultural reform" (1994: 154–55).[15] Zhang Yingjin's (1996) excellent study details similar representations in the film and literature of this period, in which the rural is represented as a backward, boring, and benighted dead weight on China's efforts to become modern. As Zhang notes, while a rural idyll was occasionally drawn in these texts to contrast with the perceived evil city (e.g., by Li Dazhao), more common was the view held by many May

Fourth writers and later *xiangtu zuojia* (native soil writers), who saw China's countryside as "the country of no hope" and a site of life that is "backward, ignorant, intolerable, stubborn, stagnant, suffocating, and sterile" (1996: 15). Lee and Nathan (1985) also describe the twentieth-century "decline" and "estrangement" between city and countryside wherein "urban intellectuals . . . speculated about the peasant mind as if the villages were on another planet" (394). Interestingly, these images and representations parallel the process of "internal orientalism" that Louisa Schein has insightfully examined in the context of Han (gendered) minority relations in China (1996b, 1997, this volume).

These images of conflict, on the other hand, contrast dramatically with those offered in such foundational accounts as Frederick Mote's on "an urban-rural continuum . . . as an aspect of Chinese psychology. . . . reinforc[ing] the organic unity of rural and urban" (1977: 103). Nor do they square easily with Rhoads Murphey's influential vision of traditional China, which suggests that "There was no denigration of rural circumstances and values, but rather, on the part of many of the urban elite, a longing for the countryside, to which they would retreat whenever they could" (1984: 192).

Clearly, these divergent accounts are the result of their reference to different types of urban elites, one of the traditional imperial order, as Murphey calls it, and the other of the postimperial twentieth century. On the other hand, the two sets of urban elites may not have disagreed had they the same object in mind in the first place. Murphey's image of the retreat of wealthy and mobile gentry and officials to the pastoral countryside to reflect, do art, poetry, and scholarship in their pavilions is surely not what twentieth-century intellectuals have had in mind in their musings on the Chinese countryside. Nor, of course, does this account of "retreat" exhaust the totality of "rural circumstances and values." Indeed, it would seem to scarcely touch it, as the vast majority of rural inhabitants has been typically muted in the historical record.

A similar difference in attitude that may prove to be more apparent than real is that between post-Mao urbanites and the revolutionaries of the Maoist era generally. Thus, Mao's and others' widely remarked "anti-urban bias," would seem to contrast with more recent cosmopolitan distinctions that valorize the urban.[16] Certainly, they are different. On the other hand, Kirkby (1985) and Fung (1981), for example, show persuasively that Maoist policies toward the urban were designed to make urban places work better, albeit along radically different lines, rather than deriving from some visceral aversion to them. Mao was clearly critical of China's cities and demonstrably championed the countryside. But it seems helpful to stress that he was critical of cities as they were then organized and functioning. Designs intended to control and shape cities in a new image do not necessarily reflect the desire to obliterate them. Further, as Whyte and Parish (1984) note, along with Kirkby and others, the Communists' relation with and attitudes toward the cities also grew out of the fact that they were effectively expelled from them by the Nationalists after 1927.

But Wait, This Is Not My Beautiful Nongcun! Apart from these issues, however, another fuzzy problem that should be nagging at you right now, to return to the Rural Channelers' entreaty for more urbanity in the Shanghai hinterland, is the point that this episode is not even taking place in "the countryside" in any completely transparent respect. Songjiang Township has been a settled market town site since at least the Song period (and possibly the Tang or even the Sui).[17] In 1959, it was officially designated a satellite town of Shanghai, and it had a population in the 1990s of some 91,000 (Fung 1996). In what sense, then, had the "rural" even been accessed by the Rural Channel in the first place? The Vice Chairman of the Workers Union was heading a workers union, after all, not a peasant association. The Director of the Workers Club was similarly not leading a peasants club. And Li Mei, the fashion-conscious suburbanite, obviously had strong ties, social and stylistic, to all the cosmo she could manage of Shanghai. So where are the peasants?

Here there emerges a set of vexing spatial and definitional issues about where "the urban" stops and where "the rural" stops, and where either might begin, and I would like to handle these in a particular way: I would like to sidestep them. But not simply for cowardly reasons. Here I find alignment with that aspect of the foundational works of Mote, Skinner, Elvin, Murphey, and others that emphasizes the porousness and heavy-traffic interactions historically between country and city in the scapes of China. For the Shanghai region, border fuzziness and permeability have been fundamental for centuries. What Elvin calls its characteristic "shifting landscape" (1977: 442) refers to its deltaic geomorphology but also conveys the dynamism of its waterway trade history. More recently, it has been the site of a tremendous and generalized sociospatial blur. The demographic flows alone convey a sense of Shanghai as a space of flux. Its population in 1945 was ten times what it was in 1842, the year before it was declared a treaty port after the Opium War (Wakeman and Yeh 1992: 1). In just the years between 1910 and 1927, the population doubled, from 1.3 to 2.6 million (Goodman 1995: 2). Further, as Goodman's extremely illuminating study shows, these population shifts entailed dramatically intensified interaction among diverse identity groups, especially those organized in terms of native-place associations. She notes that "throughout the late nineteenth and early twentieth centuries, immigrants comprised at least 75 percent of the total figure" of the Shanghai population (ibid.). Even more recently, during the PRC era, when "hard edges" were supposed to obtain between city and country (Davis et al. 1995; Naughton 1995), what Lynn White refers to as the "connections between the green and grey cities" of Shanghai (1981: 257; cf. White 1996 and Fung 1981, 1996) continued to be extremely fluid and to defy neat taxonomies into urban and rural categories.

Thus, the fixing of boundaries of various sorts in the Shanghai region proves to be impossible, whether it is between the rural and urban, the rustic and urbane, or the modern and backward. This is a liberating assumption in my view, not a defeating one, and it is akin to insights emerging in widely divergent discussions, from fresh examinations of "space, identity, and the politics of difference,"[18] to those of media audiences, cultural identity, "poetics and performance," and dialogism and hermeneutics,[19] all of which place emphasis on boundary permeability and the impossibility of closed systems, however equally constant are human efforts to "fix" across these lines, to "center," in Vincent Crapanzano's (1992b) image.

Yet these are not just recent perspectives. Eric Wolf wrote for decades on the fundamental interconnectivity among social and cultural units and the need to attend to "the total social field of which they are a part" (1955: 455) and to recall and adopt from even "the diffusionists . . . their distrust of the automatic or organic coherence of culture" (1984: 396). Indeed, as Wolf points out, much earlier expressions of flux and blur across sociocultural space, as we might call it today, include those of Alfred Kroeber (1948) on peasants as "part-societies and part-cultures," always only in relation to "a larger population" (284), and Alexander Lesser (1961) on "social fields" and the need to "conceive of human societies—prehistoric, primitive, or modern—not as closed systems, but as open systems" rather than assuming "the myth of the primitive isolate" suggested in the works of Robert Redfield and others (42).[20]

Thus, to discern the experience of things like "urbanism as a way of life" (Wirth 1938), "the cultural role of cities" (Redfield and Singer 1954), or similar objects pursued by the influential Chicago school of "human ecology" and urban studies, we must proceed, in contrast to the strategies employed by these pioneer urbanists,[21] from the assumption of interflow, of always negotiable boundaries. As Nan Ellin shows in *Postmodern Urbanism* (1996), a rich and insightful survey of Western urban design theory and trends since the 1960s, reconceptualizations of the city as far back as Marx and H. G. Wells stressed the breakdown of "the distinctions between city, suburbs, and countryside" (245; cf. Ellin 1999). She shows further that by now urbanists, urban designers, and architects have abandoned such projects as "searching for the essence of urban" (Guldin 1996: 265) and instead tend to offer blurrier images like "the 'non-place urban realm' . . . the 'anti-city' . . . the 'centerless city' . . . the term 'post-urban' . . . collage city . . . the megaburb, the technoburb . . . cyburbia . . . exopolis . . . the new city . . . and the 100-mile city" (Ellin 1996: 245).

This is not at all to deny, say, Mumford's point that "the psychological import of the wall must not be forgotten" (1938: 55) or to suggest that there is no discernible difference between urban and rural and even less that conceptualizations of such differences make no difference in everyday social life. They demonstrably do, as the above episode seeks to convey. Such distinctions, such essentialisms in action, like identity practice in general, are fundamental human manufactures. It's what we do, whether at the level of freezing or fixing phonemes, however momentarily, or at the level of valorized distinctions among marks of fashion and style in bodily comportment. Stressing the nonfixity of such boundaries as those between urban and rural thus does not deny the existence of them but rather allows fuller if more complicated access to them by extension, for it forces us to log into their ethnographic detail in process, practice, and production, across dynamic social fields, rather than seeking taxonomies of their ontological presence or absence within. It is socially significant that identifications of urbanity and rurality are being formulated in the diverse fields of Shanghai and that they are forming the basis of social action and interaction. It was also socially significant that critical commentary on the alienation of city life appeared in the eighteenth- and nineteenth-century poetry of Wordsworth and Tomson (Williams 1989) and that of the Song poet-official Su Dongpo (Murphey 1984: 190) long before Simmel and Wirth's go at it, just as such essentializing conceptualizations about the country and city, if of a different content, are alive and well across China today, as Guldin (1996) documents so well. However, these aren't bespeaking an "essence of urban" that sits fixed somewhere, like a stake in the ground, waiting to be located, pulled up, and replotted on the graph of the urban-rural continuum.

What they do express is precisely the disruption of dichotomies by interflowing cacophonies amid the flux and open-endedness of social fields, be they urban, rural, "desakota," or something in between, and the availability of these fields to serve as locations of the negotiation, coproduction, and contestation of cultural identities as socially empowered/-ing practices, always in-production. Thus, the fields of Shanghai are indeed being tilled, inscribed, and reconfigured, as Lefebvre suggests, as "spaces governed by conflicts and contradictions" ([1974] 1991: 404).

There is, however, another important particular: especially in the era of enthusiastic and officially mandated "reform and openness to the outside world" (*gaige kaifang*), this tilling or reproduction of space, as Lefebvre, Wolf, Harvey, Anagnost, and a host of others might also note, is a consummately global process, one proceeding for its own re-presentation to "the evaluative gaze of foreign capital," in Anagnost's phrase (1994: 279). This evaluative gaze of global capital—and its thus far insatiable appetite, we might add—constitutes a primary principle giving shape to the spaces of Shanghai in the 1990s. It imparts "selective, preferred directionalities," to combine insights of Raymond Williams, Stuart Hall, and Eric Wolf, respectively, to the ideas, identities, and distinctions being put into social practice on these fields.[22] Urbanity, rustic, backward, and modern need contain no fixed content in order to be useful concepts for the flow of global capital, as the mere proliferation of these and other identities, distinctions, and marks of significance offers an even greater volume of commodifiable surfaces.

Thus, "the proliferation of local identities, all of whom may be speaking the same language but producing meanings of their own" (Anagnost 1994: 278), is an ongoing process in the newly reorganized scapes of Shanghai. Entreaties—some more and some less "violent" in Lefebvre's sense of all abstraction entailing a certain violence—by figures perceived as relatively cosmopolitan forwarded to figures perceived as relatively rustic, whether they live in towns or villages or indeed within dense cityscapes, to "sophisticate up," to become more poised, urbane, and cosmopolitan, are being put into play in the newly reconfigured, globally connected spaces of Shanghai. And, as the Vice Chairman's deflamed filter, fidgeted to oblivion, suggests to me, these entreaties are conveying effective meaning, although it remains incompletely unified and always contestable. For the diverse figures of the Shanghai hinterland, the Rural Channel urbanites know what (at least part of) *xiaosa* is, and it matters. Just as in the earlier movements of urbanites *xiaxiang*, the Vice Chairman or his equivalent knew effectively what *gou geming* ("revolutionary enough") meant, and that mattered too.

But in the post-Mao, post-Communist era of globally produced social spaces in China, there is now, in this interface between China's "urban" and China's "rural," greater room than ever for the proliferation and diversity of such meanings and identities. Globally produced space, space configured and inscribed by global capital, is simply *vaster* social space. The work of meaning/identity in the age of commodified and electronic reproduction, again to sample a patch from Benjamin (1969), is something that takes place on an almost unthinkably large terrain. One of the consequences is that, at the same time that there is significant effectivity in the hinterland of cosmopolitan estimations, there is also, on another level, greater room for contest and negotiation over who's speaking, who's inscribing, and who's representing. Moreover, in the fields of Shanghai, in stark contrast to the hypodermic image of cities "dispatch[ing] urban culture into the hinterland in a systematic and insistent fashion" (Strand 1995: 402), the discursive contest has been decidedly joined by local figures seeking to rewrite a bit of that terrain.

Blurry Urban Interflow Some More   Back in Songjiang County, there was a quiet man at lunch at the Workers Club. He had sat there just listening to the conversation about mutual benefit between the crew and its hosts, the limits of science, the strengths of *qigong* and so forth. I was unsure who he was or why he was there, though Li Mei had mentioned he was from a local factory.

His interests soon became clear, for when the crew reiterated its desire to tape some locals, including young, old, male, and female, Li Mei and the quiet man chimed in to report that the manager at his factory was a twenty-six-year-old man. Perfect.

Taking leave of our kind hosts at the Workers Club and expressing gratitude to the Vice Chairman and Club Director and our desire to return soon, we piled into the van. The driver excelled against the odds. Dodging pedestrians, cyclists, vehicles of assorted types, and chickens, and peppered with now frantic, now teasing directives from our gallery of navigators, he finally got us back out among the flood-irrigated rice fields heading for our next stop.

For the crew, the most striking thing about the Shanghai Angli Bio-technological Foods Factory, a modest complex on the edge of Songjiang Township bordering the rice fields, was its state of readiness for our arrival. Some calls had been made. With our equipment extracted from the odd berths of the van, we were immediately taken to a reception room, where a handful of people were waiting. Tea was served in summer glasses as we took our places around a prepared table, and cigarettes flew up and down and across the table, from both sides but with the delicate balance in volume deftly siding with the hosts. Across the table sat two sanitary figures in professionally white coats, both looking very technical and scientific. The man was in his fifties, with an attractive and intelligent, if stressed, face. The woman was in her thirties, sharp, serious, and focused. Other figures sat back or away from the table. The young factory manager, also dressed in white, busied himself supplying cigarettes and filling tea glasses or having it done.

Suddenly it was obvious. We'd been ushered into a full-throttle pitch session, a deft maneuver in the post-Mao gold rush for ever-precious publicity.

The Bioscientist Man began. Trained at and still affiliated with a top university in Shanghai, he had helped develop a *koufuye*, or "oral liquid," for Shanghai Angli. Angli Yihao Koufuye—"Only/High-Powered #1 Oral Elixir"—was good, high-powered stuff all right, a "modern bio-engineered product," according to the packaging of the samples festooning the table. He told stories of its success and was clearly proud of its wonders. But there was an anxiety seeping through his presentation as well, and it soon brought a rather abrupt halt to the introduction. Marketing was killing them, he said. The sky-high costs of advertising were prohibiting them from distinguishing *Angli Yihao* from the countless other koufuye products out there, and " . . . we were hoping you could help."

With that and some uncomfortable resignation, he turned it over to the Bioscientist Woman. Whatever mystery might have remained regarding the purpose of our unexpected reception here at Shanghai Angli was now immediately resolved. She was very happy to host us and tell us about Angli Yihao, she said, how it prevents aging and does many other miraculous things. She launched into a presentation in the curious discursive style that has emerged in reform era China in which the language of marketing and commercial persuasion bears a striking resemblance to that of the political campaigns and "struggle" of the Mao era, referencing and reproducing some of its tropes and figures of ardent commitment, passionate belief, and fever-pitched tries of persuasion. The stock rhetorical devices were of course familiar to the crew, sitting them back in their seats even more, somewhat taken aback but ultimately sensing the inevitability as well. Even the other hosts, and indeed the woman herself, seemed to recognize the routine. Winding down finally, and a bit self-consciously, she closed by reiterating her colleague's concerns and hopes for the Rural Channel's promotional assistance.

There was a pause. The crew had pretty much powered down.

"Well!" offered Chen Ming, un-reclining from his chair, trying to pipe up, seem awake, and preempt any hurt feelings, "we've certainly gained a lot of fine knowledge regarding your factory and product here": echoes of his toast at lunch, it seemed. "It's just a pity that we don't have time to hear more about it. . . . See, what we really came out here for is to . . . "

Qu Tanrong was perhaps less tactful. He'd been listening, sitting, smoking. He'd been the target of most of the Bioscientist Woman's eye contact and language alike. Initially, I'd assumed this was simply due to his magnetic good looks and central seat. But then there was the Sony 330 video camera in front of him, too, randomly placed on the table but directly between him and her, serving then as the fulcrum over which her communiqués were delivered and aptly illustrating how the issue "on the table" was in fact on the table and all about representation, imagery, and publicity. *Xuanchuan,* the common term for "propaganda," is no longer even primarily about political propaganda, as in the Mao era. Its multi-valent connotations center now around the cluster of meanings involving commercial publicity, plugs, public relations practices, and straight-ahead advertising.[23]

"Look," began Qu, "you're really talking to the wrong people here. See, our unit in the Rural Channel is Arts and Entertainment. We've come out here to make a kind of commercial ourselves. For ourselves, for our own show. You know?" He explained that the crew would be happy to explain the situation to Special Topics, the more appropriate unit of the Rural Channel for this sort of thing, that we indeed hoped to maintain this relationship and return for further projects, but that what we really were after on this particular day were some statements of local interest in *Nanqiang Beidiao* committed to videotape.

The Bioscientist Man, apparently feeling a bit sullied by this dip into crass promo-commercialism, apologized for their urgency, saying, "Your face is very wide." So just this opportunity to tell the crew of the wonders of Angli Yihao was worth it to them. He added, to further account for their stress, that it was a very busy time for them at the factory, where they were currently rather understaffed. Sure they could help us. As the factory manager was sent to find a young woman to join him on camera, Mao Yinghua leaned over to explain to me that this was a problem in many rural enterprises: planting season comes along, and people choose or have to work in the fields, leaving factories like this one understaffed.

The factory manager returned shortly with a young factory woman. The woman was not introduced and said nothing. Her gloves and hair-stuffed hat were the same lab white as her coat, and she was preoccupied, clearly having been interrupted, and perspiring. After a few words about what we wanted, we adjourned and headed for a shooting locale.

By the time we reached a small building just behind the reception room, she had resumed her work, hurriedly changing hoses and switching valves amid the industrial plumbing attached to and connecting two large vatlike boilers in an open, airy room divided horizontally by a platform, with a boiler on each level. She glanced our way a few times, waiting for instructions, but otherwise worked busily, the brilliant greens of sun-drenched rice paddies glowing through the open windows behind her. Finally, we were set up. Chen Ming began to coach the two young "candid" commentators now gathered near one of the boilers. With the VTR and monitor set up next to the tripoded camera and in the hands of the pros, I was moving about taking pictures.

But suddenly we were making a change, moving to another location. I asked Mao and Qu why, as we hoisted the equipment and followed Chen Ming, who had decidedly left the building and was discussing the matter with Bioscientist Woman, Bioscientist Man, the factory manager, and Li Mei. The factory people don't like the backdrop, the guys told me, too generic and no tags of their factory or any of their products. Mao and Qu said they preferred the boiler room setting themselves, "but what are you going to do? These people want a little publicity out of it, a little *ruan guanggao*."[24] There were several other options, exteriors and interiors of various sorts, but soon it became clear that Chen Ming and the factory people were leading the group down the driveway toward the factory entrance. Li Mei came back and confirmed the evident: they wanted to shoot the scene with the factory entry gate and signage in the background. Well that was it for Mao and Qu, who had only reluctantly left the previous setting. This was all the excuse they needed. Insisting that the signage idea was way too forced and predictable, they stopped, feet planted, and insisted: "Back to the boiler room!"

So we started back. The factory people, with Chen Ming negotiating and navigating through the treacherous social waters along with them, again scampered in front of Mao, Qu, and myself but went back in the other direction toward the first reception room, where they hastily began preparing an adjacent room for the shot, arranging boxes and bottles of Angli Yihao and other enterprise significata in a glass case behind a table, trying to get the persuasion through Chen Ming to the other two to effect a more beneficial backdrop.[25] But by this time Mao and Qu were determined: nope, boiler room. And we finally set up there again.

Now came negotiations on the linguistic component of this high-stakes representational practice. Chen Ming resumed going over the lines with the young and attractive factory manager and the factory woman. The former was placed in the foreground, the latter in the background, both roughly "working" as they were being interviewed. The lines were simple and straightforward.

FACTORY MANAGER: People always say we young people don't like traditional Chinese opera. But the truth is not that we don't like it; we just don't understand it. I would like to see some programs introducing opera knowledge and history and so on.

FACTORY WOMAN: Yeah, I actually like Yueju [one variety of local opera], especially [Moumou's] performances. And so do all my friends!

The two amateurs performed well, and the crew was pleased. As we began to dismantle and head off however, Qu couldn't resist asking the young factory woman, before she sped back to work: "Do you really like it?" She'd already been notably perturbed by other aspects of the shoot, as when Chen Ming's habit of holding a shot long enough after the delivery of a line to enable him to do dissolves or other editing maneuvers, prompted her to continue speaking, ad-libbing what she thought the crew wanted to hear, further explaining with evident imaginative and well-intended effort what she liked about traditional opera and why, only to be told that none of that was necessary: "All we need is your line." But this really tripped her up. "*Keyi,*" she shrugged, or something like "It's okay I guess," with the implied note of "Like, what do you want?" And back to work she went. Qu didn't press it but was clearly unpersuaded.

With much remaining undone to achieve Chen Ming's desired demographic, we packed our complimentary bottles of Angli Yihao and modest marketing info sheets and bade farewell to the anxious and ultimately dissatisfied folks at Shanghai Angli. We drove along the dirt roads transecting nearby rice paddies. We stopped, rather randomly, where we could see some people planting rice shoots in the watery fields, piled out with our equipment, and started off along the built-up footpaths separating the paddies in search of others willing to reflect in our not-so-candid camera. Juxtaposing, when not altogether obliterating, the wide, spread-toed, barefoot imprints in the clayey paths with those of our own sneakers, high heels, and one broken pair of resoled wingtips from a Brooklyn Salvation Army Store, we were now looking for the elderly component of the intended sample of ruralites. But first we had to stop when we came upon a young man with his pant's legs rolled up, almost knee-deep in muddy water, who had happened to reach that end of his paddy as we walked by. He'd been furiously transplanting the shoots, working backward, plunging the roots of the fine green blades quickly into the mud ten inches apart, three across, step back, three across, step back. Chen Ming caught him. "Sure, whatever," he said, although he continued to plunge the odd shoot into the water whenever he could.

Again the voice was not his, but he was at least provisionally willing: "We peasants work hard, and after a long hard day in the fields, some dinner, and a wash, we like to watch television, especially [Moumou-style] opera." Ever meticulous Chen Ming had some reservations about part of it, and managed a couple of takes but soon got the message from the young man, who'd been anxiously glancing at the other two planting next to him who were pulling away toward the other end of the paddy, that he had more pressing matters to attend to. We thanked him for letting us interrupt his work . . . "but, by the way, could you point us in the direction of some older people we might interview, those people in the next paddy over there maybe"? He shrugged, said he didn't know them, and began making up for lost ground.

We returned to the van, where the driver slumbered in idling air-conditioning parked next to freshly built homes of the rural "nouveau riches" (baofahu). Sweat was trickling down Chen Ming's face, but he trudged off nonetheless in pursuit of an older woman wielding a hoe-type implement, who flatly said no, nonnegotiable, and then on to another, who finally acquiesced by nodding us toward a storage shed and threshing ground out in the middle of the paddies. Here we found our seniors, a barefoot couple of no apparent relation and very apparent tremendous age, who in turn obligingly presented Chen's pitch for the programming promised on Nanqiang Beidiao. With the heat, our exhaustion, and respect for their age, these two required only a couple of takes apiece.

We ended our fruitful day in Songjiang with a visit to two of its tourist attractions along our route home: Square Pagoda, built in the eleventh century, and Drunken-Poet Bai Pond, in the heart of a lovely garden where a Ming painter had once lived, followed by a Qing official, who renovated and named it after the Tang poet Bai Juyi, famous lover of wine. By the time we reached the latter, however, it had gotten late and we were told, crossing the road, that the place was closed. The crew was unfazed. Collectively, reflexively, they made for the side gate, where we met a gatekeeper good at his job. Closed, sorry, nope, see ya. He didn't seem remotely movable. Once he was appropriately decorated, however, and looking like a walking vendor with all the cigarettes dropped in his shirt pocket, between his fingers, and behind his ear, the man gave in. But he had conditions, and he was serious about them: one quick walk around and only two at a time. As Chen, Mao, and I took our turn at the gate, a man sharing a wink and a nod with the gatekeeper momentarily crept through, tackle box and fishing pole in hand. Glances of clarity, registered recognition, and low-grade embarrassment were exchanged, and the gatekeeper got grumpier.

It was a fitting end to a day of interflowing interests across the radically transforming fields and spaces of Shanghai. Urbane sophisticates carrying explosively powerful technologies to the hinterland, seeking to fix and represent "peripheral" identities,[26] both affected local cultural practice and were in turn forced to confront or conform to local maneuvers. A complex kind of "gift economy," in Mayfair Yang's (1994) phrase, but this one in post-Mao *xuanchuan* or reform-era representation, had to be engaged throughout, from the *guanxi* with entrée-providing, suburban sophisticate Li Mei to the check-in, future-oriented meeting with the local officials and the bartering with the people at Shanghai Angli. Productive in very specific ways, it is a calculus of "the convergence of consumer desire in DeLillo's (1997) phrase, " . . . not that people want the same things, necessarily, but that they want the same range of choices." Or are confined to them.

Global Access Contest Joined: Getting Urbane, Getting Modern Reconfigured for and by global capital, the fields of Shanghai are thus sites and occasions of social contests in a new key. Surfaces geomorphological, bodily, and digital are being fragmented, segmented, partitioned, and identified, then constantly re-all-of-that again to make themselves available for the inscriptionings of commoditized value per the agreed, if never finally so, standards of global capitals.[27] The outcomes of the contesting identity practices, the contest of positions, are always on one level an empirical matter. If Shanghai Angli failed on that day in 1992 to completely achieve its desires, if the Vice Chairman was indeed slightly terrorized by the urbanites' urbanity, and if the local Songjiang TV station that had so publicly and tragically lost its young director had been just a retransmitter of nonlocal programming without extensive production facilities of its own—if, that is to say, there was in fact on this day asymmetry in who had voice and the power to represent—certainly these were not fixed states of affairs but rather always fluid ones, temporary dichotomies amid the cacophonous, plurivocal, "baroque textures of . . . everyday life" (Crapanzano 1985: xiv) to be lived in everyday and everyplace practice, perhaps even ethnographically explored and represented, but never finally fixable more firmly than this either way.

Yet there is a historically unifying common cause across these fields that has exercised and practically dominated intellectual life in China for generations—from the late Qing reformers to May Fourth and other nationalists, including the Communists—and that is the project to craft a livable modernity, emically understood: to make China modern, to progress, develop, advance, and improve the quality of life. Surely, the zeitgeist of the current reform era as well (Rofel 1992), the quest to become "modern," has been an abiding, pervasive, and shaping reality in China for generations (cf. Ballew 1991, 1992).[28] As Jonathan Friedman points out, however, "modernity is a local product of commercial global systems, that is, a form of identification, or perhaps *habitus,* that arises in determinate local transformations of conditions of existence" and further, "its embodied images and things inform processes of identity formation throughout the larger world" (1994: 212–13). That such essentializing fixity, as I've emphasized, is a human impossibility does not deter our compulsion to fix nonetheless, however fleetingly. For, as Friedman goes on to note, the category "modernity" has as "one of its central features . . . precisely the principle of alterity, by which all specific forms and practices are necessarily arbitrary and temporary" (213).

Thus, as the peculiar tilling of the Shanghai sociospatial fields proceeds apace, the historically urgent task of constructing a Chinese modernity takes place in a very specific context, however internally modulated and constantly in process, which imparts upon this task a "selective, preferred directionality." Global capital and the interflow of its substantive "modernity" together configure this as a space of hegemony. It does not dictate the concrete forms and contents of the identity practices played out in this space. It never does, as hegemony is a never-ending story, an always incomplete history, an unfixed condition antisecured by, if nothing else, the tyranny of the simple sweeping second hand, the constancy of change, of motion in the system.[29] Such hegemonic contexts and the identities practiced therein, again like phonemes, have no essence. They are never perfectly *present*, in either dimension, temporal or spatial. They are rendered nouns only regrettably and misleadingly, much as culture is, suggesting and offering fixed essences despite their intractable impossibility. They are thus only the efforts to (em)-practice such would-be stable essences—the ever-fleeting if no less vital "centers that cannot but must hold"—that we might see or experience in the lived world. But they always happen in a contextualizing space configured by determinate processes not necessarily of their own making.

Thus, it seems useful to recognize the occasional/spatial limits to the project of constructing "alternative modernities" posed by such hegemonic contextualization, to acknowledge that the locally lived response to ever-intensifying interflows of globalization is not always and everywhere "of the jolly and 'creative' sort," following Friedman (1995: 422), often suggested in studies of the local in the global, but also is the site of interested power.[30] Such celebrations of alterity and resistance, while compatible with our own sense of alternative identities, if not positively schizophrenic/rhizomatic ones (Deleuze and Guattari 1983), and indeed preserving of the alterity required by anthropology and area studies, often turn on familiar reiterations of broad cultural diversity in a very wide world. When Kala-oκ performance and knowledges deemed "alternative" because they contain an alternative content (Moore 1996) are offered as proof that the dynamic cultural parameters of globally mobile capital are radically fragmented at local levels, reworked out of recognition and indeed out of effectivity, then we have lost track of the relations and processes of something that matters quite a lot: cultural power, empowered practice, (em)power(ed)/knowledge. We forget the basic structuralist lesson—even if it comes forcefully from supposed 'poststructuralists' like Foucault and others—that resistance of necessity has an object, that to which it is contrasted or opposed, even if this opposite itself never stays still or present and is always but discursively inscribed.[31]

Thus, it was the effectiveness and success, however partial and fragile, of the fragmented and partitioning culture of global capitals and modernities that so frequently appeared in the Shanghai counties that year, not merely their happy failure, or "the happy juxtapositions of many different sets . . . between center and periphery" (Wolf 1967: 463). This effectivity appeared in disparaging remarks on the backward peasants and the producers' own backward equipment, in the high-impact estimations of hairdos, personal accessorizing skills, "growth" and leisure spending per capita, and myriad other bright marks of "modernity" and "urbanity," of symbolic capital-laden distinctions, and in the sacralization of Deng Xiaoping's allegorical indifference to the color of the cat (black or white, as long as it catches the mouse), and the question whether China's economy is surnamed socialist (*she*) or capitalist (*zi*), as long as it *develops*, according to powerfully agreed indicators.

It was also evident in the fact that dear hapless Chen Ming's *Nanqiang Beidiao* itself was bound for low ratings on the Rural Channel, whose audience, as the Shanghai Angli factory woman could have predicted, would strongly favor pop music videos from around the world for its music television. Or, in Qu's only partially exaggerated remark one day, as Paul Newman and Orson Welles sweated through *The Long Hot Summer* on a Rural Channel office TV set, "See, Chinese culture is already gone!" And most overtly this effective global cultural flow showed up repeatedly in straight-ahead interview statements from STV production professionals that the substance of China's modernity should closely resemble that of the West. As the Rural Channel director himself put it in one of these interviews, "In fact, modernization is itself precisely Westernization."

Interested Interflow One of the first uses in English of the term *urbanity*, according to the *Oxford English Dictionary*, appears in the 1848 first volume of Macaulay's *The History of England*, where he refers to "that exquisite urbanity, so often found potent to charm away the resentment of a justly incensed nation" ([1848] 1934: 338). It refers to King Charles II's apology for his "unconscionable time dying" and the trouble it might have caused to those attendants who'd stood around his bed all night watching for it in 1685, apparently not a characteristic note of royal consideration and concern, but, for Macaulay, a positively exquisite note in the symphony of what would later be called, say by Max Weber, political legitimacy. It is of course about another time and another place, but it speaks to a process at the heart of the representations and identity practices related above from the dynamic fields of the Shanghai Municipality. In their work crafting a version of modernity replete with much of the palette of global capitalist renderings of "modernity" and its radically persuasive imagery of the good life, progress, and development, and in their carrying this imagery of *xiaosa* out to the Shanghai countryside, Rural Channel producers were mediating, if not channeling, an urbanity potent indeed to charm away resentment, such as any resentment that may develop locally/occasionally over the ways in which global capital interflow is reconfiguring, reinscribing, and reidentifying the spaces of Shanghai. The "modern" and "urbane" answer such potentially troublesome reactions with a shimmering vision of liberating possibilities.[32]

There are, that is, such things as "DevelopMen" in the world, to borrow a typo from more recent Songjiang xuanchuan people, and they are radically persuasive creatures.[33] DevelopMen are prepackaged to the hilt, dripping with the signatures of internationally consensual distinctions and rhetorical power. They *know* about things like progress, development, growth, decline, efficiency, backwardness, and modernity. They're seductively good to think with, incorrigibly, almost irresistibly. They are inscribed in textbooks and white papers and music videos and nightly business reports. They work at the World Bank and the IMF, at the U.S. Departments of Commerce and State, and in the countless academic departments, ostensible NGOs, and private commercial firms and financial institutions that are so extremely well wired with these policymakers. They are very urbane.

Alternative urbanities, then, like alternative modernities, are in this context identities hard to figure, hard to imagine. That the task must be joined, however, is nothing short of globally, environmentally, and humanly imperative. We can talk about sliding signifiers, decentered subjectivities, and epistemological relativism until the cows come home, as my sharecropper grandfather might have said, but environmental sustainability, for example, is about more than just language games. If global-ambition consumer capitalism, flash with the signs of the Modern, allows for—again, even demands—local difference in the contents of consumption, is it sufficient to merely celebrate the happy alterity and bypass the comfy linkages with systemic power and asymmetry, as well as the rather uncomplicated and deadly serious idea that the world can positively choke on too much plastic and fossil fuel emissions? In failing to critically address the effectivity of the rhetorics and identities of a particular modernity—the RuggedIndividualConsumer*Moderne,* or, You Are What You Buy—we are shying away from an important task, indeed, shirking an imperative responsibility.[34]

In the van on the road back from Songjiang that day, looking at the two enormous satellite dishes blossoming in a distant field as the sun went down, I remembered the point made on an earlier occasion by the head of the A&E unit, a bright, gifted, young leader and dear friend. "Even if, say, traditional Chinese opera disappears," he'd said, or some other artifact of quintessentially "Chinese" culture seems to wither as China logs in ever more forcefully to global capitalism, well, even if this were to happen, "China will still be China." For sure, I say. But for the sake of local identity-making practices and the global community alike, perhaps it will do well to remember how pleasurably yet temporarily satiated will be the empowered structures and processes of that spectacular and radically effective "urbanity," that exquisitely potent, resentment-lifting, and consumately charming *xiaosa*.

Cut To: A Quick Postscript from Shanghaivelocity Speedworld 2000, And You May Find Yourself . . .   Noticing two or more fascinating things: 1) The Shanghai Jiaoda Angli Group is now a massive and publicly traded pharmaceutical conglomerate and among the largest advertisers on TV, buying heavy volume on both national and local channels, the latter now provided by not one but four local stations, including five channels from Shanghai Cable TV alone; 2) The STV Rural Channel is not among these newly proliferated channels—it no longer exists; 3) The reasons for these things are incredibly interesting!

Same as it ever was.

But if you change your mind . . .

Notes

The main things that have made this article and/or research possible are: the insights, kindness, and friendship of many dear friends in the Shanghai film and TV world, especially Dong Zhongmin, Zhang Jianya, Zhao Yingwu, Zeng Yinjie, Li Xuegong, Li Lin, Zhang Jingchao, Zhao Qing, Huang Qi, Qu Cheng, Hua Jian, Lou Shifang, Bei Long, Pu Shengqi, Zuo Yijian, Yu Qiduo, Wang Ren, Zheng Jian, Huang Baohua, Sun Xiaogang, Wang Guoping, and Quan Xiaolin; institutional support from the Ph.D. Program in Anthropology at the City University of New York Graduate Center, the Wenner-Gren Foundation for Anthropological Research, the National Science Foundation, the Shanghai Academy of Social Science, and the Center for Asian Studies at Arizona State University; insightful advice and abiding support from Vincent Crapanzano, Jane Schneider, Faye Ginsburg, and Eric R. Wolf, whose inspiring scholarship and human care have made the world a better place even if his recent passing made it sadly poorer; the kind invitation from Nancy Chen, Connie Clark, Suzanne Gottschang, and Lyn Jeffery to participate in this volume and the workshop on which it was based; detailed and insightful comments from Lyn Jeffery and Connie Clark on earlier drafts of this piece; additional helpful remarks from Louisa Schein, Ellen Hertz, Paola Zamperini, Greg Guldin, Tim Oakes, Stevan Harrell, and an anonymous Duke University Press reviewer; terrific supports from colleagues in the ASU Interdisciplinary Humanities Program, especially Kent Wright, Helen Morales, Nora Taylor, John Lynch, Paul Privateer, Shannon Steigerwald, and Charles Dellheim; many years of many contributions from Nan Ellin; and last but most, daily lessons in truth, beauty, and the good, delightfully unencumbered by the banal and dreary shackles of epistemological doubt, from my daughter and very favorite thing, Theodora Ballew. To all of these dearlies I shall remain most eternally grateful.

1   Curiously, the explanation I most often heard was that the derivation of this link was from the Cantonese pronunciation of *eight,* a high-toned *bat* according to a press reviewer, even though of course Cantonese is not local language in Shanghai. I'm grateful for this reviewer's suggestion to clarify this.

2   From *Brief Introduction* (1992: 1) which elaborates the mission: "The Rural Channel will publicize/propagandize (*xuanchuan*) rural and agricultural work in a prompt and timely fashion and popularize the scientific, educated, and prosperous countryside. It will explore and probe rural reforms, and showcase today's rural customs and conditions, and the styles and scenes of the times for the contemporary peasant. It will serve as a helping hand in peasant life and an adviser to agricultural production." All translations are my own unless otherwise indicated.

3   These personal names are fictitious.

4   Fung (1996) suggests that Howard-inflected planning ideas were implemented in the Shanghai area only with the satellite town projects of the late 1950s, although they had been first propounded in China by Sun Yat-sen, who was also the first to advocate the development of Shanghai's Pudong area (cf. Yeh 1996 and MacPherson 1996). Chan (1996) and MacPherson both note that greenbelts and satellite town planning had also been part of the 1946 master plan for Shanghai, while MacPherson's account suggests that they may even have been part of planning efforts begun by native Chinese in 1926–27, which achieved remarkable success during the following decade despite the war with Japan.

5   Geremie Barmé's recent achievements (1996; see also 1999) provide rich accounts of this and other artifacts of "the cult of the great leader." See also Hou Dangsheng's 1996 piece on these portraits as cab driver talismans.

6   Benchmark discussions of the urban-rural continuum include those in Elvin (1977); Mote (1977); Murphey (1984); and Skinner (1977a, 1977b). Strand's (1995) discussion of urban-rural relations points to Rawski (1985), pointing to Liu (1970) arguing that at least by the late Ming, in Strand's words, "cities now began to dispatch urban culture into the hinterland in a systematic and insistent fashion" (1995: 402).

7　The role in China of such networks of guanxi have received extensive scholarly attention. For recent accounts, see Yan (1996); Kipnis (1997); Wilson (1997); and Yang (1989, 1994).

8　The term was *duixiang*, which can also mean a prospective marriage partner or girlfriend/boyfriend.

9　The Vice Chairman was evidently aware that TV programming is supposed to use putonghua more or less exclusively in Shanghai. In fact, there would prove to be some shows, including parts of episodes of *Nanqiang Beidiao*, in which Shanghainese was allowed. It depended on the context and appropriateness, I was told by the head of the A&E unit. For example, when a well-known Shanghai opera star hosted one episode of *Nanqiang Beidiao*, she was allowed to use Shanghainese in her introductions to segments; and of course the segments, this time featuring Huju, Shanghai's local opera, were in Shanghainese as well. This prominent performer believed strongly that Shanghainese should be more common on local shows.

10　I am grateful to Lyn Jeffery for remarking on the semantic nebulousness of the term *xiaosa*. I've understood and translated it as including the equally nebulous notion of "urbanity" based on a dictionary entry listing "urbane" as its meaning but mostly based on explanations I was given by people in Shanghai. Still, it should be kept in mind that the term is multivalent.

11　This figure is from Whyte and Parish (1984: 19), who specify that it covers only the decade after 1968 and compares to a *total* urban population of only some 100 million. White (1996) makes the important point that urban-rural relocations had occurred long before the *shangshan xiaxiang* movements of the Cultural Revolution (1966–76), such as in Shanghai in the mid-1950s, when numbers were more vast than at any time during the Cultural Revolution, but that the former are far less remarked because they involved workers rather than the vocal and literate intellectuals of the latter movements.

12　Bernstein (1977), Selden (1993) and White (1978, 1996) treat the movements extensively. For an evocative fictional account of the encounter between urbanites and ruralites engendered by this program, see Liu Zhen's "The Girl Who Seemed to Understand" (1983).

13　I am grateful to a press reviewer for pointing to the limits of this whole analogy, given the difference in scale—four TV producers in one day hardly compare to 17 million youth over a decade. My intention is indeed to stress the differences as much as the similarities, for example, that while the Rural Channel and earlier shangshan xiaxiang movements share the quality of being urban-to-rural Projects on a Mission, officially mandated by the state, the language, broadly speaking, through which they operate is vastly different, as the above episode seeks to show. I cannot quite agree, however, that the analogy breaks down because the Rural Channel project is too narrow. Indeed, it is only more narrow on one end, so to speak, in that the urbanites involved are so few. With television, however, these few urbanites can engage such vast numbers of people—and, of course, with spectacular sights and sounds. This in my view is quite consequential, just as the earlier, more physical movements *xiaxiang* were.

14 Rural industrialization in China has been widely examined. Naughton (1995a) expresses the enthusiasm of many observers about the efficacy of rural industrialization in getting neoclassical-economic indicators up or down, as the case may desire. China studies in the West have largely ignored, or silenced, the powerful ideological function served by these ways of seeing political economy. Despite their long-noted limitations in accounting for economic process and practice even in capitalist economies (see Nell 1973, for example), such analytical discourses are of course quite effective in the global spread of capitalist structures and process. Yet isn't this worth a more critical look? It would seem safe to say, for example, that far fewer Eastern Europeans and Russians believe as wholeheartedly now, in the late 1990s, in the beneficent invisible-hand power of "free" markets or the explanatory efficacy of supply and demand, per capita GNP, productivity and growth rates, and the like as did prior to 1989, when very sophisticated analyses, well-entrenched theories, and vast literatures made these categories out to be analytical—and prescriptive and proscriptive—manna from on high, Modern and Scientific.

15 Cohen also refers to the more extensive treatment of this history by Hayford (1990) and Potter and Potter (1990).

16 Mao's writings are indeed replete with fodder for this characterization from his identification of the peasantry as the "vanguards of the revolution" ([1927] 1975) to the 1942 mandate that literature and the arts serve the peasants (as well as workers, soldiers, and even petty bourgeoisie) in his "Talks at the Yenan Forum" ([1942] 1967). Fei Xiaotong is, among others, pegged as harboring the antiurban bias, not least because he wrote in the late 1940s that "at present the growth of great urban centers is like a tumor from which China is suffering" (1953: 138). Recent comments or reemphases on a generalizable Maoist antiurban bias are present in Naughton 1995, Kipnis 1997, and Tang 1996a. Profound thanks go to Connie Clark for drawing my attention to Kirkby's critique of antiurban bias characterizations.

17 Johnson (1995) says that Songjiang is the new name for Huating, a market town from the Song of the late tenth century (36–37). Elsewhere, however, she writes that "the identities of several new port towns begin to emerge in the Sui and early Tang periods . . . [including] Songjiang on the Huangpu River" (29). One press reviewer pointed out that Songjiang was urban before Shanghai and that the area was long known as Su-Song-Tai.

18 This was the title of the first issue of *Cultural Anthropology* under Fred Myers's editorship, a theme issue edited by James Ferguson and Akhil Gupta. Apart from the latter's joint and individual pieces, see especially Malkki (1992) and Rofel (1992).

19 Shifts in audience studies toward more processual, active viewer perspectives are insightfully traced by Morley (1992) and Hay, Grossberg, and Wartella (1996).

20 Lesser in turn draws the social field notion from British social anthropology, citing Firth's point that "Fields of social relations, not clear-cut societies, must be the more empirical notion of social aggregates" (1961: 28).

21 An excellent discussion of the Chicago school of urban studies is that in Hannerz (1980).

22   Williams (1973) writes of "selectivity" in effective dominant culture, Hall (1980) of "preferred readings" encoded in media texts, and Wolf (1984) of "characteristic directionality" imparted to ideas by modes of mobilizing social labor (but see also Wolf's [1999] more recent and extended treatment of the relations between ideas and power). Central to each of these ideas is their insistence on a lack of closure, their recognition with Gramsci (1971) of the fundamental incompleteness of hegemony.

23   This shift is evident in the translation of the term into English in two widely used dictionaries. In the popular *Pinyin Chinese–English Dictionary,* compiled between 1971 and 1978, *xuanchuan* is defined as "conduct propaganda; propagate; disseminate; give publicity to." It is attached to other characters or compounds to mean: "propaganda car/instrument (or means) of propaganda or publicity; mass media/ propagandist/picture poster/propaganda (or publicity) material." In the reform era *Concise English-Chinese Chinese-English Dictionary* (1986), however, *xuanchuan* is defined as folows: "I (verb) 1. Disseminate; publicize; propagate . . . [as in] publicize traffic regulations [and] make known the importance of environmental protection; 2. Spread propaganda; propagandize . . . [as in] both parties are busy propagandizing about their own policies. II (noun) 1. Dissemination; 2. Propaganda . . . [as in] there has been too much propaganda about the horror of war." Obviously, these are fascinating shifts reflective of larger social ones that have occurred in the past couple of decades.

24   This nebulous and very interesting category covers infomercial-type content but also, for example, the kind of publicity a store gets from a story on the news or a newsmagazine, or that bestowed upon an enterprise or even a development zone by virtue of its hosting a variety show, though these may also be denoted by the term *xuanchuan.*

25   Mu Zhenqing was out of the loop here. On this occasion, this was due primarily to her inexperience, this being one of her first shoots. Women production personnel, from actors to editors to producers and directors, often did have to deal with a variety of gendered asymmetries in their work however, which I examine more fully elsewhere (2000).

26   Much like this text in your hands, of course.

27   I draw here also from Castells's (1989) description of urban space being transformed into "space of flows superseding the meaning of the space of places . . . a variable geometry of production and consumption, labor and capital, management and information—a geometry that denies the specific productive meaning of any place outside its position in a network whose shape changes relentlessly in response to the messages of unseen signals and unknown codes" (348). I only object to the imagery of supersession and denial here, which seems counter to that of flow to the extent it implies closure. The geometry of Shanghai, at least, is certainly still changed by vividly *seen* signals and *known* codes in addition to these more nebulous ones.

28   Important recent discussions of modernity in China may be found in Anagnost (1993a, 1997); Chow (1991); Duara (1995); Lee (1999); Liu (1995, 1996); Ong (1996, 1997b); Rofel (1999); Tang (1996b); and Yang (1988, 1996, 1997), among others.

29 These are fundamental qualities of hegemony consistently stressed by every serious employer of the notion I have read, a fact often forgotten by critics who can't resist the easy mockery of that straw figure, total domination, in which no one actually believes anyway, least of all people who find hegemony or something like it useful to think with, from Gramsci to Williams, Wolf, Hall, Eagleton (1991, 1996), Jameson (1998), Berman (1982, 1992), or even Chomsky (1998).

30 A range of excellent work (e.g., Appadurai and Breckenridge 1988, 1990, 1996; Appadurai 1990, 1996; Yang 1996, 1997; Ong 1996, 1997b; Chatterjee 1993) contains moments of this relative emphasis, which hopefully is the best way to conceptualize the distinction. Marcus's (1986; cf. Marcus and Fischer 1986) influential call to specifically seek out that which at local levels is resistant or oppositional to the culture of the world system seems to foreclose attention to the points where and when this does not appear. It does, however, serve the disciplinary legitimacy crisis— that is, no difference in the globalized world, no need or room for anthropology, find difference. For a recent examination of the "alternative modernity" problem, see the special issue of *Public Culture* on precisely this theme (Gaonkar 1999).

31 As Stuart Hall notes, when Foucault calls for "not a theory of the knowing subject, but rather a theory of discursive practice" (1970: xiv, quoted in Hall 1996: 2), it is indeed a call for the decentering, but "not the abandonment or abolition of 'the subject' . . . [rather] a reconceptualization—thinking it in its new, displaced or decentered position within the paradigm" (Hall 1996: 2).

32 Cf. Thomas Frank's (1997) insightful piece on what he calls "liberation marketing," advertising that represents consumer capitalism as a space of nonconformity and self-determination rather than one of uniform conformity and cogs in machines; think car commercials, ads for e-commerce, ISPs, telecoms, or anything featuring phrases like "outside the box." The irony of course, as Frank notes, is that consumer capitalism needs liberated consumers, but only within limits. "Be your own dog" or whatever, just keep defining self/citizen as Consumer; get liberated and be unique and innovative, just do it at the mall or something and otherwise stay calm; and everything (read: consumer capitalism) will be just fine.

33 For a taste of how Songjiang people have more recently been using new opportunities to reinscribe and represent their place, if still in relation to Shanghai, try the following exercise. Log on to "Shanghai on Internet" (1998) on the World Wide Web at ⟨www.sh.com⟩, and click on "Districts & Counties." This will take you to a page blinking at the top with "Shanghai Needs Investment," listing hyperlinks to the thirteen districts, six counties, and one new area now comprising the Shanghai Municipality, each with its own animated, rotating gold star. Click on "Songjiang County." Your first greeting, again blinking at the top, will be "Investment & DevelopMen [*sic*]" followed by several more hyperlinks that elaborate this peculiar identity-making project.

34 Two excellent and provocative films addressing the relations between identity, consumption, media, and environmental sustainability are *The Ad and the Ego* (Boihem and Emmanouilides 1996) and *Advertising and the End of the World* (Jhally 1998).

Ellen Hertz Face in the Crowd: The Cultural
Construction of Anonymity in Urban China

The starting point for my reflections in this chapter was the following
play on words: if face is a central discourse in the description of social
interactions in China, how then are we to account for that set of interactions that urban sociology has traditionally qualified as "faceless"? Faceless interactions in the sociological literature are interactions between
people who do not know each other, who most probably will never know
each other, and yet who, unlike strangers crossing paths on a country
road, belong somehow to a common collectivity, a collectivity we may
provisionally label "the urban." Both European social critics observing
the accelerating cadence of urbanization in Paris and Berlin (e.g., Simmel
[1903] 1965) and American sociologists watching the overnight metro-
politanization of Chicago and other U.S. cities (see, e.g., Wirth 1938)
placed great analytical weight on anonymity as a defining characteristic
of the urban experience.[1] In trying to think about specifically urban
forms of face in China, I noted, however, that the socioanthropological
literature on urban China makes virtually no reference to facelessness. In
other words, the anthropology of urban spaces in China lacks an account
of the cultural construction of anonymity. My question became, then,
where does facelessness disappear to in the Chinese context and can its
absence be accounted for by the presence of face?

As I reflected on this double metaphor of face, it seemed to me that
exploring its implications provided new perspectives onto the models
underlying the description of Chinese society, as reflected in both Western socioanthropological theory and Chinese urban discourse. In both
metaphors, relations between people are described in terms of the pres-

ence or absence of the front portion of their heads. However, whereas "face" is the translation of the indigenous discourse of *mianzi/lian*,[2] facelessness is a concept taken straight from the Western sociological literature with no obvious equivalent in the Chinese. Furthermore, the implications of the two usages—in terms of what is known and unknown about the social actors involved, what is seen and unseen, and the kinds of sociality that results from this knowing and seeing—are quite different. In short, face and facelessness operate in the context of contrasting forms of "imagined community" (Anderson 1983).

As Anderson has noted, "all communities larger than primordial villages of face-to-face contact (and perhaps even these) are imagined. Communities are to be distinguished, not by their falsity/genuineness, but by the style in which they are imagined" (1983: 15). In this chapter, I argue that face works—as concept and as practice—within a vision of the Chinese collectivity modeled on the Gemeinschaft, a bounded community for which "the rural" serves as exemplar. Loss of face is then the loss of social standing in the opinion of known or knowable (that is to say, imagined) others. But the "loss of face" associated with facelessness is otherwise, for what is lost is precisely the relation to those particularized others through whom one secures a certain sense of self. If the discourse of face is based on a model of the Chinese collectivity as "community," it is the experience of facelessness that figures the collectivity in terms of "society" (Gesellschaft).[3]

Of course, the Western socioanthropological emphasis on gemeinschaft—and hence on face—in the Chinese context can be at least partially explained by the traditional Great Divide that structures the field. Others, premoderns of various stripes, have always been thought of in communitarian terms and as opposed to "Us," those who live in gesellschaft. By borrowing Tonnies' famous distinction, I in no sense wish to reinstate the evolutionary scheme that served as the backdrop for his theorizing. We do, however, need to account for the fact that, despite China's long history of urbanization, no indigenous concept of anonymity has been articulated.[4] In this chapter, I will not attempt to survey this long history. Rather, I wish to examine the particular forms that experiences of anonymity take in contemporary PRC China. I will argue that both face and facelessness are characteristic moments in the Chinese urban experience. Furthermore, these moments are not contradictory but represent the variety of modes of sociability that structure urban life across cultures (Hannerz 1980). What needs to be explained, then, is their particular cultural inflection, their availability (or unavailability) as experiences feeding the elaboration of cultural discourses, and the terms in which these discourses operate.

In what follows, I briefly run through the well-known literature on face as a modality of Chinese selfhood, drawing out some of its implications for urban life. I then analyze a variety of forms of faceless interaction characteristic of Chinese cities in general and Shanghai society in particular. My examples draw on fieldwork I carried out on the Shanghai stock market in 1992, where the question of anonymous socioeconomic exchange was central to the construction of this new institution of Chinese modernity. If I give more weight to facelessness than face, and, within the category of facelessness, to some experiences than others, this is not because I believe they represent some cultural essence of urban China but rather because so little writing on contemporary China has drawn these experiences within the purview of its analysis.

Face and the "Relational Construction of Personhood"   The centrality of face in the description of Chinese society is attested by the outpouring of literature it has occasioned (see Hu 1944; M. Yang 1945; Jacobs 1979; Cheng 1986; Hwang 1987; Jankowiak 1993; Smart 1993; M. M.-H. Yang 1994; Zito 1994; and Kipnis 1995).[5] Face operates with reference to a conglomerate of institutions and values that might be characterized as communitarian: it involves the loyalty associated with kinship, the reciprocity that makes good neighbors, and the embedded, stable social relations that are typically thought to characterize the rural context. The "persistence" of these relationships in an urban setting is frequently associated with a particular concept of the self. In Mayfair Yang's analysis, for example, the centrality of face is intimately tied to the Chinese "relational construction of personhood" in which "threats to one's face constitute threats to one's identity, which is constructed relationally by internalizing the judgment of others in oneself" (1994: 196). Thus, face is credited as one of the bases, if not the basis, for articulating the distinctive conception of the person that governs the individual's relation to society in China (see, e.g., Liang 1949; Fei 1992; and Hsu 1967). But what is this distinctive conception, and how, more specifically, is it linked to a communitarian mode of sociality?

In her seminal article "The Chinese Concepts of 'Face,'" Hsien Chin Hu explores "two sets of criteria by which prestige is gained and status secured or improved" (Hu 1944: 45), articulated through the dual notions of lian and mianzi. More important for our purposes than the distinction between these two forms of face is the fact that both mianzi and lian function against the backdrop of "public opinion," the known or knowable consensus of "society" as to the standards of correct conduct. Hu's examples indicate that this public is, in her own terms, "amorphous" (48), ranging in size and composition from a rural lineage (55), to a place of employment (urban or rural) (55), to the national citizenry (57), to the entire international "community" (48).[6] Yet neither she nor the Chinese "ego" (in Hu's rather scientistic terms), who suffers from the "consciousness that [this] amorphous public is . . . relentlessly condemning every breach of morals and punishing with ridicule" (48), appears to question the reality of this superegolike configuration. How does ego ascertain that an "amorphous public" has formed to judge her or that its judgment flows in the direction she imagines? That no such proof is needed is an indication that more than a code of honor and prestige is at issue here: rather, the discourse of face works simultaneously to apply "community standards" and to call into being the very community whose standards it is supposed to apply.

The concept of face thus figures society as community, transposed beyond the face-to-face village setting and applied to urban, national, and even transnational contexts. Consequently, when working in urban settings, analysts have tended to overlook the potential for faceless interactions present in the city and have emphasized instead those forms of face-to-face encounters in which face operates in recognizably "Chinese" ways—governing relations between employees in the workplace, between business partners in the market, between neighbors, between political leaders and followers, and so on (see, e.g., Bruun 1993; Jankowiak 1993; Yang 1994; and DeGlopper 1995). The result of this paradigm of sociality is a focus on embedded, long-term networks of reciprocity and competition in structuring urban Chinese society.

There are many reasons why this focus is justified. In China's long history of urbanization, urbanites have shown considerable ingenuity in inventing institutional relations between strangers that organize them into recognizable—and more importantly—trustworthy groupings: guilds, *hui,* and surname- and native-place associations have thoroughly structured urban life and tempered the individualizing effects of commercialization in imperial and Republican China. The advent of industrialization in the early twentieth century called forth further inventions, the most durable being the *danwei* system (see Yeh 1996). Indeed, one analyst has drawn an out-and-out equation between "danwei culture" and "urban culture" in Beijing during the Maoist era (Li 1993). In its totalizing form, the danwei provided its occupants with a place to work, sleep, eat, and receive all life essentials without leaving the walled enclave that marked the boundaries of their "unit." The urban danwei had the capacity, then, to reduce to an absolute minimum those moments when urbanites came into contact with the urban, if by *urban* we mean the phenomena of facelessness, alienation, and individualization associated with urban spaces in the early formulations of the Western sociological tradition.

With the "ten years of chaos" occasioned by the Cultural Revolution, urban Chinese threw themselves into another, more indirect but equally important mechanism for minimizing the facelessness of the urban setting. That mechanism is the *guanxi* system, that complex flow of gifts and services that has for centuries structured and continues to structure, with different moral-ideological implications, rural as well as urban life today (cf. Yang 1994 and Yan 1996). The guanxi system, as Yang perceptively notes, is a particularizing system. Viewed diachronically, there may be good reason to interpret its reappearance in post-Maoist China in Yang's terms: as a "reaction-formation in the social body" against the universalistic ethics of self-sacrifice, national identity and state loyalty promulgated under state-sponsored collectivism (Yang 1994: 297). Viewed synchronically, however, we can draw attention to one of its less remarked upon consequences: the guanxi, like the danwei, system has the effect of insulating urban Chinese from the experience of facelessness always present in the city but particularly destabilizing, perhaps, under conditions of rapid marketization and economic reform. The guanxi system, whether viewed positively as the expression of "human feelings" (*renqing*) or negatively as corruption (Hertz 2000) locates its practitioners in webs of communitarian contacts and distinguishes them as individuals from the faceless universalized monades who make up the crowd, the masses, or "the People."

We can trace, therefore, a malleable but persistent tendency toward sociocultural resistance to facelessness in urban settings, that manifests itself in a variety of ways. The strongest and most interesting illustration of this resistance can be found in a common Chinese consumer view of prices and value. One of my best-connected acquaintances in Shanghai once boasted to me that because of his extensive guanxi network he never paid the market price for anything he bought. In his extreme formulation, buying at market price would have meant a loss of face because it demonstrated that he was merely one consumer among the masses, not connected enough to command his own price. Others I talked with shared his assessment, though not his obsessive relation to face. Indeed, some admitted that now that commodity shortages were no longer a problem they preferred buying on the market like everybody else in order to save themselves the immensely time-consuming work of activating their guanxi network. Nonetheless, they concurred that buying at a discount gave face and that face increased proportionately with the size and frequency of the discounts accorded. As a corollary, it followed that the "fair" price of capitalist market ideology was almost by definition not a "good" price precisely because it applied to everybody indiscriminately, thereby depriving the buyer of that form of exchange-based surplus value available only through the guanxi system—face.[7]

Urbanity, Facelessness, and Collective Identification   The importance of face and the particularistic networks underlying it in both the rural and urban contexts need not be questioned. My purpose here is simply to draw attention to those other moments of metropolitan life—individually evanescent but structurally constant—that urban anthropology in China has tended to overlook, those moments when the identities provided by the relational conception of personhood are temporarily muted and urbanites must construct a sense of self in the crowd. In what terms are we to account for the "loss of face" that is facelessness?

Such an account must start from the fact that the Chinese language does not present us with a convincing translation for the English term *faceless*. Furthermore, in contrast to the rather commonplace register on which this term operates in English, all of the possible translations into Chinese ring either bookish or borrowed. The closest one can come is the English *anonymity,* but that term poses problems that merit examination. In the Shanghai Renmin Chubanshe English-Chinese dictionary, *anonymity* is translated either as *niming* (hidden or concealed name) or *wuming* (without a name, but also indefinable, indescribable). These two terms are generally used not as nouns but as adjectives, as in "an unknown hero" (*wuming de yingxiong*) or "an anonymous letter" (*niming-xin*). Note that the two translations have very different connotations: in the first example, the anonymous (wuming) hero has been violently stripped of his (the masculine form is appropriate here) particular identity (name), literally and figuratively sacrificed to the collective cause; in the second example, the anonymous (niming) letter writer has chosen to conceal her identity, indeed, quite literally her face, for reasons that are eminently personal, not collective.

If we search for related concepts to elucidate the notion of niming, we run into notorious difficulties with the Chinese term for privacy, associated with the character *si,* which can mean personal or private but also secret, selfish, illicit or illegal. These associations must be kept in mind, but it is the alternative translation, "wuming," that concerns us most directly here. Turning then to related concepts of wuming, we find that the Chinese language abounds with terms for loneliness (*jimo, gudu, huangliang*), but this is loneliness associated with the solitude of the recluse, not the aloneness of the individual awash in the anonymous crowd. Chinese also has an extensive lexicon for describing anonymity from the point of view of those who are not anonymous—words, that is, for strangers or outsiders (*moshengren, xinlaizhe, shengke, wairen*). Thus, the notion of anonymity itself—which appears in the Western sociological tradition as a neutral term for the description of a certain brute experience of city life—presupposes a certain set of relations to the group, the self, and sacrifice that require untangling in the Chinese context. What, then, are the forms of the urban Chinese experience of anonymity or, as I prefer, *facelessness,* the experience of being part of a crowd in which one can neither have nor lose face because one's personal relation to the community is not at issue?

A first form of facelessness is familiar to anyone who has conducted fieldwork at urban sites. When cramming themselves onto a bus, sitting in the audience of a public cinema, maneuvering their bicycles through traffic, crowding around to observe an argument on the street, or trying to attract the attention of sales clerks, urban Chinese are confronted with the anonymity of city life. Most of these situations appear to provoke hostility. In Liu Xinwu's "Bus Aria" (1990), cited by Chen (1995), readers are given a bleak description of the loneliness and psychological violence associated with this crowded anonymity. The rudeness of urban sales clerks when dealing with the anonymous public is legendary and led central leaders during the mid-1980s to promulgate "civilization and politeness" (*wenming limao*) campaigns specifically targeting state service workers. I note also that, as with all aspects of urban life in China today, attitudes here are changing as Chinese firms facing an increasingly competitive transnational environment learn to submit their sales personnel to that special form of consumerist discipline that in the West has long since been naturalized as "courtesy" (Anagnost 1997: 75–97).

The hostility expressed by urbanites in situations of anonymity is often interpreted in terms of a communitarian social ideology in which particularistic relations are so positively connotated that they effectively block the emergence in China of notions of urban civility and the public good (see, e.g., M. Yang 1945 and Andrieu 1996). This "culturalist" (Rocca 1996) reading of Chinese sociality is belied, however, by the various situations in which anonymity is positively connotated in urban China. The crowd is not always a source of inconvenience and hostility. Strolling and window shopping (*guangguang jie*), favorite pastimes, involve less charged but equally important millings with the crowd as urban *flâneurs* attempt to keep up with the semiotics of commodities under the rapidly changing aesthetic codes of the reform era. Further, individuals and especially couples frequently seek out crowds as a way of escaping from the prying eyes of family, neighbors, and supervisors.[8] The particular experiences of urbanity encoded in these practices merit closer attention, as some of the chapters in this volume attest. However, these experiences fall into the category not of wuming but of niming, or si, in which the crowd serves principally as a backdrop for the expression of one's private life or personal choices. The situations that I explore in the remainder of this chapter fall into neither of the two categories of anonymity described above. Rather, they are moments of wuming in which collective identification with the crowd becomes the salient social element, imposing its codes of "public" or "mass" sociability over and against those of particularized social relations.

Collective Anonymity: The Stock Market   The importance of public or mass sociability in the experience of the urban became clear to me during ethnographic research I conducted on and around the Shanghai stock market in 1992 (Hertz 1998). At first sight, it would seem that nothing could be further from the practices of collective identification I am exploring than the advent of a market for enterprise shares in Shanghai. If we are to believe the triumphalist Western press (and much popular commentary in China as well), with the stock market the Chinese have finally abandoned their misguided collectivist slogans and recognized that the individualistic pursuit of wealth is the only route to a healthy society. In a capitalist reading, the success of this new institution—the "fever" (*re*) it has occasioned—is the natural consequence of capitalism's inherent appeal: everybody wants to make money.[9] However, over the course of my fieldwork, as I listened to Shanghai friends and acquaintances, both investors in and spectators of this mass market, I began to suspect that the operative word in this phrase was not *money*, as the Western press presumes, but *everybody*. Shanghainese have taken up the role of "stock folk" (*gumin*) with an abandon that transcends the individual calculus of self-interest posited by capitalism. Indeed, a "rational" analysis of the Chinese stock market cannot possibly explain its appeal, for the market itself is frequently characterized by investors as a zero-sum game: every winner implies a loser on the other side of the exchange, and a calculus of individual self-interest should lead one to think at least twice before risking one's savings to such an institution. Structurally speaking, then, it is not the simple desire to make money that feeds stock fever but stock fever that elicits and configures the apparently simple desire to make money. Stock markets are public markets that bring with them their own dynamics of crowds and power (Canetti [1960] 1984).

Institutionally, the stock market provided particularly fertile ground for the reworking of collective social forms. The creation of this new market called forth the creation of new discourses, both official and popular, and engendered a new series of social practices. Lack of space and computer facilities forced huge crowds of investors onto the streets and into specially constructed trading rooms. At their most intense, these crowds took on qualities described by Canetti ([1960] 1984): the social code allowed for a kind of physical intimacy in this context that would be unthinkable elsewhere, as the eager public pressed against others' most private parts in their effort to read market reports off television screens or to hear the latest market gossip reported by a presumed insider.

More importantly, perhaps, an individualized relation to price, so crucial in the giving of face in other economic settings, was impossible on the stock market. In the context of this speculative market, what counts is not the price but the price vector, the reading that "stock people" as a totality give to the market. When stock people "see positively" (*kan hao*), pressures to buy move prices up; when they "see negatively" (*kan huai*), prices drop. In the most palpable and active sense, then, "the masses"— the millions of decisions of millions of anonymous others—make the prices on the stock market. While reputation (*mingqi*) or quality (*suzhi*) were often at stake in investors' efforts to predict price movements correctly (Hertz 1998: 136–46), few avenues of appeal to face—that symbolic quantity that structures the relation between buyer and seller so as to determine value—were available in this setting.

But for our purposes here the most important construct called into being by the stock market was a new category of collective actor, "stock folk," sometimes referred to more technically as investors (*touzizhe*). Stock folk were that portion of "the People" who had thrown themselves into stock fever, a form of that more general activity of the 1990s called "taking the plunge" (*xia hai*). These stock folk hailed from every walk of life, from every social class and category, and this variety of social origins was part of what Shanghainese meant when they told me that "everybody" was playing the market. In the special room for wealthy investors that I visited regularly, one of the more respected "big players" was a woman of peasant background, in her sixties, who started investing with money her son had sent her from his temporary job in Australia. My research assistant, a graduate student in finance, had also borrowed a significant sum from family and teachers to play the market. I was introduced to the editor of a literary magazine who had made a neat fortune investing in share-purchase lottery tickets. I was also befriended by a worker from a Shanghai factory who had been hired by a group of coworkers to buy and sell for them. And the "everybody" with stock fever extended well beyond the boundaries of Shanghai Municipality. It was in part this sense of a nationwide, all-status everybody, in which the Shang-hainese saw themselves as particularly implicated, that lent the stock market much of its power of fascination.[10] To be part of this "everybody" was, at one level, to leave the relational identities of kinship, neighborli-ness, co-working and guanxi behind.

Gumin as Social Actors   Stock folk were themselves divided into two distinct types. On the one hand, we find the "big players" (*dahu*), indi-viduals who had made enough money on the stock market or elsewhere to qualify for entry into the brokerage-run "VIP rooms" (*dahushi*) for wealthy investors. In the cultural discourse surrounding "big players," these actors appear as hypertrophied individuals, capable of profiting from "the system" on their own terms (see Hertz 1998: 129–51). Thus, "big players" were culturally constructed as free both from the obliga-tions of embeddedness and from the collective identity of the crowd.

The "small" or "dispersed" players (*xiaohu* or *sanhu*), on the other hand, were all those investors who were not wealthy enough to buy themselves entry into the VIP rooms and who had thus to trade under difficult circumstances, waiting hours and sometimes days for their turn to open a stock account or place orders, straining to read information off distant computer screens, and standing in the streets sharing information under the sweltering sun.[11]

In contrast to dahu, the sanhu were not tagged with a social stereo-type; indeed, the notion of sanhu was not really applicable outside the stock market and a few other speculative markets such as the postage stamp market. Sanhu were investors from all walks of life, and the cate-gory cut across the entire spectrum of class/status distinctions in urban China. As such, sanhu were to the market what the People, the public, or the masses were to other spheres of Chinese society: a collective actor defined by its quality as a crowd of similar individuals. Sanhu were thus the subjects par excellence of stock fever, the victims of the "beehive mentality" so excoriated in popular discourse (to be examined below).

Looking closely at sanhu investing practices, however, we discover that dispersed players had learned to compensate in a great number of ways for their "dispersal." Information gathering, the most important "work" involved in "playing" the market, required that they create and participate in a wide variety of formations, organizations, and networks. These creations require careful examination, as they range in nature from the most "public," and hence anonymous, groupings to the most "social," and hence embedded, networks of long-term cooperation and loyalty. It is here that we can see most clearly the multiple codes of belonging and distancing at work in the urban setting writ large.

The most public groupings were what I have termed "crowd clusters" (Hertz 1998: 155–59). This was also the form of informal or unofficial stock market gathering that occasioned the most comment from the Shanghainese themselves, for they took the form of smallish groups (numbering five to fifty) of (mainly) men that amassed spontaneously in the streets outside brokerage houses, blocking traffic and attracting attention, throughout the day and often late into the night. As such, they represented a visible emblem of stock fever, and official discourse had much to say about the "traffic problems" (a code word for the symbolic disorder or "chaos" [*luan*]) that they created. My focus here, however, is not on the externally feverish aspects of these groupings, but on their internal dynamics.

Crowd clusters were amoebalike, attracting greater or lesser numbers of people depending on the charisma of the main participants and on the random ebb and flow of passers-by. The principal feature of these groups was that no one knew any of the other participants. But the public nature of these clusters extended beyond their anonymity, for these gatherings were characterized by a kind of mass democratic spirit with its own rules of etiquette and prestige.[12] There was no a priori ranking of speakers; those wishing to speak were free to, the only criterion being that they continue to hold the attention of their audience. Thus, these gatherings became the forum for oratorical contests in which individual investors attempted to convince the crowd of the reliability of their predictions, gossip, and analysis. Prestige was gained for humor, displays of cynicism toward the government, well-documented rumor collection, and opinions that cut against the grain. However, there were also many tempering voices ready to repeat commonly held opinions about the virtues of this or that stock or new government policy. In line with the spirit of these clusters, neither the hostility often associated with anonymity nor the exaggerated politeness of more "social" encounters (to be examined below) were in evidence. Agreement and disagreement were equally open, and those disagreed with did not spend too much time defending their honor but moved on to another topic or a neighboring cluster.

The unique nature of crowd cluster on the stock market scene is best illustrated by contrasting it with another apparently public forum for information gathering, the many adult education classes that were organized for investors in official or semiofficial settings (Hertz 1998: 164–66). These meetings generally consisted of a lecture that was open to the public (after payment of an entrance fee) and delivered by a local researcher or professor (of finance or economics), a broker or stock market official, or, in some cases, a recognized big player, preferably of not too shady a class background. The lectures, usually held at night, were advertised in the newspapers, on wall posters, and by word of mouth. However, unlike crowd clusters, these classes were not the occasion for a free and open discussion among participants. Rather, the audience listened quite passively to the speakers, preferring at question time, for example, to write their queries on little slips of paper which the speaker read aloud, rather than risking the embarrassment of asking a question publicly. In short, the official or semiofficial character of the situation transformed it from a place where anonymous public face could be displayed and negotiated to a place where official face was acknowledged and reinforced.

Another much-discussed forum for sharing information on the stock market was stock "salons" (*shalong*), which dotted the city during the year of my fieldwork.[13] These gatherings might be characterized as public-social, for they combined certain of the qualities of crowd clusters with those of adult education classes and those of informal stock market discussion groups (Hertz 1998: 159–62). In salons, a certain number of speakers with information or know-how to share were invited to give a brief presentation of their views of the market and to field questions (generally written not oral) from the audience. Thus, a preliminary hierarchy of knowledge and experience was established, replicating the setup of the adult education classes. Among these speakers, however, a degree of oratorical competition was in evidence, as speakers sought to entertain as much as to inform the public. Salons were also the forum for clique formation, as certain sanhu made visible their loyalties to influential dahu and created the bases for long-term sharing of information and strategies. As such, salons called upon processes of particularizing through which the anonymous stock folk could affiliate themselves with such-and-such a group, a dahu, or simply a piece of semipublic information. And, as with particularizing schemes in Chinese society generally, these processes called upon metaphors of kinship and brotherhood, with the master-disciple relation serving as a model for the ways in which dahu were to relate to their sanhu followers.

Gumin as Symbolic Construct An ethnographic analysis of stock folk presents us with a conundrum. As social actors, they follow contextualized and precise discursive codes governing the various public, official, semiformal, and social gatherings in which they participate, codes in which individual expression and group debate play a prominent role. However, as cultural symbol gumin stand for the most homogenized of social objects, moved by impulses that are considered both powerful and laughable. Gumin were thus the subject of a local discourse that interpreted stock fever as a form of cultural epidemic, following a pattern common to all fevers in urban China. Thus, while stock fever was certainly the largest and most symbolically charged fever in post-Mao China, it replicated a sociocultural pattern that had a well-established history, dating back at the very least to the latter years of the Cultural Revolution.[14] It is this pattern that must be examined if we wish to trace the relation between face and facelessness in contemporary urban China.

The term *fever* can apply to numerous and diverse domains of contemporary urban culture (Hertz 1998: 71–93). The defining characteristic of the fever is that everyone is doing the same thing at the same time; as such, fevers activate both a particular conception of "everybody" and a particular relation to time. Many take the form of simple commercial fads, and as such they appear to function in ways quite similar to fads in Western economies. Indeed, like the changes of fashion studied by Simmel, fevers are "part of the more general process of accentuation of time-consciousness [under modernity]" (Frisby 1985: 99). On the one hand, they are by their very nature evanescent; they are expected to come but then to go again, replaced by the next, equally evanescent focus of attention, and thus operate with a notion of time as fleeting and changeable. On the other hand, fevers play out a permanent reexpression of the modern, for fevers always work with that which is new, very often with that which is "Western" and new, or at the very least with that which places the actor at a critical distance from "tradition." Following or at least knowing about the going fever is a way of being "with it," with "it" being an entirely empty category. Fevers mimic in exaggerated form the waves of change sweeping over Chinese society generally under the policy of "reform and opening." But they also mimic the very form of modernity itself with its permanent tension between form (the modern as that which is timelessly contemporary) and content (the modern as a historically determined set of rationalizing institutions, policies, and attitudes).[15]

But the parallel between Western fads and Chinese fevers runs into difficulties when one turns to the cultural discourse surrounding these two phenomena, particularly with regard to the relation between the individual and the group, the "everybody" afflicted by re. The Chinese commentary on re makes it clear that these are moments when, by the very act of participating in the making of an everybody, one has somehow left one's individual face behind. When I discussed re with friends and acquaintances, they pointed out that fevers pose a "problem" in this sense. "Chinese have no individual personality (*gexing*)," I was told. "They always follow fashion (*gan shimao*), they have the psychology of a beehive (*yiwofeng*), they 'rush headlong into mass action' (*yi hong er shang* [a proverb])." This commentary was generally delivered with an air of contempt, as if there were something fascinating but abnormal about "the Chinese people's" lack of individuation—the collective loss of face—that fevers imply. Comparing Chinese fevers with U.S. fads, one remarks that no U.S. fad, no matter how widespread or silly—Ty toys, platform shoes, *Star Wars*—occasions the kind of homogenized self-criticism that equivalent events appear to call forth in urban China. Fads in the U.S. context seem to be about what other people do, not about what "we" are.

In tracing the roots of the malaise surrounding re in Shanghai discourse, I was led to another parallel, that between fevers in reform China and that paradigmatic instance of the voluntarily faceless crowd represented by political campaigns under Mao. During Mao's large-scale mobilization campaigns, a universalized, agglomerated People found itself amassed in ritualized spaces of revolution enacting identical gestures and crying out identical slogans. In their most extreme form during the Cultural Revolution, these campaigns enacted the control of the masses over the individual, more specifically the selfish bourgeois individual, by requiring similar dress and action of all. These moments, which once took pride of place in the Communist Party's elaboration of a uniquely Chinese and Maoist understanding of communist politics, today represent a kind of collective loss of face for a People bewildered by its own capacities to enact itself.

It is tempting to read fevers as "survivals" of these mass movements and to attribute some of the ambivalence that Chinese observers and participants expressed about fevers to an uneasiness with the parallels between these two moments of mass activity. This is a temptation to which Chinese commentators themselves yielded with a certain amount of glee.[16] On the stock market, investors and observers—particularly that large cohort of people who were adolescents during the Cultural Revolution—sometimes characterized stock fever as "revolutionary," drawing an analogy between the mass activities of stock people during the reform era and those of the People during the collectivist era. The stock market, in their terms, was a "social movement" (*shehui yundong*), "a second Cultural Revolution" (*dierge Wenhua Da Geming*).

The drawing of this parallel was simultaneously ironic and serious. As irony, it served to process discursively the enormous distance between socialist policies under Mao, which excoriated "speculation and profiteering" (*touji daoba*), and socialist policies supporting the highly speculative stock market of the 1990s. In this regard, investors in Shanghai in 1992 entertained what might be called a joking relationship with capitalism. "This is just capitalism," they would say derisively, thereby dismissing the government's strained ideological stance of "market socialism using capitalist mechanisms." Or "we're all just capitalists," they would declare, highlighting the sudden policy reversal that has made money-making rather than self-sacrifice a legitimate social activity. But calling the Shanghai stock market capitalist was meant as a critique of the government, not an analytic claim. When comparing the Shanghai market to markets internationally, these same investors were at pains to distinguish the Chinese case from all others and to highlight its "abnormal" (*buguifan*) characteristics as judged by capitalist standards.

In a less ironic mode, observers remarked that one of the things that distinguished the Chinese stock market from "Western" markets and linked it to prereform social practices was the presence of re. In this regard, it is interesting to note that the Chinese comparison between popular fevers, or "manias" (Whyte and Parish 1984: 321), and mass movements apparently dates to the late Cultural Revolutionary years. As Whyte and Parish report: "In Canton, the mania for hobbies and card games became known among some as the 'mass movement,' welling up from below, as opposed to the numerous 'political movements,' which descended from above. Among others, it became known as the 'army, air force, navy movement,' with crickets being the army, birds the air force, and goldfish the navy" (ibid.). Thus, contrary to popular discourse, it was not the revolutionary presence of capitalist mechanisms that qualified the stock market as a social movement but rather the particular form of mass participation that it called upon.

But what is this particular form? As Perry and Li's (1997) study of worker participation in the Cultural Revolution in Shanghai demonstrates, the totalitarian, mindless horde reading of the Cultural Revolution has significantly distorted our understanding of how the Cultural Revolution in particular and mass campaigns in general actually worked. Successful calls for mass action have in fact provided avenues for the expression of individual as well as group sentiment and ambition, and have divided the People as much as they have united it. Likewise, if fevers "work" to such a spectacular degree in urban China, it is because they provide an idiom for the expression of group and individual identity simultaneously: the person who wears black with the most style, who manages to go abroad under the best conditions, or who makes the most on the stock market distinguishes herself from the group on the group's terms. While some of the urbanites I met stubbornly refused any association with "fevers," and others threw themselves foolishly into the most ephemeral of passing fads, most Shanghainese played the fever game with discretion, choosing when they participated, how they participated, and with what attitude. Thus, fevers provide a means for distinguishing oneself from others in society while simultaneously articulating the changing framework within which society evaluates the individual.

The analogy between fevers and mass movements must be addressed, if only because it is an analogy drawn by the Chinese themselves. However, it need not be addressed in the terms that Chinese commentary sets for it. Enormous differences in social cause and effect separate them, and neither is linked to a "collective conception of personhood" in any essentialist fashion. What is common to manias, fashion, the Mao Craze, stock fever, and mass campaigns—but also religious pilgrimages, myths of origin, and ethnic warfare, to borrow examples from Canetti ([1960] 1984) that move us beyond the Chinese field—is a moment in their constitution during which individuals appear to give up, however briefly, the particularistic identities that define them in relation to particular others and take up a collective activity. In the terms we have developed, this phenomenon is one of *wuming*, of a "being with the crowd" that involves sacrificing one's individual identity to a collective design. At issue is the question of agency, the moment when the crowd ceases to function as a backdrop to one's individual will and purposes and starts to function as the catalyst for other purposes and other wills.[17] Fevers are moments when facelessness is actively created and sought out, when the particularizing strategies of face give-and-take are overshadowed by the universalizing ambitions of the crowd. And with facelessness "ego" ceases, fleetingly, to define himself in relation to others and defines himself, fleetingly, as others.

Conclusion: The Face of the Crowd   We are now in the position to return to the problem with which this chapter began. On the one hand, the instances of facelessness that I have examined suggest that we should resist an essentialized portrayal of a Chinese "relational construction of personhood" based on face. This does not mean that face and the particularized relations it builds upon are not important but only that they should not be construed so as to exclude the possibility of public, mass, and social groupings that call upon other constructions of personhood. On the other hand, these instances of facelessness call into question the individualist ideology that desocializes anonymity in Western settings, portraying it as a natural fact of modern urban life, an uncoded reality of numbers, volumes, and traffic patterns. In the urban Chinese context, anonymity is culturally inflected otherwise, producing discourses and practices that problematize the nature of the collectivity in relation to the individual. Anonymity may provoke hostility, provide a context for intimacy, create an arena for public performance, reproduce relations of official elite domination, or place the individual under the collectivity's spell—but it is never neutral. If one of the central goals of this volume is to examine the effects of global capitalism on social practices and cultural discourses in urban China, this cultural construction of anonymity must come into the analysis, for it inflects Chinese conceptions of markets, persons, cities and states against the liberal ideogram of the depersonified individual that lies at capitalism's core.

Notes

Many thanks to the editors of this volume, to the anonymous (*niming*) readers at Duke University Press, and to Florence Graezer, Lida Junghans, Hélène Martin, and Aihwa Ong for their critical comments. Further thanks to the participants at the Santa Cruz conference Ethnographies of the Urban for a wonderfully stimulating meeting.

1   On the European critics, see generally Frisby (1985), on Simmel, Kracauer, and Benjamin.

2   For problems posed by this translation, see Kipnis (1995).

3   Anderson's discussion of imagined community continues with the following example. "Javanese villagers have always known that they are connected to people they have never seen, but these ties were once imagined particularistically—as infinitely stretchable nets of kinship and clientship. Until quite recently, the Javanese language had no word meaning 'society' (1983: 15–16)." Here, Anderson comes dangerously close to assuming that "seeing" others means being "connected to" them, as it were, naturally. Communities are then imagined when this seeing is extended mentally beyond face-to-face encounters. But the study of gesellschaft, as opposed to gemeinschaft, is the study of people whose everyday encounters reinforce the feeling that they have no "connections," where seeing works as a form of alienation as much as a form of communion.

4   Parallel to this is the absence, noted also by Anderson for the Indonesian case, of an indigenous concept of society. On the (recent) importation from Japan of the Chinese term for society (*shehui*) and the contingencies surrounding this choice, see Lu (1992).

5   Kipnis performs a thorough ethnographic updating of Hu's analysis, highlighting the extraordinary malleability of "Chinese face-talk" (1995: 121) through time and across social place. He argues that mianzi/lian should be understood "in terms of orders of visibility" and not in the psychologizing vocabulary of "desires for prestige" employed by Hu (126). However, while he carefully avoids both essentialist and evolutionary readings of mianzi/lian, he provides no framework for analyzing the persistence of this "long-standing discourse" (144) beyond its malleability.

6   It is this international "community," and specifically the humiliation of China by foreign powers, that accounts for the importation of the concept of face from Chinese into English. Kipnis (1995) describes the trajectory by means of which the rich discourse of mianzi/lian became the impoverished Western notion of face through nineteenth-century missionary writing on "Chinese characteristics." Ervin-Tripp, Nakamura, and Guo date the first metaphorical use of the word *face* in English to a 1876 article by R. Hart describing Chinese political history. In French,

the equivalent "*face*" appeared in 1850 in a direct translation from the Chinese (1997: 3–4).

7   Lautard (1997: 126) also refers to face as a form of surplus value.

8   See Pellow (1993) on the space of privacy, or the lack thereof, in urban Shanghai.

9   The Chinese term *re* can be translated as the highly charged "fever" or the disappointingly mundane "fad." I have chosen "fever" to reflect the slightly pathological connotations that Chinese discourse itself attributes to the notion of "re," as illustrated below.

10 Much of this paragraph is borrowed from Hertz (1998: 94–95).

11 My discussion of sanhu draws on Hertz (1998: 152–73). Since the time of my fieldwork, conditions for small investor trading have improved. Brokerages have also opened intermediary rooms for "medium-sized" investors (*zhonghu*), which provide some but not all of the services of big investor rooms.

12 See also Jankowiak's (1993: 125–64) discussion of urban street argument in Huhhot with their "public" rules of face and persuasiveness, a parallel "clustering" that demonstrates that the forms of anonymous face I am describing here predate and extend far beyond the stock market.

13 For a more extended discussion, see Hertz (1998: 166–68). Stock salons were officially banned in 1994.

14 In Hertz 1998, I argue, drawing on Gates 1996, that this cultural pattern is concomitant with China's imperial tributary state and thus dates back to the Sung dynasty.

15 This tension in turn nourishes a feverish need for new coinages such as "late modernity" and "postmodernity." See Latour 1993 [1991].

16 I, too, succumb to this temptation in Hertz 1998: 71–93.

17 This formulation owes everything to Canetti ([1960] 1984), marvelously illuminated by McClelland (1989). As McClelland points out, Canetti is the only theorist of crowd behavior whose apprehension of the crowd is not short-circuited by a fascination with the power of the leader. For Canetti, the leader is a mere excretion of the crowd's collective will to action.

Bibliography

A Contemporary English-Chinese Dictionary (Dangdai yinghan xiangjie cidian). 1985. Shanghai: Shanghai yiwen chubanshe.

Adams, Don. 1970. *Education and Modernization in Asia*. Reading, Mass.: Addison-Wesley.

Adams, Vincanne. 1996. "Karaoke as Modern Lhasa, Tibet: Western Encounters with Cultural Politics." *Cultural Anthropology* 11, no. 4: 510–46.

Agelasto, Michael. 1998. "Graduate Employment: From Manpower Planning to the Market Economy." In *Higher Education in Post-Mao China*, ed. Michael Agelasto and Bob Adamson, 259–80. Hong Kong: Hong Kong University Press.

Agelasto, Michael, and Bob Adamson, eds. 1998. *Higher Education in Post-Mao China*. Hong Kong: Hong Kong University Press.

Agnew, John. 1994. "Representing Space: Space, Scale, and Culture in Social Science." In *Place, Culture, Representation*, ed. James Duncan and David Ley, 251–71. London: Routledge.

Ai Mo. 1997. "Zuo yige wanzheng de chuanxiao ren" (Being the complete MLM marketer). *Chuanxiao Yanjiu* (Direct selling review) (September): 36–38.

Allison, Anne. 1994. *Nightwork: Sexuality, Pleasure, and Corporate Masculinity in a Tokyo Hostess Club*. Chicago: University of Chicago Press.

Anagnost, Ann. 1989. "Prosperity and Counterprosperity: The Moral Discourse on Wealth in Post-Mao China." In *Marxism and the Chinese Experience*, ed. Arif Dirlik and Maurice Meisner, 210–34. Armonk, N.Y.: M. E. Sharpe.

———. 1993a. "Cultural Nationalism and Chinese Modernity." In *Cultural Nationalism in East Asia: Representation and Identity*, ed. Harumi Befu, 61–73. Berkeley: University of California, Institute of East Asian Studies.

———. 1993b. "The Nationscape: Movement in the Field of Vision." *positions* 1, no. 3: 585–606.

———. 1994. "Who Is Speaking Here? Discursive Boundaries and Representation in Post-Mao China." In *Boundaries in China*, ed. John Hay, 257–79. London: Reaktion.

———. 1995. "A Surfeit of Bodies: Population and the Rationality of the State in Post-Mao China." In *Conceiving the New World Order*, ed. Faye D. Ginsburg and Rayna Rapp, 22–41. Berkeley: University of California Press.

———. 1997. *National Past-Times: Narrative, Representation, and Power in Modern China*. Durham: Duke University Press.

Anderson, Benedict. 1983. *Imagined Communities: Reflections on the Origin and Spread of Nationalism*. London: Verso.

Andors, Phyllis. 1988. "Women and Work in Shenzhen." *Bulletin of Concerned Asian Scholars* 20: 22–41.

Andrieu, Jacques. 1996. "Chine: une économie communautarisée, un État décomposé." *Revue Tiers-Monde* 147: 669–87.

Appadurai, Arjun. 1986. *The Social Life of Things: Commodities in Cultural Perspective*. Cambridge: Cambridge University Press.

———. 1990. "Disjuncture and Difference in

the Global Cultural Economy." *Public Culture* 2, no. 2: 1–24.

———. 1996. *Modernity at Large: Cultural Dimensions of Globalization.* Minneapolis: University of Minnesota Press.

Appadurai, Arjun, and Carol Breckenridge. 1988. "Why Public Culture?" *Public Culture* 1, no. 1: 5–9.

———. 1990. "Public Culture in Late Twentieth Century India." *Items: Social Science Research Council* 4, no. 4: 77–80.

———. 1996. "Public Modernity in India." In *Consuming Modernity: Public Culture in a South Asian World,* ed. Carol A. Breckenridge. Minneapolis: University of Minnesota Press.

Armstrong, David. 1997. "The Chuppies Are Coming: Urban Professionals Are Turning China a Lighter Shade of Red." *San Francisco Examiner,* September 21, B–1.

Armstrong, Warwick, and T. G. McGee. 1985. *Theatres of Accumulation: Studies in Asian and Latin American Urbanization.* New York: Methuen.

Ballew, Tad. 1991. "The Local and Global Contexts of Television in Shanghai: Preliminary Notes." Paper presented at the American Anthropological Association Annual Meeting, Chicago, November 22.

———. 1992. "Thinking the Relativity of Resistance, or, Where Does Heterodoxy Go? A Preliminary Report from Shanghai Television Station." Paper presented at the American Anthropological Association Annual Meeting, San Francisco, December 6.

———. 2000. "Screening Modernity at Shanghai Television Station: Globalization, Media, and Cultural Identity-Making in Local Context." Ph.D. diss., City University of New York.

———. N.d. "Screening Modernity in Shanghai." Manuscript.

Balsamo, Anne. 1995. *Technologies of the Gendered Body: Reading Cyborg Women.* Durham: Duke University Press.

Barlow, Tani. 1994. "Theorizing Woman: Funu, Guojia, Jiating" (Theorizing Woman: Chinese woman, Chinese state, Chinese family). In *Body, Subject, and Power in China,* ed. Angela Zito and Tani E. Barlow, 253–89. Chicago: University of Chicago Press.

Barmé, Geremie R. 1996. *Shades of Mao: The Posthumous Cult of the Great Leader.* Armonk, N.Y.: M. E. Sharpe.

———. 1999. *In the Red: On Contemporary Chinese Culture.* New York: Columbia University Press.

Bauman, Richard, and Charles L. Briggs. 1990. "Poetics and Performance as Critical Perspectives on Language and Social Life." *Annual Review of Anthropology* 19: 59–88.

Bauman, Zygmunt. 1996. "From Pilgrim to Tourist, or, a Short History of Identity." In *Questions of Cultural Identity,* ed. Stuart Hall and Paul du Gay, 18–36. Thousand Oaks: Sage.

Beijing daxuesheng daibiaotuan mishuzu (Beijing College Team Secretariat). 1986. "Saiqian xuzhi" (Things to know before the meet). Mimeographed booklet. July.

Bell, Daniel. 1960. *The End of Ideology.* Glencoe, Ill.: Free Press.

Benjamin, Walter. [1936] 1969. "The Work of Art in the Age of Mechanical Reproduction." In *Illuminations: Essays and Reflections,* ed. Hannah Arendt, 217–51. New York: Schocken.

———. 1979. *One Way Street and Other Writ-*

ings. Trans. Edmund Jephcott and Kingsley Shorter. London: NLB.

Bennett, H. Stith. 1980. *On Becoming a Rock Musician.* Amherst: University of Massachusetts Press.

Berman, Marshall. 1982. *All That Is Solid Melts into Air: The Experience of Modernity.* New York: Simon and Schuster.

——. 1992. "Why Modernism Still Matters." In *Modernity and Identity,* ed. Scott Lash and Jonathan Friedman, 33–58. Oxford: Blackwell.

Bernstein, Thomas P. 1977. *Up to the Mountains and Down to the Villages: The Transfer of Youth from Urban to Rural China.* New Haven: Yale University Press.

Bian Yanjie. 1994. *Work and Inequality in Urban China.* Albany: State University of New York Press.

Biggart, Nicole Woolsey. 1989. *Charismatic Capitalism: Direct Selling Organizations in America.* Chicago and London: University of Chicago Press.

Bird, Jon, Barry Curtis, Tim Putnam, George Robertson, and Lisa Tickner, eds. 1993. *Mapping the Futures: Local Cultures, Global Change.* New York: Routledge.

Blim, Michael. 1997. "Can NOT-Capitalism Lie at the End of History or Is Capitalism's History Drawing to an End?" *Critique of Anthropology* 17, no. 4: 351–63.

Boihem, Harold, and Chris Emmanouilides, prod. 1996. *The Ad and the Ego: Truth and Consequences.* Presented by Parallax Pictures. San Francisco: California Newsreel. Videorecording.

Bordo, Susan. 1993. *Unbearable Weight: Feminism, Western Culture, and the Body.* Berkeley: University of California Press.

Borneman, John. 1993. "Trouble in the Kitchen: Totalitarianism, Love, and Resistance to Authority." In *Moralizing States and the Ethnography of the Present,* ed. Sally Falk Moore. American Ethnological Society Monographs, no. 5. Arlington, Va.: American Anthropological Association.

Bourdieu, Pierre. 1977. *Outline of a Theory of Practice.* Trans. Richard Nice. Cambridge: Cambridge University Press.

——. 1984. *Distinction: A Social Critique of the Judgement of Taste.* Cambridge: Harvard University Press.

Bourdieu, Pierre, and Jean-Claude Passeron. 1990. *Reproduction in Education, Society, and Culture.* Trans. Richard Nice. London: Sage.

Brace, Tim. 1991. "Popular Music in Contemporary Beijing: Modernism and Cultural Identity." *Asian Music* 22, no. 2: 43–65.

Bray, Francesca. 1997. *Technology and Gender: Fabrics of Power in Late Imperial China.* Berkeley: University of California Press.

Brief Introduction to the Shanghai TV Rural Channel (*Shanghai dianshitai nongcuntai jianjie*). 1992. Shanghai Television Station.

Brownell, Susan. 1995. *Training the Body for China: Sports in the Moral Order of the People's Republic.* Chicago: University of Chicago Press.

Bruun, Ole. 1993. *Business and Bureaucracy in a Chinese City: An Ethnography of Private Business Households in Contemporary China.* China Research Monographs, no. 43. Berkeley: University of California, Institute of East Asian Studies.

Buck Morss, Susan. 1989. *The Dialectics of*

Seeing: Walter Benjamin and the Arcades Project. Cambridge: MIT Press.

Burke, Timothy. 1997. *Lifebuoy Men, Lux Women: Commodity, Consumption, and Cleanliness in Modern Zimbabwe*. Durham: Duke University Press.

Caldeira, Teresa P. R. 1996. "Fortified Enclaves: The New Urban Segregation." *Public Culture* 8: 303–28.

Canetti, Elias. [1960] 1984. *Crowds and Power*. New York: Farrar Strauss Giroux.

Castells, Manuel. 1972. *City, Class, and Power*. London: Macmillan.

———. 1989. *The Informational City: Information Technology, Economic Restructuring, and the Urban-Regional Process*. Cambridge, Mass.: Blackwell.

Certeau, Michel de. 1984. *The Practice of Everyday Life*. Trans. Steven Rendall. Berkeley: University of California Press.

Chamberlain, Heath B. 1987. "Party-Management Relations in Chinese Industries: Some Political Dimensions of Economic Reform." *China Quarterly* 112: 631–61.

Chan, Anita, Richard Madsen, and Jonathan Unger. 1992. *Chen Village under Mao and Deng*. Expanded and updated ed. Berkeley: University of California Press.

Chan, Kam Wing. 1992. "Post-1949 Urbanization Trends and Policies: An Overview." In *Urbanizing China*, ed. Gregory Eliyu Guldin, 41–63. New York: Greenwood.

———. 1994. *Cities with Invisible Walls: Reinterpreting Urbanization in Post-1949 China*. Hong Kong: Oxford University Press.

———. 1996. "Post-Mao China: A Two-Class Urban Society in the Making." *International Journal of Urban and Regional Research* 20, no. 1: 134.

Chan, Roger C. K. 1996. "Urban Development and Redevelopment." In *Shanghai: Transformation and Modernization under China's Open Policy*, ed. Y. M. Yeung and Sung Yun-wing, 299–320. Hong Kong: Chinese University Press.

Chatterjee, Partha. 1993. *The Nation and Its Fragments: Colonial and Postcolonial Histories*. Princeton: Princeton University Press.

Chavez, Leo R. 1992. *Shadowed Lives*. Fort Worth, Tx.: Harcourt Brace Jovanovich.

Cheah, Pheng, and Bruce Robbins, eds. 1998. *Cosmopolitics: Thinking and Feeling beyond the Nation*. Minneapolis: University of Minnesota Press.

Chen, Nancy Nu-Chun. 1995. "Urban Spaces and Experiences of Qigong." In *Urban Spaces in Contemporary China*, ed. Deborah Davis, Richard Kraus, Barry Naughton, and Elizabeth Perry, 347–61. Cambridge: Woodrow Wilson Center Press.

Chen Xiangming, and William L. Parish. 1996. "Urbanization in China: Reassessing an Evolving Model." In *The Urban Transformation of the Developing World*, ed. Josef Gugler, 61–90. Oxford: Oxford University Press.

Chen Xiaomei. 1995. *Occidentalism: A Theory of Counter-Discourse in Post-Mao China*. New York: Oxford University Press.

Cheng Chung-Ying. 1986. "The Chinese Face and Its Confucian Roots." *Journal of Chinese Philosophy* 13: 329–48.

Cheng Tiejun, and Mark Selden. 1994. "The Origins and Social Consequences of China's Hukou System." *China Quarterly* 139 (September): 644–68.

Chevrier, Yves. 1991. "Micropolitics and the Factory Director Responsibility System, 1984–1987." In *Chinese Society on the Eve of Tiananmen: The Impact of Reform*, ed. Deborah Davis and Ezra Vogel, 109–34. Cambridge: Council on East Asian Studies, Harvard University.

Child, John. 1994. *Management in China during the Age of Reform*. Cambridge: Cambridge University Press.

Chomsky, Noam. 1998. "Free Trade and Free Markets: Pretense and Practice." In *The Cultures of Globalization*, ed. Fredric Jameson and Masao Miyoshi, 356–70. Durham: Duke University Press.

Chong, Denise. 1994. *The Concubine's Children*. New York: Penguin.

Chong, Woei Lien. 1991. "Rock Star Cui Jian." *CHIME (Journal of the European Foundation for Chinese Music Research)* 4 (Autumn): 4–22.

Chow, Rey. 1991. *Woman and Chinese Modernity: The Politics of Reading between West and East*. Minneapolis: University of Minnesota Press.

Chowdhury, Anis, and Iyanatul Islam. 1993. *The Newly Industrializing Economies of East Asia*. London: Routledge.

Christiansen, Flemming. 1990. "Social Division and Peasant Mobility in Mainland China: The Implications of the Hu-k'ou System." *Issues and Studies* 26, no. 4: 23–42.

Cohen, Anthony P., and Katsuyoshi Fukui, eds. 1993. *Humanising the City? Social Contexts of Urban Life at the Turn of the Millennium*. Edinburgh: Edinburgh University Press.

Cohen, Myron. 1994. "Cultural and Political Inventions in Modern China: The Case of the Chinese 'Peasant.'" In *China*

in Transformation, ed. Tu Wei-ming, 151–70. Cambridge: Harvard University Press.

Comaroff, John, and Jean Comaroff. 1991. *Of Revelation and Revolution: Christianity, Colonialism, and Consciousness in South Africa*. Vol. 1. Chicago: University of Chicago Press.

Communist Party of China, Central Committee. 1985. *Reform of China's Education Structure: Decision of the Communist Party of China, Central Committee* (May 1985). Beijing: Foreign Languages Press.

Concise English-Chinese Chinese-English Dictionary (Jingxuan yinghan hanying cidian). 1986. Hong Kong: Oxford University Press.

Cornue, Virginia. 1997. "Love, Sex, and New Social Forms: Producing Identities and Organizations in Contemporary China." Unpublished Conference Paper presented at Ethnographies of the Urban in 1990s China, University of California, Santa Cruz, September 27–28.

Cosgrove, Stuart. 1988. "The Zoot Suit and Style Warfare." In *Zoot Suits and Second Hand Dresses*, ed. Angela McRobbie, 3–22. Boston: Unwin Hyman.

Costa, Frank J., Ashok K. Dutt, Laurence J. C. Ma, and Allen G. Noble, eds. 1989. *Urbanization in Asia: Spatial Dimensions and Policy Issues*. Honolulu: University of Hawaii Press.

Crane, George T. 1994. "Special Things in Special Ways: National Economic Identity and China's Special Economic Zones." *Australian Journal of Chinese Affairs* 32 (July): 71–92.

Crapanzano, Vincent. 1985. *Waiting: The Whites of South Africa*. New York: Random House.

Crapanzano, Vincent. 1986. "Hermes' Dilemma: The Masking of Subversion in Ethnographic Description." In *Writing Culture: The Poetics and Politics of Ethnography*, ed. James Clifford and George E. Marcus, 51–76. Berkeley: University of California Press.

———. 1990. "On Dialogue." In *The Interpretation of Dialogue*, ed. Tullio Maranhao, 269–91. Chicago: University of Chicago Press.

———. 1991. "The Postmodern Crisis: Discourse, Parody, Memory." *Cultural Anthropology* 6, no. 4: 431–46.

———. 1992a. *Hermes' Dilemma and Hamlet's Desire: On the Epistemology of Interpretation*. Cambridge: Harvard University Press.

———. 1992b. "Some Thoughts on Hermeneutics and Psychoanalytic Anthropology." In *New Directions in Psychological Anthropology*, ed. Theodore Schwartz, Geoffrey M. White, and Catherine A. Lutz, 294–307. New York: Cambridge University Press.

Croll, Elisabeth. 1994. *From Heaven to Earth: Images and Experiences of Development in China*. London: Routledge.

———. 1995. *Changing Identities of Chinese Women: Rhetoric, Experience, and Self-Perception in Twentieth-Century China*. London: Zed.

CSBP (China Statistical Bureau, Population and Employment Department), ed. 1997. *Zhongguo Renkou Tongji Nianjian* (China population statistics yearbook). Beijing: Zhongguo Tongji Chubanshe.

"Cui Jian xianqi Haerbin xiaji yaogunfeng." 1996. *Yinyue shenghuo bao* (Musical life), July 12, 1.

Dai Jinhua. 1997. "Imagined Nostalgia." *boundary 2* 24, no. 3: 143–62.

Dalian Personnel Bureau (DPB, Dalian Renshiju). N.d. *Jiji tansuo, ba biyesheng jiuye zhidu gaige wenbu tuixiang qianjin* (Positive exploration: take the reform of the graduates' career system and push it steadily forward). Dalian: Dalian renshiju.

Dalian University of Technology, Dalian ligong daxue comp. 1992. *Bangzhu ni jiuye* (Helping with your career). Dalian: Dalian Ligong Daxue.

———. 1995a (Oct.) "Jiuwu jie biyesheng jiuye qingkuang jianjie" (Brief introduction to the situation of 1995 graduates' jobs). In *Daxuesheng jiuye* (University Students' Employment). No. 54. Dalian: Dalian ligong daxue zhaosheng biye fenpei bangongshi: 1.

———. 1995b (Nov.) "Dalian ligong daxue jiuliu jie biyesheng (ben, zhuanke) jiuye gongzuo shishi xize" (Rules for the implementation of 1996 graduates of DUT (3 and 4 year) career work). In *Daxuesheng jiuye* (University Students' Employment). No. 55. Dalian: Dalian ligong daxue zhaosheng biye fenpei bangongshi: 1.

———. 1997. *Dalian ligong daxue jiuqi jie biyesheng (ben, zhuanke) jiuye gongzuo zongjie* (Summary of employment work for 1997 graduates of DUT (3 and 4 year). Dalian: Dalian ligong daxue.

Davin, Delia. 1999. *Internal Migration in Contemporary China*. London: Macmillan Press.

Davis, Deborah. 1990. "Urban Job Mobility." In *Chinese Society on the Eve of Tiananmen: The Impact of Reform*, ed. Deborah Davis and Ezra Vogel, 85–108. Cambridge: Council on East Asian Studies, Harvard University.

Davis, Deborah, and Stevan Harrell, eds. 1993. *Chinese Families in the Post-Mao*

Era. Berkeley: University of California Press.

Davis, Deborah, Richard Kraus, Barry Naughton, and Elizabeth Perry, eds. 1995. *Urban Spaces in Contemporary China: The Potential for Autonomy and Community in Post-Mao China*. Washington, D.C.: Woodrow Wilson Center.

Davis, Deborah, and Ezra Vogel. 1991. *Chinese Society on the Eve of Tiananmen: The Impact of Reform*. Cambridge: Council on East Asian Studies, Harvard University.

Davis, Mike. 1992. *City of Quartz: Excavating the Future in Los Angeles*. New York: Vintage.

De Oliveira, Orlandina, and Bryan Roberts. 1996. "Urban Development and Social Inequality in Latin America." In *The Urban Transformation of the Developing World*, ed. Josef Gugler, 253–314. Oxford: Oxford University Press.

Debord, Guy. 1994. *The Society of the Spectacle*. New York: Zone.

DeGlopper, Donald R. 1995. *Lukang: Commerce and Community in a Chinese City*. Albany: State University of New York Press.

Delany, Brian, and Lynn W. Paine. 1991. "Shifting Patterns of Authority in Chinese Schools." *Comparative Education Review* 35, no. 1: 23–43.

Deleuze, Gilles, and Felix Guattari. 1983. *Anti-Oedipus: Capitalism and Schizophrenia*. Trans. R. Hurley, M. Seek, and H. Lane. Minneapolis: University of Minnesota Press.

DeLillo, Don. *Underworld*. 1997. New York: Scribners.

Deng Xiaoping. 1994. "Da yidali jizhe aolingaina-falaqi wen" (Responding to Italian reporter, August 21, 23, 1980). In *Deng Xiaoping Wenxuan* (Deng Xiao-

ping's selected works), vol. 2. Shenyang, Liaoning: People's Publishing: 344–53.

Diamond, Norma. 1988. "The Miao and Poison: Interactions on China's Southwest Frontier." *Ethnology* 27, no. 1: 1–25.

——. 1995. "Defining the Miao: Ming, Qing, and Contemporary Views." In *Cultural Encounters on China's Ethnic Frontiers*, ed. Stevan Harrell, 92–116. Seattle: University of Washington Press.

Dikotter, Frank. 1995. *Sex, Culture, and Modernity in China: Medical Science and the Construction of Sexual Identities in the Early Republican Period*. Honolulu: University of Hawaii Press.

Dirlik, Arif. 1994. *After the Revolution: Waking to Global Capitalism*. Hanover, N.H.: University Press of New England.

——. 1995. "Confucius in the Borderlands: Global Capitalism and the Reinvention of Confucianism." *Boundary 2* 22, no. 3: 229–73.

——. 1997. "Critical Reflections on 'Chinese Capitalism' as Paradigm." *Identities* 3, no. 3: 303–30.

Dirlik, Arif, and Zhang Xudong, eds. 1997. Introduction to *Postmodernism and China*, special issue of *boundary 2*, 24, no. 3: 1–18.

Donald, James. 1997. "This, Here, Now: Imagining the Modern City." In *Imagining Cities*, ed. S. Westwood and J. Williams, 181–201. New York: Routledge.

Douglas, Mary. 1966. *Purity and Danger: An Analysis of the Concepts of Pollution and Taboo*. London: Routledge.

Duara, Prasenjit. 1988. *Culture, Power, and the State: Rural North China, 1900–1942*. Stanford: Stanford University Press.

——. 1995. *Rescuing History from the Nation: Questioning Narratives of Modern China*. Chicago: University of Chicago Press.

Durning, Alan Thein. 1992. *How Much Is Enough? The Consumer Society and the Future of the Earth.* New York: Norton.

Dutton, Michael. 1992. *Policing and Punishment in China: From Patriarchy to "the People."* London: Cambridge University Press.

———. 1998. *Streetlife China.* Cambridge: Cambridge University Press.

Eagleton, Terry. 1991. *Ideology: An Introduction.* London: Verso.

———. 1996. *The Illusions of Postmodernism.* Cambridge, Mass.: Blackwell.

Ehrenreich, Barbara. 1990. *Fear of Falling: The Inner Life of the Middle Class.* New York: Harper Collins.

Ellin, Nan. 1996. *Postmodern Urbanism.* Cambridge, Mass.: Blackwell.

———. 1999. *Postmodern Urbanism.* Rev. ed. Princeton: Princeton Architectural Press.

Elvin, Mark. 1977. "Market Towns and Waterways: The County of Shang-hai from 1480 to 1910." In *The City in Late Imperial China,* ed. G. William Skinner, 441–73. Stanford: Stanford University Press.

Elvin, Mark, and G. W. Skinner. 1974. *The Chinese City between Two Worlds.* Stanford: Stanford University Press.

Ervin-Tripp, Susan, Kei Nakamura, and Jiansheng Guo. 1997. "Shifting Face from Asia to Europe." In *Essays in Semantics and Pragmatics,* ed. M. Shibatani and S. Thompson, 43–71. Amsterdam: John Benjamins.

Evans, Grant. 2000. "The Transformation of Jinghong Xishuangbanna, P.R.C." Unpublished conference proceedings, Hong Kong University, Anthropology Department.

Evans, Grant, Chris Hutton Evans, and Kuah Khun-eng. 2000. *Where China Meets Southeast Asia: Social and Cultural Change in the Border Regions.* ISEAS: Singapore.

Evans, Harriet. 1997. *Women and Sexuality in China.* New York: Continuum.

Fabian, Johannes. 1983. *Time and the Other: How Anthropology Makes Its Object.* New York: Columbia University Press.

Fang Tianlong. 1996. *Chuanxiao mijue: chenggong jingying ni de chuanxiao shiye* (Secrets of multi-level marketing: How to successfully manage your multi-level marketing career). Chuanxiao Zhifu Xilie (Multi-level marketing to wealth), no. 2. Beijing: Zhongguo Duiwai Fanyi Chuban Gongsi.

Fang Zhou, ed. 1998. *Zhongguo dangdai mingren chenggong suzhi fenxi baogao* (Report and analysis of the successful qualities of famous contemporary Chinese people). Vol. 1. Beijing: Qingnian Chubanshe.

Farquhar, Judith. 1994a. *Knowing Practice: The Clinical Encounter of Chinese Medicine.* Boulder: Westview.

———. 1994b. "Eating Chinese Medicine." *Cultural Anthropology* 9: 471–97.

———. 1996. "Market Magic: Getting Rich and Getting Personal in Medicine after Mao." *American Ethnologist* 23, no. 2: 239–57.

Featherstone, Mike, ed. 1990. *Global Culture.* London: Sage.

Fei Xiaotong. 1953. *China's Gentry.* Chicago: University of Chicago Press.

———. 1992. Foreword to *Urbanizing China,* ed. Gregory E. Guldin, ix. New York: Greenwood.

Ferguson, James. 1992. "The Country and the City on the Copperbelt." *Cultural Anthropology* 7, no. 1: 80–92.

———. 1997. "The Country and the City on the Copperbelt." In *Culture, Power, Place: Explorations in Critical Anthro-*

pology, ed. Akhil Gupta and James Ferguson, 137–54. Durham, N.C.: Duke University Press.

Fernandez, James W., ed. 1991. *Beyond Metaphor: The Theory of Tropes in Anthropology*. Stanford: Stanford University Press.

Firth, Raymond. 1951. *Elements of Social Organization*. London: Watts.

Foucault, Michel. 1970. *The Order of Things*. London: Tavistock.

Foucault, Michel. 1979. *Discipline and Punish: The Birth of the Prison*. New York: Vintage.

——. 1980a. *The History of Sexuality*. Vol. 1: *An Introduction*. Trans. Robert Hurley. New York: Vintage.

——. 1980b. *Power/Knowledge*. New York: Pantheon.

——. 1991. "Governmentality." In *The Foucault Effect: Studies in Governmental Rationality*, ed. Graham Burcell, Colin Gordon, and Peter Miller, 87–104. Chicago: University of Chicago Press.

——. 1994. *The Birth of the Clinic: An Archaeology of Medical Perception*. New York: Random House.

Frank, Thomas. 1997. "Liberation Marketing and the Culture Trust." In *Conglomerates and the Media*, ed. Erik Barnouw, et al. New York: New Press: 173–89.

Fraser, Nancy. 1993. "Clintonism, Welfare, and the Antisocial Wage: The Emergence of a Neo-liberal Imaginary." *Rethinking Marxism* 6, no. 1: 9–23.

Friedland, Roger, and Deirdre Boden, eds. 1994. *NowHere: Space, Time, and Modernity*. Berkeley: University of California Press.

Friedlander, Paul. 1991. "China's 'Newer Value' Pop: Rock-and-Roll and Technology on the New Long March." *Asian Music* 22, no. 2: 67–81.

Friedman, Edward, Paul G. Pickowicz, and Mark Selden, with Kay Ann Johnson. 1991. *Chinese Village, Socialist State*. New Haven: Yale University Press.

Friedman, Jonathan. 1990. "Being in the World: Globalization and Localization." In *Global Culture: Nationalism, Globalization, and Modernity*, ed. Mike Featherstone, 311–28. London: Sage.

——. 1994. *Cultural Identity and Global Process*. Thousand Oaks: Sage.

——. 1995. "Comments, on 'Objectivity and Militancy: A Debate.'" *Current Anthropology* 36, no. 3: 421–23.

Friedman, Jonathan, and Kajsa Ekholm. 1985. "Towards a Global Anthropology." *Critique of Anthropology* 5, no. 1: 97–119.

Frisby, David. 1985. *Fragments of Modernity: Theories of Modernity in the Work of Simmel, Kracauer, and Benjamin*. Cambridge: Polity Press, in association with Basil Blackwell, Oxford.

Fung, Ka-iu. 1981. "The Spatial Development of Shanghai." In *Shanghai: Revolution and Development in an Asian Metropolis*, ed. Christopher Howe, 269–300. Cambridge: Cambridge University Press.

——. 1996. "Satellite Towns: Development and Contributions." In *Shanghai: Transformation and Modernization under China's Open Policy*, ed. Y. M. Yeung and Sung Yun-wing, 321–40. Hong Kong: Chinese University Press.

Furth, Charlotte. 1987. "Concepts of Pregnancy, Childbirth, and Infancy in Ch'ing Dynasty China." *Journal of Asian Studies* 46, no. 1: 7–36.

Gaonkar, Dilip Parameshwar, ed. 1999. "Alter/Native Modernities, Volume I, Millennial Quartet: A Public Culture Miniseries." *Public Culture* 11, no. 1.

Gates, Hill. 1996. *China's Motor: A Thou-*

sand Years of Petty Capitalism. Ithaca: Cornell University Press.

Gaubatz, Piper Rae. 1995. "Urban Transformation in Post-Mao China: Impacts of the Reform Era on China's Urban Form." In Urban Spaces in Contemporary China, ed. D. Davis et al., 28–60. Washington, D.C.: Woodrow Wilson Center.

——. 1996. Beyond the Great Wall: Urban Form and Transformation on the Chinese Frontiers. Stanford: Stanford University Press.

Geertz, Clifford. 1980. Negara: The Theatre-State in Nineteenth-Century Bali. Princeton: Princeton University Press.

Giddens, Anthony. 1990. The Consequences of Modernity. Stanford: Stanford University Press.

——. 1991. Modernity and Self-Identity. Stanford: Stanford University Press.

Gilmartin, Christina, Gail Hershatter, Lisa Rofel, and Tyrene White, eds. 1994. Engendering China: Women, Culture, and the State. Harvard Contemporary China Series, no. 10. Cambridge: Harvard University Press.

Gilroy, Paul. 1991. There Ain't No Black in the Union Jack: The Cultural Politics of Race and Nation. Chicago: University of Chicago Press.

Gladney, Dru. 1991. Muslim Chinese: Ethnic Nationalities in the People's Republic. Cambridge: Cambridge University Press.

——. 1994. "Representing Nationality in China: Reconfiguring Majority/Minority Identities." Journal of Asian Studies 53, no. 11: 92–123.

Gold, Thomas B. 1993. "Go with Your Feelings: Hong Kong and Taiwan Popular Culture in Greater China." China Quarterly 136 (December): 907–25.

Good, Byron J. 1994. Medicine, Rationality, and Experience: An Anthropological Perspective. Cambridge: Cambridge University Press.

Goodman, Bryna. 1995. Native Place, City, and Nation: Regional Networks and Identities in Shanghai, 1853–1937. Berkeley: University of California Press.

Gramsci, Antonio. 1971. Selections from the Prison Notebooks. New York: International.

Greenhalgh, Susan. 1994. "Controlling Births and Bodies in Village China." American Ethnologist 21, no. 1: 3–30.

Grosz, Elizabeth. 1994. Volatile Bodies: Toward a Corporeal Feminism. Bloomington: Indiana University Press.

Gugler, Josef, ed. 1996. The Urban Transformation of the Developing World. Oxford: Oxford University Press.

Guldin, Gregory Eliyu. 1990. Anthropology in China: Defining the Discipline. Armonk, N.Y.: M. E. Sharpe.

——. 1992a. "Urbanizing the Countryside: Guangzhou, Hong Kong, and the Pearl River Delta." In Urbanizing China, ed. G. Guldin, 157–84. New York: Greenwood.

——. ed. 1992b. Urbanizing China. New York: Greenwood.

——. 1996. "Desakotas and Beyond: Urbanization in Southern China." Ethnology 35, no. 4: 265–83.

——. 1997. Farewell to Peasant China: Rural Urbanization and Social Change in the Late Twentieth Century. Armonk, N.Y.: M. E. Sharpe.

Guldin, Greg, and Aidan Southall, eds. 1993. Urban Anthropology in China. Leiden: Brill.

Gupta, Akhil, and James Ferguson, eds. 1997a. Anthropological Locations:

Boundaries and Grounds of a Field Science. Berkeley: University of California Press.

———. 1997b. *Culture, Power, Place: Explorations in Critical Anthropology*. Durham: Duke University Press.

Hall, Stuart. 1980. "Encoding/Decoding." In *Culture, Media, Language: Working Papers in Cultural Studies (1972–79)*, ed. S. Hall, D. Hobson, A. Lowe, and P. Willis, 128–38. London: Hutchinson.

———. 1985. "Signification, Representation, Ideology: Althusser and the Post-structuralist Debates." *Critical Studies in Mass Communication 2*, no. 2: 91–114.

———. 1996. "Introduction: Who Needs 'Identity'?" In *Questions of Cultural Identity*, ed. Stuart Hall and Paul du Gay, 1–17. Thousand Oaks: Sage.

Hall, Stuart, and Tony Jefferson, eds. 1976. *Resistance through Rituals: Youth Subcultures in Post-war Britain*. London: Harper Collins.

Hamm, Charles. 1991. "Music and Radio in the People's Republic of China." *Asian Music 22*, no. 2: 1–42.

Han Zhong'en. 1993. "Dangdai zhishifenzi yu yaogunyue ji qi wenhua zhuanxiang" (Contemporary Intellectuals, Rock Music, and Rock's Changes). *Zhongyang yinyue xueyuan xuebao* (Journal of the Central Conservatory of Music) 3:14–16.

Hannerz, Ulf. 1980. *Exploring the City: Inquiries toward an Urban Anthropology*. New York: Columbia University Press.

———. 1987. "The World in Creolization." *Africa 57*, no. 4: 546–59.

———. 1989. "Notes on the Global Ecumene." *Public Culture 1*, no. 2: 66–75.

———. 1992. *Cultural Complexity: Studies in the Social Organization of Meaning*. New York: Columbia University Press.

———. 1993. "The Cultural Role of World Cities." In *Humanising the City? Social Contexts of Urban Life at the Turn of the Millenium*, ed. Anthony P. Cohen and Katsuyoshi Fukui, 67–84. Edinburgh: Edinburgh University Press.

———. 1996. *Transnational Connections: Culture, People, Places*. New York: Routledge.

Hanyu chengyu cidian (Dictionary of Chinese proverbs). 1992. 18th printing. Shanghai: Shanghai Educational Publishers.

Hao Zaijin. 1992. "Zhongguo Liudong Renkou Baogao" (Reports on China's floating population). *Liberation Daily*.

Harrell, Barbara. 1981. "Lactation and Menstruation in Cultural Perspective." *American Anthropologist 83*, no. 4: 796–823.

Harrell, Stevan, ed. 1995. *Cultural Encounters on China's Ethnic Frontiers*. Seattle: University of Washington Press.

Harvey, David. 1985a. *The Urbanization of Capital: Studies in the History and Theory of Capitalist Urbanization*. Baltimore: Johns Hopkins University Press.

———. 1985b. *Consciousness and the Urban Experience: Studies in the History and Theory of Capitalist Urbanization*. Baltimore: Johns Hopkins University Press.

———. 1989. *The Condition of Postmodernity*. Cambridge, Mass.: Blackwell.

———. 1990. "Between Space and Time: Reflections on the Geographical Imagination." *Annals of the Association of American Geographers 80*, no. 3: 418–34.

———. 1993. "From Space to Place and Back Again: Reflections on the Condition of Postmodernity." In *Mapping the Futures: Local Cultures, Global Change*, ed. Jon Bird et al., 3–29. London: Routledge.

———. 1998. "What's Green and Makes the

Environment Go Round?" In *The Cultures of Globalization,* ed. Fredric Jameson and Masao Miyoshi, 327–55. Durham: Duke University Press.

Haug, Wolfgang Fritz. 1986. *Critique of Commodity Aesthetics: Appearance, Sexuality, and Advertising in Capitalist Society.* Minneapolis: University of Minnesota Press.

Hawkins, John. 1982. "Education Reform and Development in the People's Republic of China." In *Comparative Education,* ed. Philip G. Altback, Robert F. Arnove, and Gail P. Kelly, 411–32. New York: Macmillan.

Hay, James, Lawrence Grossberg, and Ellen Wartella, eds. 1996. *The Audience and Its Landscape.* Boulder: Westview.

Hayford, Charles W. 1990. *To the People: James Yen and Village China.* New York: Columbia University Press.

Hayhoe, Ruth. 1987. "China's Higher Curricular Reform in Historical Perspective." *China Quarterly* 110: 196–230.

——. 1989. *China's Universities and the Open Door.* Armonk, N.Y.: M. E. Sharpe.

——. 1993. "China's Universities since Tiananmen: A Critical Assessment." *China Quarterly* 134: 291–309.

——. 1996. *China's Universities, 1895–1995: A Century of Cultural Conflict.* New York: Garland.

He Zhuoqiang. 1988. "Wo ke bushi 'shentong.'" (I am not a child prodigy). *Tiyu Baol* (Sports Daily) January 1.

Hebdige, Dick. 1979. *Subculture: The Meaning of Style.* New York: Routledge.

Henderson, Gail. 1998. "Selling Drugs to China in the 1990s: The Struggle for Control over the Medical Market. Paper presented at the Association for Asian Studies Annual Meetings, Boston.

Henderson, Gail, and Myron S. Cohen.

1984. *The Chinese Hospital: A Socialist Work Unit.* New Haven: Yale University Press.

Hershatter, Gail. 1997. *Dangerous Pleasures: Prostitution and Modernity in Twentieth-Century Shanghai.* Berkeley: University of California Press.

Hertz, Ellen. 1998. *The Trading Crowd: An Ethnography of the Shanghai Stock Market.* Cambridge: Cambridge University Press.

——. 2000. "Le Bien de L'autre: Justice et Corruption en Chine Populaire." In *Monnayer les Pouvoirs. Éspaces, Mécanismes et Représentations de la Corruption.* G. Blundo, ed. Paris: Presses Universitaires de France (Nouveaux Cahiers de l'IUED Series no. 9): 99–122.

Hoffman, Lisa. 1997. "'Virtuous Wife–Good Mother' (Xianqi Liangmu) and the Working Woman in Late Twentieth Century Urban China." Paper presented at the International Conference on Gender and Development in Asia, Chinese University of Hong Kong, November 27–29.

Holston, James, and Arjun Appadurai. 1996. "Cities and Citizenship." *Public Culture* 8: 187–204.

Honig, Emily. 1992a. "Migrant Culture in Shanghai: In Search of a Subei Identity." In *Shanghai Sojourners,* ed. Frederic Wakeman Jr. and Wen-hsin Yeh, 239–65. Berkeley: University of California, Institute of East Asian Studies.

——. 1992b. *Creating Chinese Ethnicity: Subei People in Shanghai, 1850–1980.* New Haven: Yale University Press.

Honig, Emily, and Gail Hershatter. 1988. *Personal Voices: Chinese Women in the 1980s.* Stanford: Stanford University Press.

Hou Dangsheng. 1996. "Hanging Mao."

Shades of Mao: The Posthumous Cult of the Great Leader, ed. and trans. Geremie R. Barme, 211–14. Armonk, N.Y.: M. E. Sharpe.

Hsieh, Shihchung. 1995. "On the Dynamics of Tai/Tai-Lue Ethnicity." In *Cultural Encounters on China's Ethnic Frontiers,* ed. Stevan Harrell. 301–28. Studies on Ethnic Groups in China. Seattle: University of Washington Press.

Hsu, Francis L. K. 1967. *Under the Ancestors' Shadow.* Stanford: Stanford University Press.

Hu, Hsien Chin. 1944. "The Chinese Concepts of 'Face.'" *American Anthropologist* 46: 45–64.

Huang Shumin. 1998. *The Spiral Road: Change in a Chinese Village through the Eyes of a Communist Party Leader.* 2d ed. Boulder: Westview.

Humphrey, Caroline. 1995. "Creating a Culture of Disillusionment: Consumption in Moscow, a Chronicle of Changing Times." In *Worlds Apart: Modernity through the Prism of the Local,* ed. Daniel Miller, 43–68. London: Routledge.

Hwang, Kwang-kuo. 1987. "Face and Favor: The Chinese Power Game." *American Journal of Sociology* 92: 944–74.

Ikels, Charlotte. 1996. *The Return of the God of Wealth: The Transition to a Market Economy in Urban China.* Stanford: Stanford University Press.

Iwao, Sumiko. 1993. *The Japanese Woman.* New York: Free Press.

Jacobs, Bruce. 1979. "A Preliminary Model of Particularistic Ties in Chinese Political Alliances: *Kan-ch'ing* and *Kuan-hsi* in a Rural Taiwanese Township." *China Quarterly* 78: 237–73.

Jaivin, Linda. 1995. "Beijing Bastards: The New Revolution." *CHIME* 8 (spring): 99–103.

Jameson, Fredric. 1984. "Postmodernism, or, the Cultural Logic of Late Capitalism." *New Left Review* 146 (July–August): 59–92.

Jameson, Fredric. 1998. "Notes on Globalization as a Philosophical Issue." In *The Cultures of Globalization,* ed. Fredric Jameson and Masao Miyoshi, 54–77. Durham: Duke University Press.

Jankowiak, William R. 1993. *Sex, Death, and Hierarchy in a Chinese City: An Anthropological Account.* New York: Columbia University Press.

Jelliffe, Derrick, and E. F. Patrice Jelliffe. 1981. *Human Milk in the Modern World.* Oxford: Oxford University Press.

Jhally, Sut, writer and editor. 1998. *Advertising and the End of the World.* A production of the Media Education Foundation. Northampton: Media Education Foundation. Videorecording.

Ji Dangsheng, et al. 1995. "Beijing shi liudong renkou xianzhuang yu duice yanjiu" (A study of the current condition of and strategies for Beijing's floating population). *Renkouxue yu jihua shengyu* (Population studies and birth planning) 5: 75–82.

Jin Zhaojun. 1993. "Zhongguo xinshiqi liuxing yinyue chuangzuo de meixue guannian" (The aesthetic concepts involved in the creation of China's new popular music). *Zhongyang yinyue xueyuan xuebao* (Journal of the Central Conservatory of Music) 3: 5–8.

———. 1994. "Zhongguo liuxing yinyue de jushi he youhuan" (The situation and suffering of China's popular music). *Zhongyang yinyue xueyuan xuebao* (Journal of the Central Conservatory of Music) 4: 82–87.

Jinnai, Hidenobu. 1995. *Tokyo: A Spatial Anthropology.* Trans. Kimiko Nishimura. Berkeley: University of California Press.

Johnson, Linda Cooke. 1995. *Shanghai: From Market Town to Treaty Port, 1074–1858.* Stanford: Stanford University Press.

Jones, Andrew F. 1992a. *Like a Knife: Ideology and Genre in Contemporary Chinese Popular Music.* Ithaca, N.Y.: East Asia Program, Cornell University, Series title: Cornell East Asia series 57.

——. 1992b. "Beijing Bastards." *Spin,* October, 80–90, 122–23.

——. 1994. "The Politics of Popular Music in Post-Tiananmen China." In *Popular Protest and Political Culture in Modern China,* ed. Jeffrey N. Wasserstrom and Elizabeth Perry, 148–65. Boulder: Westview.

Kim, Joochul, and Sang-Chuel Choe. 1997. *Seoul: The Making of a Metropolis.* Chichester: Wiley.

King, Anthony D. 1996a. "Introduction: Cities, Texts, and Paradigms." In *Representing the City: Ethnicity, Capital, and Culture in the Twenty-First-Century Metropolis,* ed. A. King, 1–19. New York: New York University Press.

——. ed. 1996b. *Re-presenting the City: Ethnicity, Capital, and Culture in the Twenty-First-Century Metropolis.* New York: New York University Press.

——, ed. 1997. *Culture, Globalization, and the World System: Contemporary Conditions for the Representation of Identity.* Minneapolis: University of Minnesota Press.

Kipnis, Andrew. 1995. " 'Face': An Adaptable Discourse of Social Surfaces." *positions* 3, no. 1: 119–48.

——. 1997. *Producing Guanxi: Sentiment, Self, and Subculture in a North China Village.* Durham: Duke University Press.

Kirkby, R. J. R. 1985. *Urbanisation in China: Town and Country in a Developing Economy, 1949–2000 A.D.* London: Croom Helm.

Kofman, Eleonore, and Elizabeth Lebas, eds. 1996. *Writings on Cities.* Oxford: Blackwell.

Kroeber, Alfred R. 1948. *Anthropology.* New York: Harcourt, Brace.

Kwok, R. Yin-Wang. 1992. "Urbanization under Economic Reform." In *Urbanizing China,* ed. Gregory E. Guldin, 65–85. New York: Greenwood.

Lattimore, Owen. 1940. *Inner Asian Frontiers of China.* New York: American Geographical Society.

Latour, Bruno. 1993 [1991]. *We Have Never Been Modern.* C. Porter, trans. Cambridge, Mass.: Harvard University Press.

Lautard, Stéphanie. 1997. "Les réseaux d'influence." *Pouvoirs* 81: 123–37.

Lavely, William. 1991. "Marriage and Mobility under Rural Collectivism." In *Marriage and Inequality in Chinese Society,* ed. Rubie S. Watson and Patricia Buckley Ebrey, 286–312. Berkeley: University of California Press.

Lee, Ching Kwan. 1998. *Gender and the South China Miracle: Two Worlds of Factory Women.* Berkeley: University of California Press.

Lee, Leo Ou-fan. 1999. "Shanghai Modern: Reflections on Urban Culture in China in the 1930s." *Public Culture* 11, no. 1: 7.

Lee, Leo Ou-fan, and Andrew J. Nathan. 1985. "The Beginnings of Mass Culture: Journalism and Fiction in the Late Ch'ing and Beyond." In *Popular Culture in Late Imperial China,* ed. David Johnson, Andrew J. Nathan, and Evelyn S. Rawski, 360–95. Berkeley: University of California Press.

Lefebvre, Henri. [1974] 1991. *The Produc-*

tion of Space. Trans. Donald Nicholson-Smith. Cambridge, Mass.: Blackwell.

——. 1996. Writings on Cities, ed. and trans. Eleonore Kofman and Elizabeth Lebas. Oxford: Blackwell.

Lefort, Claude. 1986. The Political Forms of Modern Society: Bureaucracy, Democracy, Totalitarianism. Cambridge: MIT Press.

Lesser, Alexander. 1961. "Social Fields and the Evolution of Society." Southwest Journal of Anthropology 17: 40–48.

Lewis, J. W., ed. 1971. The City in Communist China. Stanford: Stanford University Press.

Li Bin. 1993. "Danwei Culture as Urban Culture in Modern China." In Urban Anthropology in China, ed. Greg Guldin and Aidan Southall, 345–52. Leiden: Brill.

Li Cheng. 1997. Rediscovering China: Dynamics and Dilemmas of Reform. Lanham, Md.: Rowman and Littlefield.

Li Cheng, and Lynn T. White III. 1991. "China's Technocratic Movement and the World Economic Herald." Modern China 17, no. 3: 342–88.

Li Cheng'an. 1999. "Zhongguo gaodeng xuexiao biyesheng jiuye shichang jizhi yanjiu" (A study of the mechanism of employment markets for graduates of China's higher education institutes). M.A. thesis, Dalian, Liaoning, China, Dalian Ligong Daxue. (Dalian University of Technology).

Li He. 1997. Yaogun gu'er: Hou Cui Jian cun miaoxie (Rock orphans: a portrait of the post-Cui Jian group). In Jinri xianfeng (Today's Vanguard). Beijing: Sanlian shudian.

Li Jianjun. 1995. "Zhongguo diyidaide bailing daxieyi" (A bold outline of the first generation of Chinese white collars).

Chengshi Ren (Metropolitan), June, 20–21.

Li Tinggui. 1991. Leigongshan Shang de Miaozu (The Miao on Leigong Mountain). Guiyang: Guizhou Minzhu Chubanshe.

Li Zhisui. 1994. The Private Life of Chairman Mao: The Memoirs of Mao's Personal Physician. Trans. Tai Hung-chao, ed. Anne F. Thurston. New York: Random House.

Liang Shuming. 1949. Zhongguo de wenhua yaoyi (Essential meanings of Chinese culture). Chengdu: Lu ming shudian.

Lin, George C. S. 1997. Red Capitalism in South China. Vancouver: University of British Columbia Press.

Lipietz, Alain. 1986. "New Tendencies in the International Division of Labor: Regimes of Accumulation and Modes of Regulation." In Production, Work, Territory: The Geographical Anatomy of Capitalism, ed. A. Scott and M. Storper, 16–40. Boston: Allen and Unwin.

Liu, James T. C. 1970. "Integrative Factors through Chinese History: Their Interaction." In Traditional China, ed. James T. C. Liu and Wei-ming Tu, 10–23. Englewood Cliffs, N.J.: Prentice-Hall.

Liu Kang. 1995. "The Problematics of Mao and Althusser: Alternative Modernity and Cultural Revolution." Rethinking Marxism 8, no. 3: 1–26.

——. 1996. "Is There an Alternative to (Capitalist) Globalization? The Debate about Modernity in China." boundary 2 23, no. 3: 193–218.

Liu, Lydia. 1993. "Translingual Practice: The Discourse of Individualism between China and the West." positions 1, no. 1: 160–93.

——. 1995. Translingual Practice: Literature,

National Culture, and Translated
Modernity—China, 1900–1937. Stanford:
Stanford University Press.

Liu Xinwu. 1990. "Bus Aria." In *Black
Walls and Other Stories*. Trans. D. Cohn.
Hong Kong: Rendition.

Liu Yiran. 1992. "Rocking Tiananmen." In
New Ghosts, Old Dreams, ed. Geremie
Barme and Linda Jaivin, 5–22. New
York: Random House.

Liu Zhen. 1983. "The Girl Who Seemed to
Understand." Trans. W. J. F. Jenner. In
*Stubborn Weeds: Popular and Controver-
sial Literature after the Cultural Revolu-
tion*, ed. Perry Link, 31–48.
Bloomington: Indiana University Press.

Low, Setha. 1996. "The Anthropology of
Cities: Imagining and Theorizing the
City." *Annual Review of Anthropology*
25: 383–409.

Lowe, Donald. 1996. *The Body in Late Capitalist USA*. Durham: Duke University
Press.

Lu Hanlong. 1992. "On the Intellectual
Environment for Theory Building in
Chinese Sociology." In *SASS Papers*, 4:
431–42. Shanghai: Shanghai Academy
of Social Sciences Publishing House.

Lu Jianhua. 1997. "Zouxiang xin jiegou"
(Moving toward a new structure). In
*Guanjian shike: Dangdai zhongguo jidai
jiejue de 27 ge wenti* (A critical moment:
27 problems of contemporary China in
need of urgent solution). Beijing: Jinri
zhongguo chubanshe.

Ma Yongbo. 1996. "Cui Jian fangtan lu 3"
(Interview with Cui Jian, No. 3). *Yinyue
shenghuo bao* (Musical life), July 26, 3.

Lu Wenfu. 1987. *The Gourmet and Other
Stories*. London: Readers International.

Lü Xiaobo, and Elizabeth J. Perry, eds.
1997. *Danwei: The Changing Chinese*

Workplace in Historical and Comparative Perspective. Armonk, N.Y.: M. E.
Sharpe.

Macaulay, Thomas Babington. [1848] 1934.
*The History of England from the Acces-
sion of James II*. Vol. 1. London: Dent.

MacPherson, Kerrie L. 1996. "The Shanghai Model in Historical Perspective." In
*Shanghai: Transformation and Modern-
ization under China's Open Policy*, ed.
Y. M. Yeung and Sung Yun-wing, 493–
527. Hong Kong: Chinese University
Press.

Malkki, Liisa. 1992. "National Geographic:
The Rooting of People and the Territorialization of National Identity
among Scholars and Refugees." *Cultural
Anthropology* 7, no. 1: 24–44.

Manderson, Leonore, and Margaret Jolly,
eds. 1997. *Sites of Desires, Economics of
Pleasure: Sexualities in Asia and the Pacific*. Chicago: University of Chicago
Press.

Mao Zedong. [1927] 1975. "Report on an
Investigation of the Peasant Movement
in Hunan." In *Selected Works of Mao
Tse-tung*, 1:23–59. 3d ed. Beijing: Foreign Languages Press.

——. [1942] 1967. "Talks at the Yenan
Forum on Literature and Art." In *Selected Works of Mao Tse-tung*, 3:69–98.
2d ed. Beijing: Foreign Languages Press.

Marcus, George E. 1986. "Contemporary
Problems of Ethnography in the Modern World System." In *Writing Culture:
The Poetics and Politics of Ethnography*,
ed. James Clifford and George E. Marcus, 165–93. Berkeley: University of California Press.

Marcus, George E., and Michael M. J.
Fischer. 1986. *Anthropology as Cultural
Critique: An Experimental Moment in*

the Human Sciences. Chicago: University of Chicago Press.

Martinez-Alier, Joan. 1998. " 'Environmental Justice' (Local and Global)." In The Cultures of Globalization, ed. Fredric Jameson and Masao Miyoshi, 312–26. Durham: Duke University Press.

Mascia-Lees, Frances, and Patricia Sharpe. 1992. Tattoo, Torture, Mutilation, and Adornment. Albany: State University of New York Press.

Massey, Doreen. 1993. "Power Geometry and a Progressive Sense of Place." In Mapping the Future: Local Culture, Global Change, ed. J. Bird, B. Curtis, T. Putnam, G. Robertson, and L. Tickner, 59–69. New York: Routledge.

———. 1994. Space, Place, and Gender. Minneapolis: University of Minnesota Press.

McClelland, J. S. 1989. The Crowd and the Mob: From Plato to Canetti. London: Unwin Hyman.

McClintock, Ann. 1995. Imperial Leather: Race, Gender, and Sexuality in the Colonial Contest. New York: Routledge.

Meisner, Maurice. 1982. Marxism, Maoism, and Utopianism. Madison: University of Wisconsin Press.

———. 1986. Mao's China and After: A History of the People's Republic. New York: Free Press.

———. 1996. The Deng Xiaoping Era: An Inquiry into the State of Chinese Socialism, 1978–1994. New York: Hill and Wang.

Micic, Peter. 1995. " 'A Bit of This and a Bit of That': Notes on Pop/Rock Genres in the Eighties in China." CHIME 8 (spring): 76–95.

Mitchell, Timothy. 1991. Colonizing Egypt. Cambridge: Cambridge University Press.

Mitchell, Tony. 1996. Popular Music and Local Identity: Rock, Pop, and Rap in Europe and Oceania. London: Leicester University Press.

Moore, Henrietta L. 1996. "The Changing Nature of Anthropological Knowledge: An Introduction." In The Future of Anthropological Knowledge, ed. Henrietta L. Moore. New York: Routledge.

Moore, Sally Falk. 1987. "Explaining the Present: Theoretical Dilemmas in Processual Ethnography." American Ethnologist 14, no. 4: 727–36.

———. 1993. Moralizing States and the Ethnography of the Present. American Ethnological Society Monograph 5, no. 5. Arlington, Va.: American Anthropological Association.

Morley, David. 1992. Television, Audiences, and Cultural Studies. New York: Routledge.

Morley, David, and Kuan-Hsing Chen, eds. 1996. Stuart Hall: Critical Dialogues in Cultural Studies. London: Routledge.

Mote, F. W. 1977. "The Transformation of Nanking, 1350–1400." In The City in Late Imperial China, ed. G. William Skinner, 101–53. Stanford: Stanford University Press.

Mueggler, Eric. 1991. "Money, the Mountain, and State Power in a Naxi Village." Modern China 17, no. 2: 188–226.

———. 1995. "Spectral Temporalist: The Time of Agency in Maoist Southwestern China." Paper presented at the meetings of the American Anthropological Association, Washington, D.C.

Mumford, Lewis. 1938. The Culture of Cities. New York: Harcourt, Brace.

Murphey, Rhoads. 1984. "City as a Mirror of Society: China, Tradition, and Transformation." In The City in Cultural

Context, ed. John Agnew, John Mercer, and David Sopher, 186–204. Boston: Allen and Unwin.

Nash, June. 1981. "Ethnographic Aspects of the World Capitalist System." *Annual Review of Anthropology* 10: 393–423.

Naughton, Barry. 1988. "The Third Front: Defense Industrialization in the Chinese Interior." In *China Quarterly* 115: 351–86.

———. 1995a. "Cities in the Chinese Economic System: Changing Roles and Conditions for Autonomy." In *Urban Spaces in Contemporary China: The Potential for Autonomy and Community in Post-Mao China,* ed. Deborah S. Davis, Richard Kraus, Barry Naughton, and Elizabeth J. Perry, 61–89. Washington, D.C.: Woodrow Wilson Center Press.

———. 1995b. *Growing Out of the Plan: Chinese Economic Reform, 1978–1993.* Cambridge: Cambridge University Press.

———. 1998. "China's Financial Reform: Achievements and Challenges." BRIE Working Papers, no. 112. Available at URL:http://brie.berkeley.edu/BRIE/pubs/wp/wp112.html.

Nell, Edward. 1973. "Economics: The Revival of Political Economy." In *Ideology in Social Science: Readings in Critical Social Theory,* ed. Robin Blackburn. London: Fontana.

Nonini, Donald. 1997. "Shifting Identities, Positioned Imaginaries: Transnational Traversals and Reversals by Malaysian Chinese." In *Ungrounded Empires: The Cultural Politics of Modern Chinese Transnationalism,* ed. Aihwa Ong and Donald Nonini, 203–27. New York: Routledge.

Oi, Jean. 1989. *State and Peasant in Contemporary China: The Political Economy of Village Government.* Berkeley: University of California Press.

Olwig, Karen Fog, and Kirstin Hastrup, eds. 1997. *Siting Culture: The Shifting Anthropological Object.* London and New York: Routledge.

Ong, Aihwa. 1993–94. "On the Edge of Empires: Flexible Citizenship among Chinese in Diaspora." *positions* 1, no. 3 (winter): 745–78.

———. 1996. "Anthropology, China, and Modernities: The Geopolitics of Cultural Knowledge." In *The Future of Anthropological Knowledge,* ed. Henrietta L. Moore, 60–92. New York: Routledge.

———. 1997a. " 'A Momentary Glow of Fraternity': Narratives of Chinese Nationalism and Capitalism." *Identities* 3, no. 3: 331–66.

———. 1997b. "Chinese Modernities: Narratives of Nation and of Capitalism." In *Ungrounded Empires: The Cultural Politics of Modern Chinese Transnationalism,* ed. Aihwa Ong and Donald Nonini, 171–202. New York: Routledge.

———. 1999. *Flexible Citizenship: The Cultural Logics of Transnationality.* Durham: Duke University Press.

Ong, Aihwa, and Don Nonini, eds. 1997. *Ungrounded Empires: The Cultural Politics of Modern Chinese Transnationalism.* New York: Routledge.

Orleans, Leo. 1987. "Graduates of Chinese Universities: Adjusting the Total." *China Quarterly* 111: 444–49.

Paine, Lynn Webster. 1994. "Progress and Problems in China's Educational Reform." In *China Briefing, 1994,* ed. William A. Joseph, 113–31. Boulder: Westview.

Pang, Linlin. 1993. "Matchmaking via the

Personal Advertisements in China versus in the United States." *Journal of Popular Culture* 27, no. 1 (summer): 163–70.

Pannell, Clifton. 1992. "The Role of Great Cities in China." In *Urbanizing China,* ed. Gregory E. Guldin, 11–39. New York: Greenwood.

Park, Robert E. 1952. *Human Communities.* Glencoe, Ill.: Free Press.

Parker, Andrew, M. Russo, D. Sommer, and P. Yaeger, eds. 1992. *Nationalisms and Sexualities.* New York: Routledge.

Pasternak, Burton, and Ching Wang. 1985. "Breastfeeding Decline in Urban China: An Exploratory Study." *Human Ecology* 13, no. 3: 433–66.

Patton, Paul. 1995. "Imaginary Cities: Images of Postmodernity." In *Postmodern Cities and Spaces,* ed. Sophie Watson and Katherine Gibson, 112–21. Oxford: Blackwell.

Peattie, Lisa Redfield, and Edward Robbins. 1984. "Anthropological Approaches to the City." In *Cities of the Mind,* ed. Lloyd Rodwin and Robert M. Hollister, 83–95. New York: Plenum.

Pellow, Deborah. 1993. "No Place to Live, No Place to Love: Coping in Shanghai." In *Urban Anthropology in China,* ed. Gregory E. Guldin and Aidan Southall, 396–424. Leiden: Brill.

Pepper, Suzanne. 1984. *China's Universities: Post-Mao Enrollment Policies and Their Impact on the Structure of Secondary Education, a Research Report.* Ann Arbor: University of Michigan, Center for Chinese Studies.

———. 1990. *China's Education Reform in the 1980s: Policies, Issues, and Historical Perspectives.* Berkeley: University of California, Institute of East Asian Studies.

———. 1995. "Regaining the Initiative for Education Reform and Development." In *China Review, 1995,* ed. Lo Chi Kin et al., 18.2–18.49. Hong Kong: Chinese University Press.

———. 1996. *Radicalism and Education Reform in Twentieth Century China: A Search for an Ideal Development Model.* New York: Cambridge University Press.

Perry, Elizabeth J., and Li Xun. 1997. *Proletarian Power: Shanghai in the Cultural Revolution.* Boulder: Westview.

Pieke, Frank. 1995. "Bureaucracy, Friends, and Money: The Growth of Capital Socialism in China." *Comparative Study of Society and History* 37, no. 3: 494–518.

———. 1996. *The Ordinary and the Extraordinary: An Anthropological Study of Chinese Reform and the 1989 People's Movement in Beijing.* London: Kegan Paul International.

Pillsbury, Barbara. " 'Doing the Month': Confinement and Convalescence of Chinese Women after Childbirth." *Social Science and Medicine* 12, no. 1B: 11–22.

Pinyin Chinese-English Dictionary, The. 1985 [1978]. Edited by the Hanying Cidian Compilation Group, Beijing Foreign Languages Institute English Department. Hong Kong: The Commercial Press, Ltd.

Popkin, Barry, M. Bilsborrow, J. S. Akin, and M. E. Yamamato. 1983. "Breastfeeding Determinants in Low-Income Countries." *Medical Anthropology* 7, no. 1: 130–44.

Potter, Sulamith Heins. 1983. "The Position of Peasants in Modern China's Social Order." *Modern China* 9, no. 4: 465–99.

Potter, Sulamith Heins, and Jack M. Potter.

1990. *China's Peasants: The Anthropology of a Revolution*. Cambridge: Cambridge University Press.

Pred, Allan, and Michael John Watts. 1992. *Reworking Modernity: Capitalisms and Symbolic Discontent*. New Brunswick: Rutgers University Press.

Price, Niko. 1992. "That 'Dynasty' Look: China—a Nation of New Fashion Victims." *San Francisco Chronicle*. April 5.

Qing Hongping. 1995. "Li zu shiji, jiakuai fazhan xishuangbanna luyou shiye" (Taking advantage of the present situation to revitalize Xishuangbanna's tourism industry). *Xueshu lunwen ji* (A collection of research papers from Xishuangbanna Education College) 2–3: 71–73.

Raban, Jonathan. 1974. *Soft City*. London: Hamish Hamilton.

Rai, Shirin M. 1991. *Resistance and Reaction: University Politics in Post-Mao China*. London: St. Martin's.

Rawski, Evelyn S. 1985. "Economic and Social Foundations of Late Imperial China." In *Popular Culture in Late Imperial China*, ed. David Johnson, Andrew J. Nathan, and Evelyn S. Rawski, 3–33. Berkeley: University of California Press.

Rea, Dennis. 1993. "A Western Musician's View of China's Pop and Rock Scene." *CHIME* 6 (spring): 34–55.

Redfield, Robert. 1941. *The Folk Culture of Yucatan*. Chicago: University of Chicago Press.

——. 1947. "The Folk Society." *American Journal of Sociology*, no. 52: 293–308.

Redfield, Robert, and Milton B. Singer. 1954. "The Cultural Role of Cities." *Economic Development and Culture Change* 3: 53–73.

Rickett, Allyn, and Adele Rickett. 1957.

Prisoners of Liberation. New York: Cameron Associates.

Rocca, Jean-Louis. 1996. "La corruption et la communauté: Contre une analyse culturaliste de l'économie chinoise." *Revue Tiers-Monde* 147: 689–702.

Rofel, Lisa. 1992. "Rethinking Modernity: Space and Factory Discipline in China." *Cultural Anthropology* 7, no. 1: 93–114.

——. 1994. "Liberation Nostalgia and a Yearning for Modernity." In *Engendering China: Women, Culture, and the State*, ed. Christina Gilmartin, Gail Hershatter, Lisa Rofel, and Tyrene White, 226–49. Cambridge: Harvard University Press.

——. 1999. *Other Modernities: Gendered Yearnings in China after Socialism*. Berkeley: University of California Press.

Rose, Nikolas. 1996. "Governing 'Advanced' Liberal Democracies." In *Foucault and Political Reason: Liberalism, Neo-liberalism, and Rationalities of Government*, ed. Andrew Barry, Thomas Osborne, and Nikolas Rose, 37–64. Chicago: University of Chicago Press.

Rowe, John. 1984. *Hankow: Commerce and Society in a Chinese City, 1796–1889*. Stanford: Stanford University Press.

Ruan Fangyu. 1991. *Sex in China: Studies in Sexology in Chinese Culture*. New York: Plenum.

Santiago-Irizarry, Vilma. 1996. "Culture as Cure." *Cultural Anthropology* 11, no. 1: 3–24.

Sassen, Saskia. 1994. *Cities in a World Economy*. Thousand Oaks: Pine Forge.

Schein, Louisa. 1994. "The Consumption of Color and the Politics of White Skin in Post-Mao China." *Social Text* 41 (winter): 141–64.

——. 1996a. "The Other Goes to Market:

The State, the Nation, and Unruliness in Contemporary China." *Identities* 2, no. 3: 197–222.

——. 1996b. "Multiple Alterities: The Contouring of Gender in Miao and Chinese Nationalisms." In *Women Out of Place: The Gender of Agency and the Race of Nationality,* ed. Brackette Williams, 79–102. New York: Routledge.

——. 1997. "Gender and Internal Colonialism in China." *Modern China* 23, no. 1: 69–78.

——. 1998. "Importing Miao Brethren to Hmong America: A Not So Stateless Transnationalism." In *Cosmopolitics: Thinking and Feeling beyond the Nation,* ed. Pheng Cheah and Bruce Robbins, 163–91. Minneapolis: University of Minnesota Press.

——. 1999. "Of Cargo and Satellites: Imagined Cosmopolitanism." *Postcolonial Studies* 2, no. 3: 345–75.

——. 2000. *Minority Rules: The Miao and the Feminine in China's Cultural Politics.* Durham: Duke University Press.

Schram, Stuart, ed. 1974. *Chairman Mao Talks to the People: Talks and Letters, 1956–1971.* Trans. John Chinnery and Tieyun. New York: Pantheon.

Schumpeter, Joseph. [1942] 1962. *Capitalism, Socialism, and Democracy.* New York: Harper and Row.

Schwankert, Steven. 1997. "Taking Rock to the People: A Beijing DJ Walks a Long and Winding Road." *Asiaweek,* January 10.

Seabrook, Jeremy. 1996. *In the Cities of the South: Scenes from a Developing World.* London: Verso.

SEC (State Education Commission), ed. 1992. *Putong Gaodeng Xuexiao Zhaosheng Gongzuo Nianjian* (Yearbook of ordinary higher education enrollment work). Comp. Higher Education Students Department and Higher Education Institutions Enrollment Research Association. Beijing: People's Education Press.

——. 1993. *Putong Gaodeng Xuexiao Zhaosheng Gongzuo Nianjian* (Yearbook of ordinary higher education enrollment work). Comp. Higher Education Students Department and Higher Education Institutions Enrollment Research Association. Beijing: People's Education Press.

Seeberg, Vilma. 1998. "Stratification Trends in Technical-Professional Higher Education." In *Higher Education in Post-Mao China,* ed. Michael Agelasto and Bob Adamson, 211–36. Hong Kong: Hong Kong University Press.

Selden, Mark. 1993. *The Political Economy of Chinese Development.* Armonk, N.Y.: M. E. Sharpe.

Sennett, Richard. 1994. *Flesh and Stone: The Body and the City in Western Civilization.* New York: Norton.

Sensenbrenner, Julia. 1996. "Rust in the Iron Rice Bowl: Labor Reforms in Shanghai's State Enterprises, 1992–1993." Ph.D. diss., Johns Hopkins University.

Seybolt, Peter J. 1996. *Throwing the Emperor from His Horse: Portrait of a Village Leader in China, 1923–1995.* Boulder: Westview.

Shanghai jiaotong University, ed. 1993. *Chinese-English Dictionary.* Shanghai: Shanghai Jiaotong Daxue Chubanshe.

Shanghai Jiaoyu Dianshitai (Shanghai Educational Television). 1994. *Muru weiyang* (Breast-feeding). Videorecording.

Shanghai Municipal Statistical Bureau Information Office Page. 1998. "Shanghai Basic Facts '97: Investment in Urban

Construction." URL: http://www.
shanghai-window.com/shanghai/
(April 28 access).

Shanghai on Internet web site. 1998. URL:
http://www.sh.com (April 28 access).

Shanghaishi gaoxiao biyesheng jiuye
zhidao zhongxin (Shanghai higher education graduates' career guidance center). 1998. *Recruit Book Shanghai:
Career Information, Volume 2.* Shanghai: Shanghaishi gaoxiao biyesheng
jiuye zhidao zhongxin.

Shenzhen Fazhi Bao (Shenzhen Legal
Daily). 1994. "Shenzhen sanwu buluo
toushi" (A perspective on the Shenzhen
"Three Nothing" Tribe), March 6.

Shields, Rob. 1996. "A Guide to Urban
Representation and What to Do About
It: Alternative Traditions of Urban The-
ory." In *Re-presenting the City: Ethnicity,
Capital, and Culture in the Twenty-first-
Century Metropolis,* ed. Anthony D.
King, 227–52. New York: New York Uni-
versity Press.

Shih, Shu-mei. 1999. "Gender and a
Geopolitics of Desire: The Seduction of
Mainland Women in Taiwan and Hong
Kong Media." In *Spaces of Their Own:
Women's Public Sphere in Transnational
China,* ed. Mayfair Mei-Hui Yang, 278–
307. Minneapolis: University of Min-
nesota Press.

Shishang (Trends). 1995. "Shishang zazhi
duzhe diaocha baogao" (Report on the
survey of the *Trends* readership),
March, 65.

Shue, Vivienne. 1988. *The Reach of the
State: Sketches of the Chinese Body Poli-
tic.* Stanford: Stanford University Press.

——. 1995. "State Sprawl: The Regulatory
State and Social Life in a Small Chinese
City." In *Urban Spaces in Contemporary
China: The Potential for Autonomy and*

Community in Post-Mao China, ed.
D. Davis et al., 90–112. New York: Cambridge University Press.

Shusterman, Richard. 1999. "France's *Phi-
losophe Impolitique*" (review of Pierre
Bourdieu, *Acts of Resistance: Against the
Tyranny of the Market and on Television*). *The Nation,* May 3, 25–28.

Simmel, Georg. [1903] 1965. "Les grandes
villes et la vie de l'esprit." In *L'urban-
isme, utopies, et réalités,* ed. F. Chaoy,
409–21. Paris: Seuil.

Sit, Victor. 1985. *Chinese Cities: The
Growth of the Metropolis since 1949.* Oxford: Oxford University Press.

Siu, Helen. 1989a. "Socialist Peddlers and
Princes in a Chinese Market Town."
American Ethnologist 16, no. 2: 195–212.

——. 1989b. *Agents and Victims in South
China: Accomplices in Rural Revolution.*
New Haven: Yale University Press.

——. 1993. "Cultural Identity and the Politics of Difference in South China."
Daedalus 122 (spring): 2.

Siu, Noel Y. M., and C. P. Lau. 1998. "Development Practices in the People's Republic of China." *China Report* 34, no. 1:
47–67.

Sjoberg, Gideon. 1959. "Comparative Ur-
ban Sociology." In *Sociology Today:
Problems and Prospects,* ed. Robert K.
Merton, Leonard Broom, and Leon-
ard S. Cottrell Jr., 334–59. New York:
Basic Books.

Skinner, G. William. 1964–65. "Marketing
and Social Structure in Rural China."
Journal of Asian Studies 24: 3–43, 195–
228, 363–99.

——. 1977a. "Introduction: Urban and
Rural in Chinese Society." In *The City in
Late Imperial China,* ed. G. William
Skinner, 253–73. Stanford: Stanford
University Press.

———. 1977b. "Cities and the Hierarchy of Local Systems." In *The City in Late Imperial China,* ed. G. William Skinner, 275–351. Stanford: Stanford University Press.

Sklair, Leslie. 1998. "Social Movements and Capitalism." In *The Cultures of Globalization,* ed. Fredric Jameson and Masao Miyoshi, 291–311. Durham: Duke University Press.

Smart, Alan. 1993. "Gifts, Bribes, and Guanxi: A Reconsidertion of Bourdieu's Social Capital." *Cultural Anthropology* 8, no. 3: 388–408.

Solinger, Dorothy. 1993. *China's Transition from Socialism: Statist Legacies and Market Reforms, 1980–1990.* Armonk, N.Y.: M. E. Sharpe.

———. 1994. "China's Urban Transients in the Transition from Socialism and the Collapse of the Communist 'Urban Public Goods Regime.'" *Comparative Politics* (January): 127–46.

———. 1995. "The Floating Population in the Cities: Chances for Assimilation?" In *Urban Spaces in Contemporary China: The Potential for Autonomy and Community in Post-Mao China,* ed. Deborah S. Davis et al., 113–42. Washington, D.C.: Woodrow Wilson Center Press.

———. 1999. *Contesting Citizenship in Urban China: Peasant Migrants, the State, and the Logic of the Market.* Berkeley: University of California Press.

South China Morning Post. 1993. "Matchmaker City Crosses Borders," January 15.

———. 1994. "Foreign Husbands' Warning to Brides," January 11.

Spence, Jonathan D. 1990. *The Search for Modern China.* New York: Norton.

———. 1995. "Conclusion: Historical Perspec-

tives." In *Urban Spaces in Contemporary China: The Potential for Autonomy and Community in Post-Mao China,* ed. Deborah S. Davis et al., 394–426. New York: Cambridge University Press.

Sugawara, Sandra. 1997. "Beijing Is Finally Getting Its Own Cafe/Bar Scene." *Seattle Times,* January 19, K7.

Sunday Morning Post. 1992. "China's Profitable Path of True Love," October 4.

———. 1993. "With This Ring I Flee to a Life of Hell," March 21.

Sung, Yun-Wing. 1991. *The China-Hong Kong Connection.* Cambridge: Cambridge University Press.

Tam, Maria Siu-Mi. 1992. "Class and Patriarchal Relations in Shekou: A Structuralist View." *Journal of Women and Gender Studies* 3 (March): 89–115.

Tang Xiaobing. 1996a. "New Urban Culture and the Anxiety of Everyday Life in Contemporary China." In *In Pursuit of Contemporary East Asian Culture,* ed. Xiaobing Tang and Stephen Snyder, 107–22. Boulder: Westview.

———. 1996b. *Global Space and the Nationalist Discourse of Modernity: The Historical Thinking of Liang Qichao.* Stanford: Stanford University Press.

Tsing, Anna L. 1993. *In the Realm of the Diamond Queen.* Princeton: Princeton University Press.

Turner, Bryan. 1996. *The Body in Society.* London: Sage.

Turner, Terence. 1994. "Bodies and Antibodies: Flesh and Fetish in Contemporary Social Theory." In *Embodiment and Experience: The Existential Ground of Culture and Self,* ed. Thomas Csordas, 27–47. Cambridge: Cambridge University Press.

Unger, Jonathan. 1982. *Education under Mao: Class and Competition in Canton*

Schools, 1960–1980. New York: Columbia University Press.

Urry, John. 1995. *Consuming Places*. London: Routledge.

Van Esterik, Penny. 1989. *Beyond the Breast-Bottle Controversy*. New Brunswick, N.J.: Rutgers University Press.

Verdery, Katherine. 1992. "The 'Etatization' of Time in Ceausescu's Romania." In *The Politics of Time*, ed. Henry Rutz. AES Monograph Series, no. 4. Washington, D.C.: American Anthropological Association.

———. 1996. *What Was Socialism and What Comes Next?* Princeton: Princeton University Press.

Villapando, Venny. 1989. "The Business of Selling Mail-Order Brides." In *Making Waves: An Anthology of Writings by and about Asian-American Women*, ed. Asian Women United of California, 318–26. Boston: Beacon.

Vogel, Ezra F. 1969. *Canton under Communism: Programs and Politics in a Provincial Capital, 1949–1968*. Cambridge: Harvard University Press.

———. 1989. *One Step Ahead in China*. Cambridge: Harvard University Press.

Wakeman, Frederic, Jr. 1966. *Strangers at the Gate: Social Disorder in South China, 1839–1861*. Berkeley: Calif.: University of California Press.

Wakeman, Frederic, Jr., and Wen-hsin Yeh. 1992. *Shanghai Sojourners*, ed. Frederic Wakeman Jr. and Wen-hsin Yeh, 1–14. Berkeley: University of California, Institute of East Asian Studies.

Walder, Andrew G. 1986. *Communist Neo-traditionalism: Work and Authority in Chinese Industry*. Berkeley: University of California Press.

Wallack, Lawrence. 1990. "Two Approaches to Health Promotion in the Mass Media." *World Health Forum* 1: 143–48.

Wang Anyi. 1994. *Fuxi he muxi de shenhua* (Paternal and maternal deities). Zhejiang: Zhejiang xinhua chubanshe.

Wang Chunguang. 1995. *Shehui liudong he shehui chonggou: jingcheng zhejiangcun yanjiu* (Social mobility and social restructuring: A study of Zhejiangcun in Beijing). Zhejiang: Zhejiang renmin chubanshe.

Wang Lianfang. 1993. *Yunnan minzu gongzuo huiyi lu* (A memoir and record of work among Yunnan's minorities). Yunnan wenshi ziliao xuanze (Yunnan cultural history data collections), no. 45. Kunming: Yunnan renmin chubanshe.

Wang Xiaoyi. 1993. "The Development of China's Small Towns." In *Urban Anthropology in China*, ed. Greg Guldin and Aidan Southall, 151–66. Leiden: Brill.

Watts, Michael J. 1992. "Space for Everything (A Commentary)." *Cultural Anthropology* 7, no. 1: 115–29.

Wen Fuxiang. 1996. "Enhancing Students' Overall Quality and Promoting Society's All-Around Development." In *East-West Dialogue in Knowledge and Higher Education*, ed. Ruth Hayhoe and Julia Pan, 266–79. Armonk, N.Y.: Sharpe.

Westwood, Sallie, and John Williams, eds. 1997. *Imagining Cities: Signs, Scripts, Memory*. London: Routledge.

White, Gordon. 1987. "The Politics of Economic Reform in Chinese Industry: The Introduction of the Labor Contract System." *China Quarterly* 111: 365–89.

White, Lynn T., III. 1978. *Careers in Shanghai: The Social Guidance of Personal Energies in a Developing Chinese City, 1949–1966*. Berkeley: University of California Press.

——. 1981. "Shanghai-Suburb Relations, 1949–1966." In *Shanghai: Revolution and Development in an Asian Metropolis*, ed. Christopher Howe, 241–68. Cambridge: Cambridge University Press.

——. 1996. "Shanghai's 'Horizontal Linkages' and Population Control." In *Shanghai: Transformation and Modernization under China's Open Policy*, ed. Y. M. Yeung and Sung Yun-wing, 419–67. Hong Kong: Chinese University Press.

Whyte, Martin K. 1993. "Deng Xiaoping: The Social Reformer." *China Quarterly* 135: 515–35.

Whyte, Martin K., and William L. Parish. 1984. *Urban Life in Contemporary China*. Chicago: University of Chicago Press.

Williams, Raymond. 1973. *The Country and the City*. New York: Oxford University Press.

——. 1980. "Base and Superstructure in Marxist Cultural Theory." In *Problems in Materialism and Culture: Selected Essays*, 31–49. London: Verso.

——. 1989. "Metropolitan Perceptions and the Emergence of Modernism." In *The Politics of Modernism: Against the New Conformists*, ed. Tony Pinkney, 37–48. London: Verso.

Wilson, Ara. 1988. "American Catalogues of Asian Brides." In *Anthropology for the 1990s*, ed. Johnnetta Cole, 114–25. New York: Free Press.

Wilson, Scott [Wei Lajiao]. 1997. "The Cash Nexus and Social Networks: Mutual Aid and Gifts in Contemporary Shanghai Villages." *China Journal* 37: 91–112.

Wirth, Louis. 1938. "Urbanism as a Way of Life." *American Journal of Sociology* 44: 3–24.

Wittfogel, Karl A. [1957] 1981. *Oriental Despotism: A Comparative Study of Total Power*. New York: Vintage.

Wolf, Eric R. 1955. "Types of Latin American Peasantry: A Preliminary Discussion." *American Anthropologist* 57: 452–71.

——. 1967. "Understanding Civilizations." *Comparative Studies in Society and History* 9: 446–65.

——. 1984. Culture: Panacea or Problem?" *American Antiquity* 49, no. 2: 393–400.

——. 1999. *Envisioning Power: Ideologies of Dominance and Class*. Berkeley: University of California Press.

Wolff, Janet. 1997. "The Global and the Specific: Reconciling Conflicting Theories of Culture." In *Culture, Globalization, and the World System: Contemporary Conditions for the Representation of Identity*, ed. Anthony D. King, 161–74. Minneapolis: University of Minnesota Press.

Xiang Biao. 1993. "Beijing you ge zhejiangcun" (There is a "Zhejiang Village" in Beijing). In *Shehuixue yu shehui diaocha* (Sociology and Social Investigation), nos. 3–5.

Xiang Biao. 1995. "Zhejiangcun zhaji #15" (Notes on Zhejiang Village). In *Zhongguo nongmin* (Chinese Peasantry), 12: 54–8.

Xiao Jin, and Mun C. Tsang. 1999. "Human Capital Development in an Emerging Economy: The Experience of Shenzhen, China." In *China Quarterly* 157: 72–114.

Xinhua News Agency. 1996. "Beijing Issues Child Welfare White Paper." *Foreign Broadcast Information Services*, April 3, 1996.

Xiong Yu. 1993. "Analysis of the Changes in Fertility Culture of the Minority Nationalities in Beijing." In *Urban Anthropology in China,* ed. Greg Guldin and Aidan Southall, 256–67. Leiden: Brill.

Xu Jiangshan. 1996. "Shoudu shimin wenming gongyue chutai" (The civilization code for capital residents makes its stage entrance). *Renmin Ribao* (People's daily), March 11, 1.

Yan Yunxiang. 1996. *The Flow of Gifts: Reciprocity and Social Networks in a Chinese Village.* Stanford: Stanford University Press.

Yang, Martin C. 1945. *A Chinese Village: Taitou, Shantung Province.* New York: Columbia University Press.

Yang, Mayfair Mei-hui. 1988. "The Modernity of Power in the Chinese Socialist Order." *Cultural Anthropology* 3, no. 4: 408–27.

———. 1989. "The Gift Economy and State Power in China." *Comparative Studies in Society and History* 31, no. 1: 25–54.

———. 1994. *Gifts, Favors, and Banquets: The Art of Social Relationships in China.* Ithaca: Cornell University Press.

———. 1996. "Tradition, Traveling Anthropology, and the Discourse of Modernity in China." In *The Future of Anthropological Knowledge,* ed. Henrietta L. Moore, 93–114. New York: Routledge.

———. 1997. "Mass Media and Transnational Subjectivity in Shanghai: Notes on (Re)Cosmopolitanism in a Chinese Metropolis." In *Ungrounded Empires: The Cultural Politics of Modern Chinese Transnationalism,* ed. Aihwa Ong and Donald Nonini, 287–319. New York: Routledge.

Yau, Esther. 1989. "Is China the End of Hermeneutics? Or, Political and Cultural Usage of Non-Han Women in Mainland Chinese Films." *Discourse* 11, no. 2: 115–36.

Yeh, Anthony G. O. 1996. "Pudong: Remaking Shanghai as a World City." In *Shanghai: Transformation and Modernization under China's Open Policy,* ed. Y. M. Yeung and Sung Yun-wing, 273–98. Hong Kong: Chinese University Press.

Yeh, Wen-hsin. 1996. *Provincial Passages. Culture, Space, and the Origins of Chinese Communism.* Berkeley: University of California Press.

Yeung, Yue-mand and Xu-wei Hu, eds. 1992. *China's Coastal Cities: Catalysts for Modernization.* Honolulu: University of Hawaii Press.

Yin Shaoting. 1986. "Shuo Zhang" (Speaking of miasma). *Yunnan difang zhi tongxun* (The communication annals of places in Yunnan) 4: 69–74.

Yu Ruizhou, ed. 1999. *Xin jiuye shidai* (New era of employment). Beijing: Gaige chubanshe.

Zhang Jianpeng, ed. 1999. *Xue shenme zhuanye hao* (How to choose a major). Beijing: Xueyuan chubanshe.

Zhang, Li. Forthcoming. *Strangers in the City: Reconfigurations of Space, Power, and Social Networks Within China's Floating Population.* Stanford: Stanford University Press.

Zhang Minxuan. 1998. "Changing Conceptions of Equity and Student Financial Support Policies." In *Higher Education in Post-Mao China,* ed. Michael Agelasto and Bob Adamson, 237–58. Hong Kong: Hong Kong University Press.

Zhang Qingwu. 1988. "Basic Facts on the Household Registration System." *Chinese Economic Studies* 22, no. 1: 22–85.

Zhang Yingjin. 1996. *The City in Modern Chinese Literature and Film: Configurations of Space, Time, and Gender.* Stanford: Stanford University Press.

Zhang Youyi, and Wang Zhilin. 1991. "Liudong renkou yu huji guanli" (The floating population and Hukou regulation). *Renkou yu fazhan* (Population and Development) 4.

Zhang Zaixing, and Zixiang Han. 1993. "Zouchu hundun: wailiu mingong xingtai genzong caifang shouji" (Coming out of chaos: Interview notes on the inner world of migrant peasant workers). In *Dushi li de moshengren* (Strangers in the city), ed. Linxu Wang, 377–411. Shanghai: Shanghai shehui kexueyuan chubanshe.

Zhao Bin. 1997. "Consumerism, Confucianism, Communism: Making Sense of China Today." *New Left Review* 222: 43–59.

Zhongguo Shangbao (China trade news).

1995a. " 'Xiwang zhongguo you geng duode meiren dansheng' " (I hope China has even more beautiful people emerging), June 25, 1.

——. 1995b. "Motuo dasai bushi xuanmei bisai" (The model competition is not a beauty contest), June 25, 1.

Zhou, Kate Xiao. 1996. *How the Farmers Changed China*. Boulder: Westview.

Zito, Angela. 1994. " 'Silk and Skin: Significant Boundaries' or 'Bodies and Vessels.' " In *Body, Subject, and Power in China*, ed. Angela Zito and Tani Barlow, 103–30. Chicago: University of Chicago Press.

Zito, Angela, and Tani Barlow, eds. 1994. *Body, Subject, and Power in China*. Chicago: University of Chicago Press.

Contributors

Tad Ballew teaches in the Interdisciplinary Humanities Program at Arizona State University.

Susan Brownell's first book, *Training the Body for China: Sports in the Moral Order of the People's Republic*, was based on her experience as a collegiate athlete in China, followed by a year of study at the Beijing University of Physical Education. She is Associate Professor of Anthropology at the University of Missouri, St. Louis, and is currently doing research on fashion models, cosmetic surgery, and the changing politics of appearance in China.

Nancy N. Chen is Assistant Professor of Anthropology at the University of California, Santa Cruz. Her book manuscript "Breathing Spaces: Qigong, Psychiatry, and Body Politics of Late Twentieth Century China" is under revision for publication.

Constance D. Clark teaches in the Department of Women Studies at San Francisco State University. She presently is revising her manuscript on migration, work, and marriage in southern China.

Rob Efird is a Ph.D. candidate in sociocultural anthropology at the University of Washington.

Suzanne Gottschang is Luce Assistant Professor of East Asian Studies and Anthropology at Smith College. She is currently revising her manuscript on the politics of mothering in China.

Ellen Hertz teaches social-cultural anthropology at the University of Lausanne, Switzerland. She has written an ethnography of the Shanghai stock market and is currently exploring an ethnographic approach to international institutions, including the United Nations Working Group for Indigenous Populations and the World Trade Organization.

Lisa Hoffman received her Ph.D. in cultural anthropology at the University of California, Berkeley, and currently lives and teaches in Hong Kong.

Sandra Hyde completed her doctorate degree in 1999 in the Joint Medical Anthropology Program at the University of California, Berkeley and San Francisco. Her dissertation was entitled "Sex, Drugs, and Karaoke: Making AIDS in Southwest China." She currently holds a postdoctoral fellowship in social medicine at Harvard University.

Lyn Jeffery is a doctoral candidate in cultural anthropology at the University of California, Santa Cruz. She currently is completing her dissertation on the cultural construction of transnational marketing networks in mainland China.

Lida Junghans received her Ph.D. in anthropology from Harvard in 1999. Currently a consultant, she is working on a manuscript that uses ethnographic material from the People's Republic of China to explore the connections between temporalities and ideologies.

Louisa Schein is Associate Professor of Anthropology at Rutgers University. She is the author of *Minority Rules: The Miao and the Feminine in China's Cultural Politics.* Her articles have appeared in *Modern China, Cultural Anthropology, Social Text,* and *Identities.*

Li Zhang is Assistant Professor of Anthropology at the University of California, Davis. She is the author of *Strangers in the City: Reconfigurations of Space, Power, and Social Networks within China's Floating Population* (Stanford University Press, forthcoming).

Index

Breast-feeding, 89–90, 92–94, 103 n.1; promotion of, 95–96; as "scientific"/modern, 96; and sexuality, 95, 97–101; women's decisions about, 101–2. *See also* Health; Health care; Hospitals; Sexuality

Brides, 104, 105, 111, 112, 114–17, 121; video, 116

Canetti, Elias, 283, 293 n.17

Capital, 12, 16, 143; cultural/symbolic, 56–57, 230, 238; flow of, 179, 212, 255; foreign, 11, 48, 190; global, 63 n.12, 93, 255, 256, 263, 264, 265, 267; and labor, 11; and nation-state, 3, 10; as principle of analysis, 4

Capitalism, 3, 4, 5, 10, 282; consumer, 267, 273 n.32; and culture, 268; entrepreneurial, 92; global, 2, 4, 15, 92, 266, 268, 291; and the individual, 92, 292; and mobility, 104–5; and modernity, 92; and modernization, 102; morality of, 25; and power, 267; and socialism, 25, 36, 44; and space, 15–16, 104; and stock folk, 289; and time, 93, 104. *See also* Market socialism

Cardin, Pierre, 133, 134, 139

Castells, Manuel, 272 n.27

Censorship, 78–79

Certeau, Michel de, 240 n.2

Chan, Kam-wing, 241 n.4, 269 n.4

Chengdu (city), 29, 85 n.6, 133

China Fire (*Zhongguo huo*; record company), 78, 86 n.19

Chinese Communist Party (CCP), 3, 5, 20, 24, 39, 187, 198

Chixinjie (Festival of Eating the New Rice), 232–34, 238, 241 n.7

Chuanxiao. *See* Multilevel marketing (MLM)

Chuanxiao Yanjiu (Direct Selling Review; magazine), 36

Cities, 1, 5, 7; as apogee of commodity fetishism, 227; and bodies, 123, 124, 125, 168; borders of, 6, 7, 9, 14, 228, 253–55; coastal, 8, 9, 47, 49, 185; and consumerism, 225; and countryside, 4, 9, 251; images of, 122, 123, 125; migration to, 9, 106; as objects of desire, 7, 122, 225; and practices of well-being, 180; reconceptualizations of, 245, 254; and socialism, 5–7, 168, 185. *See also* Anonymity; Urban, the; Urban Migrants; Urbanization

Citizens: production of, 13, 24–25, 92

Citizenship: urban, 7, 107, 201; variegated, 56

Civilization Code, 129

Civilization, 125, 126, 196; and bodies, 166; campaigns to promote, 281; Han women and, 150; and the urban, 4. *See also* Beijing; Spiritual civilization (*jingshen wenming*)

Class, 4, 38, 50, 54, 104, 127, 141, 229, 230, 239; labels, 48; urban, 127; white-collar, 126

Clinics. *See* Hospitals

Cohen, Myron, 20 n.1, 250

College graduates, 10, 42 n.16, 49, 56–57, 58, 135; and labor markets, 10, 45; as products, 59–60; rural, 54, 61 n.4, 237. *See also* Guidance (*zhidao*); Job assignment system; Mutual choice; Social mobility; Universities

Colonial culture, 81–82

Colonialism: internal, 154; Japanese, 47–48

Commodification, 12, 13; of bodies, 14, 118; of culture, 13, 233; of ethnicity, 14; of *guanxi*, 205; of health care, 168, 171; of labor, 59–60; of land, 4; of medicine, 166; of social relations, 24, 34; of tradition, 13; of yaogun, 70

Commodities, 4, 11, 14, 167, 196–97, 225–26, 229, 231–33, 241 n.2

Competition, 14, 198; in labor market, 50, 51, 53, 58, 115; for space, 194. *See also* Sports; Supermodel Contest (1995)

Confucianism: and education, 56; and marketing, 34, 42 n.21; and modernity, 92; and sexuality, 151, 153

Consumer culture, 4, 9, 12, 180–81; foreign, 4, 239; and health, 166–68, 180; transnational, 93

Consumerism, 12, 24, 95, 229; and cosmopolitanism, 225, 238–40; and health care, 173–74, 177; and identity, 24, 26, 40 n.4; and motherhood, 13, 90, 96–97, 98. *See also* Commodities; Consumption

Consumption, 3, 15, 56, 68, 125, 158, 160, 241 n.2, 247, 267; and cosmopolitanism, 225, 238–40; and culture, 123, 225–27, 229, 231, 234, 240; and gender, 177, 181; and health care, 4, 16, 94, 165–67, 171–72, 174–81; and identity, 24, 26, 40 n.4; and modernity/urbanity, 90, 237, 239–40; and MLM, 24, 27, 35; and power, 181; rationed, 200; of sex, 150–52, 159; and socialism, 12; of yaogun, 73, 83. *See also* Commodities; Consumerism

Corruption, 23, 36, 168; and crime, 205, 215, 218; and *guanxi*, 278

Cosmopolitanism, 26, 58, 90, 104, 111, 120, 126, 127, 132, 150, 231, 239; and concepts of beauty, 137–40; and consumption/consumerism, 225, 238–40; imagining of, 226–27, 238–40; and nationalism, 141; and rurality, 229, 240, 250, 255; and the urban, 4, 13, 17–18. *See also* Beijing; Cities; "Imagined cosmopolitanism"; Jinghong (city); Multilevel Marketing (MLM); Shenzhen; Tianjin; Xishuangbanna

Courtship, 18, 19, 232

Crime/criminality, 128, 151, 201, 204; attributed to floating population, 202, 206, 208, 209, 211, 212, 216; and corruption, 205, 218; origins of, 213–16. See also *Heishehui* (criminal syndicates); Migrant space(s); Multilevel Marketing (MLM); Piracy

Cui Jian, 69, 71–72, 77, 78, 81–83, 85 n.8

Cultural production: 4, 10, 123, 225, 228, 229, 232, 234, 237–38, 240

Cultural Revolution (1966–1976), 6, 54, 63 nn.13, 15, 65 n.21, 131, 147, 148, 162 n.8, 172, 235–36, 239, 270, 278, 288, 289, 290

Culture, 4, 10; and capitalism, 268; commodification of, 13, 233; of consumption, 92–93, 95, 225–26; consumption of, 123, 225, 231, 234, 240; elite, 13, 126, 132, 134, 136; flows of, 141, 266; global, 126, 141, 226; industry, 28, 83; local, 131, 141, 232; minority, 13, 238; national, 125, 131; objectification of, 234, 239; popular, 126, 141, 233; and power, 197, 265; and the state, 4, 24, 234; traditional, 42 n.23, 153, 226, 229, 236–37; transnational, 136. *See also* Beijing; Body culture; Colonial culture; Consumer culture; Youth: culture of

Dahu (big players on the stock market), 284, 286, 287. *See also* Stock market

Dai Jinhua, 1

Dalian (city), 29, 50, 57, 62 nn.6, 7, 133; history of, 47–48; hukou transfers to, 53, 64–65 n.19; labor allocation in, 52–53, 54–55, 59–60; universities in, 44

Dalian City Talent Market, 52, 57

Dalian University of Technology (DUT), 43–44, 53–59, 61 nn.1, 2, 62 n.7, 64 nn.16, 17, 19; 65 n.23

Daling qingnian (aging youth), 108, 112, 122 n.1

Dang'an. See Dossier

Danwei (work unit), 2, 6, 110, 147, 149, 169, 171, 178, 184, 185, 187, 200 n.6, 247; and *difang*, 191–92, 193–95, 197; and urban sociality, 278

DeLillo, Don, 263

Deng, Xiaoping, 8, 48, 62 n.10, 217, 266

Desakota, 8, 255

Health care (*cont.*)

tion, 4, 16, 92, 165–67, 171–72, 174–80; rural-urban inequalities in, 164–67, 172–73, 179, 180; social geographies of, 16, 174; and socialism, 16, 165–66, 172–73, 178, 181; and time, 174, 178; and urban space, 170–71, 177. *See also* Hospitals; United Nations Children's Fund (UNICEF); World Health Organization (WHO)

Hegemony, 212, 264–65, 272 n.22, 273 n.29

Heishehui (criminal syndicates), 149

Henan (province), 135

Hershatter, Gail, 144

Hinterland, 8, 15, 123, 145, 150, 154, 249, 252, 256, 263

HIV/AIDS, 145, 150, 151, 161 n.2

Hong Kong, 9, 25, 28, 30, 48, 71, 75, 78, 86 n.20, 113, 114, 136, 159

Hospitals, 4, 13, 16, 90, 92, 172–73, 176–78; "Baby-Friendly," 89, 93–94; and consumer culture, 92–93, 95; and modernity, 13, 91, 93; promotion of body images in, 89–91, 101, 102; promotion of breast-feeding in, 91, 97–98; and the state, 92, 96, 175, 179

Household registration system. See *Hukou*

Howard, Ebenezer, 244, 269 n.4

Hsieh, Shihchung, 162 n.8

Hu, Hsien Chin, 277, 292 n.5

Hukou (household registration system), 5–6, 16, 45, 49, 50, 62 nn.6, 7; 106–7, 184; transfers of, 50, 53, 57, 58, 64–65 n.19, 107, 201, 204, 205, 221 n.2

Hunan (province), 146, 241 n.4

Identity/ies, 19, 66 n.26; 89, 103, 105, 121, 131, 138, 186; and consumption, 24, 26, 40 n.4; cultural, 233; and face, 276; market, 12, 25, 34–36; national, 9, 14, 141; practice(s) of, 263–66, 268, 273 n.33; sexual, 159; and the state, 12, 24; urban, 125, 128, 130, 131, 137, 150, 154, 236, 254–56; white collar, 126; and work, 25, 55

"Imagined cosmopolitanism," 13, 31, 160, 226

Individual, the, 31, 37, 55, 57, 59; and capitalism, 92, 292; and the collectivity, 19, 92, 181; in Cultural Revolution, 288; and health practices, 171; through face, 276, and cosmopolitanism, 26; and mass movements/fevers, 290–91; performance of, 32; and socialism, 31; and the state, 13, 92

Industrialization: British, 250; rural, 3, 8, 9, 271 n.14; urban, 5; and urbanization, 5, 228

Investment, 8; foreign, 48, 49, 195; hierarchies of, 15; for MLM, 27

Iron rice bowl, 44, 187, 190

Jankowiak, William, 293 n.12

Japan and Japanese, 5, 8, 14, 23, 26, 28, 31, 37–38, 47, 86 n.20, 29; 105–6, 108–10, 113–14, 116–22, 269 n.4

Jiangsu (province), 108, 120, 133, 185

Jiangxi (province), 159, 197

Jilin (province), 133

Jinghong (city), 14, 143–47, 149, 151–57, 159, 161 n.3; as cosmopolitan, 150, 160

Job assignment system, 63 nn.14, 15, 237; and central planning, 50; continued use of, 53–54; as mode of population control, 46; move away from, 43, 47; reforms in, 49, 51, 59, 60. *See also* College graduates; *Fenpei* (direct assignments); Labor allocation system; Market(s), for labor; Mutual choice

Johnson, Linda, 271 n.17

Jones, Andrew, 73, 85 n.9

Karaoke, 134, 143, 147, 247, 265; as sign/practice of urbanity, 231–32

Kipnis, Andrew, 292 nn.5, 6

Kroeber, Alfred, 253–54

Kunming (city), 85 n.6, 133, 145, 146, 148, 161 n.2

Kwok, R. Yin-wang, 5

Labor, 3; and capital, 11; commodification of, 59–60; contract, 49; distribution of, 11, 54; flow of, 45, 105, 107, 147, 198, 212; rural, 5–6, 8, 18, 48, 115; and the state, 50, 59; surplus, 8, 48; talented (*rencai*), 48–49. *See also* College graduates; Employment office/employers; Labor allocation system; Market(s), for labor; Migrants; Migration; Workers

Labor allocation/distribution, 11, 60; and assignments, 49–50, 237; and guanxi/connections, 53–54, 57; and guidance, 50–52, 54, 63–64 n.16; rationalization of, 51, 53, 58–59, 66 n.26; reforms in system, 49, 52–54; and talent markets, 52–53. *See also* College graduates; *Dalian* (city); *Fenpei* (direct assignments); Guidance (*zhidao*); Job assignment system; Market(s), for labor; Mutual choice

Lao Ge (record producer), 78

Laos, 146, 147, 148, 161 n.4

Las Vegas, 148

Lautard, Stephanie, 293 n.7

Lee, Leo Ou-fan, 251

Lefebvre, Henri, 2, 226, 239–40, 242, 255–56

Leisure, 9, 15, 106, 113, 149, 150, 170, 176, 231, 234, 247, 266

Lesser, Alexander, 254

Li, Xun, 290

Li Zhisui, 173

Lian. See Face

Liu Wenfu, 174, 178

Liu Xiyu (choreographer), 131–32

Local/global, 68, 105, 265, 273 n.30

Locality, 68, 93. See also *Difang* (local place)

Macao, 146

Mao Zedong, 3, 20, 43, 166, 172–73, 251–52

Maoism, 3, 18, 25, 37, 227, 251–52, 271 n.6

Maoist era, the, 45, 48, 55, 57, 59, 66 n.26, 125, 132

Marginality/marginalization, 17, 25–26, 31–32, 37–38, 205; of yaogun musicians, 84

Market(s), 4, 10, 11, 14, 15, 39; for fashion models, 138, 140; as form of rationalization, 50; for health goods and services, 16, 168, 174–75, 177, 179–80; and identity, 12, 25, 34–36; for labor, 4, 10–11, 45, 50–53, 54, 55, 58, 115; and socialist notions of, 59; and the state, 10–11, 25, 40; as temporal category, 185; as transformative/civilizing force, 25, 31, 39; and yaogun, 11, 70, 83. *See also* Black market; Job assignment system; Market socialism; Stock market

Market economy, 10, 24, 69

Market reform, 17, 71; and railway workers, 190; and sexuality, 160

Market socialism, 10, 180–81, 186, 198–99

Marketing, 258; and Confucianism, 34, 42 n.21; of health, 35; of infant formula, 92; practices, 12; social, 95; stigmatization of, 34; of urban identities, 125. *See also* Advertising; Multilevel marketing (MLM); Packaging; *Xuanchuan* (propaganda/publicity)

Marriage introduction agencies, 4, 13, 14, 104, 107, 110, 111–18; and the same, 117–18, 119

Marriage, 19, 121, 230, 232; criteria for, 106, 109, 111; foreign/transnational, 14, 104, 108–10, 113, 118, 119, 120; in Japan, 116–17; and residency, 107–8

Masculinity, 123, 177

Mass campaigns, 15. *See also* Sociality, mass forms of

Massey, Doreen, 15, 92–93, 104–5, 116, 121

Media, 1, 3, 13, 39, 70, 80, 90, 105, 106, 109, 123, 141, 170, 201, 206, 222, 229, 253

Medical system. *See* Health care

Medicine: commodification of, 166; consumption of, 4, 174–75; and place, 174; and social relations, 16. *See also* Health care; Pharmaceutical(s)

Meisner, Maurice, 3, 60, 66 n.26

Metropolitan (Chengshi ren; magazine), 126–27

Metropolitan, the, 126, 141, 235

Mianzi. See Face

Miao (ethnic minority), 18, 123; in Beijing, 234–36; and clothing, 232, 235–36, 239; and consumerism, 229; culture, 233–34; and gender, 235–37; and mobility of, 237–38; and modernity, 228–29; notions of self, 236; peasants, 228, 230, 235; and tradition, 228, 236, 239. *See also* Performance(s); Youth: culture of

Micic, Peter, 85 n.9

Migrants: as criminals, 222 n.9; critique of state, 217; as emblems of rurality, 2; as laborers, 13, 15, 49, 123, 146, 211, 237; and modernity, 219; representations of, 201–2, 206–8, 216. *See also* Crime, Floating population; *Waidi ren;* Wenzhou migrants; Zhejiangcun

Migrant space(s), 4, 7, 17, 201–2, 219; criminalization of, 202, 218; management of, 214–16, 220; subversive potential of, 203–4, 207; urban myths about, 206–8; valorization of, 212

Migration, 3, 18; and crime, 128–29; and hukou system, 107; internal, 106, 147, 154, 227–29, 237–38

Minorities (non-Han). *See* Ethnic minority/ies (non-Han)

Mobility (of people), 5, 6, 121, 187, 201, 202, 209, 210, 214, 228; of brides, 116; and capitalism, 104–5; and gender, 105, 117, 121–22; of Miao, 237–38; and power, 121; and restrictions on, 7, 9, 51, 227; and sports, 129; and travel, 146. *See also* Social mobility

Model self, the, 37

Modern, the, 15, 25; and consumer capitalism, 267; desire for, 239; and "fevers," 287; and global capital, 255, 267; practices of, 234; and sexuality, 146, 149, 151

Modernity/ies, 1, 9, 13, 16, 38, 40, 90, 92, 121, 132, 210, 229, 264–67; and alterity, 264; and consumption, 90, 237, 239–40; and ethnic minorities, 228–29, 234–38; global, 225; and health/the good life, 176; and hospitals, 13, 91, 93; and the Miao, 228–29; and migrants, 219; and nation, 92–93; performance of, 237, 239; and railroads, 183; and rurality, 17–18, 250; and sexuality, 145–46, 149–51, 160; and the state, 91–92; and urbanity, 18, 145, 238, 264, 266–67; and women, 158. *See also* Alternative modernity/ies

Modernization, 39, 44, 48, 54, 55; and capitalism, 102; of countryside, 243; and female bodies, 105; and *rencai,* 54; and Westernization, 266. *See also* Industrialization

Morality, 4; of capitalism, 25; codes of, 149, 151, 161; sexual, 146, 149, 151; and socialist campaigns, 175; urban, 145

Mote, Frederick, 251, 252

Motherhood, 4, 13, 90; ideals of, 91; and sexuality, 97; as state priority, 102

Movement. *See* Mobility

Multilevel marketing (MLM), 4, 10–12, 23, 25, 26–27; and advertising, 28–29; and bodies, 26, 35; and consumption, 24, 35; as cosmopolitan, 37–38; criminalization of, 35, 39–40; as critique of the state, 24, 31, 36, 39, 42 n.15; and dress codes, 34; as identity, 35–37; recruitment practices, 29–31, 38, 41 n.10, 42 n.15; and self-realization, 31; and the state, 24, 28; as urban form, 29. *See also* Marketing

Murphey, Rhoads, 251, 252

Musical Life (magazine). See *Yinyue Shenghuo Bao* (Musical Life; magazine)

Mutual choice, 43, 44, 46, 52, 53, 54, 59, 60, 63–64 n.16

Myanmar (Burma), 146, 147, 148, 161 n.4; rural-rural, 5, 7, 9, 106, 113, 123, 125, 129, 135; and surplus labor, 8

Nanjing, 133, 146, 185, 186, 195–97

Nanqiang Beidiao (television show), 245–48, 259, 262, 266, 270 n.9

Nationalism, 25, 38, 42 n.23, 51, 55–56, 60, 92, 130, 131, 139–40, 141

Nation-state: and flexible capital, 10; as global ethnic body, 56

Naughton, Barry, 7, 271 n.14

Network marketing. *See* Multilevel marketing (MLM)

Niming (anonymity), 280, 281

Ningxia, 38

Nongcun tai. See Rural Channel, The

Nostalgia, 226, 235, 237

One-child policy, 90, 91, 94

Ong, Aihwa, 3–4, 49, 56, 63 n.12; 85 n.4, 91–92; 119

Opera: (Chinese), 18, 243–44, 261, 262, 268, 270 n.9

Orientalism/orientalization: internal, 226, 251; self-orientalism, 119, 138

Overseas Chinese, 25, 29, 32

Packaging: of college graduates, 59; and DevelopMen, 267; of health care, 181; of the self, 34; of traditional medicine, 174; of women, 14, 111

Parish, William, 251, 270 n.11, 290

Party-state, 124, 125, 126, 128, 130, 131, 217

Patriotic professional(ism), 44, 45, 60

Patriotism, 47, 51, 54, 55–56, 60

Peasants/peasantry, 6, 149, 156, 237, 243, 262; as backward/anti-modern, 17–18, 250–51, 265; and health care, 172; images of, 168; as investors, 283; and Maoism, 18, 271 n.16, 227; Miao, 228, 230, 235; as "other," 250–51; and sports, 129–30; television programming for, 18, 243–73; and *xiaxiang* initiative, 249. *See also* Labor, rural; Rural, the; Ruralites; Rurality; Status

Performance(s): 67–68, 70, 72–76; public, 123, 124, 125, 141, 232–37

Personhood, 19, 276, 279, 291

Pharmaceutical(s), 16, 47, 165, 171, 173–77, 268; industry, 171–75, 178; state regulation of, 179–80

Piracy: of pharmaceuticals, 174, 180; of yaogun, 69, 79, 86 n.20

Place(s), 4, 15, 17, 69, 93, 174, 185–87, 197–99; eroticization of, 159; fixing, 184

Placing practices, 26, 34

Population: growth of, 5, 9; health of, 90, 94; management of, 47; quality of, 94

Post-Mao era, 7, 15, 123, 131, 132, 141, 149, 151, 229, 237, 241 n.4, 247, 257, 263

Power: and bodies, 62 n.9, 141, 220; and capitalism, 267; and consumption, 181; and culture, 197, 265; and gender, 121; and knowledge, 202, 265; of market forces, 183; and mobility, 121; and representation, 264; and space, 201–2, 213; techniques of, 45

Prestige. *See* Status

Progress(ive) (*xianjin*), 9, 16, 148, 183, 228, 236, 264, 266; vs. "backward," 185–86, 188, 196–99; "civilizing," 153

Prostitute(s), 136, 144, 146, 150–52, 155–58

Prostitution, 14, 144–46, 149–51, 159, 206–7; as opportunity for women, 152, 157–58

Publicity. *See* Advertising; Marketing; *Xuanchuan* (propaganda/publicity)

Public-private dichotomy, 19, 145

Pukou (town), 185, 186, 188–92

Qigong, 16, 167–71, 177–80, 256–57

Qingdao (city), 29

Railway: as place, 186–87; use of, 184

Railway workers, 4, 15, 16, 183; comparative advantages of, 189–90, 192; as disadvantaged, 193–95; effect of market reforms on, 190; hierarchy among, 194, 195–97;

Railway workers (*cont.*)
history of, 187; liminality of, 185, 188; and "place," 185. *See also Danwei* (work unit); *Difang* (local place); Nanjing; Pukou (town); Shanghai

Rationalization: of labor allocation, 50, 54; of social divisions, 59, 60

Re. See Fever; Stock fever

Red Star (Hong Xing) record company, 78, 80, 86 nn.19, 23, 24

Redfield, Robert, 241 n.3, 254

Renao (liveliness), 165, 168

Rencai (talented personnel), 48, 61; markets for, 52; and modernization, 54

Renqing (human feelings), 278

Residence, 14, 204; permits, 107–10, 113, 129; restrictions on, 227; rights to, 122

Rock music, 4, 10, 11, 12, 67, 81, 143. See also *Yaogun* (rock and roll)

Rofel, Lisa, 38, 61 n.2; 62 n.9

Rural, the, 246, 252; ambivalence toward, 236–37, 249, 250; and authenticity, 227; as backward, 17–18; encounters/interpenetration with the urban, 8, 145, 181, 226–27, 252–56; and face, 276–77; and gemeinschaft, 275; and Maoism, 3, 18, 251–52; nostalgia/longing for, 226, 237, 251; as symbolic, 240; as traditional, 236. *See also* Peasants/peasantry; Ruralites

Rural Channel, The (*Nongcun tai*), 18, 242–43, 247, 249, 250, 256, 257–59, 268, 266, 269 n.2; and "the rural," 246, 252

Rural factories, 5, 18, 257–60

Ruralites/rural residents: as consumers, 173; and higher education, 61 n.4; and MLM, 23, 28–29, 31, 37–38, 62 n.4. *See also* Athletes; Peasants; Sports

Rurality, 2, 3, 4, 7, 8, 19; and anthropology of China, 19; and backwardness, 17, 250–51; and criminality, 210; and ethnicity, 13; and health, 166; and modernity, 17–18, 250; and MLM, 28, 37; notions of, 26; as "Other," 18; and the

urban, 3–4, 8, 15, 17, 18, 240; and urbanity/cosmopolitanness, 8, 229, 240, 250, 255. *See also* Rural, the

Rural-urban: inequalities, 6, 38, 127, in health care, 164–67, 172–73, 179, 180; differences, 8, 200, 229, 254; as dualism, 5, 19, 45, 107, 145, 227; migration, 7, 9, 106, 113, 123, 125, 129, 135. *See also* Urban-rural continuum

Sanhu (small players of stock market), 284–87, 293 nn.9, 11. *See also* Stock folk

Sassen, Saskia, 225

Self: and face, 275–76; the making of, 25, 96, 106, 226, 238; realization, 31, 95

Sennett, Richard, 166, 168, 181

Sex, 144, 153, 156, 159; as commodity, 150; and consumption, 150–52, 159; and desire, 145. *See also* Sexuality

Sex industry, the, 150, 153, 161 n.2; and the state, 151, 155, 157

Sex tourism, 4, 144, 147, 152, 155. *See also* Jinghong (city); Xishuangbanna (Dai Nationality Autonomous Prefecture)

Sexuality, 13, 89, 106, 121, 150, 160, 235; and breast-feeding, 95, 97, 98–101; and Confucianism, 151, 153; and ethnic minorities, 235; and the modern, 145–46, 149–51, 160; and motherhood, 97; and the state, 149; and tradition, 101; and the urban, 146. *See also* Eroticization; Morality; Sex

Sex workers, 135–36, 151, 162 n.10. *See also* Prostitute(s)

Shandong (province), 133, 173

Shanghai, 7, 9, 18, 29, 45, 47, 49, 58, 85 n.6, 131, 145, 146, 148, 168, 172, 185, 186, 189, 192–95, 225, 243–45, 250, 252–57, 263–67, 269 n.4, 270 nn.9, 11; 271 n.17; 272 n.27; 273 n.33, 279, 282–84, 289–90; and fashion industry, 133; and food culture, 125; images of, 124, 125, 134; and prostitution, 144; Talent Market, 55

Shanghai Angli Biotechnological Foods Factory, 257–63, 268

Shangshan xiaxiang. *See* Xiaxiang

Shanxi (province), 133

Shenzhen, 13, 14, 29, 105, 106, 110, 114, 117–20, 133, 237; as cosmopolitan, 104, 111; marriage agencies in, 112, 116; migration to, 106, 113; residency in, 107–9, 113

Shishang (Trends; magazine), 126

Si (privacy), 280, 281

Sichuan (province), 85 n.6, 144, 146, 155–57, 241 n.5

Singapore/an, 9, 14, 86 n.20, 105, 106, 114–16, 119, 121, 146, 243

Sipsongpanna, 146. *See also* Xishuangbanna (Dai Nationality Autonomous Prefecture)

Siyueba (April Eighth Festival), 234–35

Skinner, G. William, 186, 192, 252

Social mobility, 57, 62 n.5, 109; and college graduates, 44–45, 49, 54, 56–57; and marriage, 104, 108, 120; and move to the city, 228; and naturalization of distinctions, 58–59, 66 n.26; and social/cultural capital, 56–57; and urban desires, 45, 58, 62 n.5

Social networks/connections, 44, 54; and MLM, 24, 179. See also *Guanxi* (social connections)

Social order, 17, 128, 202, 204, 206–7, 212–15, 218

Socialism, 149; bankruptcy of, 24; and capitalism, 25, 36, 44; and cities, 5–7, 168, 185; and consumption, 12; education, 12; and global capitalism, 3–4; and health care, 16, 165–66, 172–73, 178, 181; and individualism, 31; and urbanity, 3–4; and welfare system, 45; and womanhood, 13. See also *Danwei* (work unit); Job assignment system; Maoism; Maoist era, the; Market socialism

Socialist economies: features of, 15

Sociality, 277; mass forms of, 283, 285–87, 288–90; urban, 276

Songjiang (county), 244–47, 256, 262–63, 267–68, 271 n.17, 273 n.33

South Korea, 9, 136

Space, 10, 16, 17, 141, 145; as anonymous, 106; and capitalism, 3, 15–16, 104; competition for, 194; and global capital, 93, 256; national, 45, 183; and place, 93, 199; politicization of, 15; and power, 201–2, 213; privatization of, 69; and social distinctions, 197; and the state, 4, 15, 198, 205; and time, 15, 93, 183, 185, 198; and urbanity, 240. *See also* Migrant Space(s); Urban Space(s)

Spatialization: of market, 11; of social landscape, 17; of time, 16, 184

Special Economic Zone (SEZ), 9, 14, 237

Spiritual civilization (*jingshen wenming*), 128, 197

Sports, 115, 129, 130; and nationalism, 139, 141

State, the: and athletes, 130; and bodies, 166–67; bureaucratic distribution of labor, 11; and capital, 10–11; civilizing project of, 15; and consumerism, 24, 92; continued significance of, 43–47; and control of population, 6, 47, 201, 216, 220; and cultural production, 24; and culture, 4, 234; and fashion industry, 134, 136; and floating population, 217, 220; and health care/of citizens, 13, 92, 94–95, 98–99, 102, 165, 166–78, 179–80, 181; and hospitals, 92, 96, 175, 179; and identity, 12, 24; and individualism, 13, 92; and labor distribution, 11, 45; legitimacy, 17, 215, 218; and markets, 10, 11, 25, 40; and marriage introduction agencies, 117–18, 119; and means of production, 50; and minorities, 18; and motherhood, 102; and MLM, 11, 24, 28, 31, 35, 36, 39–40, 42 n.15; and pharmaceuticals, 179–80; reproductive poli-

State, the (*cont.*)

cies, 13, 102; and the sex industry, 151, 155, 157; and sexuality, 149; and society, 7, 15, 17, 201, 216–17, 220; and space, 4, 15, 198, 205; and subject formation, 15, 45–47, 60; and technology, 179; and television programming, 249; and time, 15; and tourism policies, 160; and urbanization, 7; and yaogun, 70, 78–79, 82–83. *See also* Corruption; *Hukou* (household registration system); Market socialism; Party-state; State-run industry/enterprises

State bureaucratic distribution of labor, 11

State Education Commission, 44, 53, 61 n.4

State-run industry/enterprises, 6, 10, 23, 44, 47, 49, 56, 69, 134, 188. See also *Danwei* (work unit)

Status, 6, 18, 29, 54; and prestige, 226, 229–30, 235, 237–39; of women, 120. *See also* Peasantry; Social mobility

Stock fever, 282–85, 287; as epidemic, 287; as social movement, 289

Stock folk (*gumin*), 282–84; and capitalism, 289; as social actors, 284–87

Stock market, 19, 276; forms of sociality in, 282–87

Students, 67, 70, 73

Subject formation/subjectivity, 12, 15, 90; and the state, 15, 45–47, 54, 60; and the urban, 168

Supermodel Contest (1995), 13, 123–24, 133, 136–40

Suzhi (quality, essence), 37, 59–60, 166, 200 n.8, 283; and habitus, 210–12

Tai (ethnic minority), 144, 145, 150, 158; dress, 144, 155, 157; eroticization of, 152–54, 160; Han images of, 153–55, 158; language and culture, 14, 153–54, 161 nn.1, 2, 162 n.8. *See also* Tai-Lue

Taiji (tai ch'i), 170

Tai-Lue, 146, 149, 161 n.2, 162 n.9

Taiwan: and Taiwanese, 8, 9, 23, 25–30, 32, 37–38, 50, 71–72, 86 nn.19, 20, 29, 135, 148

Talent, 48–49, 59, 62 n.7; state use of, 50. See also *Rencai* (talented personnel)

Tang Dynasty (rock band), 78

Technology/ies, 1, 3, 12, 232, 263; biomedical, 165, 173–74, 178–79; of bodies, 124, 141; contraceptive, 176; of gender, 123, 137–38, 140–41; of representation, 249; state regulation of, 179; video, 114–15

Television programming, 5, 18, 243–46, 248, 270 n.9

Temporality, 15, 185

Territorialization of virtue, 185, 197

Thailand, 117, 146, 147, 157, 161 n.4, 162 n.9

Tianjin, 7, 125, 128, 133; as cosmopolitan, 126–27

Tibet, 80, 231

Time, 15; epochal, 183; and global capitalism, 3, 93, 104; and health care, 174, 178; and place, 184; and space, 93, 198; spatialization of, 16, 184; and the state, 15

Tourism, 125, 147, 158, 160

Tourists, 13, 14, 144, 146–48, 159–60

Tradition: and beauty, 13, 137–40; commodification of, 13; Confucian, 56; and marriage, 106; meanings of, 105, 118, 119–20, 121, 239; and sexuality, 101; and socialism, 31

"Traditional business," 26, 36

Traditional medicine, 174, 180

"Traditional women," 14, 105, 114, 116, 119–21. *See also* Beauty

Travel, 144, 180

Treaty ports, 5, 126–27

Trends (Shishang; magazine), 126

Tsing, Anna, 25–26

Underurbanization, 7

United Nations Children's Fund (UNICEF), 89, 94, 101

United States, 28, 37–38, 42 n.14, 86 n.20, 140, 172

Xiaxiang, 147, 249, 256, 270 nn.11, 13

Xijiang (village), 229–35, 238

Xinjiang (province), 38, 85 n.6

Xishuangbanna (Dai Nationality Autonomous Prefecture), 143–44, 161 nn.1, 3, 4, 162 n.7; as cosmopolitan, 145; as Han fantasy, 158–60; history of, 146–49, as site of desire, 160–61. *See also* Ethnic minority/ies (non-Han); Prostitution; Sex tourism

Xuanchuan (propaganda/publicity), 69, 75, 259, 263, 267, 269 n.2, 272 nn.23, 24. *See also* Advertising; Marketing

Yang, Mayfair, 12, 25, 45, 263, 276, 278

Yangge, 16, 167–71, 176

Yaogun (rock and roll), 11, 69, 85 nn.5, 9; as advertisement, 74–75, 76, 86 n.25; in Beijing, 70–71; and Chineseness, 71, 81–82; as commodity, 70; and consumers, 83; diversification of, 82; and the market, 11, 70, 83; vs. "pop," 71–72, 80; profitability of, 70, 75–81, 84; promotion of,

79–80; state regulation of, 70, 78–79, 82–83; and Westernness, 71, 72, 75, 81. *See also* Cui Jian; *Yinyue Shenghuo Bao* (Musical Life; magazine)

Yinyue Shenghuo Bao (Musical Life; magazine), 79, 80, 81, 86 n.26

Youth, 4, 18, 232; culture of, 236, 238–40, 249. See also *Daling qingnian* (aging youth)

Yueju. *See* Opera (Chinese)

Yunnan (province), 85 n.6, 143, 146, 147, 161 nn.1, 2, 3

Yuppie (*yapi*), 126

Zhang, Yingjin, 250

Zhang, Youdai (disc jockey), 77

Zhejiang (province), 35, 113

Zhejiangcun (in Beijing), 17, 201–3, 206–7, 212–19, 221 n.4

Zheng Jun, 80, 86 n.24

Zhidao. See Guidance (*zhidao*)

Zhiliang (quality), 59–60, 200 n.8